MW01253185

MARGINALISATION IN CHINA

IGU Marginal Regions Series

Series Editor: Walter Leimgruber, University of Fribourg, Switzerland

Marginality studies have become imperative in a world which is increasingly being divided into haves and have-nots. This series, published in collaboration with the IGU Commission on Evolving Issues of Geographical Marginality, covers a wide range of topics, including cultural, ecological, economic, political and social aspects of marginality, as well as the marginalization process. The series brings together high quality research monographs and edited volumes from all over the world.

Marginalisation in China

Perspectives on Transition and Globalisation

Edited by

HEATHER XIAOQUAN ZHANG
University of Leeds, UK

BIN WU
Cardiff University, UK

RICHARD SANDERS
University of Northampton, UK

ASHGATE

Published by
Ashgate Publishing Limited
Gower House
Croft Road
Aldershot
Hampshire GU11 3HR
England

Ashgate Publishing Company
Suite 420
101 Cherry Street
Burlington, VT 05401-4405
USA

Ashgate website: http://www.ashgate.com

British Library Cataloguing in Publication Data
Marginalisation in China : perspectives on transition and
globalisation. - (Marginal regions)
1. Marginality, Social - China 2. Globalization - Social
aspects - China 3. China - Economic conditions - 1976-2000
4. China - Economic conditions - 2000- 5. China - Economic
policy - 1976-2000 6. China - Economic policy - 2000-
I. Zhang, Heather Xiaoquan II. Wu, Bin, 1957 Nov. 6-
III. Sanders, Richard, 1947- IV. IGU Commission on Dynamics
of Marginal and Critical Regions
305.5'6'0951

Library of Congress Cataloging-in-Publication Data
Marginalisation in China : perspectives on transition and globalisation / edited by Heather Xiaoquan Zhang, Bin Wu, and Richard Sanders.
p. cm. -- (Marginal regions (and in association with IGU - dynamics of marginal and critical regions))
Includes bibliographical references and index.
ISBN 978-0-7546-4427-9
1. China--Economic policy--1976-2000. 2. China--Economic policy--2000- 3. Globalization--Economic aspects--China. 4. Regional economic disparities--China. 5. Marginality, Social--China. 6. Equality--China. I. Zhang, Heather Xiaoquan. II. Wu, Bin, 1957 Nov. 6- III. Sanders, Richard,
1947-

HC427.92.M387 2007
338.951--dc22

2007002932

ISBN 978-0-7546-4427-9

Printed and bound in Great Britain by MPG Books Ltd, Bodmin, Cornwall.

Contents

List of Figures

List of Tables

Notes on Contributors

Philip Andrews-Speed is Professor of Energy Policy and Director of the Centre for Energy, Petroleum and Mineral Law and Policy at University of Dundee, UK. He leads the Centre's China Programme, which covers research, consultancy and professional training in the energy sector. The focus of his research is on energy policy, regulation and reform, and on the interface between energy policy and international relations. His recent publications include *Energy Policy and Regulation in the People's Republic of China* (Kluwer Law International, 2004).

Yiying Cao is currently a doctoral candidate at the University of Northampton, UK, writing her PhD thesis on Agricultural Biotechnology in China. She has undergraduate and post-graduate degrees from China Agricultural University, Beijing and before becoming a visiting scholar at the Institute of Development Studies, University of Sussex in 2001, worked as a researcher at the China Centre for Agricultural Policy, the Chinese Academy of Agricultural Sciences, Beijing.

Yang Chen is Senior Lecturer in Economics at the University of Northampton, UK and Assistant Director of the China Centre there. An economics graduate of Nankai University, Tianjin, she completed her MBA at University of Liverpool in 1999 before successfully completing her PhD at the University of Leicester in 2004, writing her thesis on Changes in Ownership and Property Rights in China-in-Transition. She has published widely in the areas of the 'New Economy', property rights and corporate governance in contemporary China.

Ian G. Cook is Professor of Human Geography and Head of the Centre for Pacific Rim Studies, Liverpool John Moores University, UK. His main research interests are on China's Environment, Ageing in China and Health Inequalities. He is co-author/co-editor of six books and, the forthcoming, *New Perspectives on Aging in China* (ed, with Jason Powell), Nova Science Publishers, New York.

Mingzhu Dong is a PhD candidate in the Department of Social Policy at the London School of Economics and Political Science, UK. She is also an affiliate of the Centre for Analysis of Social Exclusion at LSE. Her work focuses on employment and social exclusion in China.

Mark Duda is a Research Fellow at Harvard University's Joint Center for Housing Studies, where he edits a joint working paper series with Tsinghua University's Institute for Real Estate Studies that examines housing economics, policy, and finance in urban China. His work focuses on housing economics and policy in China and the US.

Trevor Dummer was Senior Lecturer in Human Geography at Liverpool John Moores University, UK, where he is an honorary research fellow. He is currently a researcher at the Canadian Centre for Vaccinology, IWK Health Centre, Halifax, Nova Scotia. His PhD, from the University of Newcastle upon Tyne, was in geographical epidemiology. He has published widely in the area of health-environment interactions and, with Ian Cook, on changing health inequalities in China.

Markus Eberhardt holds a bachelor's degree in Modern Chinese Studies from University of Leeds, and Masters' degrees in Development Economics from the University of East Anglia and in Economics from University of Oxford, UK. He has spent in excess of three years living and working in China, most recently researching sourcing strategies of UK and US manufacturing subsidiaries. He is currently studying for a doctorate in Economics at University of Oxford.

Zhiqiang Feng, PhD, is a Research Fellow in the School of Geography and Geosciences at University of St Andrews, UK. He also works for the Scottish Longitudinal Studies Centre and the Centre for Interaction Data Estimation and Research. His research interests are in geography of health, health inequality, longitudinal analysis, migration, and applications of geographical information systems. His research has been published in journals such as *British Medical Journal*, *Journal of Epidemiology and Community Health*, *Computers*, *Environment and Urban Systems*; *Habitat International*; *The Geographical Journal*, etc.

Ka Lin, PhD, is Professor in the Department of Sociology, Nanjing University, China. He was a Senior Research Fellow in Department of Social Policy, University of Turku, Finland. He is also a docent at Department of Social Policy and Social Work, University of Tampere and a docent at Department of Social Policy, University of Turku. His research areas include comparative social policy, welfare theory, cultural study of welfare, gender and family policy. His recent publications include articles in *International Journal of Social Welfare*, *International Social Security Review*, *European Journal of Political Research*, *Social Policy & Administration*, *Acta Sociologica* and *Comparative Sociology*.

Katherine Morton, PhD, is a Fellow in the Department of International Relations at The Australian National University. Her recent publications include 'Surviving an Environmental Crisis: Can China Adapt?', *The Brown Journal of World Affairs*, Vol. XIII, No. I, Summer/Fall 2006, 'The Emergence of NGOs in China and Their Transnational Linkages: Implications for Domestic Reform', *Australian Journal of International Affairs*, Vol. 59, No.4, December 2005, and *International Aid and China's Environment: Taming the Yellow Dragon*, Routledge Studies on China in Transition, Routledge, 2005.

Richard Sanders is Reader in Political Economy at the University of Northampton, UK and Director of the China Centre there. A graduate of University of Cambridge, he gained his MA and PhD degrees in London, writing his thesis on The Political Economy of Chinese Ecological Agriculture. He lectured for two years in the early

1990s at Beijing Foreign Studies University, China. He has published widely in the areas of Chinese political economy, rural development, environmental protection and property rights.

Jun Tang is General Secretary of the Chinese Academy of Social Sciences' (CASS) Social Policy Research Centre and a research professor at CASS' Institute of Sociology. He is also former director of the Social Security Research Group of China's Ministry of Civil Affairs. He has published extensively in areas of human development, rural and urban poverty, social security and social policy reforms in China.

John Q. Tian received his PhD from Cornell University and is now associate professor of government at Connecticut College in USA. His research interest includes Chinese and East Asian political economy. He has published a book *Government, Business and the Politics of Interdependence and Conflicts across the Taiwan Strait*, Palgrave-Macmillan, 2006, and various articles in *Journal of Contemporary China, Canadian Journal of Development Studies* and *Issues & Studies*.

John Thoburn is Professor of Development Economics at Ritsumeikan Asia Pacific University in Japan. He taught at the University of East Anglia in Norwich, UK, from 1967 to 2006, where he is now Emeritus Reader in Economics. Most recently he has been working on China and Vietnam in relation to the impacts of the end of the Agreement on Textiles and Clothing in 2005 on developing country garment exporters.

Bin Wu obtained his PhD from University of Hull, UK, and now works as a researcher at Cardiff University, UK. His current research focuses on the impacts of globalisation on Chinese labour mobility at national and international levels. He has taken many research projects on the global labour market for seafarers, transformation of Chinese seafarers for international shipping, the mobility and impact of Chinese migration to Italy. He is author of the book, *Sustainable Development in Rural China: Farmer Innovation and Self-Organisation in Marginal Areas* (Routledge, 2003).

Heather Xiaoquan Zhang, PhD, is Senior Lecturer in Chinese Studies at the Department of East Asian Studies, University of Leeds, UK. She specialises in China's development, gender, migration, poverty, social exclusion and marginalisation, and social policy. She has pioneered research on AIDS in China from a development and well-being perspective, and has published widely, including journal articles in *Development and Change, The Journal of Peasant Studies, Journal of International Development, Women's Studies International Forum, Geoforum, Public Administration and Development*, etc.

Li Zhang is Assistant Professor in the Department of Geography and Resource Management, the Chinese University of Hong Kong. His research areas include migration, urbanisation, regional development in China. He has published a number of articles in international journals, including *The China Quarterly, International*

Journal of Urban and Regional Research, Urban Studies, Geoforum, Habitat International, International Regional Science Review, Asian Survey, and *China Economic Review.*

Chapter 1

Introduction: Marginalisation and Globalisation in Transitional China

Heather Xiaoquan Zhang and Richard Sanders

Despite the general acknowledgement of China's achievements in terms of rapid and sustained economic growth during the last 28 years, scholars, policy makers and practitioners concerned with human development and well-being may question whether such achievements can compensate for the environmental and social costs wrought as a result. A close examination of the distribution of the costs and benefits of economic growth amongst the Chinese population raises important issues, including, for example, the degree to which economic development and social well-being are related to each other and the extent and means by which the benefits of China's growth can be more equitably shared. Other questions present themselves. How can the many downsides of rapid societal change be avoided or effectively addressed and what are the roles of the state and of civil society in so doing? What new institutions need to be put in place and what reforms should be made to existing institutions?

We intend to analyse the above issues and challenges using the concept of *marginalisation*. This concept, we maintain, refers to the processes and consequences of economic, political and social changes leading to the (re)centralisation and control of scarce resources, including natural, financial, social and political capitals, from marginal areas, sectors and groups to core areas, sectors and groups: for example, from the rural to the urban or from the people as a whole to elites. Marginalisation is not a new phenomenon in China. Yet the market reforms and economic transition since the late 1970s, and in particular since the mid-1990s, characterised as they are by intensifying globalisation, have rendered the phenomenon more salient. Growing inequalities and polarisation in all aspects of life have interwoven with the emergence of new forms of poverty, vulnerability and social disadvantage and with environmental degradation and natural resource depletion. All this has reshaped socio-economic and power relations, creating 'winners' and 'losers', and generating greater uncertainty, insecurity and risks in livelihoods, as well as compromising the ways individuals, families and communities respond, adapt to and absorb external shocks.

Marginalisation in China cannot be fully understood without taking into account the impacts of globalisation, broadly interpreted as a process through which the world is becoming increasingly interconnected and interdependent in respect of economy, society, culture, environment and polity (cf. Beck, 2000; Castells, 1996; Giddens, 1990; Martin, 2004). Studies on globalisation have gained increasing currency in international academic and policy making circles in recent years. The globalisation discourse, however, is often marked by heated debates about the benefits and costs, advantages and disadvantages, winners and losers in its process and about its impact on poverty, inequality and environmental and social sustainability globally, nationally and locally (cf. Dasgupta, 1998; Masina, 2002; Stiglitz, 2002). Indeed, examining the development path and outcomes of post-reform China, we may well argue that globalisation has been a significant influence on the processes and patterns of marginalisation in the country, as a result of the induced changes in the exercise and modalities of power over resources and the consequent (re)distribution of costs and benefits at various levels.

Since the market reforms initiated in the late 1970s, China has sustained impressive rates of economic growth of approximately 9% per annum, a remarkable achievement when compared with other developing regions of the world. A major factor contributing to this has been China's increased integration into the global economic system. The pace of globalisation further accelerated with the country's accession to the World Trade Organization (WTO) near the end of 2001. China's decision to strive for WTO membership was based on the leadership's optimistic perception of globalisation's potential for economic opportunities and benefits, discounting the likely challenges and costs that it might pose to vulnerable sectors of the economy and society. Similarly positive predictions predominate in academic circles and policy domains both within China and without (cf. Chang, et al., 2001). And while it is undeniable that China has actively participated in globalisation and that certain regions, sectors and groups have been able to take advantage of this, it is also arguable that too much emphasis has been placed on narrow growth indicators as evidence of the positive impact of globalisation on China at the expense of a more critical scrutiny of the ways in which globalisation has engendered differential effects on Chinese society. Whereas China is frequently applauded as a success story in relation to globalisation, relatively less attention has been paid to its negative impacts and to the often drastic socio-economic and cultural changes wrought by it on the lives and livelihoods of disadvantaged groups, sectors and regions, and their implications for poverty, inequality, vulnerability and marginalisation.

Marginalisation as a consequence of a skewed process of redistribution of scarce resources involves a range of actors and complex interest relations. In this regard, perhaps, China can be deemed as unique in the developing world not only in terms of the extent of socio-economic differentiation and inequality amongst different regions, sectors and social groups which have emerged during the era of transition, but also in terms of the various initiatives that the government has taken to tackle the problems. Such initiatives are, in part, linked to the legacies of state socialism associated with an earlier part of the People's Republic's developmental history but are, additionally, heavily influenced by official apprehension at the possibility of political instability caused by growing social discontent. There is also, within China, a cultural tradition, which values egalitarianism and reciprocity and nurtures diverse and strong familial, kinship and social networks. With respect to trends in China's political reform, it should be noted that democratic election of local government officials has already been initiated at village and township levels and that the new leadership of the Chinese Communist Party in the early twenty-first century has started paying more attention to marginal regions and peoples and vulnerable and disadvantaged groups (*bianyuan yu ruoshi qunti*) manifest, for instance, in the new emphasis on a people-centred approach (*yiren weiben*) to development, on urban-and-rural balanced and holistic development (*chengxiang tongchou fazhan*) and on the need for a more harmonious and inclusive society (*hexie shehui*). However, how such rhetoric is to be translated into reality remains to be seen. While neo-liberal discourses of globalisation, marketisation and *de facto* privatisation have continued to shape the reform agenda, the extent to which the problems of marginalisation in China will be successfully tackled remains doubtful.

Whilst the concept of *marginalisation* is gaining increasing prominence in an understanding and analysis of the more recent changes and emerging forms of inequalities in China, there has been a lack of systematic and interdisciplinary employment of a *marginalisation lens* to reveal, delineate and better understand the processes, patterns, trends, multiple dimensions and dynamics of the phenomenon, the challenges that it has posed and the consequences and implications for development and for well-being of the Chinese people. In this context, this volume constitutes the first attempt to address the issues as identified above through such a lens, thereby contributing to the debate over marginalisation and its interactions with globalisation and transition in China. It brings together a wide range of domestic and international experts and disciplinary perspectives, combining empirical research and conceptual analysis in an attempt to map out the contour of China's development landscape in the reform era. As such, the research presented here has significance for various domestic and international policy arenas in respect of tackling marginalisation, poverty and social exclusion effectively and striving for the achievement of the UN Millennium Development Goals.

This volume is structured in two parts. Part 1, China in Transition: Inequality, Poverty and Marginalisation, contains six chapters. In chapter 2, Richard Sanders, Yang Chen and Yiying Cao discuss the question of marginalisation in the Chinese countryside since the rural reforms using data from the 2003 Rural Household Survey of the National Bureau of Statistics of China, and informed by recent evidence presented in the *Chinese Farmers Report*, officially banned in the country, containing first-hand accounts of the precarious, marginalised status of many Chinese farmers nowadays, in particular the rural poor. The chapter testifies to the enlarging inequalities in China, illustrated by a high and still rising Gini Co-efficient in recent years, not just between urban and rural areas, but *within* the countryside itself, and offers a range of explanations for such a state of affairs. It is clear from their analysis that some farmers face such a barrage of interlocking disadvantages – geographical, employment, educational, ethnic, social, political and personal – that it is hardly surprising that they remain mired in absolute poverty. Still others experience perceived relative marginalisation as institutional factors – to include excessive fees, taxes, arbitrary actions of local officials, continuing structural constraints on mobility and opportunities, regressive fiscal policy and so on – combine to sideline them, often to such an extent that the expression of their grievances, in the absence of appropriate mechanisms of political representation, leads to violent conflicts with the authorities. The chapter argues that unless the new Chinese leadership of President Hu Jintao and Premier Wen Jiabao seriously faces up to the farmers' predicament and finds effective ways of alleviating the increasingly marginalised 'farmers' burden', their 'balanced and holistic development' blueprint will remain a pipedream.

In chapter 3, Jun Tang, Mingzhu Dong and Mark Duda analyse another critical group of Chinese adversely affected during China's transition: those who have been laid off from state-owned enterprises (SOEs), which, in the fierce competition of a market-oriented economy and faced with hard budget constraints, have had to downsize their workforces, with some even facing bankruptcy. The authors highlight a critical feature of the pre-reform (but, to a much lesser extent, the post-reform) social structure, that of the work unit or *danwei*, which provided workers with not only life-long employment and wage income but also access to a package of welfare benefits, frequently to include pensions, subsidised housing, medical care, primary and secondary education for their children and, most significantly, an associated sense of community belonging and social inclusion. Against this backdrop, being laid off during the industrial restructuring has involved much more profound effects than just losing a job. For not only does it mean, for workers, losing their wage incomes but it also involves separation from welfare benefits at precisely the time when they are needed most. And with the loss of wages, social benefits and their sense of social belonging, the workers involved experience 'transition' from insider to outsider status, from a state of relative social inclusion to one of marginalisation – indeed a 'double marginalisation' – in terms of access to the market and the state. Using evidence from a number of studies in China, to include a study carried out by the authors in Wuhan, central China, at the turn of the last century, Tang, Dong and Duda show that government re-employment policies are frequently ineffective and that those laid-off workers who do find themselves re-employed may well do so in the increasingly large informal sector, which are inadequately regulated and likely to carry little or no social benefits. They conclude that laid-off workers experience great difficulties in finding secure or full-time jobs again and, in consequence, suffer from considerable marginalisation in multiple dimensions. They argue that unless strong institutional support in the form of a fundamental reform of the social security system is provided for those laid-off, in particular with resources necessary for them to weather the storm, the SOE laid-off workers will continue to suffer from double marginalisation, preventing China from building a truly harmonious society and achieving common prosperity.

In chapter 4, Philip Andrews-Speed looks at marginalisation in China's energy sector, using the case of township and village coal mines (TVCMs). He charts the rise and fall of TVCMs since the early 1980s, and the important role that they have played in the national economy through their contribution to China's energy supply during its industrialisation drive. Throughout the 1980s, TVCMs played no small part in generating employment for local and migrant populations, as well as revenues for local governments, thus alleviating poverty in many rural areas endowed with coal reserves. At the same time, however, many TVCMs contributed to local environmental problems, posed harsh and dangerous working conditions, were mired with official corruption driven by the possibility of huge material rewards and were a source of large numbers of industrial accidents resulting in fatalities and injuries, problems which increasing official regulation of the mines in the 1990s and 2000s have failed to solve. The author concentrates on the period after 1998, when overcapacity in the coal industry, competition with larger state-owned coal mines and new government regulations combined to produce a wave of closures, resulting in increased unemployment and aggravated rural poverty in many areas. The lack of policies and programmes to prepare the coal mine communities for absorbing such external shocks and, for the remaining mines, the continued violation of miners' rights to life, decent working conditions and pay, all mean that material and social deprivation, vulnerability and marginalisation remain typical in small TVCMs and their surrounding communities.

In chapter 5, Li Zhang examines the marginalised status of rural migrant workers (*mingong*) in Chinese cities. Zhang employs a model of 'urban accumulation' to explain a wide range of discriminative practices and policies adopted by urban authorities nowadays against rural migrants, including, for instance, restrictions imposed on migrant workers in the labour market by barring them from better-paid, more secure jobs of higher-status through attaching conditions of eligibility, to include possession of permanent urban household registration *(hukou*), and the exclusion of migrant workers from the newly introduced social security schemes like pension, health and workplace injury insurances. 'Urban accumulation', in this context, is construed as a process of reallocation and (re)centralisation of resources as possessed by migrant workers by the more powerful from rural peripheral to urban core areas. Zhang identifies and analyses recent developments and trends in relation to rural-urban migration in China, including such phenomena as urban residential segregation manifest in the emergence of the so-called urban villages, or *chengzhongcun*, which are in fact, residential enclaves of migrant communities in large cities, and the 'commodification' of the *hukou*, which involves the selling of permanent residency rights to those who can afford it in order to allow urban governments to expand their revenue bases. The consequences, Zhang points out, are the exploitation and marginalisation of migrant workers, reducing them to *de facto* second-class citizens in Chinese cities.

The issue of social and citizenship rights of the Chinese is further explored by Zhiqiang Feng in chapter 6, which focuses on China's more recent health system reforms and their impacts on poverty, inequality and marginalisation. Feng examines the universalistic and egalitarian approach to healthcare provision during the first three decades of the People's Republic, when, despite China's low average income level, life expectancy increased from 35 to 68, infant mortality declined from 250 to 40 deaths per 1,000 live births and malaria was effectively brought under control. He argues that these remarkable achievements were largely attributable to the official emphasis on preventative healthcare and an equitable public health policy of 'Health for All'. He demonstrates that these were realised through three major institutionalised schemes, namely, the public-funded medical care system (*gongfei yiliao*) for the public sector employees, the labour medical security system (*laobao yiliao*) for permanent workers in SOEs and large collective enterprises, both urban-based schemes, and the cooperative healthcare system (*hezuo yiliao*) in rural areas. In more recent years, however, there has been a state retreat from its previous commitment to preventative healthcare and health for all as market principles have been steadily introduced into the health system. Thus we find in China today a health service which has received low levels of public funding (much lower than in most comparable countries), where services, to include state hospitals are being privatised, where health insurance schemes are patchy at best and where the direct costs of healthcare, including medicines, diagnosis and treatment, have risen sharply to a level which seriously hinders access by large sections of the Chinese population and has led to a *reduction* in its utilisation despite an increase in the numbers falling ill. Feng argues that this is a profound form of social exclusion, marginalising disadvantaged and vulnerable groups, such as migrant workers in urban areas and the urban and rural poor, and that, if the situation is to be remedied, the Chinese government needs to reconstruct healthcare as a public or semi-public good, not to be treated just like *any* good in the marketplace, and to provide strong support in terms of the funding, organisation and delivery of healthcare and the urgent development and scaling up of new health insurance schemes.

In chapter 7, Ka Lin, adopting an institutional approach, delineates the changing patterns of poverty as it has been linked to social exclusion and marginalisation in China since 1949. The institutional perspective differs from the approaches to poverty studies currently predominant in China in that its overarching concerns are not the measurement and incidence of poverty. Rather, it focuses on institutional responses to poverty problems and the changing state poverty reduction strategies in different historical periods. Lin analyses the dynamics of the national profile of poverty during the past half century or more, focusing on the ways in which increased marketisation of the economy in the reform years has reconfigured Chinese society in respect of shifting social stratification as well as class and power relations. This has generated new patterns of poverty and inequality: it has not just worsened regional inequality, but has created new sources and forms of inequality *within* regions, to include relative poverty and deprivation, social exclusion and marginalisation. Lin shows that while the incidence of absolute poverty in rural areas has fallen significantly since the initiation of the reforms, recent development has witnessed the emergence, rise and, to some extent, entrenchment of urban poverty and social exclusion to include the SOE laid-off workers, the unemployed and many rural migrants. Lin charts three stages in the development of the Chinese government's responses to poverty since 1949, characterised by a state-organised collective welfare system in the first phase (the pre-reform years) followed by a state-initiated growth-led anti-poverty strategy, particularly targeting regional poverty, from the early 1990s onwards, and, since the late 1990s, by increased state intervention through the introduction of more redistributive policies and mechanisms to include various social insurance schemes and the improvement of social security and social assistance programmes. Examining the strengths and weaknesses of the three approaches to poverty, social exclusion and marginalisation, Lin concludes that the neo-liberal solution to poverty – the single-minded pursuit of economic growth through market-based reforms which has, until recently, characterised the reform years' institutional responses to poverty – is overly simplistic and inadequate. He therefore calls for a better balance between growth- and redistribution-oriented approaches to poverty and marginalisation in order to achieve the goals of equity, welfare and social cohesion.

Part 2 – Marginalisation in the Era of Globalisation in China – entails six more chapters exploring the links between marginalisation and globalisation. In chapter 8, Bin Wu, based on secondary data and supplemented by the author's empirical research on Chinese seafarers, looks at the marginalisation of a special group, overseas contract workers, who have gone abroad through authorised recruitment agencies to provide labour services for foreign employers in the years of China's reform and opening up to the outside world. While increasing globalisation of the Chinese economy has witnessed greater labour mobility both nationally and globally, leading to a growing number of such contract workers, Wu argues that insufficient attention has been paid to the distribution of benefits and costs among the different actors and agents involved in the process, especially in a sending country like China. Wu charts the organisational changes in China's overseas labour service regime since the early 1950s, and in particular in the post-reform years. He points out that the results of the more recent changes in the recruitment and management of overseas labour services, however, have left these workers increasingly marginalised: Chinese overseas contract workers have fared considerably worse than those of other countries, partly because of a triangular relationship between the foreign employer, the overseas labour service broker and the contract worker. The indirect contact between the employer and the employee in such circumstances means that the Chinese overseas contract worker is vulnerable to exploitation, insecurity and violation of rights by domestic recruitment agencies as well as overseas employers. The overseas contract worker and his or her family have to shoulder all the costs and risks, by, for example paying high charges to the recruitment agent, while gaining disproportionately less of the potential benefits of working abroad in that the domestic labour broker determines their wages based on the levels in the Chinese domestic labour market rather than those in the host country. Wu argues that, today, the overseas labour service market remains chaotic and difficult to regulate. This, combined with the official prohibition of labour organisation, including trade union membership, has exacerbated the situation, rendering Chinese overseas contract workers even more marginalised and powerless in defending their rights and interests.

In chapter 9, John Tian takes up and reinforces many of the issues raised by Sanders, Chen and Cao in chapter 2 with regard to the difficulties currently faced by many Chinese farmers which have contributed to their increasing marginalisation in recent years, in the light of China's accession to the WTO in late 2001. At that time, many cautious observers, both inside and outside China, felt that China had conceded too much in its drive for WTO membership and that the interests of Chinese farmers in particular had been sacrificed in the negotiations with the USA. Adopting the approach of political economy, Tian's chapter revisits the pre-WTO anxieties, examines the post-WTO developments, in particular in terms of the policy adjustments in response to the challenges posed by the WTO, and evaluates their impact on and implications for Chinese agriculture. Interestingly, Tian shows that despite the much greater concessions made by China than by other WTO members in the opening up of its domestic agricultural market to include, for instance, eliminating state subsidies for agricultural export and substantial reduction of tariffs on agricultural import, Chinese agriculture and farmers have fared better than the critics expected and the many feared disruptions have not occurred owing to a combination of a favourable global market situation, appropriate policy measures and institutional changes. He suggests that, paradoxically, it was *because* of the many challenges which WTO membership brought about to farmers' livelihoods at a time when farmers were already suffering considerable hardship (and sometimes violently expressing their grievances at their plight) that prompted the Chinese government to adopt a battery of new measures designed to alleviate farmers' burdens, to include tax-for-fee changes and the abolition of agricultural taxes. However, he warns against complacency. He is particularly concerned that the recent improvement in farmers' income could be short-lived owing to a power vacuum at the local level created by political and fiscal constraints resulting from the combined effects of recentralisation of financial resources and the dual reforms of village governance and rural taxation. Tian predicts, therefore, that many of the challenges facing Chinese agriculture will remain for the foreseeable future.

The impact of WTO membership on the textile and clothing industries is the subject of the chapter jointly written by Markus Eberhardt and John Thoburn. Concentrating on the years leading up to the turn of the last century as China attempted a major restructuring of the industries in preparation for WTO entry in 2001, the authors provide a description of the process and discuss its employment implications and the social costs involved. It is fascinating to read, even in an industry which was expected to benefit significantly from China's WTO membership, that the restructuring deemed necessary to remain competitive caused considerable disruption and marginalised many groups of textile workers: almost two million textile workers lost their jobs in 1997/8 alone as a result of the government-initiated enterprise restructuring and overall, there was a 28% drop in employment in the sector during the last decade of the twentieth century. Many workers, particularly the older and less skilled, lost their jobs in SOEs together with their social welfare benefits, and in consequence, suffered from marginalisation in their economic and social lives. The authors argue that the optimistic projection of the impact of China's WTO entry on job creation failed to take full account of the effects on employment of intensified import competition in the Chinese domestic market as China lowered import barriers under its WTO accession agreement.

Heather Xiaoquan Zhang in chapter 11 turns to an examination of the marginalisation of migrant workers in Chinese towns and cities from a fresh perspective: health and well-being. While acknowledging the positive role that rural-urban migration can play in rural poverty reduction and livelihood diversification, Heather Xiaoquan Zhang, in common with Li Zhang in chapter 5, perceives the legacy of the *hukou* regime as a major institutional constraint responsible for pushing many migrants to the margins of Chinese society with their equal citizenship rights barely recognised. She shows that rural migrants continue to suffer from discrimination, marginalisation and social exclusion and that this state-of-affairs, together with the many emerging health hazards in China in a context of increased inequality and globalisation, has exacerbated the vulnerabilities of rural migrants to ill-health, compounding their marginalised status and constituting serious threats to their livelihoods, welfare and well-being. In an attempt to develop a conceptual framework for an understanding of the relationship between migration and development in China, Zhang demonstrates that the sustainable livelihood analysis, taking an actor-oriented approach, holds the potential for such a framework. She points out, however, that the framework so far has not paid much attention to health as an essential livelihood component, a significant omission in that health can determine its *sustainability* and outcomes. By an extensive review of literature, Zhang's chapter explores the conceptual linkages between migration, health and sustainable livelihoods and argues that while being a useful conceptual tool, the livelihood framework needs to be broadened by incorporating a health and well-being perspective. This can be achieved by broadening our understanding and interpretation of (a) *access* – by going beyond the emphasis on a single economic dimension of employment entry to include, in particular, access to public goods such as healthcare, (b) *sustainability* – by including not merely environmental but also human sustainability; and (c) *human capital* – by perceiving health as the basic constituent of livelihood; and by paying greater attention – beyond individuals and households – to institutions, structures and power in shaping livelihoods and their sustainability or vulnerability.

Continuing the investigation into health-related issues, chapter 12 by Ian Cook and Trevor Dummer highlights changes in access to healthcare wrought by the reforms in the context of globalisation, changes which have aggravated the vulnerabilities of marginalised groups, such as the elderly, the unemployed, women, ethnic minorities and rural migrant workers. They present a tilted development landscape of post-reform China where globalisation has led to significant spatial and social discrepancies between regions and areas. In this regard, they examine the role of inward foreign direct investment, which has flowed overwhelmingly into China's coastal regions, in enlarging the developmental gaps between the eastern seaboard and the hinterlands, as a consequence, for example, of growing wage differences and differentials in local and regional government revenues, leading to a huge array of inequalities which affect healthcare provision, as well as health and well-being outcomes. Cook and Dummer examine the critical health issues facing China today and paint an alarming picture in which, despite China's overall increases in prosperity, a large number of endemic diseases are actually on the *rise,* to include schistosomiasis, tuberculosis, malaria, viral hepatitis and Dengue fever. Added to these are the new epidemics and health hazards, such as HIV/AIDS, SARS and Avian Flu. The authors analyse these in the context of changes and reforms in healthcare provision wrought in the years of transition and globalisation which have increased the pressures on healthcare to marketise, to 'modernise' and to employ new technologies to tackle health problems. They point out that such forces, however, have been partly responsible for the country's deteriorating health services and exacerbated inequalities in access to healthcare, compounding the marginalisation of particular groups of people, to include the rural poor. The authors suggest that institutional support, in the form of, for instance, more equitable health insurance coverage for those marginalised and most negatively affected by globalisation would bring both economic and social benefits, and thus be of crucial importance in terms of reducing poverty and promoting welfare in China.

The theoretical links between modernisation, globalisation and marginalisation are further explored by Katherine Morton in chapter 13, where the author adopts a critical approach by problematising Western social thoughts and philosophy and their informed faith in 'modernity' and 'progress'. Morton looks at the influences of such ideas on Chinese intellectuals and leaders both historically and contemporarily. For Morton, the present-day discourse of globalisation resonates, to a large extent, with the modernisation school of thought and the dominant idea of 'human progress', manifest in the desire for greater material wealth, has a strong tendency to overlook the inequalities and social injustices that have occurred as a direct consequence of the 'modernisation' of China. Instead of seeing those marginalised as victims, however, Morton focuses on the agency of people in marginal places, that is, the work of grassroots non-governmental organisations (NGOs) in making a difference to the lives of the marginalised and disadvantaged by evoking the ideals of compassion, mutual help and self-development. Basing her analysis of marginalisation firmly within the context of social justice – or lack of it – Morton argues that NGOs have, under certain conditions, the capacity to allow marginalised groups, those suffering most from forms of social injustice and from the downsides of modernisation and globalisation, to gain some redress. She provides us with fascinating evidence from her recent fieldwork on two NGOs in China's remote western Qinghai province predominantly inhabited by ethnic minority groups, the Sanchuan Development Association and the Snowland Service Group, that, despite the difficulties they have faced, sometimes as a result of government restrictions, they have the potential capacity to mobilise people and resources and thereby alleviate hardship without destroying tradition. Morton suggests, however, that not all NGOs will be successful in so doing and that a number of factors are crucial to their success: the NGOs must be grounded firmly within their 'grassroots', allowing community-wide participation and local knowledge to be the foundations of policy and action; they must possess the tradition of communal self-help supported by strong community spirit and a sense of human compassion; it is helpful to have charismatic local leaders who possess broader social and political capital and they must be linked and networked with wider civil society both nationally and internationally. Above all, NGOs must be transparent and patient advocates of social justice and their success should be measured less by immediate policy outcomes and more by their ability to effect broader attitudinal changes, albeit gradually and incrementally.

Overall, this volume challenges the development paradigm dominant in China for the past 28 years of transition by examining the flipside of modernisation and globalisation and their consequences and implications for marginalisation. As a whole the voice uttered here calls for a critical evaluation of and reflection on policies and practices that are informed by such a paradigm and which tend to justify inequalities and social injustice as an 'inevitable' outcome of 'modernity' and 'progress'. Instead, we hold that marginalisation, as it is intertwined with poverty and social exclusion, is unacceptable and should be forcefully tackled through institutional changes, social policy making and effective responses from both the state and civil society.

References

Beck, Ulrich (2000), *What Is Globalisation?* Polity: Cambridge and Oxford, UK.

Castells, Manuel (1996), *The Information Age: Economy, Society and Culture, Vol. 1: The Rise of the Network Society*, Oxford: Blackwell.

Chang, Chun, Fleisher, Belton M. and Parker, Elliott (eds.) (2001), Special Issue of *China Economic Review*, No. 1.

Dasgupta, Biplab (1998), *Structural Adjustment, Global Trade and the New Political Economy of Development*, Zed Books: London and New York.

Giddens, Anthony (1990), *The Consequences of Modernity*, Polity, Cambridge, UK.

Martin, Ron (2004), 'Editorial: Geography: Making a Difference in a Globalising World', *Trans Inst Br Gergr*, No. 29, pp. 147-150.

Masina, Pietro P. (ed.) (2002), *Rethinking Development in East Asia: From Illusory Miracle to Economic Crisis*, Curzon: Richmond.

Stiglitz, Joseph (2002), *Globalisation and Its Discontents*, W.W. Norton: New York.

PART 1
China in Transition: Inequality, Poverty and Marginalisation

Chapter 2

Marginalisation in the Chinese Countryside: The Question of Rural Poverty

Richard Sanders, Yang Chen and Yiying Cao

Introduction

In April 2005 the villagers of Huankantou in the countryside of Zhejiang province rose up against the authorities. They rioted, set up road blocks, repelled a thousand riot police, putting more than thirty into hospital, smashed police buses and left cars burned out and windows broken. In so doing they became merely the latest in a very long list of rural dwellers who have, over the last two decades, felt the need to resort to violence in protest at the conditions in which they have found themselves. In Huankantou, villagers blamed official corruption, the seizure of village land for an industrial park and the siting of a highly polluting chemical works therein. When the authorities refused to listen to their grievances, they took to the streets (Watts, 2005, p.1).

The disaffection of Huankantou's villagers and countless more like them, many accounts of which appear in the groundbreaking – though officially banned – Chinese Farmers Report by Chen and Chun (2004), is eloquent testimony to the growing social polarity in contemporary China, a country where national income per head has been rising by 9-10% a year for two decades, where increasing numbers of urban millionaires have been created, where a well-off urban middle-class has taken shape, driving cars, living in stylish villas and taking regular holidays and, indeed, where hundreds of millions of people in both town and countryside have been taken out of poverty in record time. For while the majority of the 1.3 billion Chinese have enjoyed significant material fruits of recent economic growth, there are a large number of mostly rural Chinese for whom relative poverty, and in some cases absolute poverty, impacts powerfully on their daily lives. In 2003, for the first time since records began, the numbers of rural Chinese living in absolute poverty, defined as earning less than 637 yuan a year[1] – less than two yuan a day- rose by 800,000 to over 29 million (Xinhua, 2004), as did, at 85 million, the numbers living on less than PPP$1 a day, the World Bank poverty threshold (Watts, 2004). The Chinese Poverty Alleviation and Development Office blamed this rise on unexpected natural disasters and were relieved that the figures fell again in 2004. But it is clearly not only the

1 At current (2006) exchange rates, US1$ = approximately 8 yuan.

absolute poor in rural China who feel left behind in the general rush to get rich quick but the many farmers, like those in Huankantou, residents of one of the richest provinces in China, who feel sufficiently aggrieved at the conditions in which they live their lives that they resort to desperate means to change them. Such desperation is surely ample testimony to the extent to which many rural poor feel marginalised in contemporary China.

Links between poverty and marginalisation are neither necessary nor inevitable. In the Mao years, poverty was endemic in the Chinese countryside yet the rural institutional environment, in the form of the three 'nested layers' (White, 1993, p.95) of the communes (*gongshe*), brigades (*dadui*) and production teams (*xiaodui*), was created (and recreated) to ensure the peasants were at the centre of the Chinese revolution of the time. While most Chinese peasants were poor, they were not marginalised. Since the start of the reforms and the sweeping away of the communes, however, sections of the Chinese rural population have remained absolutely poor and/or, in terms of their felt experiences, marginalised and powerless as most others have gained relative advantage.

This chapter will attempt to provide explanations as to how this state-of-affairs has come about, engaging with questions not only associated with the urban-rural divide but with those to do with inequality within the countryside. Using recent 2003 data from the National Bureau of Statistics of China on the contemporary conditions of rural households,[2] it will attempt to provide a full account of the extent of rural poverty and its location and a clear explanation of its multiple causes, to include questions of government policy, institutional and other changes in the countryside and environmental degradation and pollution. The chapter will continue by discussing the current prospects for poor and increasingly marginalised farmers and conclude by suggesting appropriate institutional responses to alleviate their problems.

The Urban-Rural Divide

The Maoist Legacy

Though divisions between the urban and rural China have accentuated dramatically in the reform period since 1979, institutional discrimination between town and countryside began well before then. Indeed, it is arguable (Sanders, 2000a, p.24) that the one clear thread linking state policy towards agriculture in both pre- and post-reform periods has been that, despite differences in emphasis (Yao, 1994, p.4), the Chinese countryside has consistently been squeezed of surpluses in the interests of the heavy industrial and urban sectors. As White (1993, p.96) argued, under Mao,

> state policies towards agriculture.... were not designed to encourage rural development merely for its own sake, but to link agriculture and other sectors of the rural economy into an overall economic strategy which benefited industrialisation.

---

2 The authors would like to thank the China Centre for Agricultural Policy (CCAP), Chinese Academy of Agricultural Sciences, Beijing for access to the NBSC database.

We argue that little has changed since. The institutionalised discrimination referred to above stemmed from government policy designed to ensure that a rapidly increasing urban, industrial population could be fed cheaply. It led to a widening of the 'price-scissors' (*jiandao cha*) in which the prices of industrialised inputs to agriculture were allowed to rise while the state procurement prices for farm outputs were kept low, squeezing any farmers' surpluses in the interests of urban areas. The disasters unleashed on the rural population by the Great Leap Forward of 1958 and the subsequent famine of 1959-61, in which up to 30 million peasants were feared to have died of starvation, and countless more reduced to penury, illustrated the potential 'invisibility' of farmers and their problems. Even after the Great Leap was abandoned, farmers' per capita income from workpoints increased by only 10.5 yuan between 1965 and 1976, an increase of less than one yuan a year, just enough to buy a packet of cigarettes while private household earnings from sidelines, banned as 'capitalist tails' (*zibenzhuyi weiba*) during the Cultural Revolution, were seriously reduced (Howard, 1988). In 1978, per capita earnings from collective sources averaged only 74 yuan and a quarter of all peasants had a per capita income of less than 50 yuan. As Howard (1988, p.44) comments, "peasants succinctly expressed their predicament with a common complaint that they were being 'roped together to live a poor life'".

And peasants were further trapped in poverty by the system of household registration (*hukou*) which meant that the rural population was denied rights of migration to urban areas, alongside the planned labour allocation system. All this denied farmers the entitlement to work and welfare, in terms of education, medical treatment, low-cost housing and pension benefits that urban residents enjoyed (Du, 2001, see also the chapter by Li Zhang in this volume).

The Reform Period

When the reform period began in 1979, average per capita net incomes in urban areas [343.4 yuan] were already more than 2.5 times those in rural areas [133.6 yuan] (China Statistical Yearbook, 2004, p.357). In the very early years of the reforms, increases in farm incomes were generated through a significant increase in outputs as rural incentives sharpened with decollectivisation and with the rise in state procurement prices for agricultural produce. With average net per capita annual income up to 397.6 yuan by 1985, rural households' incomes were only 1:1.85 of their urban counterparts. But the trend was reversed thereafter. By 1990, rural incomes as a ratio of urban incomes fell to 1:2.2, by 1995 to 1:2.7 and by 2000 to 1:2.8. In 2003, the ratio widened dramatically, to 1:3.2. While average annual per capita incomes of rural households had climbed to 2,622 yuan, those of urban households increased to 8,472 yuan (China Statistical Yearbook, 2004, p.357). Indeed Zhao Renwei (2001) of the Chinese Academy of Social Sciences estimates that the real income disparity might well be greater once the welfare benefits of urban residents are taken into account. The reform period has thus worsened the relative position of farmers inherited from the pre-reform years and the income disparity between urban and rural households continues to widen today (see Figure 2.1).

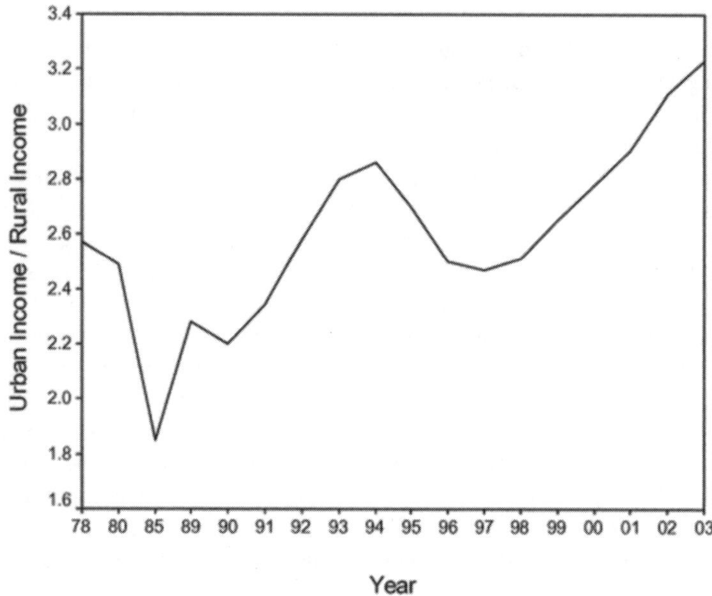

Figure 2.1 The urban/rural income multiple
Source: Compiled by the authors from China Statistical Yearbook 2004, p.357.

State policy and institutional inertia appear to be the primary factors responsible for this state-of-affairs. There is plenty of evidence to suggest that the price scissors effect continues to hurt farmers, as crop prices stagnate while farm expenditure on chemical fertilisers and seeds have continued to rise. Between 1985-1995, for example, in the heat of the restructuring of state-owned enterprises which led to the laying-off of large numbers of urban workers, the administered prices of major agricultural products was reduced in order to maintain order and social stability in urban areas. The price of rice was reduced from 2 yuan to below 1 yuan per jin,[3] while the price of eggs was reduced from 3.5 yuan to less than 1.8 yuan per jin. Thus while farmers increased their outputs, their sales revenues fell (Lu, 2000).

But these detrimental effects on farmers have been reinforced by other policy initiatives, to include the increasingly onerous levying of fees and charges by the state at provincial and particularly local levels. There is a wealth of evidence (see, for example, Bernstein and Lu, 2000) to suggest that the fiscal burden for farmers (*nongmin fudan*) has magnified alarmingly. As farmers from Huibei village in Anhui province complained to Chen and Chun (2004, p.7),

> expenditures on seeds, fertilisers, irrigation and hiring machinery keep rising and on top of production costs, local cadres levy all sorts of additional fees. The wheat production has to exceed 990 jin per mu,[4] otherwise we make a loss. But, as you know, in Huibei, it is

3 A *jin* is half a kilogram.

4 A *mu* is one sixteenth of a hectare.

very rare to get 900 jin per mu and on average we get only 600 jin per mu. We can hardly sustain our own living with farming; how can we pay numerous additional fees?

Another institutional factor continuing to reinforce the urban-rural divide remains the hukou[5] system (see also the chapter by Li Zhang in this volume). While the strict household registration system of the past has been relaxed, allowing rural-urban migration to take place, it does so by penalising migrants to the city at the expense of rural residents. Wages for migrants are frequently lower and social welfare benefits often non-existent, reducing the incentive for rural people to migrate and reducing the remittances of those that do – frequently an important source of household income to those left behind (see Unger, 2002, p.175). To these and other forms of institutional and policy discrimination against farmers, we return later in the chapter.

The Gini Coefficient

The Gini Coefficient is the most common index of income inequality used by economists, its values varying between 0 (perfect equality) and 1 (perfect inequality). Though under Mao the rural population was indeed subject to both policy and institutional discrimination, various estimates of the Gini Coefficient at the end of the 1970s suggest that, at around 0.26 (see Brugger and Reglar, 1994, p.126), China's income distribution was one of the most equal in the world. In the 1980s and 1990s, however, there was a notable retreat from equality (Riskin, Zhao and Li, 2001; Khan and Riskin, 2001). Today, with a Gini Coefficient of 0.45 (World Bank, 2004) higher than in either the USA or UK, it is one of the most unequal. With a growing number of urban millionaires, this high figure across China as a whole might well have been expected. However, the fact that the Gini Coefficient within the Chinese countryside is, on a number of estimates (Unger, 2002, p.172) above 0.4 suggests that it is not merely the result of an urban-rural divide that poverty and marginalisation exist in rural China.

Intra-Rural Poverty

Regional Differences

Much of the differences in incomes between rural households can be explained by geography. Since the start of the reforms the provinces on the eastern, and particularly, south-eastern seaboard of China, have made spectacular economic advances while those in the centre of China have made less spectacular advance and those provinces in western China have progressed at a much lower pace. The results are that the net per capita income of rural households varies dramatically on a regional basis. While the national average income of rural households in 2003 was 2,622 yuan, the provincial variation around the mean was substantial, the richest rural households

5 The system in which every individual is given a household registration *(hukou)* in a particular city or county in China which gives him/her social benefits not available elsewhere.

being in suburban Shanghai and Beijing, and in Zhejiang province, which are either leading metropolises of the country, or the eastern province in the coast region, 2.5, 2.2 and 2.1 times the national average respectively, the poorest being in Guizhou, Gansu and Shaanxi, all western provinces, with average rural incomes of 0.59, 0.64 and 0.64 of average rural incomes respectively (China Statistical Yearbook 2004 p.383). This makes the average rural income in Shanghai over 4 times higher than those in the poorest provinces. These provincial, regional differences are relatively easy to explain in that the reform and open policy (gaige kaifang) inevitably impacted most on those provinces geographically positioned to gain fastest from international trade and slowest on those geographically positioned least favourably to do so. But geographical position does not wholly explain either rural poverty or marginalisation. After all, Huankantou is a village in Zhejiang province where rural incomes are amongst the highest in China. And villages in provinces across China would have diverse experiences and outcomes in relation to poverty and marginalisation. To the reasons for this we now turn.

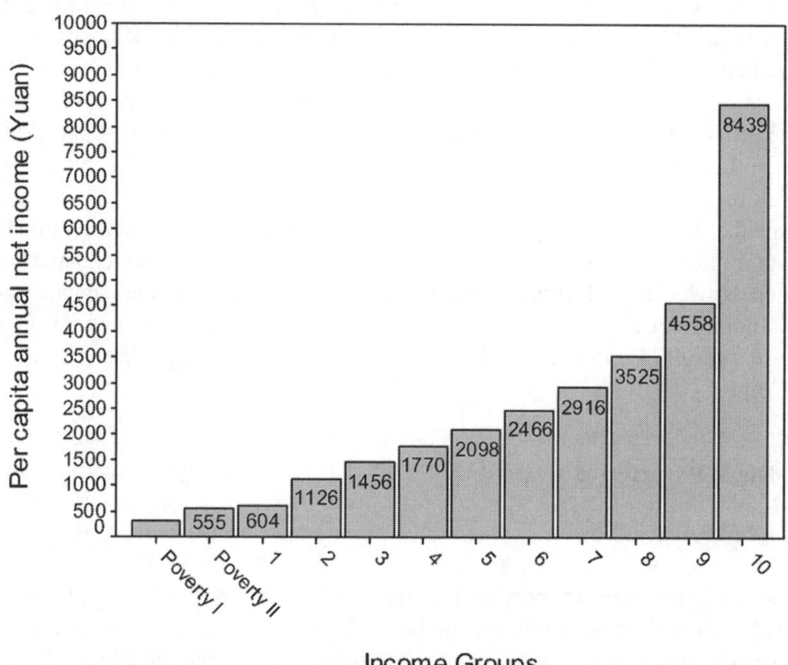

Figure 2.2 Per capita annual net income by decile

Poverty I represents those below Chinese poverty threshold (637 yuan p.a.)
Poverty II represents those below World Bank poverty threshold (PPP $1 per day)
Source: Compiled by the authors from the 2003 NBSC Rural Household Survey.

The National Bureau of Statistics of China's (NBSC) Rural Household Survey 2003

The NBSC's database on rural household income in 2003 presents a picture of multiple causation of rural poverty. It divides rural villages into ten equal deciles in order of household income level and additionally records information for those below the Chinese poverty line, 637 yuan p.a., (poverty I) and those below the World Bank poverty threshold, PPP$1 per day (poverty II). The lowest decile has an average per capita household income of 604 yuan, the highest an income of 8,439 yuan, a fourteen-fold discrepancy (see Figure 2.2). The database then distinguishes these deciles on a range of variables.

From the wealth of statistics provided, we have identified a number of variables which correlate strongly with income distribution. The importance of geography is reinforced by the data. While the average per capita annual net income of rural households is 2,895 yuan, it varies from 4,170 yuan in the South East (comprising Shanghai, Jiangsu, Zhejiang, Fujian, Jiangxi and Shandong) to 1,989 yuan in the South West (comprising Chongqing, Sichuan, Guizhou, Yunnan and Tibet). However, there are also other crucial geographical variations.

Nationally, 41% of villages are located in plains, but amongst the lowest decile less than 30% are so located while amongst the top decile, more than 60% are. Meanwhile, although nationally 23% of villages are located in mountainous regions, amongst the poorest decile, 36% are in mountainous regions, amongst the top decile, only 11%, strongly suggesting that geographical location in relation to topography is of considerable significance. Indeed, correlating the income rank of villages with their ranking in terms of percentages located in plains using the Rank Spearman Correlation Coefficient, we get a perfect positive correlation, when correlating income rank with ranking in terms of location in mountainous regions, we get a perfect negative correlation. Villages located in plains are much more likely to be richer than those in mountainous regions (see Figures 2.3 and 2.4).[6]

Another geographical pointer to income disparity is the distance of a village from the nearest town, railway station or port. The poorest villages are 2.5 times less likely to be within 2 kilometres of the county town than richest, but 23% more likely to be more than 20 kilometres from it. As to the distance to the local railway station or port, the poorest villages are more than 3 times as likely to be 20 kilometres or more distant than the richest villages.

Industrial Change

The reform era ushered in a new dimension of industrial change. While a green light to urban industrialisation was part of the process, the heroic rates of economic growth experienced nationally were substantially the result of industrialisation in the Chinese countryside as a result of the mushrooming of the township and village enterprises (TVEs). In the 1980s, many rural cadres, leaders of the now liquidated

6 The NBSC's Rural Household Survey database implies a third topographical category of hilly land, between 'mountainous areas' and 'plains'.

communes and freed from the restrictions on sideline activities imposed largely during the Cultural Revolution, turned their hands to producing chemicals, paper, bricks, clothing, bottles, indeed just about any industrial product that could turn a profit. This resulted in a huge explosion of industrial enterprises and output in rural areas, providing new opportunities of factory employment to farmers, either within their villages or in the nearest township or county.

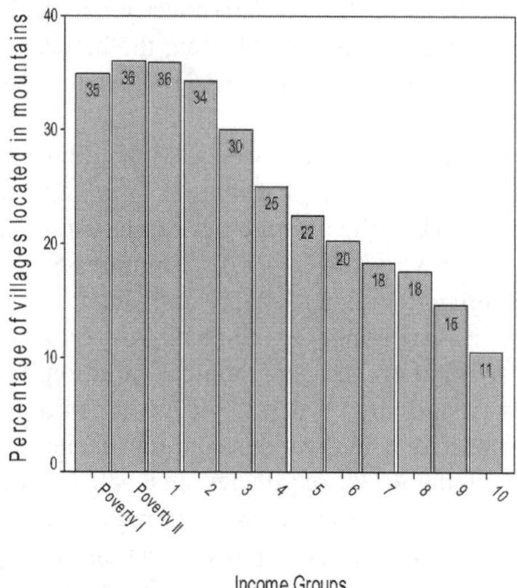

Figure 2.3 Percentage of villages located in mountains by income decile
Source: Compiled by the authors from the 2003 NBSC Rural Household Survey.

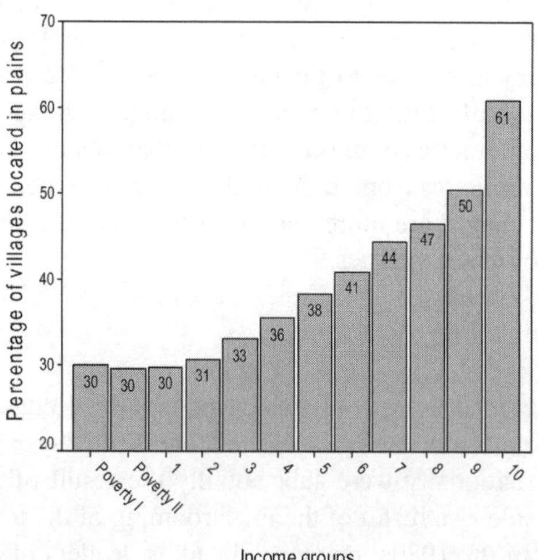

Figure 2.4 Percentage of villages located in plains by income decile
Source: Compiled by the authors from the 2003 NBSC Rural Household Survey.

All recent empirical evidence suggests that the availability – or otherwise – of employment in a nearby TVE is a major factor in creating disparities in income levels between rural households. The NBSC's database suggests that, in the poorest decile of villages in 2003, there was only one TVE and 26 TVE workers, in the richest decile, 8.7 TVEs and 286 TVE workers. This has huge impacts on household income. In the poorest decile of villages, per capita wage income (income largely from working in TVEs) in 2003 was 805 yuan, in the highest decile it was 11,430 yuan (see Figure 2.5). And of course, the richest households earn far higher proportions of their much larger incomes from wages. In Shanghai, no less than 78.9% of the average per capita rural household income of 6,654 yuan stems from wages, in Yunnan only 18.75% of 1,697 yuan does so (China Statistical Yearbook, 2004, p.383).

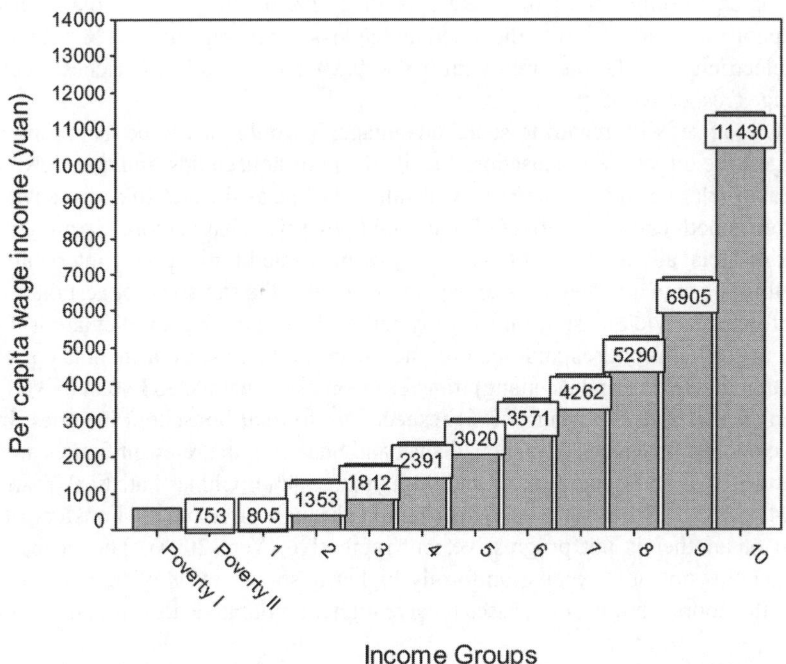

Figure 2.5 Per capita wage income by decile
Source: Compiled by the authors from the 2003 NBSC Rural Household Survey.

Geographical and Industrial Advantage

Disparities in incomes between rural households is therefore partly to be explained by whether or not the household possesses various forms of advantage. Certainly, geographical advantage, or lack of it, is a major cause of income inequality between rural households. Proximity to the East and South East seaboard is a major boon to households, as is location in plains rather than mountainous areas, as is proximity to nearby towns, railway stations and ports. Overlapping this geographical advantage, however, is industrial advantage, with opportunities for wage employment in TVEs correlating very strongly with levels of rural household income across China as a whole and helping to explain why, even in mountainous regions, far from the south eastern seaboard, from towns and railway stations, some villages are very much richer than others.

Social Advantage

It is unsurprising that the poorest villages ranked in terms of household income should also be those with least social advantage, measured in terms of the existence of roads, telephone networks, electricity and television coverage. According to the 2003 NBSC database, amongst the poorest decile of villages, 17% had no roads compared to only 4% of the richest decile. 7.7% of the poorest villages had no telephone network, 1.7% of them had no television coverage and 1.1% of them had no electricity at all, compared with 0.8%, 0.3% and 0.6% in the richest decile of villages respectively.

Of course, with regard to social advantage, it would clearly be inappropriate to suggest the direction of causation. Inevitably, poor households find themselves in a spiral of relative and, in some cases, absolute decline as the lack of social advantage becomes both cause and effect of household poverty. What is more alarming is that lack of social advantage is not in any way compensated for by policy intervention in the form of state directed transfer payments. Indeed, the statistics suggest that policy reinforces the vicious spiral of poverty rather than operating to alleviate it. In the two major metropolises and one province with the highest rural incomes per head (Shanghai, Beijing and Zhejiang) transfer incomes contribute 353 yuan (5.3%), 365 yuan (6.5%) and 232 yuan (4.3%) respectively to total household incomes. In the three poorest provinces (Guizhou, Gansu and Shaanxi), the relevant figures are 80.6 yuan (5.1%), 58.8 yuan (3.5%) and 90.9 yuan (5.4%) (China Statistical Yearbook, 2004, p.383). The system of redistribution through government transfers of one kind or another is not progressive, but regressive (Yep, 2004). The richest rural households not only receive uniformly higher absolute levels of transfer incomes than the poorest but in some cases receive higher amounts relative to their income.

Political, Educational and Ethnic Advantage

The NBSC 2003 rural household income database provides other clues as to the cause of income disparity. In the poorest decile of villages, only 3.1% of households have village leaders as members, in the richest decile it is 11.5%, suggesting strongly that political leadership at local level translates into political advantage which can frequently be income earning. Educational advantage is also statistically significant, with the poorest villages having more than four times the number of illiterate residents and less than 40% of the numbers graduating from high school as the richest villages. Ethnic advantage also must be taken into account. Indeed the 2003 NBSC survey suggests that ethnicity is one of the major factors in explaining disparities in incomes. For while over 20% of the poorest villages comprised ethnic minorities, only 3.6% of the richest villages did so. The richest households were overwhelmingly Han households.

Personal Factors

Despite the enormous disparities in incomes between one rural village and another, inevitably within villages there are also income disparities to be partially explained by differing levels of political, educational and ethnic advantages discussed above. Inevitably other factors will play a part, however, to include death, disability, illness, old age and infirmity of household members, what Estes (2000) would call "case poverty". The breaking of the 'big pot' resulting from the abolition of the communes has meant that such personal misfortune remains a crucial factor in keeping poor households poor.

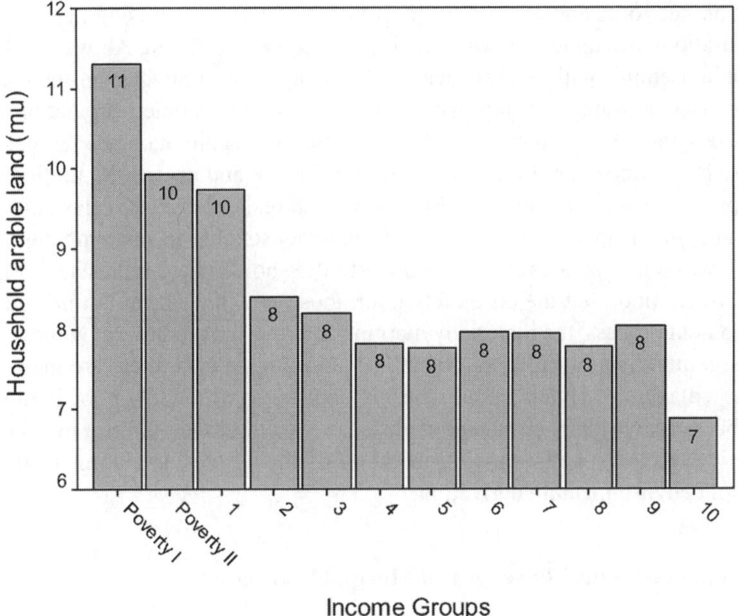

Figure 2.6 Household arable land (*mu*) by income decile
Source: Compiled by the authors from the 2003 NBSC Rural Household Survey.

Other factors leading to income discrepancies within villages include the differential impacts of marriage settlements, impacting badly on households with female children and of outward migration. One perhaps counter-intuitive inference from the NBSC 2003 rural household income survey, however, is that there is no positive correlation between household poverty and either family size or size of landholding. Indeed, in the lowest income decile, the average family size is 4.35 and the figure falls, as the income decile rises, to a figure of 3.0 amongst the highest income decile, providing a perfect negative rank correlation between household size and income levels. There is also a strong negative correlation between income levels and available arable land, those households in the lowest income decile having, on average, 9.74 mu of available land, those in the highest income decile, having only 6.87 mu, implying, amongst other things a very low marginal productivity to both land and labour in the Chinese countryside (see Figure 2.6).

2003 NBSC Rural Household Survey: A Summary

The NBSC's database thus provides a multi-dimensional picture of inequality and poverty in contemporary rural China. The poorest villages, and as a result the poorest villagers, are most likely to be located far from the eastern seaboard, in the central, western and south western provinces. They are more than likely to live in mountainous regions, a long distance from a county town, far from a nearby port or railway station. The poorest villages are likely to have fewer roads, telephone links, television networks and electricity lines, their residents comprising above average concentrations of ethnic minorities and the least well educated. Above all else, the poorest households will be dependent primarily upon farming for their income, with little or no opportunity for employment in local TVEs to supplement that income.

In 2004 there were 26 million Chinese whose per capita incomes fell below the Chinese government's poverty threshold of 637 yuan and another 52 million whose per capita incomes fell below the World Bank's threshold of PPP$1 day (Lu, 2005). Thus, altogether approximately 1 in 11 rural households in contemporary China fall below the internationally agreed poverty threshold. These represent not merely the relatively poor, but the absolutely poor, those who have been left behind in the development process, the materially marginalised in China today. Yet while there are very large numbers of villagers objectively so marginalised, there are many more, like the villagers of Huankantou, who may not be so absolutely poor in monetary terms but perceive themselves marginalised as a result of their inferior income status in relative terms as well as their perception of themselves as victims of political, social and environmental deprivation.

Perspectives on Rural Poverty and Marginalisation

Relative Poverty and Farmers' Protests

The very large number of rural protests, frequently leading to rioting and violence, grew in scale and number throughout the 1990s and beyond (see, for example, Bernstein and Lu, 2000, Yep, 2004) and are testimony to both absolute and perceived relative marginalisation. The immediate causes of such protests are many and various but a common thread to most has been feelings of powerlessness in the face of a combination of increasing fiscal burdens imposed by local officials, official indifference to the fate of rural households, corruption by local cadres and environmental degradation and pollution. The increasingly unreasonable fiscal burden on rural households became a serious cause for concern as early as 1987 as local governments, given greater fiscal autonomy associated with government decentralisation in the early 1980s, began to abuse that autonomy by imposing or increasing a number of rural taxes or introducing a new range of fees and levies (Bernstein and Lu, 2000, Yep 2004). As decentralisation has continued, the burdens of such taxes, fees and levies imposed by local officials has been exacerbated. Meanwhile, farmers grievances have included the lack of accountability amongst officials for the revenues raised, the arbitrariness and unpredictability of the levies, the failure of officials to deliver services paid for, the imposition of multiple charges for the same services, official banqueting and the deduction of levies from procurement payments or the issuing of IOUs[7] leaving farmers with little or no earnings at all. Responses have included official indifference in some cases or official brutality and callousness in others. In some reported cases, farmers, unwilling to pay their fiscal burdens have suffered serious injury, even death (Bernstein and Lu, 2000, p.747, Chen and Chun, 2004, chs. 1-3).

The Farmers' Burden

To add insult to injury, the fiscal burden on farmers in the form of taxes, levies and fees is regressive. As Unger (2002, p.176) reports, a survey in the mid-1990s based on 500 rural households selected randomly from poor regions across China concluded that taxation was highly regressive, with households in the lowest quintile paying a higher absolute amount of tax than those in the top quintile. Several other surveys quoted by Unger confirm the severe regressiveness of rural taxation.

One of the perennial difficulties facing research in China is the reliability of the statistics. Clearly, it is difficult for the state to target poverty alleviation if it is not easy to identify the poor. The problem is compounded, however, when local officials are complicit in deliberately falsifying the numbers in order to make things appear better than they really are in order to please their superiors. This phenomenon is well explained by Chen and Chun (2004, p.9) as they recount the predicament of the villagers of Baiji village, Xiuning County, Anhui Province:

> As a village in a county that is close to Huangshan, Baiji farmers are supposed to be better-off, however the facts are: among the 620 households, 514 (82.95%) are living in poverty and classified as pinkun hu; average annual income in Baiji is only 700 yuan, most households live in mud built tree-skinned roofed houses; there is no basic medical care and farmers cannot afford any medical treatment.
>
> Although most farmers lived in poverty, the village was deleted from the list of counties in poverty several years ago and was classified as 'escaped from poverty' (*tuo pin*) as a result of misleading statistics cooked up by corrupt village cadres. Being classified as 'escaped from poverty', heavier taxes and additional fees were levied on poor farmers which made the poverty of Baiji farmers still worse.

The sheer numbers of officials to support at local level magnifies the farmers' burden. According to Xiangang Li of the Rural Economic Research Centre, there are 13.16 million cadres at the county level or below, implying that, on average, 68

7 Credit notes (I owe you).

farmers are levied taxes and fees to support one cadre. In the words of local farmers in Lixing County, Anhui Province, "dozens of people in uniforms govern one farmer in a straw hat" (Chen and Chun, 2004, p.173).

At the same time, many local officials have added to the perceived relative marginalisation of poor farmers by indifference or connivance in local environmental degradation and pollution. Much has been written by scholars both within China and without on the precarious state of the Chinese natural environment (see, for example, Smil, 1984, Edmonds, 1995, Sanders, 2000a). Suffice it to say that many of the threats to that environment result from inappropriate activities in rural areas to include the overuse of chemical fertilisers, pesticides and herbicides, which, on the one hand, are both expensive and suffer from diminishing marginal returns while, on the other, cause a range of environmental ills, to include land degradation, desertification, soil erosion, and leeching of nitrates into soils and water courses (Sanders, 2000b), as well as spelling danger to health for those who use them. But just as overtly threatening to the natural environment in the countryside – through atmospheric, solid waste and water pollution- have been TVEs, frequently involved in some of the most polluting industries, to include the making of chemicals, paints, bricks and paper, operating with little or no knowledge of environmental impacts, or, if the knowledge is there, widespread indifference to them. As environmental education and state concern for environmental protection have spread in China throughout the 1990s, more and more local environmental protection bureaux (EPBs) have been established, but their funding has been variable –those furthest from the urban centres the least well funded – and their powers frequently compromised by the determination of other village or township cadres to expand industrial employment and earn profits thereby. Where ETBs have imposed fines on polluting enterprises, enterprise managers have frequently treated them as costs well worth paying. As a result, as in Huankantou village, environmental pollution based on official indifference and connivance adds injury to insult for rural dwellers and reduces them to marginalised status.

Institutional Factors: The Household Responsibility System

Perhaps the most significant of the early reforms under Deng Xiaoping was the abandonment of the communes and their replacement by the Household Responsibility System (HRS) in the late 1970s and early 1980s. Communal land and property were divided up equitably but parsimoniously amongst households on a 15 year leasehold basis (since renewed for 30 years) and each household was contracted to produce a certain amount of grain for the state to be sold at state determined procurement prices. Once the household had fulfilled its contract to the state, it could either consume any surpluses produced or sell them in newly legalised rural markets at the going market rates. The HRS thus determined for most farmers the incentive system in which they would operate, the prices they would receive, the size of plots they would farm, the stocks of capital they could use, the land tenure system to which they were subject and the crops they would plant. Little in terms of principle has changed since: farmers still farm very small plots on an individual household basis with a contract to supply grain or taxes to the state and have user but no exchange rights over the land.

The structural position within which farmers have found themselves since the reforms is such that, unlike in North America or Europe, there is little or no opportunity for farmers to get rich through farming alone. Farmers farm very small holdings, the average allotment of arable land being 8 mu (NBSC, 2003). Since that 8 mu may well not be contiguous but may comprise two or three plots, the legacy of a highly equitable post-commune distribution system whereby all households were allotted equal amounts of good and bad land, the opportunities for farmers to enjoy the benefits of economies of scale are non-existent. The size of household plots determines an overwhelmingly labour-intensive agriculture by limiting the size and scale of agricultural machinery that can be used, even if the household could afford it. Meanwhile the land tenure system associated with the HRS, whereby land cannot be sold, means that there are negligible opportunities for farmers to expand the size of their operations. As a result, the efficiency of Chinese agriculture remains very low. In that procurement prices are determined largely in the interests of keeping grain prices down, it is hardly surprising that the key to increasing farmer household incomes has been the opportunity to earn non-farm income, primarily in the form of income from employment in local TVEs or as remittances from household members who have migrated to the cities to find work.

Other Institutional Factors

Meanwhile other policy and institutional factors continue to discriminate against farmers. These factors include (a) the lack of credit facilities for the rural poor in reform China (Unger, 2002) and, as mentioned above, (b) adverse movements in the 'price scissors', aggravating the terms of trade for farmers, (c) the hukou system, which continues to restrict migration from the poorest households and reduces remittances therefrom, (d) excessive and regressive taxation at local level, biting into the net incomes of farmers and (e) the current failure of the state system of transfer payments to redress the balance, indeed its contribution to exacerbating inequality.

The predicament of farmers is, indeed, a sorry one.

Government Approach and Policy Options

The accounts of increasing rural unrest, leading to rioting and violence, has spurred the Chinese government into a range of policy initiatives in the last ten years or so to alleviate the farmers' predicament and thereby ensure social stability and the avoidance of 'chaos' (*luan*). In the mid 1990s, the Chinese government announced a range of targeted poverty alleviation programmes (Unger, 2002; Khan and Riskin, 2001; Zhang, Huang and Roselle, 2003). Meanwhile China's Campaign to "Develop the West", first announced in 1999 and currently ongoing (Goodman, 2004; Tian, 2004), was designed to increase the material opportunities of all those, often farmers, who reside in the western regions of China. In 2002, then Premier Zhu Rongji, in his government report to the National Peoples Congress, emphasised repeatedly the importance of alleviating farmers' burdens in order to achieve stability and growth. More recently, the Chinese government's tax-for-fee (*feigaishui*) initiatives (Yep, 2004; see also Tian's chapter in this volume), designed to replace the arbitrary imposition of fees and levies by local officials on farmers with a system of clearly defined, transparent taxation determined centrally has attempted to reduce the arbitrary and regressive nature of taxation on poor farmers.

However the success of the targeted poverty alleviation programmes is debatable (Ravallion and Chen, 2004) and clearly not complete (Zhang, Huang and Roselle, 2003). One of the reasons for their limited success has been errors in targeting, partly the result of inadequate statistics (see above), debates around the validity of the statistics (Gustafsson and Zhong, 2000), politicisation of the poverty headcount (Park and Wang, 2001) and poor administration, such that only one of the three designated programmes is actually progressive (Park, Wang and Wu, 2002).

The "Develop the West" campaign clearly has the aims of reducing socio-economic inequalities, particularly in non-Han areas of China, but despite superficial appearances to the contrary, according to Goodman (2004, p.317) the campaign represents more of an adjustment to current regional policy than a radical departure from it, not least because of "debate and imprecision about its goals, processes and finance". Tian (2004) calls for greater clarification and quantification of policy goals, a reinforceable legal system, greater government efficiency and deeper economic reform in rural areas if the "Develop the West" campaign is to be successful in reducing China's widening economic inequalities. Meanwhile, the "tax-for-fee" initiatives, for Yep (2004, p.69), merely reflect the state's inability to adapt its financial mechanisms to the rapidly changing economic structures in China and are doomed to failure unless the government faces up squarely to current institutional deficiencies with regard to questions of redistribution and accepts the need for far more radical change.

Conclusions

We argue that marginalisation stems from both absolute and relative poverty in the countryside. Despite the enormous strides that China has taken in reducing rural poverty over the last 28 years, it is clear from all recent data to include the NBSC's 2003 Rural Household Income Survey and, indeed from our own experiences of fieldwork in a large numbers of provinces in rural China, that the problem of absolute poverty has not been eradicated, that depending upon where the line is drawn, there are between 25 million to 80 million (3% to 9% of the rural population) absolutely poor rural Chinese and that these numbers have become increasingly impervious to change. Indeed, in 2003, the numbers rose. But the problem of absolute poverty is compounded by perceived relative poverty, its existence illustrated in the pages of Chen and Chun's Chinese Farmers Report and in the many reports of rural discontent which reach the front pages of the western press, to include the rioting in Huankantou in 2005.

The reform period in China has ushered in market processes as opposed to planning as the principal means of allocating scarce resources. It is hardly surprising, therefore, that inequality has increased since 1980. After all, even advocates of the market recognise that market signals operate on the basis of inequality. Unless prices and incomes are different, market forces cannot work. So it is futile to expect further market-based reforms to redress imbalances, indeed quite the reverse. In most developed nations, the problem of inequality and the redress of poverty is left to state interventionist, redistributive policy to deal with. In such countries, taxation is often highly progressive, as is the system of redistributive payments, which allows the poor to enjoy, in some cases, absolutely and, in all cases, relatively higher levels of welfare and other transfer payments than the rich.

But in contemporary rural China, we find a very different state-of-affairs in which many poor rural households, unfavourably geographically located and without the various forms of advantage – industrial, social, political, educational, ethnic, personal and the like necessary to achieve rapid welfare enhancement – and already facing forms of institutional and policy discrimination to include the effects of the widening 'price-scissors' and the hukou system, are subject to a state redistributive policy, both in the form of taxation and transfer payments, which is actually regressive, making the net distribution of income even more unequal than ever. State policy systematically discriminates against poor farmers. It is hardly surprising that the rural Gini-Coefficient is not only remarkably high for a nominally socialist country, but rising.

And it is clear that the poverty alleviation programmes advanced to date, including the Tax-For-Fee initiative and a greater degree of democratisation, have been motivated to a great extent by the central government's determination to deal with unrest in the countryside and ensure rural political stability rather than an interest in advancing the welfare of the poor on grounds of equity and social justice. We argue that, while the questions of inequality and poverty in the Chinese countryside continue to be handled largely in the interests of political expediency, prospects for the poor, both absolutely and relatively, will remain dim. While China remains in thrall to a market-based ideology which, in its very essence, demands inequality, there is little hope of a reverse from it and marginalisation will become ever more entrenched.

Meanwhile, other macro-economic and international developments associated with the globalisation process, to include China's membership of the World Trade Organisation threaten to exacerbate the problems for rural households (see Tian's chapter in this volume). President Hu Jintao and Premier Wen Jiabao are associated with the Chinese government's recent advocacy of 'balanced development' and the Construction of the New Socialist Countryside Movement launched in early 2006. However, unless they face up to the systematic discrimination by the state against poor rural households as a result of a welter of policy and institutional arrangements and unless the government radically alters local governance structures and outcomes and significantly increases its overall investment in rural areas, to include increases in investment in agricultural R&D, irrigation, rural education, health care, the sustainability of the rural environment and rural infrastructure (see Fan, Zhang and Zhang, 2004) on the basis of a policy commitment so to do, that advocacy will always have a hollow ring.

References

Bernstein, Thomas and Lu, Xiaobo (2000), 'Taxation without Representation: Peasants, the Central and Local States in Reform China', *The China Quarterly*, 163, pp.742-763.

Brugger, B. and Reglar, S. (1994) *Politics, Economy and Society in Contemporary China*, MacMillan, London.

Chen, Guidi and Chun, Tao (2004) *Chinese Farmers Report* (Zhongguo Nongmin Diaocha), Renmin Wenxue chubanshe, Beijing. (In Chinese).

Du, Rensheng (2001) 'We are Heavily Indebted to Peasants', Foreward to Li, Changping (2002) *Wo xiang zongli shuo shihua (I Told the Truth to the Premier)* p.2, Guangming Ribao chubanshe, Beijing.

Edmonds, R.L. (1995), *Patterns of Lost Harmony*, Routledge, London and New York.

Estes, Richard J. (2000), 'The "Poverties": Competing Perspectives and Alternative Approaches to Measurement', Paper presented at the "Rich and Poor" conference, ISA Work Group 6, Social Indicators and Social Reporting, Berlin, quoted in Lindberg Dennis N (2001), *Rural Poverty in China in Changing Contexts*, International Sociological Association Annual Conference, University of Oviedo, Spain.

Fan, Shenggen, Zhang, Linxiu and Zhang, Xiaobo (2004), *Reforms, Investment and Poverty in Rural China*, University of Chicago Press, Chicago USA.

Goodman, David S.G. (2004) 'The Campaign to "Open Up the West": National, Provincial and Local Perspectives', *The China Quarterly*, 178, pp.317-334.

Gustafsson, Bjorn and Zhong, Wei, (2000), 'How and Why has Poverty in China Changed'. A Study Based on Microdata for 1988 and 1995, *The China Quarterly*, 164, pp.983-1006.

Howard, Pat (1988), 'Breaking the Iron Rice Bowl', M.E.Sharpe, New York.

Khan, A.R. and Riskin, C. (2001) 'Inequality and Poverty in China in the Age of Globalization', Oxford University Press, Oxford.

Li, Binglong, (2002) 'The Progress of Poverty Alleviation in China: Experience, Problems and Implications for the Asia-Pacific', Paper presented to the Meeting of the Advisory Panel on ESCAP/UNDP Initiative to support the achievement of the Millennium Development Goals in Asia and the Pacific Region, Bangkok.

Lu, Chun, (2005), *2004: Monitoring Report of China's Rural Poverty*, Beijing Youth Daily, April 22.

Lu, Xuyi (2000), 'Walk Out of the Dilemma of "Urban Rural Separation, One State Two Systems"', *China Agricultural Economy*, 6.

National Bureau of Statistics of China (2004), *China Statistical Yearbook*, Beijing.

Park, Albert and Wang, Sangui (2001), *China's Poverty Statistics*, China Economic Review, 12, pp.384-398.

Park, Albert, Wang, Sangui and Wu, Guobao (2002), 'Regional Poverty Targeting in China', *Journal of Public Economics*, 86, pp.123-153.

Ravallion, Martin and Chen, Shaohua (2004), 'China's (Uneven) Progress Against Poverty', World Bank Research Working Paper 3408, Washington DC.

Riskin, Carl, Zhao, Renwei and Li, Shi, (2001) 'The Retreat from Equality: Highlights of the Findings', in Riskin, Zhao and Li (eds.), *China's Retreat from Equality*, M.E.Sharpe, London and New York.

Sanders, Richard, (2000a), *Prospects for Sustainable Development in the Chinese Countryside*, Ashgate, Aldershot, UK.

Sanders, Richard (2000b), 'Political Economy of Chinese Ecological Agriculture: a case study of seven Chinese eco-villages', *Journal of Contemporary China*, 9(25), pp.349-372.

Smil, Vaclav (1984), *The Bad Earth*, M.E.Sharpe, New York.

Tian Qunjian (2004), 'China Develops its West: Motivation, Strategy and Prospect', *Journal of Contemporary China*, 13 (41), pp.611-636.

Unger, Jonathan (2002), *The Transformation of Rural China*, M.E. Sharpe, New York.

Watts, Jonathan (2004), 'China Admits First Rise in Poverty since 1978', *The Guardian,* London, 20 July.

Watts, Jonathan (2005), 'A Bloody Revolt in a Tiny Village Challenges the Rulers of China', *The Guardian*, London, 18 April.

White, Gordon (1993), *Riding the Tiger, The Politics of Economic Reform in Post-Mao China*, Macmillan, London.

World Bank (2004), Fact Sheet: The Gini Coefficient, Legislative Council Secretariat, Research and Library Services Division, Washington DC, pp.4-5.

Xinhua (2004), '800,000 More Chinese Live in Poverty in 2003', China Daily, Beijing, July 20. Accessed from www.chinadaily.com.cn/english/doc/2004-7/20/content_350069.htm, retrieved April 19, 2005.

Yao, Shujie, (1994), *Agricultural Reforms and Grain Production in China*, Macmillan, London.

Yep, Ray (2004), 'Can "Tax for Fee Reform" Reduce Rural Tension in China? The Process, Progress and Limitations', *The China Quarterly*, 177, pp.42-70.

Zhang, Linxue, Huang, Jikun and Roselle, Scott (2003), 'China's War on Poverty: Assessing Targeting and the Growth Impacts of Poverty Programmes', *Journal of Chinese Economic and Business Studies*, 1 (3), pp.301-317.

Zhao, Renwei (2004) 'Increasing Income Inequality and its Causes', in Riskin, Zhao and Li (eds.), *China's Retreat from Inequality*, M.E. Sharpe, London and New York.

Chapter 3

Marginalisation of Laid-off State-owned Enterprise Workers in Wuhan

Jun Tang, Mingzhu Dong and Mark Duda

China's ongoing transition from central planning to a socialist market economy has engendered drastic economic and societal change. While such a transition would be challenging for any country, China's problems are compounded by the legacy of integration between the urban labour market and social welfare through the *danwei* system. For many workers, the unravelling of state ownership of the means of production and the exposure of state-owned enterprises (SOEs) to market competition has therefore not simply meant the loss of an income but also separation from their social benefits package at precisely the time when they need it most (Zheng and Hong 2004, Tang 2002a, and Cai and Yang 2000). For these workers, 'transition' has been experienced as a shift from insider to outsider status vis-à-vis the dominant social and economic systems – a move from relative social inclusion to a state of social marginality.

This chapter explores the nature and persistence of social marginality among former SOE workers in urban areas. Despite its importance, this topic has not been systematically addressed. The chapter therefore represents an initial step in the exposition of marginality among China's urban unemployed. It principally uses a case study of laid-off workers in the industrial city of Wuhan in central China to delineate and explore material conditions among this group and compares them to those of other residents. In doing so, it establishes a platform from which future studies on the underlying causes of and potential remedies for the types of marginality uncovered here can be examined.

The chapter begins with a discussion of the co-evolution of China's social welfare and employment systems, demonstrating the depth of the consequences suffered by laid-off SOE workers as a result of the ongoing dismantling and restructuring of these systems. It then reviews the policy steps taken to address the urban unemployment problem generated by the economic and social transition. Next, it develops a framework for assessing social marginality based on related work in China, Europe, and the post-Soviet states. Finally, it explores marginality using survey data on the material conditions and labour market outcomes among two sets of workers in Wuhan.

The empirical analysis focuses on the consumption aspects of marginality, finding that levels of deprivation among the laid-off group are severe in both absolute and relative terms. It also makes clear that there is little reason to expect either unemployment or underemployment following layoff to be a temporary phenomenon for most unemployed workers nor any reason to be optimistic that labour markets alone will help integrate these individuals into the broader social system. The chapter concludes by suggesting ways that marginality might be reduced by rethinking the basis of reemployment policy.

The Link between Work, Social Welfare, and Marginality in Urban China: 1949-2006

The relationship between work, welfare, and marginality in urban China has evolved in three phases since 1949. The first phase, from 1949 to 1978, was characterised by the deployment of the *danwei* system in which individuals were linked to the state resource allocating mechanism through their work units. During the second phase, from 1979 to 1994, this system was weakened as reforms created social divisions both by separating some workers from 'the system' and by allowing others to amass wealth and status. Subsequently, in the third and ongoing phase, this process has deepened and accelerated, producing widespread social divisions and marginality on a large scale.

The Urban Labour Market in the Planned Economy: 1949-1978

Beginning in 1949, a series of reforms led to the progressive nationalisation of the commercial and industrial sectors of the Chinese economy, along with virtually all urban real estate. Industrial production took priority as the government pursued policies intended to redirect the economy away from its agrarian base. Meanwhile, social welfare provision and the labour market were merged through the *danwei* system in which individuals were allocated to work units providing housing, schooling, medical care, pensions, other basic necessities and social welfare along with employment. Relative to alternative forms of social organisation the *danwei* system reduced the cash basis of a low value-added economy and minimised the number of individual allocation decisions made by economic planners. It also saved higher-level policymakers from taking direct responsibility for welfare provision because such decisions were lodged with work unit level cadres.

Over time the system's initial advantages became drawbacks, contributing to the underperformance of the national economy. Central economic planning led to low levels of allocative efficiency and constrained job growth (Yao 2005). The fact that control was exercised politically, though not entirely at odds with productivity and profitability goals, meant that the end results often had little complimentarity with them. Labour mobility was minimal due to the links between employment, social welfare benefits and other in-kind remuneration. By the second half of the 1970s conditions had changed sufficiently that the administrative orientation of the *danwei* system had become problematic, causing policymakers to begin experimenting with quasi-market allocation mechanisms (Ji 1998).

As this period of socialist economic production drew to a close, Chinese cities were characterised by extremely low levels of income inequality (though urban-rural differences were substantial). Most urban households were attached to the state resource allocating system via their work units. As a result, the subsequent period in which reforms were progressively introduced saw not only a managed opening of the economic system to competitive pressures, but also a steady drift away from the previously high level of social cohesion as groups disadvantaged by the economic transition first tasted 'outsider' status and benefits accrued to those able to proactively adjust to the transition environment.

Gradual Labour Market Reform: 1979-1994

Introduction of the 'household responsibility system' (*jiating lianchan chengbao zerenzhi*) for agricultural producers is widely considered the beginning of the reform period. It did not, however, signal a wholesale shift in the allocative mechanism of the urban economy toward a more market-oriented basis and away from command and control. In contrast, the first round of reforms targeting the industrial sector were intended to solidify, rather than supplant, the state sector by 'correcting' the shortcomings of the SOEs in order to improve productivity (Yao 2005, Fan and Nolan 1994). As a result, the early years of the reform period did not see dramatic increases in marginality among urban workers.

Progressively, however, reforms began laying the groundwork for more substantial change. In 1986, the 'production responsibility and contract system' (*jingji zerenzhi yu laodong hetongzhi*) was introduced to define worker and enterprise rights in recruitment. Whereas previously workers were tied to work units for life, this change introduced flexibility for both parties. The wage system was also reformed to include bonus payments designed to stimulate productivity – SOE workers whose enterprises met government-set targets received better housing, health care, and other benefits, beginning a process of social differentiation.

The impact of these changes on the SOE sector was initially modest, however, and most enterprises continued to under-perform (Yao 1997, Hay *et al.* 1994, Groves *et al.* 1994). This was due in part to SOEs' cost structure – even as they became relatively less competitive SOEs continued to bear responsibility for the welfare benefits, including in many cases operating schools and hospitals, of their workers, while the new types of enterprises did not. In sectors hit hardest by reforms, such as textiles, both incomes and welfare benefits declined as the enterprises themselves were effectively bankrupt (see Eberhardt and Thoburn's chapter of this volume). Fan (1996) shows that a class of 'working poor' emerged among workers whose *danwei* were essentially bankrupt and unable to afford either their 'theoretical wages' or 'theoretical welfare.'

Overall, during the 1979-1994 period China's economy improved not by 'fixing' SOEs but largely through the introduction of new types of firms and new forms of employment (Buckley 2001). As a direct but unintended result, many workers in the growth (i.e. non-state) sector of the economy saw an end to their access to social welfare benefits, since no meaningful system of social protection was devised to cover most workers outside the public sector. The coexistence of a partially market-based economy and the state productive sector enhanced the process of differentiation and diversification across social groups. As a result of these trends, marginality became an increasingly possible social status in urban China, though this period offered only a hint of subsequent levels of inequality.

Initiating Fundamental Reform: 1994-Present

In 1993 at the Third Plenum of the Fourteenth Chinese Communist Party (hereafter CCP) Central Committee, Chinese leaders took the decisive step of initiating reforms to the foundation of the command economy – the State-Owned and the Collectively-Owned Enterprises (COEs). The latter differ from SOEs in that ownership belongs to their workers, rather than to the state, though many were established under the direction of local level governments or SOEs. A new system was envisioned based on 'clarified property rights, clearly defined responsibility and authority, separation of enterprises from the government, and scientific management.'[1] Reforms were designed to improve productivity by 'reducing redundancy and improving efficiency' (*jianyuan zengxiao*).

Unlike the earlier changes, these reforms would have far reaching effects on urban low-skill workers. Policies guided by the principle of 'focusing on the big and giving up the small' (*zhuada fangxiao*) allowed smaller and medium-size SOEs to escape state control either by failing, being privatised or through transformation into joint-stock companies. Larger SOEs were also encouraged to seek more flexible forms of ownership and many were restructured into share-holding corporations.

The changes led to severe and immediate employment effects for many urban workers. As SOE reforms became more widespread after 1997, many firms were allowed to fail and others required massive layoffs in order to compete with foreign rivals and domestic upstarts. In both cases large numbers of workers lost both salaries and benefits. The official national unemployment rate reached 5% though estimates of the actual rate are as much as five times higher (cf. Giles, Park and Zhang 2005, Cai 2003).

The combination of a shrinking state sector and a burgeoning private sector has meant the shift of a significant share of employment to 'informal' work – jobs not regulated by the standard labour contract scheme, and in which employers do not participate in the social insurance system. As a result, benefits of the growth in informal employment (to include increased labour mobility and flexibility, 'buffer' employment for laid-off workers attempting to re-enter the labour market and jobs for rural migrants) are offset by the fact that these jobs typically carry little or no social benefits package (Cai 2005). In addition to exposing many workers to poor working conditions in return for low wages and little job security, the growth of informal employment has therefore fostered a retreat of the social security system.

Collectively, the reforms of the last decade have substantially increased the supply of unskilled and low-skilled labour, holding down wages at the bottom of the urban wage structure, especially in areas with concentrations of obsolete industries. Because the *danwei* system still provides the framework for welfare policy most of

1 Several Decisions on Establishing Socialist Market Economy by the Central Committee of Chinese Communist Party (*Zhonggong Zhongyang Guanyu Jianli Shehui Zhuyi Shichang Jingji de Ruogan Jueding*). P1. Supplement. *China Daily*. Beijing. 17 November 1993.

this vulnerable low wage labour force has little or no access to social welfare. The present patchwork system creates enormous differences in the quality and range of benefits available to Chinese citizens and, with the exception of the Minimum Living Standard System (MLSS – '*zuidi shenghuo baozhangxian zhidu*'), intended to cover the absolutely worst off in society, is regressive in the extreme. As a result, the upshot of economic reform for many laid-off SOE workers has been marginalisation via both reduction in income and exclusion from the system through which state resources, including social welfare benefits, are tapped.

The Impact of Reemployment Policy

As noted above, because China's low wage/high employment system led to overstaffing on a massive scale, reforms designed to improve economic efficiency inevitably generated substantial unemployment. Initially, the government's response to the redundancy issue emphasised the SOEs' re-absorption of surplus workers through the formation of subsidiaries which were supported by favourable tax treatment and other incentives (Lee 2000). Even during this early stage not all redundant workers could be accommodated this way, however, and some workers were furloughed while officially retaining their relationship to the *danwei*. In some cases they received retraining and/or partial wages. As reform deepened and more enterprises were allowed to go bankrupt, however, it became necessary to systematically provide transitional assistance for substantial numbers of jobless workers for whom the firm's demise meant the end of their historical source of both income and social benefits. This was achieved by mandating provision of three years of wages for laid-off SOE workers to be funded by the sale of use rights to the land formerly occupied by now bankrupt enterprises (Lee 2000).

With the onset of more aggressive reform, efforts were made to distil the lessons of city and provincial level experiments with reemployment policy conducted during the mid 1990s. These culminated in a 1998 conference entitled 'Safeguarding the Basic Living Standards of Laid-Off workers in SOEs and Their Reemployment' which was organised by the CCP Central Committee and the State Council. Following the conference a decentralised system was promulgated based on reemployment service centres established within enterprises themselves to deal with *xiagang* (i.e. laid-off) workers and provide their living stipends and insurance or pension benefits, as well as reemployment services such as job counselling (Bidani *et al.* 2005).[2] The reemployment service centre model predominated during a period of heavy layoffs from 1998 to 2001 but was phased out by 2003 (Bidani *et al.* 2005). In its place, workers still in the system and those newly laid off moved directly to 'unemployed' (rather than *xiagang*) status.

2 The term *xiagang* (literally, 'step down from the post') indicates that workers whose jobs are terminated are still retained by the work unit with partial or no pay (Lee 2000). The term is an official status pertaining to workers for a fixed period of years following job termination, after which their official status changes to unemployed if they have not found work.

Examining the effectiveness of the reemployment service centre approach based on a variety of Chinese sources, Lee (2000: 928-930) found that official estimates claimed roughly half of *xiagang* workers had found work in the latter half of the 1990s. In contrast, he pointed out that a study of 54,000 *xiagang* workers by the All China Federation of Trade Unions found that a much lower 18% had been reemployed. Furthermore, a study of 5,000 *xiagang* workers in Harbin (a city with a high concentration of laid-off workers) revealed that most (79%) of those who found work after periods of layoff did so through their individual efforts or social networks and not through the auspices of the enterprise or government. Lee (2000) also noted that most successfully reemployed workers found work either as proprietors or employees of small service sector businesses. As a result, one key determinant of reemployment success appeared to be the general macroeconomic climate in the city.

Lee and Warner (2004) examined the effectiveness of the reemployment policy approach used in Shanghai – where reemployment centres functioned mostly for distributing living allowances rather than providing reemployment services – through a series of in-depth interviews with policy makers, managers, trade union representatives, workers and unemployed individuals. They found that a relatively high share (45%) of all laid-off SOE workers had been reemployed by the end of 2000. They attributed this success largely to the city's robust economic climate and labour market and note that, given Shanghai's unique economic conditions, the value of replicating the Shanghai approach elsewhere, and particularly in areas such where laid-off workers constitute a large share of the population, is questionable.

Bidani and colleagues' (2005) study offers results more relevant to urban areas with concentrations of obsolete industries. Working in Shenyang and Wuhan, they used a quasi-experimental design to examine the effectiveness of reemployment service centre retraining programmes over the period 1998-2000. Controlling for a variety of demographic, occupational, and welfare benefit status variables they found that, overall, retraining had no effect in Shenyang but increased the likelihood of reemployment roughly 10 percentage points in Wuhan. Drilling deeper into the data revealed that the effect of training was consistently nonexistent across subgroups in Shenyang but that in Wuhan it was twice as strong for men as for women and existed only for those who had at least a junior high school education. Although this study was the most ambitious attempt to determine the effectiveness of reemployment policy the results can only be considered suggestive because of the potential for selection bias in the construction of the treatment (training) and control groups. Sorting into the two groups was not done randomly, rather the data collection was retrospective following self-sorting by the participants themselves.

Song (2003) looked beyond the service centre model, pointing out that governments have tried a variety of other approaches to reemployment. These include both efforts to influence labour supply (e.g. education, job-training, limiting rural-urban migration, mandating retention of redundant workers as condition of privatisation) and to increase labour demand (e.g. promoting growth of the service industry, subsidising the hiring of laid-off workers through tax incentives). Song (2003) found, however, that few published evaluations of these idiosyncratically developed and deployed policies existed and those that did revealed minimal impact on reemployment outcomes.

In a related study focused on the formation of associations of laid-off workers in Dalian that are designed to reintegrate laid-off workers into society rather than focusing on employment alone, Ge (2004) found that policy *can* have an effect. Study participants were drawn from the pool of unemployed residents receiving MLSS benefits and organised into community service associations for the purpose of mutual support and collective participation in income generating activities. Government provided meeting space and guidance for the associations, along with social outings and community service opportunities, but no actual retraining services. After several years, participants were found to be more likely to be employed and to hold more positive attitudes toward life in general. The positive outcome from Ge's (2004) study is encouraging and supports a holistic approach to social reintegration, while also emphasising the challenge in terms of time and resources involved in improving outcomes for laid-off workers.

Zhou's (2001) in-depth interviews of eighty-one poor urban residents indicated that the apparently weak effect of reemployment policy may result not only from poorly designed policies implemented by disinterested or distracted governments, but also from pessimism among the target population. Interviewees believed government assistance could only help secure basic needs but would not otherwise influence living standards or help them find work, making them less likely to participate in programmes such as retraining. Other surveys have shown that unsuccessful job seekers from the former SOE pool have low opinions of their own labour market competency, leading them to decide against dedicating funds to cover the out-of-pocket costs associated with reemployment activities (Tang 2002b).

Other explanations for the failure of former SOE workers' reemployment efforts range from insufficient motivation and dependence on government assistance (Lai and Chan 2002) to lack of experience in managing their own careers (Tsui 2002). Some have also claimed that this failure is related to the collapse of laid-off workers' social networks – since a disproportionate amount of their social capital is tied up in the enterprise itself, the demise of the firm leaves them linked largely to others in similarly challenging circumstances and disconnected from the broader society (Bian 2002, Zhao 2002).

Taken together, results of the reemployment studies make several points relevant to the discussion of marginality. The first of these is that retraining alone is not sufficient to make many former SOE workers viable labour market participants. Second, overall the policy approaches and specific programmes pursued to date have not been subjected to any meaningful impact evaluation through which best practices could be identified and distilled. Third, different policies may be required based on different local economic conditions. Finally, the studies reviewed here show, perhaps unsurprisingly, that termination from SOE employment is akin to a loss of one's place in society and not simply of a job. As a result, policies aimed at a more comprehensive form of social validation and reintegration, while perhaps more difficult to implement, may offer a better long term prognosis for those marginalised through SOE layoffs.

A Framework for Examining Labour Market Marginality in China

Empirically examining levels of absolute and relative marginality among laid-off workers requires an analytical framework. However, there is no broadly accepted approach to studying social marginality in general (Gurung and Kollmair 2005), much less in the context of urban China under transition. We make use of key elements of the past approaches used to understand these and related issues to devise a framework that captures key elements of the issues raised in the preceding sections of this chapter.

One important theme in efforts to examine marginality is the centrality of labour market status. Production and resulting consumption are among the most fundamental activities through which individuals participate in society, making unemployment of central concern due to linkages with other social problems such as poverty (Atkinson, 1998), neighbourhood deterioration (Lupton and Power 2002), low self-esteem (Britton 1998), and poor psychological health (Kieselbach 2004, Fryer 1992, Jahoda 1979). Labour market separation has also been shown to cause disadvantages for the children of the unemployed that impact socioeconomic status inter-generationally (Piachaud and Sutherland 2002, Machin 1997). Even those who question the overall explanatory power of employment regarding social outcomes in some contexts (e.g., Gallie 2004) allow that it is at the heart of such issues, cautioning only that causation is complex and involves feedback loops that are difficult to unravel, rather than arguing that employment status is unrelated to marginalisation and exclusion. In general, labour market status occupies a 'first among equals' position in efforts to understand urban social marginality.

A second theme emerges from the Post-Soviet literature, which argues that the transition context itself is an important influence on marginality that needs to be reflected in empirical analysis and that the factors of interest are not necessarily the same as those in the more developed economies where much of the theorisation has taken place. Tchernina (1996: 2), for example, offers the following four dynamics as important drivers of expanding marginality in transitional Russia: (1) the dismantling of the old society causing radical changes in traditional social guarantees and rights; (2) the impoverishment which occurred on a mass scale, negatively affecting virtually all but a thin stratum of 'new rich'; (3) the continued adherence by some social groups to socialist values, making the perception of their outsider status more acute; and (4) the creation of new institutions of social protection and security which failed to function adequately during the transition period.

Tikhonova's (2004) empirical analysis of Russian data illustrates the importance of the transitional context. The study intentionally focused on households that 'look at first glance like ordinary members of Russian society', in that they have permanent housing, a certain degree of income security and the right to social services, benefits and allowances. The author finds that psychological factors are critical, as disadvantaged groups complained of having little control over their lives and expressed bitterness, disappointment and shame about their situations. Regarding the role of employment specifically, Tikhonova (2004) finds that social exclusion in transitional Russia is less often generated by unemployment than by 'insecure, heterogeneous, and differentiated employment.'

A third point, the importance of poverty, income inequality, and the inability to tap state resources as drivers of marginality, emerges from the Chinese language literature. Many Chinese studies tend to deal descriptively with the nature of absolute poverty and/or problems faced by the extreme poor (cf. Tang and Wang 2002, Zhan 2004, Zhou 2001). Studies of income inequality show that the problem has become increasingly severe recently. Meng (2004), for example, argues that since 1995 increased urban inequality is mainly a result of large-scale layoffs.

Related studies of 'socially disadvantaged groups' (*shehui ruoshi qunti*) – defined as those that cannot access key resources (Wang 2003, Chen 2000) and identified by Lu (2002) as service workers in the commercial sector, industrial workers, peasants, and the un-/under-employed – emphasise the fact that social status in China is defined by an ability to tap into organisational (i.e. government and party) resources, in addition to economic ones. The emerging literature on social exclusion and marginality in China also focuses on accessing resources through the state. Wu (2004), for example, claims that marginality in contemporary urban China should be understood as a process of co-evolution between interest politics and markets. This process benefits the elite and leaves those outside 'the system' enduring a 'double marginalisation' resulting from both institutional and market mechanisms. Similarly, Xie (2003) claims that mainstream society and the political/legal system actively exclude vast swaths of the population. Li (2005) argues that because society, the legal system, and the economy are still very much in flux, successive changes often reverse the positions of 'winners' and 'losers' in the reform process.

Taken together the discussion in this section implies the following elements of a framework for assessing marginality among laid-off SOE workers in urban China. First, employment issues should be at the centre of this research. Second, categories and variables analysed should reflect specific aspects of transitional China. Third, material conditions are important both in terms of private consumption and access to resources through the system. Fourth, marginalisation is a dynamic process involving the interaction between both the market and the political system. In addition, the framework should reflect several stylistic aspects of existing empirical work not discussed here but common in studies of other countries (cf. Poggi 2004, Bohnke 2001) in which analyses begin by exploring cross-sectional data descriptively to document levels of relative marginality across groups and then present inter-temporal analysis showing the likelihood of escaping marginality over time.

Based on these principles we deploy a framework with the following characteristics: (1) we analyse our sample based on labour market status with the varying status categories designed to reflect the specific conditions of the Chinese labour market; (2) we examine material conditions of households in the various employment status categories; (3) we define consumption to include access to state resources; and (4) we look at changing labour market status inter-temporally in order to reflect the changes associated with transitional economic conditions. Table 3.1 summarises our indicators and those of four other studies conducted outside of China. Our research uses similar consumption indicators as these other studies but we divide production indicators into subcategories that reflect the specific Chinese context.

Table 3.1 Societal marginalisation indicators

Study/Location	Consumption	Production
Burchardt *et al.* (2002) UK	Household earns less than half of mean income	Not working (long-term illness, unemployed, disabled, early retired)
Poggi (2004) European Union	Adequate income; housing/ neighbourhood conditions; able to take week's holiday	Unemployed
Bohnke (2001) Germany	Household income less than half of mean; deprivation index score; housing/neighbourhood conditions	Unemployed at least twelve months
Tikhonova (2004) Russia	The right to medical assistance, culture, education; housing	The right to secure, paid work
Tang *et al.* (this volume) China	Household income; basic expenditures; schooling; housing; welfare access	Employment status; state/private sector; formal/ informal work

Empirical Analysis of Societal Marginality among Laid-off Workers

After describing the data used in the analysis, this section presents an empirical examination of marginality among former SOE workers in Wuhan in two steps. It first examines key social marginality indicators across employment status groups. It then looks at reemployment histories of laid-off SOE workers to assess their ability to escape conditions of relative marginalisation.

Data

Because China does not have a comprehensive panel survey sufficiently detailed for the examination of multidimensional societal marginalisation over time we use two household surveys from a single metropolitan area to investigate various aspects of societal marginalisation. Although conditions vary across municipalities, results presented here should be generalisable at least to middle and large cities with significant shares of former SOE workers, especially those in the provinces of Liaoning, Heilongjiang, Jilin and Hubei, where heavy industry was concentrated under the centrally planned economy.

The first data set comes from a study conducted by the Chinese Academy of Social Sciences (CASS) in 2004 in order to examine the coverage and effectiveness of the three main social insurance schemes (medical, pension and unemployment insurance). It provides comprehensive demographic and socio-economic information, as well as information on expenditures and access to social benefits. As such, it is a rich data source for both marketplace consumption and access to resources provided by 'the system' across different employment status groups.

Sampling in the CASS survey occurred as follows. First, five of Wuhan's eighteen districts were chosen at random. Then two sub-districts within each district and two communities within each sub-district were selected, also at random. Next, fifty households in each community were randomly chosen and the adult (over age eighteen) family member whose birthday was closest to August 1st was selected for interview. This process generated a sample of 500 respondents of varying ages and roles within the family. Because our research was interested only in working age households we eliminated those beyond the mandatory retirement age, producing a final sample of 424 respondents.

The second Wuhan dataset is from a study of reemployment among former SOE workers by Bidani and colleagues (2004) conducted in May-June of 2000 by the World Bank. There were two sampling frames, the first of which was a computerised list provided by the Wuhan Labour Bureau of all workers involved in training programmes in the city. The second frame was a similar listing of all former SOE workers laid off prior to the period July-September 1998. The former was the source of a treatment (retrained) group and the latter a control (not retrained) group. A roughly equal number of individuals were chosen at random from these lists, generating a sample from which we deleted individuals laid off prior to 1993 (because there were relatively few of them in any given year and part of our analysis relies on constructing layoff year cohorts) and those for whom no income information was reported, to reach a total of 1,427 observations.

In addition to year of layoff, the survey contains retrospective employment information semi-annually for the 1998-2000 period. We use the data to track earnings and employment outcomes for layoff year cohorts. Although there is some heterogeneity in terms of reemployment outcomes between the treatment and control groups we treat the dataset as comprising a single sample. Since, unlike the World Bank team, we are not investigating the outcomes of policy interventions but rather the reemployment prospects of laid-off workers in general, this method accurately reflects the fact that the pool of laid-off former SOE workers in Wuhan contains both those who received and did not receive retraining. To the extent that a bias is introduced, it stems from the overrepresentation of retrained individuals, which makes the modest levels of reemployment success we detect overstate the actual overall reemployment success rates in the city. This survey is one of the few sources of quasi-longitudinal reemployment data, either for Wuhan or elsewhere in urban China and as such provides a rare opportunity to examine the persistence of marginality.

Overall, the data used in our analysis fall short of the ideal of a large, national, representative, methodologically tested, longitudinal survey. However, they are reasonably well-suited to the purpose of investigating marginalisation among laid-off SOE workers in urban areas that formerly had large state sectors. Ultimately, the empirical results presented here should be bolstered by analysis using purpose-designed surveys along the lines of the British Household Panel.

Labour Market Status and Consumption Indicator Scores

The first set of empirical results deal with cross-sectional consumption patterns using the CASS data. In keeping with the focus on un/under-employment among urban households, the data are split by labour market status and include only working age households headed by non-retired adults. Joblessness (40% of the sample) is self-identified by respondents. The employment sector among the employed was determined to be 'state' (24%) if the respondent works in party or government *danwei* or an SOE. Formal private sector employment (11%) was determined based on whether the current employer provides at least one of the four key types of social insurance (pension, unemployment, medical, and work injury), with other employment considered informal (25%).

As shown in Table 3.2, results across most expenditure categories show the unemployed in the worst position and informal sector workers also doing poorly relative to other employed respondents. The income panel, for example, indicates that the jobless 'earn' only about half as much cash-income from all sources as informal sector workers ('income' for the jobless includes money provided by friends and relatives, transfers, pensions, and earnings from rental housing). Informal sector workers' cash earnings, at 1,500RMB per month, are lower but not dramatically lower, than those of state formal and private formal sector workers, respectively. These findings are similar to those of Li and Knight (2002) who show that the probability of falling into poverty of households with the household head unemployed is 0.34 times higher than otherwise.

The unemployed and informal sector workers also spend much less on all basic necessities each month. Jobless respondents reported spending 45%, 63%, and 69% less on food than informal, state formal, and private formal sector workers, respectively. At 50%, the share of income devoted to this most basic need, is substantially higher among the unemployed than any other group. Because meals are in some cases provided and/or paid for by work units for state formal sector workers, these figures may understate the true differences among the groups.

Jobless families also spend much less on clothing and transportation relative to the other groups. Further, they devote less to medical care, which, given their lesser access to medical benefits (shown below), seems almost certain to indicate that they are denying themselves care rather than that they are healthier than other groups. Such a finding would be consistent with the work of Tang (2002b) who found that more than 60% of his low-income household sample did not seek medical care when sick. This finding is significant in terms of understanding the mechanisms of perpetuated disadvantage because poor health and lack of health care have been shown in diverse contexts to perpetuate poverty and social exclusion (Tikhonova 2004, Li and Knight 2002, Li 2002, Piachaud 1997, see also chapter by Lin in this volume).

With rates of 83% and 73%, private formal and state formal sector workers in Wuhan are more likely to be homeowners than either informal sector workers (62%) or the jobless (58%). Independent of tenure status, the unemployed occupy the smallest housing units and enjoy the least living space per capita. They are also more likely to live in deteriorating older homes.

Expenditures on school fees appear fairly similar across the four employment categories, with the median ranging from 700RMB to 1,000RMB. We have no controls for school quality, however, which varies markedly. Perhaps reflecting this is the fact that relatively small shares of households in the state formal and private formal sectors pay extra in order for their children to attend better schools. Since, presumably, these groups have resources to devote to upgrading their children's education if they thought it necessary, the fact they generally do not do so means that school quality is viewed as sufficient, perhaps due to the marshalling of resources at the work unit level.

Table 3.2 Labour market status and consumption levels in Wuhan, 2004

Labour Market Status	Jobless	Informal	State formal	Private formal
Income				
Monthly median (RMB)	800	1,500	1,800	2,000
Basic Expenditures (median monthly)				
Food (RMB)	400	582	650	700
Clothing (RMB)	30	150	115	300
Medical (RMB)	40	90	100	100
Transportation (RMB)	50	150	150	200
Housing				
Owner share (%)	57.7	61.7	73.7	82.6
Median total living space (m^2)	33.6	44.1	44.8	49.0
Median living space per capita (m^2)	10.0	14.0	14.0	16.3
Share in structure < 5 years old (%)	10.7	12.5	20.8	24.4
Share in structure >10 years old (%)	67.5	64.4	57.4	53.3
Schooling				
Median annual school fee (RMB)	900	700	1,000	700
Share paying to upgrade schooling	4.1	15.9	9.9	10.9
Upgrade amount paid (RMB)	1,815	6,000	2,000	1,150
Social Welfare				
Medical insurance (%)	34.3	12.2	81.2	71.7
Old age pension (%)	67.8	40.2	88.1	93.5
Unemployment insurance (%)	13.2	7.5	44.6	45.7
Work injury insurance (%)	n/a	7.5	31.7	30.4
Sample Size	170	107	101	46

Note: Total sample sizes for housing panel, median annual school fees, and median upgrade amount have sample sizes lower than those listed on the table, at 276, 245, and 39, respectively.

As mentioned throughout this chapter, access to state resources via social welfare varies with employment status. And consumption over the course of a lifetime is significantly affected by the level of access to welfare benefits. The table here includes residual benefits from former state employers for respondents in the three other categories. Even so, the differences are dramatic, with private formal and state sector workers much more likely to enjoy each of the four benefits. Interestingly, larger shares of unemployed workers report having pensions, unemployment, and medical insurance than informal sector workers, suggesting that this may partially explain the decision to engage in informal work after being laid off. This finding is consistent with that of Giles and colleagues (2005) whose models indicate that access to unemployment insurance significantly reduces the likelihood of reemployment among men (but not women) in urban China.

Overall, the cross-sectional consumption results are consistent with the notion that unemployed workers are marginalised relative to households in other labour market classes. Their incomes and basic consumption lag even behind informal sector workers and they are generally less likely to own their housing or enjoy spacious and/or high quality housing. Relative to those in the formal sector, whether private or state, they have greatly diminished access to key forms of social insurance. However, they are more likely to have these benefits than those in the informal sector. In combination, these findings suggest that, relative to other groups in urban China, both the unemployed and informal sector workers are marginalised in terms of their incomes, consumption of key necessities, and access to 'the system' via welfare benefits.

The Persistence of Unemployment

As noted earlier, changes over time are an important part of the marginality picture in social settings. For purposes of the current research, the areas of greatest interest are movements among employment categories and the duration of unemployment spells. These are important from a social policy perspective due to the nature of labour market dynamics in urban China. As industry sectors are reformed and exposed to increased competition, laid-off workers are clustered in terms of skills sets and geography, both of which tend to worsen reemployment prospects and to reduce wages for those that manage to procure work. This section therefore examines the pattern and extent of reemployment following SOE layoff, with an eye toward identifying evidence of structural processes producing a marginalised urban underclass.

Empirical results in this section use data from the World Bank reemployment study. Because the sample includes only laid-off SOE workers it allows us to examine the likelihood that workers most directly affected by reforms are able to re-enter the labour force. In order to screen out those who might treat layoff as a form of unplanned early retirement, we restrict the sample to workers under age fifty at the time of layoff. We also eliminate workers laid off prior to 1993 both because there are few of them in any given year and because reforms and labour market developments were more idiosyncratic prior to the more focused period of reforms beginning around 1994. Table 3.3 summarises the reemployment outcomes of these workers as of July 2000.

Table 3.3 Labour force outcomes by layoff year, July 2000

Layoff Year	1998 Share Employed (%)	2000 Share Employed (%)	2000 Median Wage (RMB)	Sample Size
1993	34.9	35.3	450	114
1994	38.4	39.5	480	172
1995	43.2	42.7	500	192
1996	38.3	36.8	500	209
1997	37.2	41.3	500	293
1998	n/a	38.9	500	447

Note: Employed share includes both part-time and full-time work. Wages are monthly. Data are as of July 1998 and 2000.

The table highlights several aspects of reemployment outcomes among laid-off SOE workers. First, the likelihood of reemployment (both part-time and full-time are included) is relatively low, with the reemployed share topping out at 43% among the layoff year cohorts. The table also shows a plateauing effect, with little change over the 1998-2000 period for any cohort. Year of layoff has little effect on reemployment prospects as the share reemployed is similar for all cohorts in both 1998 and 2000. Similarly, there is little difference in the median salaries of those that are working. At around 500RMB per month, these medians, while low, are well above Wuhan's MLSS threshold of 150RMB per month at the time.

Table 3.4 examines the type of employment attained by those laid-off workers that become reemployed. It continues to paint a picture of similarity rather than difference across layoff year groupings. There is little variation in the likelihood of working full-time, with about three quarters of those reemployed finding full time work, regardless of layoff year. It also indicates little variation in the likelihood of self-employment. About two-thirds of reemployed workers in all years are working for others, with the bulk of the remainder engaged in small scale self-employment involving no non-family employees ('Self-Empl.' column). A minority have established businesses allowing them to employ at least one worker.

Taken together the results presented in this section present a consistent picture of the labour market and reemployment possibilities facing laid-off workers in Wuhan. Of the reemployed, the majority work at small scale self-financed activities or are employees, most likely in the informal sector. The fact that the reemployment rate is low and consistent across layoff years, and wages are also low, suggests that there is little to 'pull' workers into the labour market. Rather it is personal financial circumstances that 'push' some into low-wage, low-skill work. Overall, SOE layoff has marked the end of productive work for the majority, and even those reemployed have seen their standards of living and social status decline.

Table 3.4 Employment characteristics by layoff year, July 2000

Layoff Year	Part-time (%)	Full-time (%)	Employee (%)	Self-Empl. (%)	Employer (%)
1993	23.8	76.2	60.0	34.1	5.9
1994	31.8	68.2	60.0	40.0	0.0
1995	22.2	77.8	67.9	30.9	1.2
1996	22.1	77.9	61.0	37.7	1.3
1997	30.0	70.0	62.5	35.8	1.7
1998	23.4	76.6	70.7	27.0	2.4

Note: Self-employed indicates that the business has no paid workers. 'Employer' refers to self-employed individuals who have at least one paid worker.

Conclusion: Addressing Marginality among Laid-off SOE Workers

The empirical results of the analysis presented in this chapter can be summarised as follows. First, laid-off SOE workers comprising large shares of both the unemployed and the informal sector workforce are marginalised with respect to their income and consumption. Relative to others, these groups have low incomes, spend significantly less on necessities including food and medical care and endure worse housing conditions. Reflecting China's transitional social policy environment, the unemployed and informal sector workers are also the *least* organisationally and institutionally supported in terms of social welfare.

Looked at over time, it is clear that laid-off SOE workers face considerable challenges re-entering the labour force. Only a minority of workers in our sample were reemployed after periods ranging from two to seven years, and only three-quarters of this reemployed minority found full-time work. In both cases, and irrespective of whether individuals are self-employed or working for others, wages are low, though they do substantially exceed the MLSS benefit trigger level. Although more strict statistical controls are necessary to draw definitive conclusions, it seems clear that laid-off former SOE workers as a group will continue to have problems finding work and will experience little upward mobility in labour markets.

The co-existence of material deprivation, disadvantaged position *vis-à-vis* the social security system, and long-term un/under-employment indicates that jobless former SOE workers are severely marginalised, as are those doing informal work. Importantly, escape from their marginal social position is hindered not only by their weak skill sets and attitudes inherited from the command economy, as is often alleged, but also by the fact that they are denied institutional resources necessary to help them find meaningful roles in the new economy.

The implications of the findings summarised above for current government efforts to address marginality by reintegrating laid-off workers into the mainstream economic and social systems are fairly straightforward. Specifically, the approach of ensuring the most basic material conditions sufficient for survival, which implicitly guides current efforts to deal with unemployment now that even the retraining programmes have been abandoned, will achieve neither widespread reemployment success nor the more ambitious goal of reintegration into the broader social system in areas hit hard by SOE layoffs.

A marginalisation perspective on the challenges facing the urban unemployed would begin by focusing on integrating laid-off workers back into the social mainstream along the lines of Ge's (2004) work, rather than emphasising either income support or reemployment in isolation. From this viewpoint, the key to any attempt to build a truly harmonious society and achieve common prosperity is the reform of the social security system to provide laid-off individuals the resources and support necessary to weather a traumatic reversal of life circumstances while setting them up for productive re-integration into the social mainstream. Such changes would indeed differ fundamentally from current practice but removing barriers and unleashing the potential of the unemployed to improve their own circumstances is the only way that their marginality can be effectively addressed.

Of course, alternative conceptions of the appropriate role of government in society and/or pragmatic assessments of what government can reasonably be expected to achieve under current conditions may argue against setting a goal as ambitious as ending marginality among the urban unemployed. In such cases, government should concentrate on two interrelated challenges. It should first develop a workable social protection system and then ensure that it is deployed in progressive or at least neutral fashion, in order to end the 'double marginalisation' (i.e. separation from both market *and* state resources) that the urban un/under-employed currently endure.

References

Atkinson, A.B. 1998. 'Exclusion, Employment, and Opportunity'. In *Exclusion, Employment, and Opportunity*. A.B. Atkinson and J. Hills (eds.). London: CASE.

Bian, Y. 2002. 'Chinese Social Stratification and Social Mobility'. *Annual Review of Sociology* 28(1).

Bidani, B., Blunch, N., Goh, C. and C. O'Leary. 2005. *Evaluating Active Labor Market Programs in Two Chinese Cities*. Revised version of World Bank report 24161-CHA. March.

Bidani, B., Betcherman, G., Blunch, N., Dar, A. Goh, C., Kline, K., and O'Leary, C. 2004. *Has Training Helped Employ the Xiagang in China?: A Tale of Two Cities*. World Bank, Poverty Reduction and Economic Management Unit, East Asia and Pacific Region, Report No. 24161-CHA.

Bohnke, P. 2001. *Nothing Left to Lose? Poverty and Social Exclusion in Comparison: Empirical Evidence on Germany*. Social Science Research Unit (WZB) discussion paper FS III 01-402.

Britton, A. 1998. 'Employment and Social Cohesion'. In *Exclusion, Employment, and Opportunity*. A.B. Atkinson and J. Hills (eds.). London: CASE.

Buckley, C. 2001. 'Context: Reform and Labor Mobility in China'. In D. Drury and M.M. Arneberg (eds.) *No More Forevers: The Chinese Labor Force in a Time of Reform*.

Burchardt, T., Le Grand, J. and Piachaud, D. 2002. 'Degrees of Exclusion: Developing a Dynamic Multidimensional Measure'. *Understanding Social Exclusion*. In J. Hills, J. Le Grand, and D. Piachaud (eds.). Oxford: Oxford University Press.

Cai, F. 2003. 'On the Priority of Employment in Social Economic Development Policy'. *Chinese Journal of Population Science* 3. (In Chinese)

Cai, F. 2005. 'New Thinking on Expanding Employment'. *Qianxian* 5. (In Chinese)

Cai, F. and Yang, T. 2000. 'The Political Economics of Urban-Rural Income Gap'. *Social Sciences in China* 4. (In Chinese)

Chen, C. 2000. *Discussion on the Socially Disadvantaged Group*. Beijing, Shidai Chubanshe. (In Chinese)

Fan, P. 1996. 'The Urban Low-Income in China: Sociological Research on the Urban Working Poor'. *Chinese Social Science* 4. (In Chinese)

Fan, Q. and Nolan, P. 1994. *China's Economic Reform*. London: Macmillan Press LTD.

Fryer, D. 1992. 'Psychological or Material Deprivation: Why Does Unemployment Have Mental Health Consequences?' In E. McLaughlin (ed.) *Understanding Unemployment: New Perspectives on Active Labor Market Policies*. London: Routledge.

Gallie, D. 2004. *Resisting Marginalization: Unemployment Experience and Social Policy in the European Union*. Oxford: Oxford University Press.

Ge, D. 2004. *Embeddedness, Autonomy and the Identity Rebuilding of the Disadvantaged People*. Centre for Social Policy Studies of the Chinese Academy of Social Sciences.

Giles, J., Park, A. and Zhang, J. 2005. 'What Is China's True Unemployment Rate?' *China Economic Review* 16(2): 149-170.

Groves, T., Hong, Y. McMillan, J. and Naughton, B. 1994. 'Autonomy and Incentives in Chinese State Enterprises'. *Quarterly Journal of Economics* 109: 183-209.

Gurung, G.S. and Kollmair, M. 2005. *Marginality: Concepts and Their Limitations*. IP6 Working Paper 4.

Hay, D., Morris, D., Liu, S. and Yao, S. 1994. *Economic Reform and State-Owned Enterprises in China 1979-87*. Oxford: Oxford University Press.

Jahoda, M. 1979. 'The Impact of Unemployment in the 1930s and 1970s'. *Bulletin of the British Psychological Society* 32: 309-314.

Ji, Y. 1998. *China's Enterprise Reform: Changing State/Society Relations after Mao*. London, Routledge.

Kieselbach, T. 2004. 'Psychology of Unemployment and Social Exclusion: Youth Unemployment and the Risk of Social Exclusion'. In D. Gallie (ed.) *Resisting Marginalization: Unemployment Experience and Social Policy in the European Union*. Oxford: Oxford University Press.

Lai, J.C.L. and Chan, R.K.H. 2002. 'The effects of job-search motives and coping on psychological health and re-employment: a study of unemployed Hong Kong Chinese'. *International Journal of Human Resource Management* 13(3): 465-483.

Lee, G.O.M. and Warner, M. 2004. 'The Shanghai re-employment model: from local experiment to nation-wide labor market policy'. *China Quarterly* (177): 174-189.

Lee, H.Y. 2000. '*Xiagang*, the Chinese Style of Laying Off Workers'. *Asian Survey*. 40(6): 914-937.

Li, B. 2005. 'Urban social change in transitional China: a perspective of social exclusion and vulnerability'. *Journal of Crises and Contingency Management* 13: (54-65).

Li, L. 2002. 'System Transition and Stratification Change – "Double-Reproduction" of Social Stratum Relations'. *Chinese Social Science* 6. (In Chinese)

Li, S. and Knight, J. 2002. 'Three Poverties in Urban China'. *Economic Research Journal* 10.

Lu, X. 2002. *Report on Social Strata in Contemporary China Research.* Beijing: Shehui Kexue Wenxian Chubanshe. (In Chinese)

Lupton, R. and Power, A. 2002. 'Social Exclusion and Neighbourhoods'. *Understanding Social Exclusion*. In J. Hills, J. Le Grand, and D. Piachaud (eds). Oxford: Oxford University Press.

Machin, S. 1997. 'Intergenerational Transmissions of Economic Status'. In P. Gregg *et al.. Jobs, Wages and Poverty: Patterns of Persistence and Mobility in the New Flexible Labor Market.*

Meng, X. 2004. 'Economic Restructuring and Income Inequality in Urban China'. *Review of income and wealth* 50(3): 357-379.

Piachaud, D. 1997. 'A Price Worth Paying? The Costs of Unemployment'. In J. Philpott (ed.) *Working for Full Employment*. London: Routledge.

Piachaud, D. and Sutherland, H. 2002. Child Poverty. *Understanding Social Exclusion*. In J. Hills, J. Le Grand, and D. Piachaud (eds.). Oxford: Oxford University Press.

Poggi, A. 2004. *Persistence of Social Exclusion in Italy: A Multidimensional Approach*. XIX National Conference of Labor Economics, Modena.

Song, S. 2003. 'Policy Issues of China's Urban Unemployment'. *Contemporary Economic Policy* 21(2): 258-269.

Tang, J. 2002a. 'New Trends in Poverty and Anti-Poverty in China'. In X. Ru *et al.* (eds.) *Analysis and Projection of Social Situation in China.* Beijing: Shehui Kexue Wenxian Chubanshe. (In Chinese)

Tang, J. 2002b. *Social Exclusion and Living Condition of the Urban Poor*. Sociology Research Institute, China Social Science Academy Discussion Paper 13.

Tang, J. and Wang, Y. 2002. 'Social Exclusion in the Policy Process of Minimum Living Standard Scheme in Urban China'. *Sociology Research Institute, China Social Science Academy Discussion Paper* 54. (In Chinese)

Tchernina, N. 1996. *Economic Transition and Social Exclusion in Russia*. Geneva, International Institute for Labor Studies.

Tikhonova, N. 2004. 'Social Exclusion in Russia'. In N. Manning and N. Tikhonova (eds.) *Poverty and Social Exclusion in the New Russia*. Aldershot: Ashgate.

Tsui, M. 2002. 'Managing transition: unemployment and job hunting in urban China'. *Pacific Affairs* 75(4): 515-534.

Wang, S. 2003. 'Give Policy Support to the Disadvantaged Groups in the Reform'. *Journal of Peking University (Humanities and Social Sciences)* 6. (In Chinese)

Wu, F. 2004. 'Urban Poverty and Marginalization under Market Transition: The Case of Chinese Cities'. *International Journal of Urban and Regional Research* 28(2).

Xie, X. 2003. 'Analysis on the Realization of Political Rights of Chinese Peasants from the Perspective of Social Exclusion'. *Jiangxi Social Sciences* 10. (In Chinese)

Yao, S. 1997. 'Profit Sharing, Bonus Payment, and Productivity: A Case Study of Chinese State Owned Enterprises'. *Journal of Comparative Economics* 24: 281-296.

Yao, S. 2005. *Economic Growth, Income Distribution and Poverty Reduction in Contemporary China*. London: New York, RoutledgeCurzon.

Zhan, S. 2004. Behavioural Choices of Low-Income Residents in Regeneration and Their Marginality. *Sociology Research Institute, China Social Science Academy Discussion Paper* (157). (In Chinese)

Zhao, Y. 2002. 'Measuring the Social Capital of Laid-Off Chinese Workers'. *Current Sociology* 50(4).

Zheng, H. and Hong, D. 2004. 'Hidden Troubles of Social Safety and Countermeasures in Transitional China'. *Journal of the Renmin University of China* 5. (In Chinese)

Zhou, X. 2001. *Voice of the Urban Poor - Report on Participatory Urban Poverty Analysis in Beijing*. Asian Development Bank.

Chapter 4

Marginalisation in the Chinese Energy Sector: The Case of Township and Village Coal Mines

Philip Andrews-Speed

Introduction

Small-scale mines, whether partly mechanised or artisanal, have long been a source of concern to policy makers and advisers in the international mining sector. This mining activity may bring short-term economic benefits to a country, to the workers and to the mining communities, but the medium and long-term costs are considerable, in terms of environmental destruction, waste of mineral resources and loss of life (International Labour Organization 1999). Further, the economic benefits to the workers and mining communities are usually not sustainable, in that they usually do not generate sufficient revenue for reinvestment in alternative economic activities once the mineral deposits are exhausted (Heemskerk 2005). Many of these mines are illegal or, at best, 'informal' (Lahiri-Dut 2004). As a result, those involved tend to lie at the margins of society from the social, economic and political perspectives.

China has long been home to the world's largest small-scale mining sector, in terms of both output and employment, and coal accounts for a large proportion of this output and employment (Gunson and Yue 2001). For more than twenty years these small-scale coal mines were owned and operated by collectives at township and village level, and thus they have come to be known as township and village coal mines (hereafter referred to as 'TVCMs')

Since the mid-1980s China's TVCMs have played an important role in the national economy through their significant contribution to the nation's energy supply. Yet, throughout this period they have been a source of controversy on account of their poor record in relation to the waste of coal resources, environmental destruction and loss of human life. Over the years the government has launched a number of campaigns to improve the management of these mines but with only limited success.

The aim of the chapter is to examine the development of China's TVCMs and to analyse the extent to which these mines have reduced or exacerbated marginalisation and poverty. This account identifies a number of recurring themes. On the one hand, the expansion of the TVCMs has been driven by the nation's economic growth and the subsequent demand for energy, by fiscal decentralisation and the consequent pressure on local governments to generate revenue, by the potential for mine owners, mine managers and local officials to make private profits, and by the opportunities for unemployed workers to earn money. On the other hand these driving forces have not been balanced by effective policies and regulatory mechanisms to constrain the negative impacts of this mining. Central government appears to have lacked a coherent long-term policy framework which could have effectively linked economic growth, energy production, sustainable development and social equity. The regulatory systems for exploitation of natural resources and for environmental protection have remained undeveloped, as have the policies and systems for labour protection. Finally, conflicts of interest at local government level have persistently undermined central government policies.

This chapter begins by showing how these mines have contributed to both the national energy supply and to poverty reduction, before proceeding to examine the negative impacts of the mining activity. The subsequent sections describe the response of the government in the 1980s and 1990s to these rising social costs and identify some of the main constraints to the effectiveness of these measures. The chapter continues by documenting some of the impacts of the campaign to close the TVCMs in the late 1990s and how the resurgence of demand for energy from 2002 led to a reappearance of many of the problems of the previous decade.

TVCMs as a source of energy

The growth of the small-scale coal mines in China was driven by two types of factor: the need for energy at a national and local scale, and the need for employment and for local revenues. This section examines how the TVCMs came to play such an important role in energy supply, from their slow development under the planned economy to the acceleration of production under the more open economy of the 1980s and 1990s.

Slow emergence as a source of energy under the planned economy

From 1949 till the early 1980s China's heavy industries and primary industries, such as mining, were governed by planned output and consumption and were run by state-owned enterprises. State-owned mines, at the central and local level, accounted for nearly all the nation's coal production. Commune and collective mines operated outside the plan, beyond the arm of the state and provided only a small proportion of output, mainly to satisfy local energy needs. This proportion amounted to less than 10% of national production for most of this period, and was usually less than 5%. The period of the Great Leap Forward in the late 1950s was exceptional. At that time national coal output increased three-fold and production from collective and commune mines accounted for nearly 20% of the national total (Thomson 2003).

Most of the collective and commune mines were worked by local inhabitants in order to produce coal for local energy supply (Thomson 2003). Coal prices were fixed at low levels. As a result the TVCMs had little incentive to sell their output, the large state-owned mines struggled to cover their costs and coal was in short supply across much of the country.

The 1970s saw the development of the 'two-legs' policy as the government decided that the large and the small coal mines should both contribute to the nation's energy supply. Those mines not owned by the state were permitted to sell their output at prices determined by the market. This initiative provided these small-scale mines with a financial incentive for the first time. But state investment was still mainly directed at the large mines in the north of the country and on infrastructure to take this coal to the south (Gao 1999). During the 1970s the output of the small-scale coal mines grew nearly four-fold from 31 million tonnes to 114 million tonnes by which time they accounted for 18% of national coal production. They were starting to play a significant role in the national economy.

Rapid expansion in the opening economy

The early 1980s saw the start of the sustained high levels of growth that were to characterise China's economy for more than two decades. The government encouraged diversification with respect to both ownership of enterprise and nature of output, and certain sectors of the economy were gradually released from the grip of 'the plan'. An important initiative was to introduce the term 'township and village enterprise' (thereafter TVE) to replace the old 'commune and brigade enterprise' as part of the highly successful drive to stimulate economic activity in rural areas (Zweig 1997).

With the economy growing at 8-10% per year, the supply of energy was required to grow at 6-8% per year (BP 2005). Though the proportion of coal in China's primary commercial energy supply had fallen from 95% in the early 1950s to 75% by the mid-1980s, coal has remained the mainstay of the domestic energy sector on account of the large scale of the nation's coal resources.

The year 1983 saw the publication by the Ministry of Coal Industries of a report entitled 'Eight Measures on Accelerating the Development of Small Coal Mines' which was approved by the State Council and actively supported by the then Prime Minister, Zhao Ziyang (Thomson 2003). The principal aim was to raise the level of national coal output by whatever means were necessary, and to encourage coal production for local consumption, thus easing the pressure on the railways and waterways. State-owned coal companies and coal bureaux were to provide active support to small-scale mines, prices were reformed to allow profits to be made, tax allowances were offered, and banks were encouraged to make loans to TVCMs. At the same time, the local government coal bureaux were to provide advice and support in the fields of technology and safety.

The need for energy supply also provided a stimulus for many local governments. Their economies became increasingly dependent on the new township and village enterprises (hereafter TVEs) which themselves required a reliable supply of energy. Most of China's coal reserves and large-scale coal mines lie in the north of the country; but much of the demand growth was occurring in the south and east. Not only did transportation add significantly to the cost of coal supply, but throughout the 1980s and 1990s, the supply of coal across China's was constrained by the shortage of transport capacity, particularly on the rail network (Wright 2000; World Bank 1995). As a result, local governments in areas with undeveloped coal deposits had a direct incentive to exploit them in order to support local industries. Many of these deposits were small in scale or complex in structure and not suitable for mining at a large scale. Thus, small-scale, low technology operations ensured that deposits were exploited that might otherwise have been left unused (Zhong 2003).

The official government plan drawn up in 1985 forecast that the annual output of the TVCMs would rise from 146 million tonnes in 1982 to 400 million tonnes by the year 2000. This target of 400 million tonnes was reached by 1991 and the annual output peaked at 659 million tonnes in 1995. By this time the TVCMs were producing 48% of the nation's coal and had accounted for more than 70% of the incremental coal output in the previous fifteen years (State Planning Commission 1997). The last phase of growth was most impressive. After coal prices were released from government control in 1993, the TVCMs' output rose by 180 million tonnes in just two years from 1993-1995, accounting for 90% of the national incremental output (Hong, Wang and Li 1998).

By the mid-1990s the number of TVCMs exceeded 80,000 and they employed as many as 4 million people (Wang 2006; Hong et al 1998). Even in 1999, after a widespread campaign to close tens of thousands of mines, an estimated 2.5 million people worked in TVCMs (Zhong 2003). Whilst many of these TVCMs were indeed owned by township and village collectives, a substantial proportion were privately owned and a small minority were owned by a variety of other government and state institutions. The role of private ownership varied greatly from province to province. TVCMs in provinces with a strong industrial base and a powerful presence from state coal mining companies tended to be owned by collectives, for example in Shanxi and Hebei Provinces. In more remote provinces, such as Yunnan and Guizhou, private ownership accounted for as many as 80% of the TVCMs (Ye and Zhang 1998).

Although nearly all of China's thirty-two provinces, municipalities and autonomous regions had some TVCMs, about 92% of these mines lay in just 16 provinces (Hong et al 1998). In the mid-1990s the TVCM output as a proportion of total coal production varied from as little as 29% in Hebei in the north to as much as 82% in Guizhou in the south. The scale of the mines also varied greatly, depending on the geological nature of the deposits and the effectiveness of the local supervisory agencies in merging mines into more efficient units. In Jiangxi Province, the production capacity of 88% of the TVCMs lay below 10,000 tonnes per year, with only 2% of the TVCMs having capacities in excess of 30,000 tonnes. In Shandong Province where the coal deposits were larger and the mining industry was more developed, 33% of the mines had capacities above 30,000 tonnes per year and only 18% lay below 10,000 tonnes per year (Ye and Zhang 1998).

In general terms the larger the mine the more likely it is to be partly mechanised, to be under government regulation to at least some degree, to be managed in a commercial manner and to employ more than one hundred people. The smaller mines tend to be informal, non-mechanised and often entirely illegal, artisanal operations employing ten to twenty workers (Ye and Zhang 1998; Wang 2006).

TVCMs and poverty reduction

A second stimulus to the rapid development of the TVCMs lay in their perceived role in alleviating poverty, on the part of both local government and individuals. With the majority of the population living in rural areas away from the main cities, the national government realised that rapid economic growth was more likely to be achieved if this rural population were actively involved. Two key steps were taken. First the development of TVEs was encouraged. Second, the national government started to decentralise the economy and the fiscal system, in order to provide direct incentives for local governments to promote local economic growth and development. At the same time there was a tacit admission that privately-owned enterprises could be created, albeit at a small scale, through which individuals were permitted to accumulate wealth. As a result, opportunities for private profit arose for local enterprises, entrepreneurs and government officials (Chen 2000; Zweig 1997).

Local governments and local communities, particularly at county, township and village levels, saw a range of economic gains from the growth of the TVCMs in their localities. These took the form of taxes and revenues paid to the local government, new industries which developed to supply and service the coal mines and in response to the growing supply of cheap energy, improved local infrastructure and facilities, and the employment of significant numbers of otherwise redundant agricultural workers. In many remote and otherwise poor locations, the TVCMs provided a vital engine for economic growth and development (Ye and Zhang 1998; Rui 2004).

Although TVCMs, and indeed TVEs in general, were officially collectively owned by the residents, in reality many local governments acted as owners of the enterprises within their jurisdictions (Chen 2000). Local government leaders provided vital support to TVEs in the form of preferential access to low interest loans. They had the power to redistribute revenues between TVEs, to provide tax breaks to favoured enterprises, to appoint managers and to permit the systematic under-reporting of economic activity (Oi 1998; Chen 2000; Ma and Ortolano 1999; Unger and Chan 1999). Other factors which allowed the TVEs to compete effectively against the larger state enterprises included their greater exposure to market forces, their greater flexibility and autonomy, and their generally harder budgetary constraints (Kwong and Lee 2000).

The further consolidation of the close relationship between local governments and their TVEs was created by the ambiguous nature of the ownership rights. Authority over major decisions and rights over the assets drifted gradually from the local government to the TVE (Li and Ye 1998). At the same time, the families of the local officials, in their private capacity, were, in some cases, able to gain control over assets. This has led, in effect, to *de facto* privatisation of collective or public assets (Walder and Oi 1999; Chen 2000). Thus the self-interest of local government officials progressively replaced the community interest as the driving force behind the success of the TVEs (Sargeson and Zhang 1999). Indeed, many truly private enterprises took on the cloak of TVEs in order to protect themselves against discrimination (Chen 2000).

In addition to the financial incentives for individual government officials and their relatives, the TVCMs provided an employment opportunity to millions of workers. From the late 1970s China's economic reforms had led to a steady increase in the number of unemployed or underemployed people, both in the countryside and in the cities. At the same time, the rules on migration were gradually relaxed to allow rural workers to move to other locations on a temporary basis. As a result the workforce in TVCMs included both local and migrant workers.

The apparent lack of nation-wide, systematic statistics on the structure of the TVCM workforce in the mid and late 1990s is not surprising given the informal and often illegal nature of many of the mines. Fieldwork by the author and associates in Shanxi Province and Chongqing Municipality in the period 1999-2002, along with others' research such as that of Ye and Zhang (1998) suggest that a number of generalisations may be made for the late 1990s.

The workforce, even within a single mine, might include both local and migrant workers. Migrant workers came both from neighbouring counties or from other provinces. Local labour might have included workers from large-scale mines using their knowledge and skills to gain extra income, and workers laid off from large-scale mines or other state-owned enterprises, as well as local people. In poorer regions the TVCM workforce tended to be dominated by local people, in richer areas by migrants. This distinction clearly derived from the dangerous and unpleasant working conditions in the TVCMs which deterred all but the most needy. In Shanxi Province in 1999 a commonly quoted wage for TCVM workers was one thousand RMB per month, with opportunities for bonuses (author's fieldwork 1999) allowing migrants to send several thousand RMB per year back to their families.

Negative impacts of the TVCMs and government counter-measures

The negative impacts of TVCMs

Whilst the benefits described above were mostly economic and short-term in nature, the negative impacts of TVCMs were much more varied and longer-term. These negative impacts were felt at both national and local levels and may be considered under four main headings: waste of natural resources, distortion of markets, environmental damage, and health and safety. The first two are mainly economic in nature, whilst the rest relate more closely to the livelihoods of local communities and mine workers. It is health and safety issues which are of greatest concern in this chapter.

From the economic perspective the most damaging accusation which may be levelled at China's small-scale coal mines is that they have wasted otherwise commercially viable coal resources. In most cases this waste has taken the form of leaving coal *in situ* which can now never be exploited commercially. Recovery rates for TVCMs are estimated to lie in the range 10-20%, compared to 60-80% for the large state-owned mines (Thomson 1996, 726-750; Coal Industry Advisory Board 1999; Zhong 2003; Horii 2001).

The second negative impact of the TVCMs concerns their distortion of the coal markets through inequitable competition with the state-owned mines. The TVCMs were able, through legitimate and illegitimate means, to avoid or substantially reduce a wide range of costs which burdened the larger mines. These included the cost of equipment, safety measures, electrical power, welfare, insurance, taxation and many other costs which a large, modern enterprise has to bear. As a result the cost of production for a TVCM was one-half to one-third of that of a state-owned mine and therefore TVCMs could massively undercut the larger mines in the coal market (He 1999; Wright 2000). This has two drawbacks. Firstly, the state-owned mines were unable to sell much of their output and state investment was therefore wasted. Secondly, by avoiding all these costs the TVCMs were not contributing anything to compensate for all the negative externalities such as the waste of coal resources, the environmental damage and the human cost of the operations.

A major legacy of China's TVCMs takes the form of environmental damage. This damage affects three facets of nature: land, air and water. Systematic quantitative data on the environmental damage caused by TVCMs is sparse, but the available information suggests that of all China's township and village industrial enterprises, coal mines have been the largest contributors to the production of solid waste, industrial dust and soot, sulphur dioxide and waste water (Andrews-Speed et al 2003a).

In areas of intense TVCM activity, these mines have caused substantial physical destruction of agricultural land through the creation of solid waste dumps, through the subsidence of land above abandoned workings, through the contamination of soils by dust, and through the erosion of topsoil (Smil 2000; Zhong 2003; Wright 2000). The dust which arises from TVCMs contaminates both the land and the air, and it has two sources. One is the mines themselves and their associated waste tips (Gunson and Yue 2001); the other is the chimneys of those enterprises which burn the coal from TVCMs. Not only do many TVCMs often exploit coal which is of lower quality than that required by larger mining enterprises, but rarely do they wash the coal to remove the waste rock before selling on to customer. As a result the end-users, often other TVEs, emit large quantities of ash or dust on combustion of the coal (Thomson 1996; Horii 2001).

The impact of small-scale coal mines on China's water has taken two main forms. Firstly, the discharge of solid waste or waste water into rivers and lakes reduces the quality of the water. Higher sediment loads may increase the frequency of flooding, and extreme cases may completely block or divert a river (Smil 2000; Wright 2000). In provinces such as Shanxi, some coal mining villages have found themselves without any supply of clean water at all. Secondly, poorly managed mining can result in changes in level of ground water, which in turn can cause either flooding of agricultural land or a shortage of water.

In the 1990s the safety record of China's TVCMs started to make headline news in the national press and was recognised by the relevant international agencies as being of serious concern (International Labour Organization 1999). Despite repeated campaigns to crackdown on dangerous mines, the statistics show that the fatality rate in the TVCMs was several times that in the large state-owned mines, and significantly higher than those mines administered by local government (see Table 4.1). The fatality rate in all three types of coal mine fell during the 1980s and 1990s. In the large state-owned coal mines the rate declined from 5 fatalities per million tonnes of output in 1980 to a steady level just above 1.0 fatality per million tones in the 1990s. This is equivalent to US coal mines in the 1950s (Wang 2006). Over the same period the fatality rate in China's local state-owned mines fell from about 10 to 4-5 fatalities per million tonnes and that of the TVCMs fell from about 15 in 1980 to 6-8 fatalities per million tonnes in 1998 (Wang 2006; Horii 2001). These fatality rates from China's TVCMs in the 1990s are equivalent to that in Belgium coal mines 150 years ago and that of Indian coal mines in 1950 (Wright 2004; Wang 2006).

The largest single cause of accidents in China's coal mines, especially in the TVCMs, is gas explosions (Wright 2004; Wang 2006). Methane gas is an essential component of most forms of coal and has long been recognised as being extremely dangerous. The gas can be released from the coal either gradually or suddenly. It can accumulate in underground cavities such as those made by mine workers, and can explode with the slightest spark. Unlike roof falls which generally kill a relatively small number of people, gas explosions have the power to cause large numbers of fatalities. Prevention of such accidents requires the use of safety lamps, the installation of effective ventilation, and the implementation of rigorous safety procedures and training programmes. The mining industry in the United Kingdom successfully introduced these technologies and practices more than 100 years ago, with a dramatic impact on the frequency of gas explosions. The Chinese coal mining industry has yet to achieve this level of success, even in the larger mines (Wright 2004).

These figures for fatalities, horrific as they are, fail to enumerate non-fatal injuries and a range of health problems experienced by small-coal mine workers. The health impact of the TVCMs include both the direct influence on those taking part in the mining, particularly lung problems, and indirect influence on local communities in the form of epidemics, drugs and crime (Sun et al 1997; International Labour Organization 1999; He 1999).

Government counter-measures and their effectiveness

The period 1986 to 1996 saw different levels of government in China take a range of measures to address the challenges posed by the TVCMs. These included issuing new laws and regulations, reforming institutional structures and carrying out periodic campaigns to close TVCMs or rectify conditions in these mines.

A Mineral Resources Law was first passed in 1986, with implementing rules appearing eight years later. The Law was revised in 1996 and a package of regulations was issued in 1998. For the first time in its history, China had a systematic set of rules concerning mineral exploration and production rights, and the transfer of these rights. These are now administered by the Ministry of Land and Resources.

A second category of laws and regulations was directed at the operations of coal mines, and cover everything from development and production plans, to safety and marketing. During the period 1994-1996, a number of measures were implemented for the coal industry as a whole. Specific rules to manage coal production licenses were issued in 1994 and 1995. These were soon followed by a Coal Law, which sought to establish a new framework for production. The Ministry of Coal Industries was the sponsor of these documents. It, along with the subordinate coal bureaux at the various levels of local government, was responsible for implementation, including the issuing of coal production licenses.

Table 4.1 Coal output and fatalities related to coal mining, 1996-2005

	1996	1997	1998	1999	2000	2001	2002	2003	2004	2005
All coal mines										
Coal output mmt	1374	1325	1232	1,044	999	1106	1382	1736	1956	2110
Fatalities in coal production	5544	6071	6275	6,469	5,796	5670	6995	6434	6027	5986
Fatality rate, per mmt	4.03	4.58	5.09	6.20	5.80	5.13	5.06	3.71	3.08	2.84
Major state-owned mines										
Coal output mmt	537	529	503	513	536	619	712	830	919	1010
Fatalities in coal production	560	710	524	572	747	781	905	894	854	972
Fatality rate, per mmt	1.04	1.34	1.04	1.12	1.39	1.26	1.27	1.08	0.93	0.96
Local state-owned mines										
Coal output mmt	220	225	212	214	194	223	263	294	295	
Fatalities in coal production	850	912	901	947	827	1044	1022	881	816	557
Fatality rate, per mmt	3.86	4.05	4.25	4.43	4.26	4.68	3.89	3.00	2.77	
TVCMs										
Coal output mmt	639	529	516	317	270	264	418	612	742	
Fatalities in coal production	3993	4154	4575	4,666	3,933	3,645	5068	4659	4357	4457
Fatality rate, per mmt	6.25	7.85	8.87	14.72	14.57	13.81	12.12	7.61	5.87	

Note: The sum of the sub-totals from the different classifications may not equal to figures from all coal mines, as some mines lie outside the three classifications. mmt = million tonnes.

Sources: China Coal Industry Yearbooks 1998, 1999, 2000 (Beijing: China Zhongguo Meitan Gongye Chubanshe) and State Administration for Coal Mine Safety, unpublished data.

Safety Supervisory Bureau, http:///www.chinacoal-safety.gov.cn/, retrieved 18 March 2006.

A third category of laws and regulations relate to the protection of the environment and the management of the land. Most of these have very wide application, but make specific reference to and have application to the mining industry. Those relating to general environmental protection and specifically, to water and soil, fall under the remit of the State Environmental Protection Agency. Those relating to land administration and reclamation were promoted by the Ministry of Land and Resources.

The final set of regulations applies specifically to township and village mines, and not to large-scale, state-owned coal mines (Table 4.2). These measures fall into two time periods. From 1980 to 1986, the annual output of the TVCMs rose from 100 million tonnes to 300 million tonnes, their contribution to China's total coal output increasing from one-sixth to one-third (Thomson 2003). Belatedly, the State Council issued a Circular in 1986, which sought to bring order to a chaotic regulatory situation, whilst at the same time, calling for higher levels of production. The Circular called on all levels of government to improve the standard of regulation for TVCMs, and to draw up local administrative provisions to implement the new Mineral Resources Law and the Regulations on Mine Production Safety.

Table 4.2 Selected relevant laws, regulations and measures relating to the operation of township and village coal mines 1986-1996

Name of instrument	Year
Circular of the State Council on the Implementation of Industrial Management of Township and Village Enterprise Mines	1986
Administrative Measures for the Township and Village Enterprise Mines in Shanxi Province	1986
Measures for Reorganisation of the Township and Village Enterprise Mines in Shanxi Province	1986
Administrative Regulations for Township and Village Coal Mines	1994
Implementation Measures for the Administrative Regulations for Township and Village Coal Mines	1994
Regulations for Small Coal Mine Safety	1996
Law on Township Enterprises	1996

The two measures listed in Table 4.2 from Shanxi Province are examples of the response of provincial governments. These address a wide range of issues such as engineering and safety standards, inspection procedures, the role of different levels of government, the responsibilities of mine managers, employee contracts, and the legal status of TVCMs. As the province with the largest output of coal in China, both aggregate and from TVCMs alone, Shanxi Province was frequently under pressure to improve the management of its TVCMs, and during the 1980s and 1990s ran a number of rectification campaigns.

The impact of these wide-ranging measures appears to have been limited however. On the positive side, the official statistics showed that the fatality rate in the TVCMs declined substantially during the 1980s and 1990s, as mentioned above. Set against this is the fact that as many as 75% of the estimated 80,000 TVCMs in operation in the mid-1990s were illegal, as they lacked either a mining licence or a production licence or both. Not only does this show that the regulatory system for TVCMs was largely ineffective over this period but also it calls into question the reliability of the accident statistics, for illegal mines are unlikely to report fatalities unless the accident is sufficiently large to be reported in the mass media. Further, no evidence has been presented that either the coal recovery rates or the environmental behaviour of TVCMs improved over this period.

Constraints on the effectiveness of government measures

The inability of China's government to effectively regulate the country's small-scale coal mines during the 1980s and 1990s derived from a combination of factors relating to financial incentives and to legal and regulatory structures and systems. In simple terms, the power of the financial incentives at local level to continue mining and to ignore the external costs was greater than the power of the regulatory system to constrain or discourage such behaviour.

A number of parties had direct financial incentives to keep the mines in operation. The local governments needed to encourage local enterprises, to generate wealth and to raise tax revenue. Many of the same local officials held private interests in these mines. The mine owners, who themselves may have had close connections with local officials, focused on short-term financial returns, as did the mine managers and workers.

All four parties were acting as rational agents seeking to maximise their financial benefits (Wright 2004; Wang 2006). Most mine workers had lower educational levels (Zhong 2003), received little information and training on safety, and had little job security. The mine owners and managers were driven by profit, and a number of factors would have discouraged them from taking a long-term view with respect to external costs. The frequent oscillations in the price of coal and in the government's policy towards TVCMs would have exacerbated their focus on short-term profits. Installing equipment to raise the level of coal recovery and the standards of safety and environment is a fixed capital cost which would have had a disproportionate cost impact on smaller operations. As a significant proportion of mine workers are rural labourers, and many of them migrants, who lack political organisation, representation and influence, there has been a conspicuous imbalance of power between capital and labour in such coal mines. As a consequence, safety measures, and technical and safety training have been constantly ignored in the scramble for profits.

Two problems existed within local government which allowed the financial incentives to carry greater weight than the regulatory responsibilities: collusion and a fundamental conflict of interests. In cases where individual local government officials held private interests in the mines, they were able to collude in order to support these operations and to obstruct the enforcement of government policy.

Within local government itself lay a conflict between its desire to promote local economic growth and its obligation to enforce national laws and policies, and to safeguard the safety of miners (Andrews-Speed et al 2003a; Wang 2006).

Legal and regulatory structures and systems were insufficiently powerful to counteract these financial drivers for two main reasons. The first relates to the deficiencies in the regulation of the mining sector, and the second concerns the regime for protecting labour.

Though China now has a substantial number of laws, regulations and administrative measures, which apply directly or indirectly to township and village coal mines, this body of law suffers from the same weaknesses as Chinese law in general. Laws governing mineral resources, land management, environmental protection and coal mining operations, including safety, have been developed and promoted by institutions with noticeably different agendas. This, combined with the reactive nature of these regulatory initiatives and the endemic vagueness of much Chinese law, has led to duplication, inconsistency and ambiguity (Andrews-Speed et al 2003a).

The country's first law on Safety in Mines was approved in 1992, though this law and its supplementary regulations focused on the large state-owned mines and was not appropriate to township and village mines (Wang 2006). Only in 1996 did the government issue specific regulations on the safety of small-scale coal mines.

A further weakness of the laws and regulations was the low levels of the penalties for non-compliance. Though most of the regulations did indeed specify a range of administrative and criminal penalties, these tended to be small in comparison with the profits available to mine owners and managers. For example, the maximum level for fines for a violation of safety standards or for an accident causing fatalities or serious injuries was RMB 50,000 in the late 1990s (Wright 2004; Wang 2006).[1]

More important than the deficiencies in the laws and regulations were those in the administrative structures and systems for implementation (UNDP/World Bank 2004). The large number of levels of administration between the key levels of policy formulation in central and provincial governments and implementation at township or village level provided great scope for policy modification, inadequate implementation and direct obstruction.

The second major weakness of the administrative system was the sheer number of vertical reporting lines, which converge downward on the hapless TVCM manager. The Bureaux for Coal Administration and for Geology and Mineral Resources carried the brunt of the workload and responsibility for the effective regulation of TVCMs, but a number of other agencies have greater or lesser roles to play. These will have included the local bureaux reporting to Ministries of Agriculture, of Land Administration, of Labour, of Public Security, and of Public Health, as well as the local Environmental Protection Bureaux (Andrews-Speed et al 2003a; Wang 2006). Such a large number of agencies were certain to result in duplication, overlap, ambiguity, confusion, poor coordination and contradictions in the formulation and

1 This maximum level of penalty is defined in such documents as the Coal Law (1996), Administrative Regulations for Township and Village Coal Mines (1994) and Regulations for Small Coal Mine Safety (1996).

implementation of policy for TVCMs, as well as providing a disincentive for mine mangers to report on account of the excessive workload.

A shortage of manpower and funds was a further obstacle to effective performance by all levels of government. Coal Bureaux at the county level were overwhelmed by the task of trying to monitor and regulate as many as 80,000 TCVMs across the country in the mid-1990s, with staffing levels established principally to oversee local state-owned operations (Andrews-Speed et al 2003a; Wang 2006).

The second relevant aspect of the legal regime relates to labour rights. Since Liberation in 1949, China's systems for social security and labour protection have possessed two main characteristics: they have been directed at urban residents and delivered through the work unit. Rural residents and urban residents without work units lay largely outside the established systems. Further, they have had no formal political voice to draw attention to this exclusion (Li 2004).

The content of the Labour Law passed in 1994 was eminently laudable in its aspirations for social insurance and employment services, but, like most Chinese laws, was exhortatory and vague. Before 2003 no attempt was made to include rural workers. Even amongst the urban workforce the take up of the various types of insurance amounted to only 14% in the case of unemployment insurance, 11% for medical insurance and 6% for workplace injury insurance (Reutersward 2005). This low level may be attributed to the fact that most uninsured are employed in the informal sector, where enforcement of labour protection regulations and laws tends to be problematic.

The Labour Law empowered the establishment of inspectorates in local Labour Bureaux with the power to inspect working conditions, working hours, wage levels, and wage payments, to ensure compliance with social insurance regulations and to deal with complaints against employers (Reutersward 2005). As with many other local agencies, these inspectorates were under-resourced and have been unable to fulfil their mandates (Zheng 2006).

The final dimension of labour rights which directly impacted the management of TVCMs during the 1990s was the low level of compensation payable by mine owners to the families of mine workers injured or killed in accidents. Under general civil law in the 1980s, the obligations for employers to compensate workers for death or injury were very vague and no quantities were specified.[2] A more specific decree was issued in 1996 which covered funeral expenses, a pension to relatives amounting to 40% of the deceased worker's monthly salary to the spouse and lower proportions to other close relatives, and a once off payment of up to 60 times the monthly wage.[3] The average level of compensation was 10,000-20,000 RMB with a maximum of 50,000 RMB (Xinhua News Agency 2003; Fu, 2005). As is the case with the penalties for accidents and safety violations, this level of payment was far too low to act as an incentive to mine owners to invest in improving their infrastructure, technology and practices, and to take seriously the lives, health and livelihood of miners.

2 See Article 119 of the General Principles of the Civil Law of the PRC, April 1986.

3 See Article 25 of Trial Methods for Insurance for Work-Related Injury to Enterprise Workers, promulgated by the State Council in October 1996.

Mine closure and unexpected outcomes

The closure campaign and accompanying measures

The year 1998 marked a dramatic turning point for China's energy sector, and in particular the coal industry, for two reasons. First, in March of that year the government announced a fundamental restructuring of the state energy companies and government agencies (Andrews-Speed et al 2000). Second, it became apparent early in the year that the decline of total primary energy consumption which had appeared during 1997 was almost certain to continue. The drop in demand particularly affected the coal industry, and stock-piles reached levels in excess of 200 million tonnes. By 1999 the end-use of coal had fallen to 37% below the level for 1996 (Sinton and Fridley 2000).

This substantial oversupply of coal posed a major threat to the larger state-owned mines into which large amounts of government investment had been directed over the previous years. The obvious culprits were the township and village mines which were able to sell at prices well below the costs of the state-owned mines. Senior government officials were quite explicit that the campaign to close TVCMs was directly influenced by the need to reduce the oversupply and to protect the state-owned mines (Zhang 1999). Other considerations included rationalising the structure of coal production, raising coal prices, improving the financial health of the major state-owned coal mines, and the need to close illegal and unsafe TVCMs (Wu 1999; Zhang 1999).

The TVCM closure policy announced in 1998 was part of a wider programme of coal industry reform which included the closure of some large mines and the bankruptcy of selected large coal mining enterprises (Zhang 1999; Huang 2000). The 1998 campaign was not the first directed at small-scale coal mines. Shanxi Province, for example, had launched rectification programmes in 1985, 1989, 1992, 1994 and 1996. However this was the first systematic attempt by central government to bring order to a chaotic sector across the whole country. For the first time, the highest authorities in the country put their weight behind such a campaign.

Official documents clearly identified and categorised the TVCMs targeted for closure (State Council 1998). Compensation would be paid only to those mines operating within the licence areas of state-owned mines and which had mining and production licences. Mines operating outside the licence areas of state-owned mines, which had mining licences but no production licences were given the opportunity to raise their technical and safety standards and apply for a production licence before the end of February 1999. The smaller mines in this category were encouraged to merge with other mines to provide the financial and technical benefits of scale (Wang 2000; Creedy et al 2006). All other TVCMs operating without the requisite licences were to be closed.

The key levels for the implementation of the policy were the provincial and county governments. Provincial governments had the responsibility to draw up a strategy for the province and to negotiate or allocate closure targets for lower levels, whilst county governments had the task of implementing the closures. In Shanxi Province, TVCM closure offices were established at each level of government. To monitor progress, the central government sent out inspection teams (Anonymous 1999; Chang 1999).

The view of the central government in 2001 would appear to have been that the TVCM closure programme had been a success. According to official accounts, the level of annual national coal production was brought down from nearly 1,400 million tonnes in the mid-1990s to about 1,000 million tonnes in 2000 and 2001. The number of TVCMs in operation was cut dramatically from 83,000 in 1997 to 23,000 in early 2002, with a consequent drop in the TVCM annual output from 710 million tonnes in 1996 to 255 million tonnes in 2001. By 2001 stockpiles were down, coal prices had risen and the overall profitability of the coal industry was starting to grow. At the same time the level of exports continued to increase (Shi 2002). Thus the state-owned mines had been protected and the key objectives of the closure programme might be said to have been achieved.

Three lines of evidence suggest that a substantial difference exists between the actual and the reported number of mine closures. Firstly, a number of Chinese commentators and officials reported that local officials were submitting false statistics during the closure campaign (Shi 2000; Lin et al 2000; Huang 1999; Wright 2000). Some were deliberately falsified and others were inaccurate because "closed" mines had subsequently been re-opened. Large numbers of mines were continuing to operate illegally even in 2001 (South China Morning Post 2001).

A second line of evidence comes from the energy statistics. A substantial divergence between official figures for coal production and coal consumption in China since 1998 cannot be explained solely by a draw-down on stockpiles, but suggests that the level of unreported coal production was substantial (Sinton 2001).

Finally, official accident statistics for TVCMs show that the number of fatalities per million tonnes of output was higher in the period 1999-2002 than it was in the preceding three years. Indeed the absolute number of fatalities per year was higher, even though reported production levels were lower (see Table 4.1). Given that the effectiveness of management and regulation of the legal mines should have improved as part of the effort to upgrade these mines, this disturbing trend in fatalities probably has two related causes: a lower level of management and regulation of illegal mines, and a high level of unreported coal output. Alternatively, these figures may just be a result of more complete reporting of fatalities.

Together these three lines of argument support the widely held view that the gap between reality and official statistics concerning the closure of TVCMs was substantial, and that a large and unquantifiable number of illegal TVCMs remained in operation throughout the closure campaign.

At the same time as they closed many TVCMs and sought to legalise and rationalise the remainder, the government carried out a radical reorganisation of the entire institutional structure governing the coal industry, with a particular focus on safety. The Ministry for Coal Industries was abolished in 1998, and a limited range of functions was allocated to the newly-created State Administration for Coal Industries. One of the key functions of this new department was to raise the standard of safety in China's coal mines. A further reorganisation in 2001 abolished the State Administration for Coal Industries and replaced it with the State Administration for

Coal Mine Safety which lay alongside the newly-created State Administration for Work Safety.

Between 1999 and 2003 these two agencies issued a substantial body of guidelines and procedures relating to safety and inspections, including the Regulations for Coal Mine Safety Supervision in the year 2000 and the Law on Work Safety in 2002 (see Table 4.3; Wang 2006). These documents increased the maximum level of penalty for safety violations from the previous level of 50,000 RMB to 150,000-200,000 RMB, depending on the nature of the offence. Further the relevant managers and officials could be removed from office and the coal mine ordered to close.

Table 4.3 Selected relevant laws, regulations and measures relating to the operation of township and village coal mines 1999-2005

Name of instrument	Year
Circular on Collecting Information about Safety Inspection	1999
Regulations for Coal Mine Safety Supervision	2000
Law on Work Safety	2002
Procedures for Administrative Sanctions on Safety Violations	2003
Guidelines for Coal Mine Safety Assessment	2003
Regulation on Licences for Safe Production	2004
Provisions for Implementing Safety responsibility and Preventing Severe Accidents in the Coal Mines in Shanxi Province	2004
Provisions for Administrative Penalties against Illegal Coal Mines in Shanxi Province	2005

Source: Modified from Wang, 2006.

A further significant change which accompanied the closure campaign was the transfer of ownership of many mines from the township or the village collective to private hands. Such privatisation of TVEs had been taking place throughout China, and few now remain as collectives (Li and Rozelle 2003; Green 2005). Though this privatisation should have led to a clear separation of the interests of government and enterprise, this was not fully achieved. Indeed, many local government officials continued to retain a private interest in the mines and the financial incentives were, if anything, enhanced by the privatisation. This will be discussed below.

Socio-economic impacts of the closure campaign

At least three parties suffer economic loss when a small-scale coal mine is closed. The owner of the mine loses their investment and future cash-flow. The local government loses tax revenue, in addition to any losses it sustains as partial or whole owner of the mine. Finally, the workers lose their livelihood, whether they be local people or migrants.

Although the official argument might have been that the redundant workers should be redeployed to other TVEs, in most areas this would have been difficult to achieve as the local enterprise sector as a whole was going through difficult times as a result of both market competition and the administrative closure of small, polluting enterprises in other sectors. Migrant underemployed rural workers formed major part of the TVCM labour force in some provinces, and hundreds of thousands will have lost their jobs if the number of TVCMs closed was indeed as high as has been reported. At the same time, local governments dependent on fiscal revenues from TVCMs may have lost as much as 10 billion RMB per year as a result of the closures (Andrews-Speed et al 2003b).

The closure campaign was carried out in such haste that little or no thought seems to have been given to planning for its economic or social impacts. The closure of the TVCMs took place against a background of rising rural unemployment and migration to the cities. From the mid-1990s the rate of growth of rural employment in non-agricultural activities declined sharply. From 1996 to 2002 China's total rural population declined whilst total urban population rose by some 130 million (National Bureau of Statistics of China 2003). This reflected both movement from the countryside to the cities as well as the progressive urbanisation of the countryside. Further, these figures do not include the mobile population of about 200 million, who worked in the cities and towns but were deemed rural residents based on their *hukou* registration status (Wang 2004).

The available evidence suggests that few or no systematic support mechanisms were put in place to deal with the negative impact of the mine closure campaign on communities (Shi 1999). Indeed it was the lack of attention to these issues which led to the formidable and sustained resistance to the closure policy by local governments and communities.

Evidence from across the country and from a detailed study in Chongqing Municipality (Andrews-Speed et al 2003b; Andrews-Speed et al 2005) shows that most local governments responded to the economic challenge in one of four ways:

1. By complying with the mine closure campaign and successfully developing alternative economic activities;
2. By complying with the mine closure campaign but failing to develop alternatives;
3. By complying with the mine closure campaign but raising output in the remaining mines;
4. By failing to comply with the mine closure campaign and allowing mines to continue in operation.

The choice of response made by local governments seems to have depended to a great extent on local economic, social and political circumstances. In relatively wealthy areas, with good communications and an already diversified economy, new economic activities and employment opportunities could be created with moderate ease. In more remote and poor areas which were more dependent on the TVCMs for economic development, rapid diversification of the local economy faced greater constraints and in many places little progress was made. These are the communities which paid the price of the sudden and unplanned implementation of the TVCM closure policy and the lack of attention paid at any time by the higher levels of the Chinese government to preparing the local communities to absorb the shocks of the closure of small-scale mines.

Resurgence of output and re-emergence of problems

The year 2002 saw the start of a surge in China's economic growth and, most relevant to the coal sector, in demand for energy. Over the years 2003 and 2004, the average annual rate of growth of primary commercial energy consumption was approximately 15%, and the growth of demand for coal was marginally higher. These figures are more than double the average over the previous two decades (BP, 2005). Total annual output of coal rose from 1,382 million tonnes in 2002 to 1,956 million tonnes in 2004 (Table 4.1).

This rapid growth in demand for energy in general and for coal in particular was triggered by the deliberate policy of the central government to encourage economic growth through investment in infrastructure and heavy industry. The large state-owned coal mines were unable to expand their production capacity at such a rate, neither were the railways and road transport fleets able to expand their transport capacities. The price of coal rose across the country by as much as 60% between 2001 and 2004 (U.S. Energy Information Administration, 2006). This provided a clear economic signal to all coal mines which were able to expand their production capacity. The TVCMs were able to raise their output faster than the large state-owned mines, for they could resort either to re-opening previously 'closed' mines or to developing new capacity in existing mines with a minimum of investment.

The available official data showed that output from TVCMs increased by 80% from 2002 to 2004, whilst output from the large state-owned coal mines grew by only 30% (Table 4.1). Even allowing for the unreliability of the output data from the TVCMs, it would appear that these small-scale coal mines accounted for more than 50% of the incremental output over this period even though they produced only 30% of the nation's coal in 2002.

The tightness of the coal markets and consequent high prices provided a great opportunity for the owners of the newly-privatised TVCMs. Those who were able to keep their costs low, through paying low wages and paying scant attention to safety measures, were able to make substantial profits. Indeed, entrepreneurs from coastal China travelled to the coal fields of Shanxi Province to take advantage of these new opportunities (O'Neill 2004).

The available information on coal mine fatalities suggests that the total number of fatalities in both major state-owned coal mines and in TVCMs rose dramatically from 2001 to 2002 and then declined in 2003 and 2004, before rising again in 2005 (Table 4.1). Though as total coal output was rising, the fatality rate per tonne continued to decline. Comparisons with earlier periods are fraught with difficulties. Between 1998 and 2002 systematic under-reporting of coal production would have resulted in fatality rates being over-stated. In the mid-1990s, at the peak of the TVCM boom, the number of fatalities was probably under-reported and, indeed, may remain so today.

Regardless of arguments concerning the reliability of the fatality statistics, it became clear to China's government by 2005 that it was not winning the battle to enforce higher safety standards in the coal mining industry. Despite the fact that growth of demand for coal was slackening and prices starting to decline, the number of deaths in all coal mines remained close to 6,000 and the number of accidents involving 10 deaths or more rose by 35%. Though many of the larger accidents necessarily took place in local or major state-owned mines, the TVCMs still accounted for the majority of fatalities.

The profit incentives for the private owners remained powerful, and the willingness of many local officials to enforce the regulations was compromised by their dual role as regulator and owner. Further, the mine owners probably realised that they faced a window of opportunity for such profits, for two reasons. First, in 2005 the government seemed determined to reduce the rate of economic growth which would necessarily impact the demand for coal, and especially for coal from TVCMs as the major state-owned mines brought new capacity into production. Secondly, in 2005 the government launched a series of new measures at central and provincial levels to improve the management of all coal mines. Thus some mine owners might have had only a year or two of operations before either the prices fell or their mines faced enforced closure.

These measures took a number of forms. At the beginning of 2005 the State Administration for Work Safety and the State Administration for Coal Mine Safety were elevated in status from vice-ministerial to ministerial level in the governance hierarchy (Wang 2006). Officially this further enhanced their authority. However, the authority of these institutions continues to be constrained by the fact that most of the inspectors are recruited, employed and paid by the respective level of government at which they operate. Thus a conflict of interests persists between the economic and safety goals of local government.

As in 1998, a campaign was launched to close large numbers of coal mines which were either unsafe or having very low recovery rates. The target of 4,000 closed mines for 2005 was exceeded, with a total of 5,290 being closed, most of which would have been TVCMs (Interfax 2006a). Further plans to merger small-scale mines were announced (Interfax 2006b). A total of six billion RMB was set aside to invest in safety in 2006 and 2007, but most of this will have been for state-owned mines, not for TVCMs (Interfax 2006c). To address the conflicts of interest at local level, government officials across the country were ordered to divest their interests in coal mines, and this campaign continued into 2006 (Xinhua News Agency 2005b, 2006).

At the provincial level, Shanxi led the way with a number of initiatives. Minimum compensation levels were raised from 50,000 to 200,000 RMB per fatality, and the financial penalty was increased to one million RMB per death.[4] Miners who reported dangers would receive financial rewards in the range of 300-3,000 RMB (Xinhua News Agency 2005a), and the owners of highly profitable mines were encouraged to make contributions to local welfare (Interfax 2006d). Other provinces followed by raising the level of compensation (Fang 2005; Wang 2005) and in Guangdong government officials who were also mine owners were given prison sentences for corruption and dereliction of duty relating to a specific major accident (Interfax 2006e).

Conclusions

Township and village coal mines have played an important role in China's economic development by contributing vital coal supplies both nationally and locally, by providing employment for local and migrant workers, and generating revenues for local governments. In this way they have helped to alleviate poverty in some areas. The chief beneficiaries of the direct economic benefits have been the owners of the mines, whether they be private or collective, the local governments and the communities in areas within which the TVCMs have been well managed and regulated, and those workers who have been employed in relatively well-managed mines.

But many workers, and their families and communities have been unable to reap such benefits on account of low wage levels, a lack of job security, dangerous and unhealthy working conditions, the low levels of compensation in cases of accidents, injuries or occupational diseases, and environmental destruction around the mines. These phenomena are consistent with accepted symptoms of marginality: relative material and social deprivation, vulnerability, social exclusion, living at the edge of a system, and lagging behind the rest of society in terms of development (Gurung and Kollmair, 2005).

The evidence suggests that small-scale coal mining rather than alleviating poverty may have sustained or possibly exacerbated the degree of social and economic marginalisation of certain groups, especially of those who are most vulnerable. For it has generally been the marginalised who have entered the sector as mine workers. Though many do benefit from a short-term enhancement of their incomes, most do not have job security, nor are covered by various social insurance schemes, and thus remain at the social, economic and political margins of society.

This disappointing phenomenon can be attributed to a failure of the regulatory system to provide an adequate counter-balance to the clear economic drivers and incentives for the mining industry. The country needs coal, the local government wants the revenue and, in some cases, the coal itself, the mine owners seek profits, and the workers are desperate for waged jobs, regardless of risk. The last ten years have seen significant progress by the government to address inadequacies in the

4 These new standards were provided for in the following two documents: "Provisions for Implementing Safety Responsibility and Preventing Severe Accidents in the Coal Mines in Shanxi Province" promulgated in November 2004; and "Provisions for Administrative Penalties against Illegal Coal Mines in Shanxi Province" promulgated in October 2005.

laws and regulations, especially those related to safety, labour and environment. But fundamental flaws in the systems and structures for regulation and its enforcement continue to dampen the impacts of these improvements.

The small-scale coal mines cannot be closed if demand still exists for their output (Stanway 2006). Radical improvements in the management of the TVCMs across China are likely only to be possible in the short term if demand for the output from these mines declines substantially. This will require both a reduction in the rate of growth of demand for coal and an increase in the level of investment in new, large-scale coal mines. Though China's coal industry may face overcapacity in 2006 (Interfax 2006f), recent history tells us that such overcapacity may not be long-lived.

Acknowledgments

I am very grateful to Dr Heather Xiaoquan Zhang for her sustained support throughout the writing of this chapter, and to Ma Xin, Cao Zhenning, Chen Ji and Zheng Ying for their contributions.

References

Andrews-Speed, P., Dow, S. and Gao, Z. (2000), 'An Evaluation of the Ongoing Reforms to China's Government and State Sector: The Case of the Energy Industry', *Journal of Contemporary China* vol. 9, no. 23, pp. 5-20.

Andrews-Speed, P., Guo, M., Shao, B and Liao, C. (2005), 'Economic responses to the closure of small-scale coal mines in Chongqing, China', *Resources Policy* 30: 1, 39-54.

Andrews-Speed, P., Ma, G., Shi, X. and Shao, B. (2003b), 'The impact of and responses to the closure of small-scale coal mines in China: a preliminary account', in G. Hilson (ed.) *The Socio-Economic Impacts of Artisanal and Small-Scale Mining in Developing Countries* (Rotterdam: Balkema, 2003), pp. 511-530.

Andrews-Speed, P., Yang, M., Shen, L. and Cao S. (2003a), 'The Regulation of China's Township and Village Coal Mines: a study of complexity', *Journal of Cleaner Production* 11, 185-196.

Anonymous (1999), 'A Journalist's Review: A Difficult Beginning – An Integrated Review of the Achievements in the First Stage of Closing Mines and Restricting Output in China's Coal Industry', *Coal Enterprise Management* no. 2: 16-18 (in Chinese).

British Petroleum (2005), *Statistical Review of World Energy 2005* (London: British Petroleum).

Chang, Y. (1999) 'Problems and Countermeasures in the Process of Closing Up the Mines and Restricting the Yield', *Energy Bases Construction* no.3, 15-16 (in Chinese).

Chen, H. (2000), *The institutional transition of China's township and village enterprises* (Aldershot: Ashgate).

Coal Industry Advisory Board (1999). *Coal in the Energy Supply of China* (Paris: OECD/IEA).

Creedy, D., Wang, L., Zhou, X., Liu, H. and Campbell, G. (2006). 'Transforming China's coal mines: a case history of the Shuangliu mine', *Natural Resources Forum* vol. 30, no.1. 15-26.

Fang, X. (2005), 'The economic considerations of coal mine accidents', *Coal Economic Research*, No. 7, 6-7 (In Chinese).

Fu, J. (2005), "Accident cash funds set up by coal mines", China Daily 27 December 2005. http://www.chinadaily.co.cn/english/doc/2005-12/27/content_506865.htm, retrieved 5 February 2006.

Gao, Y. (1999), 'The Cause and Effect of China's Small Coal Mine Problem: Part 1', *Coal Economic Research* no.6, 4-7 (in Chinese).

Green, S. (2005), 'China's industrial reform strategy: privatization and state control', in Green, S., Liu, G., (ed.), *Exit the Dragon? Privatization and State Ownership in China* (Royal Institute for International Affairs, London), pp.196-212.

Gunson, A.J. and Yue, J. (2001), 'Artisanal mining in the People's Republic of China', in *Breaking New Ground: Mining, Minerals and Sustainable Development*, Paper no. 74 (London: International Institute for Environment and Development).

Gurung, G.S. and Kollmair, M. (2005). Marginality: concepts and limitations. *IP6 Working Paper* No. 4. (Zurich: Development Study Group).

He, F. (1999), 'Uncovering the True Features of the Small Coal Mines: Discussion on Mine Closure and Output Reduction', *Coal Enterprise Management* no. 3.

Heemskerk, M. (2005), 'Collecting data in artisanal and small-scale mining communities: Measuring progress towards more sustainable livelihoods', *Natural Resources Forum* 29:1, 82-87.

Horii, N. (2001), 'Development of small-scale coal mines in market transition and its externality'. In N. Horii and S. Gu (eds.), *Transformation of China's energy industries in market transition and its prospects* (Chiba, Japan: Institute of Developing Economies).

Hou, Y., Wang, W. and Li, R. (1998), 'Investigations of the township and village coal mines across China', *Science and Technology Review* 12: 47-52 (in Chinese).

Huang, Y. (1999), 'Try all the Best to Accomplish the Goal in Mine Closure and Output Reduction', *Coal Economic Research* no. 6, 1 (in Chinese).

Huang, Y. (2000), 'Recasting the Brilliance of the Coal Industry in the New Century', *Coal Economic Research,* no. 12: 1 (in Chinese).

Interfax (2006a). '5,290 coal mines shut in 2005', *Interfax China Energy Report Weekly* 1-6 January, vol.5, issue 1, 6.

Interfax (2006b). 'Shanxi to merge small coalmines', *Interfax China Energy Report Weekly* 11-17 March, vol.5, issue 10, 9.

Interfax (2006c). 'China will inject US$ 750 mln into coal mines in next two years for safety', *Interfax China Energy Report Weekly* 21-27 January, vol. 5, issue 4, 8.

Interfax (2006d). 'Shanxi county requests coalmine bosses to invest in welfare programme', *Interfax China Energy Report Weekly* 18-24 February, vol. 5, issue 7, 18.

Interfax (2006e). '16 officials sentenced for Guangdong coalmine flood', *Interfax China Energy Report Weekly* 4-10 March, vol. 5, issue 9, 17.

Interfax (2006f). 'Coal industry faces overcapacity in 2006 – NDRC report', *Interfax China Energy Report Weekly* 18-24 March, vol. 5, issue 11, 10.

International Labour Organization (1999), *Social and labour issues in small-scale mining* (Geneva: International Labour Office).

Kwong, C.C.L. and Lee, P.K. (2000), 'Business-Government Relations in Industrializing Rural China: A Principal-Agent Perspective', *Journal of Contemporary China* vol. 9, no. 25, 513-534.

Lahiri-Dutt, K. (2004), 'Informality in mineral resource management in Asia: raising questions relating to community economics and sustainable development'. *Natural Resources Forum* 28:2, 123-132.

Li, B. (2004). Urban social exclusion in transitional China, Centre for Analysis of Social Exclusion, London School of Economics, CASE Paper No. 82.

Li, H., Rozelle, S. (2003), 'Privatizing rural China: insider privatization, innovative contracts and the performance of township enterprises', *The China Quarterly* 176, 981-1005.

Lin, D., Jia, Z, Yan, M., and Shi, X. (2000), 'Closure and Reduction: Where and How?' *Coal Enterprise Management,* no. 5, 6-10 (in Chinese).

Lin, N. and Ye, X. (1998), 'Chinese Rural Enterprises in Transformation: The End of the Beginning', *Issues and Studies*, vol. 34, no. 11/12, 1-28.

Ma, X. and Ortolano, L. (1999). *Environmental Regulation in China. Institutions, Enforcement and Compliance* (Lanham MD: Rowman & Littlefield).

National Bureau of Statistics of China (2003), *China Statistical Yearbook 2003* (Beijing: Zhongguo Tongji Chubanshe).

O'Neill, M. (2004). "Wenzhou spirit mines China's black gold", *South China Morning Post* December 6.

Oi, J.C. (1998), "The Evolution of Local State Corporatism," in A.G. Walder (ed.) *Zouping in Transition. The Process of Reform in Rural China* (Cambridge, MA: Harvard University Press).

Reutersward, A. (2005), *Labour protection in China: challenges facing labour offices and social insurance*. OECD Social, Employment and Migration Working Papers No. 30 (Paris: OECD).

Rui, H. (2004), 'The rise and fall of China's TVE coal mines' *Minerals and Energy*, 19: 1, 2-15.

Sargeson, S. and Zhang, J. (1999). 'Re-assessing the role of the local state: a case study of local government interventions in property rights reform in a Hangzhou district'. *The China Journal*, 42, 77-99.

Shi, W. (2000), 'New Requirements on the Policy of Mine Closure and Output Reduction', *Coal Enterprise Management*, no. 6, 10-11 (in Chinese).

Shi, W. (2002), 'China's Coal Industry on the Way to Recovery', http://www.chinacoal.gov.cn/coal/jryw/020130x1.htm/, retrieved 23 November 2004.

Shi, X. (1999), 'Analysis, Consideration and Proposals Concerning the Programme to Close Mines and Restrict the Output', *Coal Economic Research* no. 6, 18-21 (in Chinese).

Sinton, J.E. (2001), 'Accuracy and Reliability of China's Energy Statistics', *China Economic Review*, vol. 12, 373-383.

Sinton, J.E. and Fridley, D.G. (2000), 'What goes up: recent trends in China's energy consumption', *Energy Policy*, 28:10, 671-687.

Smil, V. (2004), *China's past, China's future. Energy, food, environment* (London: RoutledgeCurzon).

South China Morning Post (2001) "Illegal Coal Mines Flourish under the Noses of Local Officials," http://wwww.scmp.com/, July 5. retrieved 20 August 2001.

Stanway, D. (2006). 'Quantity versus quality: China's coal industry tries to reform itself' *Interfax China Energy Report Weekly* 1-7 April 2006, vol.5, issue 13, 25-27.

State Council (1998) *Notice Concerning the Closure of Illegal and Irrationally Distributed Coal Mines*, State Council Document No. 43, 1998.

State Planning Commission (1997), *'97 Energy Report of China* (Beijing: Zhongguo Wujia Chubanshe) (in Chinese).

Sun, Z., Zhang, Y., He, T., and Yang, C. (1997), 'Expectancy of Working Life of Mine Workers in Hunan Province', *Public Health*, vol. 111 (1997): 81-83.

Thomson, E. (2003), *The Chinese Coal Industry: An Economic History* (London: Routledge Curzon, 2003): 118.

U.S. Energy Information Administration (2006), 'Steam coal prices for industry', http://www.eia.doe.gov/emeu/international/stmforind.html, retrieved 22 March 2006.

UNDP/World Bank (2004). *Towards a Sustainable Coal Sector in China* (Washington DC: World Bank).

Unger, J. and Chan, A. (1999), 'Inheritors of the Boom: Private Enterprise and the Role of Local Government in a Rural South China Township', *The China Journal* Issue 42, 45-74.

Walder, A.G. and Oi, J.C. (1999), 'Property Rights in the Chinese Economy: Contours of the Process of Change', in J.C. Oi and A.G. Walder (eds.), *Property Rights and Economic Reform in China* (Stanford: Stanford University Press).

Wang, F. (2004), 'Reformed migration control and new targeted people: China's hukou system in the 2000s', *The China Quarterly* 177, 115-132.

Wang, S. (2006), 'Regulating death at coalmines: changing mode of governance in China', *Journal of Contemporary China*, 15: 46, 1-30.

Wang, X. (2000), 'Always Emphasise the Importance of the Task in Mine Closure and Production Reduction', *Coal Enterprise Management*, no. 2, 9-10 (in Chinese).

Wang, Z. (2005), 'Can greater compensation buy miners safety?' 11 February,: http://www.china.org.cn/english/2005/Feb/120289.htm, retrieved 20th June 2005.

World Bank (1995), *China – Investment Strategies for China's Coal and Electricity Delivery System*, Report No. 12687-CHA (Washington D.C.: World Bank).

Wright, T. (2000), 'Competition and complementarity: township and village mines and the state sector in China's coal industry', *China Information* 14: 1, pp. 13-129.

Wright, T. (2004), 'The political economy of coal mine disasters in China: 'Your rice bowl or your life', *The China Quarterly*, 179, 629-646.

Wu. B. (1999), 'Mine Closure, Output Reduction and Sector Restructuring – Promote the Healthy and Sustainable Development of the Coal Industry', in *Selected Documents on Mine Closure and Output Reduction in China's Coal Sector* (Beijing: Zhongguo Meitan Gongye Chubanshe) (in Chinese).

Xinhua News Agency (2003). 'Nation sets to improve coalmine safety', 24 October: http://www.china.org.cn/english/government/78283.htm, retrieved 15 November 2003.

Xinhua News Agency (2005a). 'China's Shanxi to reward coal miners who report hidden dangers'. 29 August, reported in BBC Monitoring – Energy.

Xinhua News Agency (2005b). 'Chinese officials ordered to withdraw investments in coal mines'. 30 August 2005, reported in BBC Monitoring – Energy.

Xinhua News Agency (2006). 'China to intensify check on officials' illicit shares in coal mines - ministry'. 17 March, reported in BBC Monitoring – Energy.

Ye, Q. and Zhang, B. (1998), *Township and village coal mines in China*. (Beijing: Zhongguo Meitan Gongye Chubanshe) (in Chinese).

Zhang, B. (1999), 'Explanation of the Closure of Illegal and Irrationally Located Mines in the Coal Sector', in *Selected Documents on Mine Closure and Output Reduction in China's Coal Sector* (Beijing: Zhongguo Meitan Gongye Chubanshe) (in Chinese).

Zheng, Y. (2006), 'Why China lacks the right environment for corporate social responsibility', China Policy Institute, University of Nottingham, Briefing Series, Issue 6.

Zhong, Z. (2003), 'Small-scale mining in China: socio-economic impacts, policy and management', in Hilson, G. (ed.), *The Socio-economic Impacts of Artisanal and Small-scale Mining in Developing Countries* (Lisse: A.A.Balkema).

Zweig, D. (1997), *Freeing China's farmers. Rural reconstruction in the reform era* (Armonk, New York: M.E. Sharpe).

Chapter 5

Living and Working at the Margin: Rural Migrant Workers in China's Transitional Cities

Li Zhang

Introduction

China's centrally planned economic system has undergone a series of reforms and the Chinese once dual-society based on rural-urban divisions has restructured substantially since the late 1970s. The systemic transformation underway has significantly altered the very basis of state control over rural-to-urban migration. The urban employment rights of rural migrants are partially legalised under the rubric of the "temporary" urban residency policy and many studies have indicated that the number of rural migrants working in cities is increasing year by year. Nonetheless, it had been widely reported that the acquisition of urban household registration status (*hukou* – the permanent right of abode in urban areas) by ordinary rural people remains stymied. As a large number of rural workers work in cities without officially lodged residency status, they are thereby marginalised. A new dimension of social stratification based on the rights of urban residence has emerged to form an important basis for inequality in Chinese cities.

There has been rising concern about the rights of rural migrant workers in the city expressed in both media reports and Chinese academia recently. Such concern stems from the perception that unequal treatment of rural migrant workers and the denial of their permanent right of urban abode are both inhumane and unjust. But few studies explore the question, on both theoretical and empirical grounds, as to why, despite the possibility of systemic reform, rural migrant workers, who are no longer strictly barred from seeking jobs in cities, are not granted the same urban residency rights as those with urban *hukou*. The purposes of this chapter are to examine how the *hukou* system, one of the Chinese core socio-economic institutions, is critical in determining the marginalised status of rural migrant workers and to investigate why most such migrants can *work* in cities but are deprived of their rights to *settle* there. It argues that the transformation of the regime of urban accumulation is the key to the marginalisation of rural migrant workers. To elaborate this, I first review the existing theses that conceptualise three pertinent concepts: social stratification, inequality and marginalisation. This is followed by a depiction of the peripheral status of rural migrant workers in cities. I finish by examining how the transformation of the regime of urban accumulation is linked to the deprivation of migrants' right to permanent urban residency.

Social Stratification, Inequality, and Marginalisation in Different Contexts

Marginalised groups in cities generally refer to those disadvantaged people who undertake a peripheral form of urban employment as a survival strategy or who are living at the bottom of a socio-economic hierarchy (Williams and Windebank, 2001). In both industrialised and developing economies, there exist many institutional barriers, in different forms and scales, to the inclusion of certain groups of people in respect of acquiring resources and opportunities on the basis of ethnicity, gender, age, religion and culture. The status of marginalised groups can be identified, among other things, by their inferior employment situations, poor living standards and minimal access to public services. Marginalisation, therefore, is closely linked to social stratification and inequality.

Social stratification, existing in all societies, refers to the division of people into socioeconomic layers or strata. People in society can be categorised into different classes by inequalities in the possession of material resources and access to various opportunities and institutions, implying that certain groups of people live in disadvantaged conditions at the margin of society. Thus unequal distribution of the society's resources creates a configuration of social stratification (Marger, 2002). Though social stratification, inequality and marginalisation exist in most if not all societies, the causal process may differ from one to another. While property relations and power are crucial in the determination of inequality and marginalisation, in China's development context, this is also manifest in the *hukou* system, which has functioned as a key socio-economic institution stratifying the Chinese population along an urban-rural cleavage (Solinger, 1999; Tian, 2003). In the pre-reform period, it divided the population into two exclusive 'castes', one (the urban non-agricultural population) economically and socially superior to the other (the rural agricultural population). Passing the dividing boundary between the two 'castes' was exceedingly difficult, if not completely impossible. In the reform era, the *hukou* system, though considerably eroded, has continued to produce similar schismatic effects at both societal and individual levels. While market principles introduced by the reforms have made urban employment available to rural migrants under certain prerequisites, the city only offers them second-class citizenship rights, in common with undocumented immigrants in other countries (Solinger, 1999). As I shall analyse in greater detail later, the marginalisation of rural migrant workers in urban China, as an indication of increasing social stratification and inequality, reflects a blending of market forces and certain official policies in the city under transition.

The regime of urban accumulation provides an analytical approach to understand the reaction of city governments towards rural migrants. The regime of urban accumulation, a concept deriving from the regulation school of political economy, refers to a reproducible relationship between production and consumption (Hirst and Zeitlin, 1992: 85). This approach contends that a set of regulations or institutional arrangements are required to ensure the coherent progress of capital accumulation for the structural change of the economy in general and for urban growth in particular. Each regime ends in a period of crisis of accumulation reproducability. A new regime begins with the development of a new mode of regulation. Originally, the regime of urban accumulation approach focused on the market economy. Yet, as I will argue below, this approach can have a wider application for the marginalisation of rural migrant workers in the context of China's urban transition.

The Marginalised Status of Rural Migrant Workers in Chinese Cities

Understanding marginalisation of rural migrant labour in Chinese cities under transition must begin with reference to the *hukou* system, which significantly affects the status of rural migrant workers in the city. In the pre-reform period, rural and urban societies were institutionally isolated from each other in important ways (cf. Chan, 1994). Except for state-organised migration, people were effectively bound to their place of birth by the *hukou* system and other interrelated institutions enforced by the state. The regulation of rural-to-urban migration was carried out by means of practices comparable to those for controlling international borders. The separate rural and urban sectors and spaces was manifest in multiple dimensions, including, for example, state investment and public services provision, resulting in the formation of a dual-society along a rural-urban divide. Many have argued that state policies consistently privileged the urban population at the expense of those living in rural areas (Chan, 1996; Fan, 2002).

The rural-urban divide has been blurred and Chinese society has become more fluid since the reforms launched in the late 1970s. Two striking features of the early reforms were the separation of utilisation and management rights from the ownership of the means of production in both the countryside and cities, and the diversification of the rural economy. As evidence of the former, in rural areas individual households were granted the right to contract, farm and manage collectively-owned land. Meanwhile, in cities, the managers of state-owned enterprises were given more management autonomy with regard to production, recruitment and pay. The best illustration of the latter was the fast expansion of township and village enterprises (hereafter TVEs). Given use rights over the land they worked, farming families could arrange their division of labour freely, something which was not allowed in the commune period. Taking into consideration the huge size of China's rural population and the per capita land limitations, this meant a release of a significant agricultural labour force from farming. The disparity of income between agricultural and non-agricultural jobs motivated a massive reallocation of labour from agriculture to industry. While factory managers were assigned output and profit targets by contract, they were granted a large measure of autonomy to decide the size and cost of their workforce. They had an incentive to take advantage of China's pool of cheap labour.

Meanwhile, inside the urban labour market, structural changes created certain better-paid jobs that attracted a more educated urban labour force. Physically-demanding manual and non-skilled jobs tend to be disdained by the urbanites. The unwillingness of city residents to take jobs that were particularly low-paid, strenuous, dirty, or monotonous caused a labour shortage even when there were unemployment and under-employment problems in cities. Thus city governments had to consider letting rural workers take up the slack in certain occupations in accordance with the needs of the urban economy, requiring state regulations to be less hostile to labour mobility than before. As a result, the rural and the urban labour markets became less segregated. Associated with this development was the rise of rural-to-urban migration. To the extent that such migration has become more and more spontaneous, many may believe that the Chinese state has been sidelined in the migration process. One team of researchers, for example, have claimed "farewell to peasant China" (cf. Guldin, 1997).

Table 5.1 Rural-to-urban migration and rural labour transfer, 1990-2000

Year	% of Urban Population	Net rural-to-urban migration (millions)	Rural employees in urban work-units (millions)	New urban labour supply directly from rural areas (millions)
(1)	(2)	(3)	(4)	(5)
1990	26.41	NA	NA	0.74
1991	26.94	6.96	11.98	0.82
1992	27.46	6.72	12.03	0.98
1993	27.99	6.87	12.71	0.98
1994	28.51	6.80	13.72	1.84
1995	29.04	6.79	14.31	1.62
1996	30.48	18.06	12.65	1.48
1997	31.91	18.09	11.53	1.00
1998	33.35	18.48	9.13	0.87
1999	34.78	18.71	9.29	0.90
2000	36.22	19.31	8.97	1.04

Sources: Column 2: National Bureau of Statistics of China (NBSC, 2002: 93); Columns 3, 4, 5: Chan and Hu (2003: 58 & 61).

The large presence of rural migrant workers in urban China began to occur in the late 1990s when the contribution of TVEs to rural non-agricultural employment decreased (Liu, et al., 2003). Many TVEs, inefficient with regard to resource utilisation and having problems of technology know-how, experienced a sluggish growth, which has been exacerbated by increasing competitions from foreign-owned or joint-venture firms. Consequently, surplus rural workers have been redirected to cities to seek employment opportunities. One can observe the increased flow of rural-to-urban migration (columns 2 and 3 of Table 5.1) and the relatively stable level of rural labour transfer from farming to the urban job market in the 1990s (columns 4 and 5 of Table 5.1). It should be noted that, given the increasing mobility of rural labour, the numbers in Table 5.1 are only indicative and the precise figures are difficult to obtain. However, what is generally agreed is that the accumulated stock of rural workers working in cities is sizeable. Nationwide rural migrant workers have become a major element of the urban labour market. Geographically, the main destinations of migration inflows are the coastal metropolises which are the main venues for foreign direct investment and where the urban economy is most dynamic (Chan, 2004).

Despite their large numbers, the residency rights of migrant workers in cities subsequent to their employment, however, remains tenuous under the *hukou* system. In this system, individuals are required to register in a particular place of residence, either the city or the countryside (Chan and Zhang, 1999). The *hukou* registration defines individual's economic and social entitlements in a specified locality. Among the entitlements, the most significant ones are the right to work and the right of abode where one is registered. Any move from one locale to another requires seeking official approval to change one's *huko*u registration, a process subject to conditions stipulated by a plethora of regulations and endorsed by state agents. The state possesses discretionary power to refuse to issue travel documents or to refuse to endorse a citizen at the abode of his/her own choice. Illegal migrants risk losing all entitlements at their destinations.

The way the system works is somewhat similar to the experience of international migrants who try to get a visa to travel to other countries. In pre-reform times, the system was the key mechanism restricting personal freedoms of movement. From the early 1980s, however, rural migrants have been given a certain degree of freedom to work and to reside in cities under the "temporary residency policy".[1] This policy is not so much defined by limitations on the prospective duration of residence as by concomitant economic and social rights in the host city. It specifies neither the maximum period of stay nor the possibility of conversion from temporary to permanent residency. Under the policy, therefore, rural workers may work and live in the city for years with the status of temporary residents but cannot enjoy the same employment opportunities as those with urban *hukou* registration. Many cities have classified jobs into three types: local regular *hukou* jobs, non-local regular *hukou* jobs, and jobs open to all but with local regular *hukou* people receiving preference (Cai, 2000; Guang, 2001). Thus, the jobs rural migrants can undertake and the maximum percentage of migrant workers to be hired in any given sector are restricted by local regulations. Restrictions on occupation entry in the city are not so much based on the requirements of particular skills as on the possession of a permanent urban *hukou*. This means that the *hukou* system no longer entirely prohibits rural migrant workers from working in the city but functions to exclude them from certain jobs, assigning them secondary status in the urban labour market.

1 A nationwide "temporary residence certificate" (TRC) system was introduced in urban areas in 1985. The key provision was that people of aged 16 and over who intended to stay in urban areas other than their place of *hukou* registration for more than three months were required to apply for a TRC. In 1995, the TRC system was extended to rural areas. It also lowered the length of stay to only one month. The TRC is valid for one year and is renewable. Although employers cannot hire any non-locals without the TRC, many ignore such regulations. For details, see Chan and Zhang (1999).

In addition to their size and temporary status, rural migrant workers can also be distinguished from other urban populations by their work situation, habitat space and access to public services. Though not necessarily unemployed, rural migrant workers mainly operate within a labour market characterised by manual intensity, low and belated pay, high overtime, an inferior degree of job security and little opportunities for promotion. Migrant workers come to cities to sell their labour power for a pittance. One report reveals that in 2004 the average monthly wage of a rural migrant worker was 539 yuan, much lower than the 1,335 yuan earned by an average urban employee with a formal urban *hukou*. Based on that wage gap, it is estimated that the overall saving on wage expenditure by employing rural migrant workers rather than urban workers was 1,146.2 billion yuan, accounting for 8.5% of China's GDP in 2004 (Kong, 2006). It has also been found that rural migrant workers are clustered in the dirtiest and most backbreaking jobs scorned by city residents (Yang, 2003). Only a very small group of workers are in non-manual categories (Solinger, 1999), with the major manual industries being construction, domestic service, low-order business services (mainly restaurants, cleaning, craftwork and repairs) and manufacturing processing. This situation has arisen partly because rural migrants possess little human capital and, most importantly, because city governments have imposed their own restrictions on the employment rights of migrant workers, undermining their life chances (Wu, 2004). The *hukou* system has played a significant role in the maintenance of the low wages paid to rural migrant workers.

Migrant workers have had to rely on their personal networks in the process of migration, e.g. job seeking and finding accommodation in urban settings. Many surveys have found that the majority of rural migrant workers look for jobs through relatives, friends and fellow villagers (Cai, 2000; Li, 2003; Li, 2004). These personal networks offer information and help for those who decide to migrate based on mutual trust, aid and the norm of reciprocity. It also helps the formation of migrant communities in cities. Urban migrant settlements are often formed by people from the same place of origin. Zhejiang village or Wenzhou village in Beijing are well-known examples of native place-based migrant communities (Ma and Xiang, 1999; Zhang, 2001). Indeed, a large number of rural migrant workers are accommodated in rental housing clustered in so-called urban villages, or *chengzhongcun*. The term *chengzhongcun*, literally meaning "a village within a city", refers specifically to such settlements that are administratively classified as villages but are located in the peri-urban or even inner-city areas. These 'villages', formerly in suburban areas, have been swallowed up by urban sprawl. With the extension of urban areas, many of them have been spatially absorbed into densely built-up areas and attract rural migrants because of an emerging housing rental market which can provide cheap, albeit often substandard, accommodation, meeting the needs of migrants. Table 5.2 shows that urban villages are a form of migrant enclave, where migrants outnumber local residents significantly in many cases. As demonstrated in other studies, the existence of urban villages as the enclave of rural migrant workers is an economic response to the demand for inexpensive housing resulting from growing rural-to-urban migration and the exclusion from the existing urban housing market of those without urban *hukou* (Zhang, 2005).[2] Of course, urban villages are by no means "garden villages" for rural migrants. Many urban villages are indeed plagued by aged housing and poorly maintained facilities and a high residential density that is beyond the capacity of the infrastructural services (Zhang et al., 2003). Put in this context, urban villages are an indication of spatial marginality to the extent that rural migrants are frequently housed in distressed communities.

Table 5.2 Ratio of migrants to local residents in selected urban villages of selected cities

Urban villages	Surveyed year	No. of migrants	No. of local residents	Ratio (local residents as 100)
Beijing				
Wabian cun	1997	2,162	2,086	104:100
917 district	1997	287	318	90.3:100
Guangzhou				
Shipai cun	2000	12,000	9,234	130:100
Sanyuan li	2000	11,000	4,200	262:100
Tangxi cun	2000	9,534	4,656	205:100
Ruibao cun	2000	60,000	2,000	3,000:100
Dongguan				
Shangyuan cun	1998	8,000	2,842	281:100
Yantian cun	1998	70,000	2,877	2,433:100

Source: Zhang (2005: 245).

Morphologically as well as socially, the formation of urban villages as enclaves of rural migrant workers adds a new dimension of spatial segregation, another visible aspect of their marginalised status. During the pre-reform period, the spatial organisation of Chinese cities was characterised by uniform and self-sufficient urban cells. Urban space was often structured around large, independent and walled work-unit compounds (Gaubatz, 1999; Huang and Clark, 2002). Nowadays, this work-unit based urban space has undergone restructuring. Changes in the spatial structure of Chinese cities have been characterised by specialisation of land use and spatial segregation. Housing becomes increasingly separated from work places and newly developing residential districts have sprawled outwards toward the urban periphery. While a fairly small number of old urban neighbourhoods have been reconstructed

2 The urban housing market is largely irrelevant to most rural migrant workers. The market price of commercialised housing has vastly outstripped their wages, as most of them are employed in urban low-paid sectors. As they lack the permanent right of abode in the city, they are not eligible to buy public housing privatised by the state. For the same reason, they are also not entitled to low-cost urban public housing.

into luxury residential districts, many dilapidated and overcrowded ones within the city proper (including the inner suburbs) have not yet been scheduled for demolition and redevelopment. One general result of the restructuring processes of these urban spaces is the creation of segregated residential districts for different classes, spatially separating luxury housing for the rich from the basic shelter of ordinary urban residents. The emergence of urban villages as the enclave of rural migrant workers represents the emergence of a new type of urban cluster within the city's built-up areas or at the edge of the city in sharp contrast to the affluent districts in terms of living landscape and has exemplified a significant dimension of spatial marginalisation in transitional urban China.

Rural migrant workers generally enjoy limited and costly access to urban welfare and social security programmes because of their 'rural' identity and 'alien' status. In the past ten years the provision of urban welfare and social security has been undergoing a transformation from an enterprise-based to a city-based process. The enterprise-based programmes of the past linked work-units with the delivery of a broad array of public services. The programmes provided only the employees of any given enterprise with exclusive access and the individual entitlement to welfare and social security was neither transferable across enterprises nor across cities. Furthermore, urban welfare benefits heavily subsidised by the state were restricted to those with urban *hukou* registration. Reforms in the areas of housing, unemployment allowance, pensions and health care held the promise of reducing social responsibilities previously assigned to employers and of shifting such responsibilities to city governments as well as to individuals. However, the reforms have not done enough to enhance the transferability of social welfare qualifications between administrative jurisdictions at or above the city level and, most crucially, to fully open urban social security systems to rural migrants who are often regarded as transients and thus ineligible for urban social security.[3] Without a permanent urban *hukou*, rural migrant workers are not entitled to low-cost public housing sponsored by city governments for urban low-income groups who cannot afford to purchase housing at full market prices. They are largely excluded from the protection of urban social safety nets, for example pension and health insurance, they are not subsidised when using urban public medical services and they have to pay much higher tuition fees for the compulsory education of their children (Cui, 2003; Han, 2003).

The Transformation of the Regime of Urban Accumulation and the Marginalisation of Rural Migrant Workers

While reckoning with an irreversible trend toward further relaxation of official control over urban employment, city governments have always sought to maintain their grip on granting the permanent right of urban abode to rural migrants for various concerns. The limited capacity of the urban economy to absorb rural migrant

3 According to one recent investigation report by the members of the National People's Congress, it is estimated that, at the national level, only about 12% of rural migrants working in the city are covered by a pension scheme (Wang, 2005). The low coverage rate may be due to the exclusion of many rural migrant workers from the scheme.

workers is one such concern, as well as the city's capacity to provide and expand public services. Reforms have released an enormous surplus of rural workers from the land. At the same time, China's cities, where there are already large pools of laid-off workers waiting for re-employment as well as large numbers of urban young people entering the labour market each year, have limited capacity to accommodate all rural migrants, given the pressure of poor performance of many state-owned enterprises.[4] How to generate substantial urban employment without a loss of economic efficiency represents a tough and critical challenge which needs to be confronted by the city authorities.

The urban job market has become more and more competitive since the late 1990s as TVEs, an important source of non-agricultural job creation in the earlier reform period, have suffered sluggish growth. Those workers formerly employed by TVEs have been propelled into the urban job market, frequently resulting in high urban unemployment, a potential source of political unrest. From the perspective of city governments, the employment of rural migrant workers is a business strategy but the employment of local residents is more or less a political decision. On the one hand, rural migrant workers are seen simply as an expedient for meeting a structural shortage of labour in the urban economy. On the other hand, political motives and power often come into play with regard to the employment of locals. The need for social stability under the employment pressure as perceived by urban authorities, as well as lack of power by rural migrants, has rendered the former reluctant, in practice, to allow significant relaxation of control over granting migrants the right to permanent urban *hukou*.

Rural Land Issues

Continued restrictions on migrants' rights to urban permanent *hukou* have to be judged not only against economic parameters such as the size of the rural population and the relatively low capacity of the urban job market, but also in relation to complicated issues with regard to the property rights of rural land. The introduction of the household responsibility system separated land ownership from its use rights by contracts and restored certain crucial elements of private farming. Collective land ownership gives villagers the right to an equal share of rural land. The right to use collectively-owned land on a continuing basis remains with any members of a given village who have worked and lived elsewhere so long as his/her membership (defined by a local *hukou*) of the village is kept. On the other hand, under no circumstances can

4 By 2002, the registered urban unemployment rate was 4%, according to the Ministry of Labour and Social Security. In cities, there were about 22 million people waiting for employment every year, while the new openings numbered about 8 million. At the same time, there were 25 million surplus rural workers who needed non-agricultural employment (China Youth Daily, May 9, 2003). Some surveys presented a much gloomier picture. The survey conducted by the Institute of Population and Labour Economics (IPLE), Chinese Academy of Social Science (CASS), revealed that the unemployment rates in five major cities – Fuzhou, Shanghai, Shenyang, Xi'an and Wuhan averaged about 8% between September 1996 and January 2002 (Anonym, 2003).

farmers alienate the land they have contracted from the village authorities, although some may lease it out on a short-term basis and appropriate a rental income.[5]

Despite the success of the household responsibility system in improving farming outputs and incomes, the use rights of migrants associated with their membership of the village to collectively-owned land complicates the issue of their obtaining permanent urban *hukou*. First, the prospect for rural migrants of keeping their land use rights provides a sense of security, reducing the risk of migration, as they would have a fall-back position if migration considerably falls short of their expectations or they are injured or suffer from serious illness, particularly in view of the many institutional barriers, discriminations and encroachment of rights that they face in urban settings. Second, the small size of land holding makes it difficult for farmers to get rich from agriculture in the absence of other income sources. However, frequent reallocations of farmland use rights would adversely affect sustaining long-term agricultural productivity because farmers have no incentive to invest on their assigned plots where they may not necessarily farm continually. Third, in the context of land providing the insurance for rural people in case of inadequate income from other sources, off-farm job opportunities by no means constitute a sufficient condition for rural migrants to give up their farmland use rights without sufficient compensation. Rural migrants therefore would normally wish to keep their membership in the village community and the associated land use rights. Meanwhile, the large sums of remittances sent back home by migrant workers indicate their strong rural attachment, whatever the motivations.[6]

The Regime of Urban Accumulation

For city governments, there are many economic and institutional justifications that can account for their not granting rural migrants the right to permanent urban *hukou*, but the transformation of the 'regime of urban accumulation' might be singled out as fundamental. Indeed, in both the pre-reform and reform periods, restricting the number of people entitled to urban *hukou* through a set of institutions seems to have provided the underlying political and economic rationality for sustaining the reproducibility of the regime of urban accumulation. In the early days of the People's Republic where the political and economic system was officially built in accordance with Marxist principles, the paradox between the Marxist assumption of the superiority of a communist system and its relatively uncongenial reality generated a political need for socialist "forging-ahead industrialisation". In order for this to be successfully financed, however, the state created a centralised fiscal system directing

5 In practice, while farmers are legally not allowed to sell the land that they have contracted from the village authorities to other private parties under the regime of collective land ownership, they can temporarily relinquish the use rights for rents. Many have, in fact, subcontracted their land-use right in order to take off-farm employment opportunities on the one hand, while obtaining land rents on the other (Liu, et al., 1998).

6 One study found that more than 70% of rural migrant workers remitted a portion of their incomes to their families in the countryside. About half of them remitted out more than 50% of their wages. The remittance from Chinese rural migrant workers was relatively high compared to the situation in other developing countries (Li, 2004: 184).

state resources to expand the heavy industrial base on the one hand, and minimising investment in consumption on the other. Under the centralised fiscal system, almost all revenue generated in the economy had to be handed over to the central coffers while financial expenditures at the local level were covered by the central budgetary plan. This system, based on the public ownership of the means of production and characterised by the state's monopoly over the revenue and expenditure of almost all economic and social units, allowed the state to construct a 'scissors gap' pricing system (under-pricing agricultural products relative to industrial products) not determined by supply and demand of the market but by its needs for accumulation and the mobilisation of resources. With fiscal centralisation, the state could minimise the resources devoted to the sectors it least prioritised and divert resources to the sectors it prioritised most.

The city was construed as the site of production for non-consumer products rather than as a conglomeration of a heterogeneous population or as a place for organising collective consumptions (Wu and Ma, 2005). While the state possessed absolute authority and discretion over the operation of the urban economy, at the same time it had to take full responsibility for providing sustenance, jobs and services for the urban population. Urbanisation, demographically defined as an increasing share of population living in urban areas, was viewed primarily as a cost incurred in the pursuit of "forging-ahead" industrialisation, since urbanisation would necessarily divert limited resources away from industrialisation. The costs of urbanisation were therefore minimised through a range of policies designed to restrict urban growth. These policies, according to Chan (1994), included tight control of rural-to-urban migration, rustication of urban residents to the countryside, the restriction of the urban dependent population, the intensive use of urban infrastructure and limited expansion of urban service sectors.

By attempting to introduce market mechanisms into the centrally planned economy, the Chinese reforms were initially couched primarily in terms of eradicating economic inefficiency within a basically unchanged political and economic system. This was done by various schemes of devolving power from higher to lower levels of government and allowing more autonomy to accrue to local units (Naughton, 1996; Gao, 1998). Nonetheless, with the introduction of market forces in shaping the national economy and society, the early regime of urban accumulation has experienced a transformation alongside the decentralisation of the financial system. This transformation has involved the functional transition of city governments from resource-receiving and finance-subsidising agents to financially more independent entities. Local expenditures in principle must be paid by local incomes. While greater power of fiscal administration has been granted to the locality, some central state's fiscal obligations have also been transferred into local governments. City governments have been mobilised as entrepreneurial agents struggling to find their own means to overcome the revenue constraints. The city, which used to be the site of planning-based industries for non-consumer products, is now recognised as the centre of commercialised consumption and the node for hybrid economic entities closely linked to the system of commodity production. With the decentralisation of decision-making and fiscal responsibility, the relationship among cities has changed from one of relative isolation and self-sufficiency to one of competition. City governments have increasingly put emphasis upon the need to make local economies more competitive. Alongside this transition, governments at all levels cannot wield the kind of unilateral and comprehensive control over rural-to-urban migration as was possible in the past. But such transformation has also seen city governments to formulate restrictive local policies and regulations with regard to rural migrants' rights and interests.

Hukou Commoditisation

One implication is that the *hukou* system has been widely used as a means of urban accumulation. Given that China's economic endowment is basically capital-scarce but labour-abundant, every local bureaucracy seeks to protect and expand its revenue by attracting investments and grants, by undertaking new projects and by escaping its financial obligations whenever possible. In the light of the need to expand the city's revenue base and to legitimately extract rents and profits, control over the right to permanent urban *hukou* has, in effect, been bifurcated by city governments into circumscribing unwanted migrants on the one hand and generating revenue on the other. The former function can be exemplified by a handful of city regulations on migration administration. Local regulations are now more powerful than laws delivered from the central government in deciding the terms and conditions for staying in a given city. Central control over the issuance of urban *hukous* has been greatly weakened, but it has been, at the same time, replaced by new local regulations. The latter can be exemplified by the widely publicised practices of commodifying the urban residency rights, including the sale of urban *hukous*, the imposition of urban 'entry charges' on prospective migrants and the granting of permanent rights of urban residency to those who can make contributions to the city, calculated mostly in terms of the amount of investment generated, the ranking of professional titles or university degrees. As early as the late 1980s, many cities started some form of urban *hukou* commoditisation practice. According to one investigation, the sale of urban *hukous* was already quite widespread in Anhui and Hunan provinces in the late 1980s (Liu, 1996). The nationwide introduction of the "blue-stamp" urban *hukou* in the early 1990s, requiring city newcomers to pay a large lump sum for urban capacity improvement (*chengshi zengrong fei*), represented another form of urban *hukou* commoditisation.[7] The price of an urban *hukou* and the charge for urban capacity improvement varied regionally and changed over time, depending largely on the perceived attractiveness and administrative status of the city (Du, 1999). Nonetheless, the price of an urban *hukou*, which was equivalent to many times the income of an ordinary migrant, was, and remains, well beyond the reach of most rural migrant workers.

7 The "blue-stamp" urban *hukou*, also called "locally-valid" urban *hukou*, is distinguished by a blue stamp, different from that in the formal urban *hukou* booklet, which is red. The specific design and implementation of the "blue-stamp" *hukou* programme is left to local governments, based on the principle of "local needs, local benefits, local responsibility, and local validity". This is a local policy of urban residency to give city governments flexibility in accordance with their own needs and interests (Xin and Yu, 1996).

Both commoditisation of the urban *hukou* and control of urban residency rights, therefore, have been necessitated by the needs of city authorities for revenue expansion. It is understandable that, for many city governments, the *hukou* system today is not so much an important means of keeping social order as an irresistible way to broaden their revenue base. Despite the fact that the central government has issued a number of directives against the sale of urban *hukous* and the imposition of urban 'entry charges' (General Office of State Council, 1988; Ministry of Public Security, 1992; Ministry of Public Security, Ministry of Finance, and People's Bank of China, 1994), local governments either ignore these or take tacit counter-measures. The practice of urban *hukou* commoditisation has not stopped. Only in two cases have economic barriers been lifted – in order to attract investors and business people for capital accumulation purposes – leading to a capital drain from rural areas – and to attract talented migrants (mainly professionals and technical personnel) – leading to a rural brain drain. Urban *hukou* commoditisation, as a source of local revenue, and the granting of urban *hukous* to those whom the city wants as a means of competing for resources, requires that the permanent right of urban residency be open only under certain conditions stipulated by local authorities. The rationale behind the conditional offer of urban residency right is therefore rather simple. Were there no control of any kind over urban residency rights, the urban *hukou* would have no commercial value. In fact, the stricter the implementation of controls over migrant entry, the more the city can charge for an urban *hukou*.

Not only revenue generation but also the liability for local expenditure has made local controls necessary. Under the new arrangements of fiscal decentralisation, city governments have to deliver public services to a mass clientele but at the same time take responsibility for their own expenditures. City governments often view the access of migrant workers to public goods and services as a drain on local resources, and accordingly try to exclude rural migrant workers by formulating discriminative and restrictive regulations and policies. One can see that the barriers to acquiring permanent rights of urban abode, though no longer the same as before, remain largely insurmountable for ordinary migrant workers. The bifurcation of the function of urban residency control, as an institution of residency permission and as a means of accruing financial benefits, not only keeps the rural-urban social partition within urban spaces but also allows cities selectivity over their inward migrants. Certain categories of people such as investors, professionals, and in particular the rich are favoured with residency rights on the one hand, while ordinary migrants are discriminated against on the other. This has created a paradox. City governments welcome cheap rural migrant workers for their contribution to urban growth and their provision of services. However, the interests of those same rural migrants are sacrificed in the process of urban accumulation. Rural migrant workers are economically exploited by virtue of their presence but they continually suffer from a denial of urban *hukou* and its associated rights. As a result, rural migrant workers have been marginalised as an underclass in Chinese cities.

Conclusion

As China has undergone transition and the systemic restructuring, social stratification and the process of marginalisation have presented more complex dynamics and new forms. This chapter argues that the marginalisation of rural migrant workers in Chinese cities is, institutionally, contingent on tenuous urban residency rights associated with the transformation of the regime of urban accumulation. In the absence of permanent rights to urban residency, rural migrant workers have become marginalised in terms of their economic and social entitlements and are pushed into second-class citizens in cities. To understand the political economy of urban residency rights in contemporary China in general, and, more specifically, the underlying forces contributing to the marginalisation of rural migrant workers, this chapter argues for the need to take the transformation of the regime of urban accumulation into account. As demonstrated in this chapter and elsewhere, it is quite evident that, in transitional urban China, rural migrant workers have, in many respects, been set apart from the mainstream of society. Thus, the *hukou* system continues to play a significant role in configuring new forms of social stratification and in urban accumulation. The system is used not only to exclude some members of society from accessing public services in urban areas but also to make the urban economy more competitive by grabbing and exploiting mobile capital and human resources as possessed by migrants. In this context, not surprisingly, the abandonment of control of urban residency rights by city authorities and the recognition of migrants' equal citizenship rights in urban settings remain a considerable human development challenge in China.

References

Anonym (2003), 'Jobless situation to stay serious for years', *China Daily Hong Kong Edition*, November 5, 2003, www.chinagate.com.cn/english/4664.htm, accessed on March 11, 2005.

Cai, F. (2000), *Issues of China's floating population*, Zhengzhou: Henan renmin chubanshe.

Chan, K.W. (1994), *Cities with invisible walls: reinterpreting urbanization in post-1949 China*, Hong Kong: Oxford University Press.

Chan, K.W. (1996), 'Post-Mao China: a two-class urban society in the making', *International Journal of Urban and Regional Research*, vol. 21, no. 1, pp.134-150.

Chan, K.W. (2004), 'Internal migration', in C. Hsieh and M. Lu (eds.), *Changing China: a geographical appraisal*, Boulder: Westview Press, pp.229-242.

Chan, K.W. and Hu, Y. (2003), 'Urbanization in China in the 1990s: new definition, different series, and revised trends', *The China Review*, vol. 3, no. 2, pp.49-71.

Chan, K.W. and Zhang, L. (1999), 'The hukou system and rural-urban migration in China: processes and changes', *China Quarterly*, no.160, pp.18-55.

Cui, C.Y. (2003), 'Meeting the needs of peasants in the city and adjusting rural-urban relations', in P. L. Li (ed.), *Peasant workers: economic and social analysis of urban-bound peasant workers in China*, Beijing: shehui kexue wenxian chubanshe, pp.161-171.

Du, W.D. (1999), 'Charges of city capacity improvement: prohibited by the central government and ignored by local governments', *Southern Weekend*, July 30, 1999, p.8.

Fan, C.C. (2002), 'The elite, the natives, and the outsiders: migration and labor market segregation in urban China', *Annals of the Association of American Geographers*, vol. 92, pp.103-124.

Gao, S. (ed.) (1998), *Studies on 20-year experience of Chinese reforms on economic system*, Beijing: jingji kexue chubanshe.

Gaubatz, P. (1999), 'China's urban transformation: patterns and processes of morphological change in Beijing, Shanghai and Guangzhou', *Urban Studies*, vol. 36, no. 9, pp.1495-1521.

General Office of State Council (1988), *Circular on stopping the overt sale of urban hukou in certain cities and counties,* issued on October 29, 1988.

Guang, L. (2001), 'Reconstituting the rural-urban divide: peasant migration and the rise of 'orderly migration' in contemporary China', *Journal of Contemporary China*, vol. 10, no. 28, pp.471-493.

Guldin, G.E. (ed.) (1997), *Farewell to peasant China: rural urbanization and social change in the late twentieth century*, M. E. Sharpe.

Han, J.L. (2003), 'Study on the education of urban marginalized groups: an investigation report on the situation of compulsory education for the children of floating population in Beijing', in P. L. Li (ed.), *Peasant workers: economic and social analysis of urban-bound peasant workers in China*, Beijing: shehui kexue wenxian chubanshe, pp.206-226.

Hirst, P. and Zeitlin, J. (1992), 'Flexible specialization versus post-Fordism: theory, evidence and policy implications', in M. Storper and A. J. Scott (eds.), *Pathways to industrialization and regional development*, London: Routledge.

Huang, Y.Q. and Clark, W.A.V. (2002), 'Housing tenure choice in transitional urban China: a multilevel analysis', *Urban Studies*, vol. 39, pp.7-32.

Kong, S.G. (2006), 'Institutions have established Chinese sweat shop factories', http://business.sohu.com/20060125/n241595015.shtml, accessed on January 27, 2006.

Li, L. (2003), 'Migrate to cities: an irrevocable process', in P. Li (ed.), *Migrant workers: economic and social analysis of urban-bound migrant workers in China*, Beijing: shehui kexue wenxian chubanshe, pp.116-133.

Li, Q. (2004), *Rural migrant workers and social stratification in China*, Beijing: shehui kexue chubanshe.

Liu, C.B. (1996), 'A follow-up investigation into 14 types of urban-rural institutions', *Economic Research Reference,* nos. 118/119, pp.2-9.

Liu, S., Carter, M. and Yao, Y. (1998), 'Dimensions and diversity of property rights in rural China: dilemmas on the road to further reform', *World Development*, vol. 26, no. 10, pp.1789-1806.

Liu, S.H., Li, X.B., Zhang, M. (2003), *Scenario analysis on urbanization and rural-urban migration in China*, Interim Report for International Institute for Applied Systems Analysis, Austria (IR-03-036).

Ma, L.J.C. and Xiang, B. (1998), 'Native place, migration and the emergence of peasant enclaves in Beijing', *China Quarterly*, no. 155, pp. 546-581.

Marger, M.N. (2002), *Social inequality: patterns and processes (second edition)*, Boston: McGraw Hill.

Ministry of Public Security (1992), *Urgent circular on stopping the overt sale of non-agricultural hukou*, issued on May 4, 1992.

Ministry of Public Security, Ministry of Finance, and People's Bank of China (1994), *Circular on stopping the continuous sale of non-agricultural hukou,* issued on August 2, 1994.

National Bureau of Statistics of China (2002), *China Statistical Yearbook 2002*, Beijing: zhongguo tongji chubanshe.

Naughton, B. (1996), *Growing out of the plan: Chinese economic reform, 1978-1993,* United Kingdom: Cambridge University Press.

Solinger, D. (1999), *Contesting citizenship in urban China*, Berkeley, CA: University of California Press.

Tian, B.X. (2003), *China's number one certificate: manuscripts on investigation of China's household registration system*, Guangzhou: Guangdong renmin chubanshe.

Wang, X.C. (2005), 'Who will provide pension for Chinese 200 million rural migrant workers after 10 years', http://cul.sohu.com/20050311/n224623923,shmtl, accessed on March 12, 2005.

Williams, C.C. and Windebank, J. (2001), 'The growth of urban informal economies', in R. Paddison (ed.), *Handbook of urban studies*, London; New Delhi: Sage Publications, pp.308-322.

Wu, F. (2004), 'Urban poverty and marginalization under market transition: the case of Chinese cities', *International Journal of Urban and Regional Research,* vol. 28, no. 2, pp.401-423.

Wu, F. and Ma, L.J.C. (2005), 'The Chinese city in transition: towards theorizing China's urban restructuring', in L.J.C. Ma and F. Wu (eds.), *Restructuring the Chinese city: changing society, economy and space*, London; New York: Routledge, pp.260-279.

Xin, Z.J. and Yu, Q.H. (1996), *Reform of the Chinese hukou system,* Beijing: zhongguo zhengfa daxue chubanshe.

Yang, Y. (2003), 'Urban labor market segmentation: some observations based on Wuhan census data', *The China Review*, vol.3, no.2, pp.145-158.

Zhang, L. (2001), *Strangers in the city: reconfigurations of space, power, and social networks within China's floating population*, California: Stanford University Press.

Zhang, L. (2005), 'Migrant enclaves and impacts of redevelopment policy in Chinese cities', in L.J.C. Ma and F. Wu (eds.), *Restructuring the Chinese city: changing society, economy and space*, London; New York: Routledge, pp.243-259.

Zhang, L., Simon X.B. Zhao and J.P. Tian (2003), 'Self-help in housing and chengzhongcun in China's urbanization', *International Journal of Urban and Regional Research*, vol. 27, no. 4, pp.912-937.

Chapter 6

Marginalisation and Health Provision in Transitional China

Zhiqiang Feng

Introduction

China achieved admirable improvements in the health status of its people in the three decades since the establishment of the People's Republic of China. Between 1952 and 1982, China's life expectancy increased from 35 to 68 years, infant mortality declined from 250 to 40 deaths per 1000 live births, and the prevalence of malaria decreased from 5.5% to 0.3% of the population (Ministry of Health, thereafter MOH, 1989, cited in Hsiao, 1995, p.1047). These achievements, which received worldwide acclaim, were attributable, in part, to a policy which emphasised disease prevention and public health and to a health care system which allowed wide and equal access to primary health care (Hsiao, 1995; Liu, 2004a; Dong et al, 2005).

Changes since the late 1970s associated with China's policy of 'reform and open to the outside world', however, have brought about profound transformations in China's health care system. Once essentially free, it now operates on a cost-recovery basis. In urban areas, many people end up with no health insurance cover at all as a result of the downsizing and bankruptcy of many state-owned enterprises (hereafter SOEs) while in rural areas, where the majority of the Chinese people live, the cooperative medical system has collapsed alongside the disintegration of the commune. There is a widening inequality in health status and health care access among different social groups and different regions (Liu et al, 1999; Wang, 2004; see also the chapter by Cook and Dummer in this volume) and many poor people are excluded completely from the health care system as a result of the escalating costs of health care services and a lack of health insurance.

With the introduction of the market, the government has reduced its share in total health expenditure. There has also been a shift emphasising curative treatment instead of prevention. Consequently, infectious diseases that had been brought under control, such as tuberculosis and sexually transmitted diseases (STDs), have re-emerged. The outbreak of severe acute respiratory syndrome (SARS) in China in 2003 exposed the weakness of China's epidemic prevention and monitoring system. However, there are some fundamental problems that underlie the entire health system in China. There is grave concern that it has deviated from its original 'Health For All' goal and that market oriented health services have reduced poor people's access to healthcare provision. Once famed worldwide for its health development and achievement, China was rated poorly at 144th out of 191 countries in the 2000 assessment of the performance of health care systems by the World Health Organization (WHO, 2000, p.202). In terms of health spending relative to income, i.e., 'fairness of financial contribution', China was ranked 188, third from the bottom (WHO, 2000, p.191).

This chapter will document and examine the changes in the health care system in China since the launch of the economic reforms. In particular, the chapter will focus on the investigation of the marginalisation of poor areas and poor social groups in terms of access to health care services. It first describes the health care system before the economic reform and then reviews the transformation of health care since the launch of the reform in the late 1970s. Subsequently, there is an examination of the problems under the reformed health care services, particularly the issue of widening inequality in health status among different social groups and regions. The final section discusses what conclusions can be drawn from experiences in China and proposes a number of policy implications.

Health care systems in China before the reform

At the formation of the People's Republic of China in 1949, a centrally planned economic system mirroring that of the former Soviet Union was established and in order to promote good health amongst the Chinese population, the Committee of the Patriotic Health Campaign (CPHC) and the Ministry of Health (MOH) were created. The CPHC was responsible for mass health education campaigns. For example, in the 1950s there were successful mass campaigns against parasite and infectious diseases at the local level, which greatly improved the health awareness of ordinary people. Meanwhile, the MOH was responsible for the organisation of health care services.

Three-tier health care services were set up in the 1960s, taking different forms in urban and rural areas. In rural areas, the tiers referred to village clinics, township health centres and county hospitals. In village clinical stations, barefoot doctors provided both preventive and primary care services. Barefoot doctors were part-time farmers and they usually received a certain number of work points for their health care services. Patients with serious illnesses were referred to township hospitals and the very ill patients were referred to county or to city hospitals. In urban areas the tiers were street health stations, community health centres and district hospitals. The referral system in urban areas worked similarly to that in rural areas. However, many large SOEs and military forces had their own clinics and hospitals which formed the first tier in the system. The government decided the number of beds and personnel for each hospital or clinic. The government also provided the funds for personnel wages and capital investment in health care institutions (Hsiao, 1995). In addition to hospitals and clinics, there are epidemic prevention centres (EPC) responsible for epidemic monitoring, control and immunisation, and maternal and children health care stations (MCH) specialising in pre- and post-natal care, obstetrical and gynaecological care and family planning services (Henderson et al, 1995; Liu, 2004a).

Health care in urban and rural areas was financed very differently. Urban medical security schemes were initiated in the early 1950s and were based on employment.

The publicly-funded medical care system (PFMS) – *gongfei yiliao* – provided coverage for employees working in state agencies, staff and students in educational institutions and military veterans. The PFMS covered most of its members' medical expenses except a small number of items, such as registration fees, tonics and plastic surgery. Generally, dependants of employees in state agencies were not covered by the PFMS. However, some individual work units provided a special programme which partially covered the health costs of dependants. The PFMS was jointly financed by the central and local governments and administered by the local departments of health and finance. A separate budget was usually allocated for this purpose (Henderson et al, 1998).

The second type of urban health security programme, the labour medical security system (LMSS) – *laobao yiliao* – provided coverage for all permanent workers in SOEs and in large collectively-owned enterprises. In contrast to the PFMS, dependents of those employees covered by the LMSS were also covered by the scheme, although only 50% of dependents' medical expenses were reimbursed. The LMSS was financed and administered separately by each enterprise. The contribution from the enterprise was equivalent to 5.0% of average wages. The LMSS programme was in fact a kind of self-protection by employees in enterprises and was set up according to the government's guideline (Henderson et al, 1998).

In rural areas, the medical security scheme, the Cooperative Healthcare System (CHS) (*hezuo yiliao*), was community-based. It took around 20 years for the expansion of the CHS from a few counties in the mid-1950s to a nationwide programme in the mid-1970s (Feng et al, 1995, p.1111). Under the CHS, the financing of health care relied on a pre-payment plan. Most villages funded their CHSs from three sources. First, the premiums came from farmers' family annual income. Second, the collective welfare fund derived partly from collective agricultural production or rural enterprises. The remaining contribution came from higher-level governments, to compensate health workers and to purchase medical equipment (Feng et al, 1995; Liu et al, 1995).

By the end of the 1970s, the PFMS covered about 8% of the urban population, the LMSS covered 60% of the urban population and the CHS covered 80-90% of the rural population (Guan, 2005, p.1; Hsiao, 1995, p.1050) although the gap in the conditions and quality of services between urban and rural areas was large and, in the latter, services were often inadequate. The differences in financing mechanisms and benefit administration between the PFMS and LMSS could be ignored in the centrally planned economic system. The government, in theory, was ultimately responsible for the well-being of all employees, no matter whether they were employed by government organisations or public-owned enterprises. With its almost unlimited power in mobilising social resources, the government could always serve as the last resort for every enterprise or institution by providing extra financial support.

Before the economic reforms, the prices of most products in China were determined by the government rather than the market. As a consequence, healthcare service prices, drug prices and staff salaries were all determined by the government. Political rather than economic considerations largely determined the pricing policy, with social equality being promoted as a basic doctrine of socialist ideology.

Therefore, both health services and drugs were generally priced as low as possible to make them accessible to all.

The health care system before the economic reform worked reasonably well. However, the system was not perfect and had many problems. The PFMS, LMSS, and CHS were all established as political undertakings. The medical costs were largely hidden from the users and financial feasibility was often ignored. For the CHS the pooling base was at the village level and the small funds involved were easily exhausted in the event of poor production or famine. Many rural communities faced serious financial constraints in terms of sustaining their CHS systems (Liu et al, 1995; Feng et al, 1995). There was also corruption inside the CHS scheme due to a lack of monitoring. Some cadres took advantages of their positions to receive expensive drugs and reimbursement of large medical bills. Barefoot doctors were not fully trained and could only provide very basic care. Urban health care services also experienced problems of inefficiency, poor quality, prolonged financial crisis, low pay, overwork and thus low motivation of the medical personnel etc. In addition, due to a lack of facilities, both urban and rural residents had difficulties in accessing the services (Ho, 1995).

Transformation of the health care system under economic transition

Changes of health related policies

The economic reform created a sea change that touched every corner of China. The market was regarded as an omnipotent driving force in all sectors including agriculture, industry, education and health. Prior to reform, health care in China was perceived as a necessary welfare benefit that the state had an obligation to provide to all. The economic reforms, however, shook the very foundation of the policy. In 1979, the then-minister of MOH proposed economic measures in the management of health care services (Cao and Fu, 2005). This proposal and a series of policy changes which followed signalled a marked change from the past. To a large extent, health care was treated more and more as a private rather than a public good.

Alongside this change, the government adopted a policy of limiting public funds available for health care. The reduction of government spending on health care was also a result of the huge losses incurred by SOEs, which were a major source of government revenue (Hsiao, 1995). Table 6.1 presents a summary of national health expenditure from 1980 to 2000. It can be seen that the government consistently reduced its input on total health expenditure from 36% in 1980, to 25% in 1990 and further down to 15% in 2000. In contrast, most governments of European developed countries provided 70-90% of health expenditure (2000-2004 figures, OECD, 2006). Even in the U.S. where health services are highly commercialised, governmental funding still accounts for 46% of total health and medical costs (2003 figure). In many developing countries today the governmental input is greater than that of the Chinese government. For example, the Mexican government input accounts for 33% (2002 figure), and in Thailand the government contributes 56% of total health expenditure (2000 figure) (Gao, 2005, p.6).

Table 6.1 National health expenditure in China 1980-2000

	1980	1990	2000
National health expenditure (billion *Yuan**)	13	74	476
(Real Terms, 1980)	13	37	117
Government (%)	36	25	15
Social insurance (%)	40	38	25
Individuals (%)	23	37	61
% of GDP	2.9	4.0	5.3
Per capita health expenditure (*Yuan*)	13	65	376
(Real terms, 1980)	13	32	93

*The exchange rate: US $1 is equivalent to about 8.07 *yuan*
Source: Zhao, 2000, cited in Hu and Ying, 2005, p.4.

The decentralisation of the government fiscal system also had a pronounced impact on the financing of health care services. The structure of government health care financing was altered so that each level of government was directly responsible for maintaining the health institutions under its administration (Henderson et al, 1998). For example, central government financed only the national hospitals, key research institutes, and medical schools while each province or county became responsible for its own health care institutions. As a result, a rich county would be able to provide relatively generous health care while a poor county had to settle for less (Hsiao, 1984).

As part of the health care reform package, hospitals and other health care services were granted a large degree of financial independence. In 1984, the MOH publicised its 'Report on Several Policy Issues on Health Reform', which officially declared that the government would loosen its control and grant health care institutions more power in administration and management (Cao and Fu, 2005). Government funding was gradually reduced to cover only basic personnel wages and new capital investments, amounting to 20-30% of hospital expenditures. Hospitals were required to obtain the revenue required for operating expenses themselves, leading to increased user fee charges. Moreover, bonus payments were introduced for doctors, nurses and other staff based on 'profit-achieving performances'. These bonus payments had to be funded from profits. A dual-track pricing system was adopted so that the government now only set prices for personnel wages, basic examinations and surgery while drugs and high-tech examinations and treatments were allowed to be priced according to the market principles. For example, hospitals were allowed to keep a 15–25% mark-up from selling the drugs at higher prices (Hsiao, 1995). The drug distribution system was also changed so as to cut cost and increase competition. Hospitals and clinics were allowed to purchase drugs from drug firms with lower prices. This policy enabled hospitals and clinics to make more profits from selling drugs.

Also, in line with market principles, the government liberalised ownership of health care institutions. As a result, private health care facilities and practices have re-emerged. Private and foreign joint-venture hospitals usually charged much higher fees to make profits. However, the regulations to govern these private health practices lagged behind and there was a lack of consistent approaches incorporating planning and market functions (Hsiao, 1995). Following the reform of property rights in the industry sector in the late 1990s when SOEs were allowed to be sold to private owners, Suqian City of Jiangsu Province became the first county to sell public hospitals in 2000. All but two of its 133 hospitals and health stations were sold to other SOEs or private businesses (Cao and Fu, 2005). This was a significant development signalling a move in official policy towards further privatisation in health care. Prior to this point, public hospitals and clinics accounted for 90% of the total in the country (Gao, 2005, 4), with private practices having only a marginal share of service provision. The reform in Suqian, however has now opened up the floodgates for the privatisation of large hospitals and healthcare facilities, which may considerably affect the patterns of inequality of healthcare provision, marginalising large numbers of people.

Marketisation of health care institutions

With pressures from the reduction of government funding and incentives to increase the income of doctors and nurses, hospitals and health stations have been transformed into cost-recovery and profit-driven institutions. The internal management system has accordingly been changed to increase doctors' 'productivity' and 'economic efficiency'. Many departments within hospitals have adopted a form of contract responsibility system in which each department has to bring in a certain amount of profits to help pay the running costs of the hospital and bonus payments (Hua, 2004).

In 1992 there was a new wave of economic reform across the country with the publication by the MOH of a new guide report, 'On Deepening the Health Reform'. Hospitals were encouraged to diversify services to make profits and to subsidise primary medical services. As a result, many special services were 'invented' to increase profits. For example, many hospitals set up special wards where the inpatient could pay a much higher fee and receive special services from the best doctors and nurses (Cao and Fu, 2005).

Drug prescription and selling became a principal source of income for hospitals and clinics, since around 20% mark-up could be kept. It was a common practice that doctors prescribed drugs according to the insurance status of patients. Therefore, insured patients were prescribed expensive drugs even when it was not entirely necessary. According to UNICEF, 60% of China's health spending goes on drugs, compared with the worldwide average of 15% (Economist, 2004). In pursuit of more profits, some hospitals even abuse their powers by overcharging patients. It was reported that about 20,000 cases of illegal overcharging by hospitals, involving 1.3 billion *yuan*, were investigated in China in the first eight months of 2001. Eleven hospitals were punished for their illegal overcharging and 25.8 million *yuan* in illicit income was confiscated (China Daily, 2001). Recently the MOH has criticised some medical institutions which put profits above the interests of patients (People's Daily, 2005). But without an effective monitoring and accountability system these illegal practices cannot be stopped. Although there was a decline in the number of in-patients and out-patients to hospitals between 2000 and 2003, profits still increased by 70% (People's Daily, 2005).

Not only has the behaviour of health care institutions changed as a result of the economic reforms but so has the behaviour of individual health professionals. This has occurred as social values have undergone dramatic changes as the ideology of collectivism has been replaced by individualism and materialism. Doctors felt frustrated when they were paid less than those in other occupations (Ip, 2005). In the early 1980s there was a popular saying 'People who hold a surgical knife are worse off than people who hold a butcher's knife'. Therefore, some doctors started to actively pursue profits, sometimes ignoring ethical standards and corruption became a widespread problem. Many doctors accepted personal bribes or 'little red bags' from patients who wanted to receive a high quality service or emergency treatment. These off-the-record payments increased the financial burden on patients (Ip, 2005; Dong et al, 2005). Although the government claimed to be cracking down on illegal practices like this, it did not have the power or resources, or the political will to monitor doctors and curb such professional malpractice.

Marketisation of health care services led to a rapid increase in medical costs. At the same time, the major causes of morbidity and mortality shifted from infectious diseases to chronic and degenerative diseases resulting from an epidemiological transition affecting health care demand. The treatment of chronic diseases such as heart disease and cancer usually took a longer time and needed more specialised techniques and facilities. Meanwhile, with the improvement of living standards and the increasing awareness of health, people required better quality health care. Moreover, many people naively believed that the more and the newer the technology, the better the medical care. As a result of these combined effects, health care costs escalated. It is estimated that the average per capita income of urban households rose by 6.5% between 1992 and 1997, whilst the average cost of an outpatient visit and hospital admission rose by 10.2% and 13.8% respectively (Gao et al., 2001, p.305).

The decline of health insurance coverage

In urban areas, the escalation of medical costs and the ageing of the population put a much greater financial burden on each enterprise which functioned as a self-insured unit for its employees and retirees. Furthermore, employees who were covered by the security schemes tended to overuse healthcare services. A survey showed that residents in China who were insured had both a higher health care utilisation rate and higher costs per episode of care than their uninsured counterparts (MOH, 1999). The LMSS fund which was based on 5.0% of average wages was no longer sufficient to cope with the increased costs. In contrast to its behaviour in the command economy, the government refused to come to the rescue and enterprises had to make up the deficits themselves. By 1990 most enterprises found that medical costs already equalled 8-9% of total payroll costs (Hsiao, 1995; Xu, 1998).

To make things worse, the market economy also meant that as independent economic units, SOEs had to make profits to survive. However, many SOEs could not compete against private and foreign joint ventures and earned no profits at all. This arose partly because of mismanagement and partly because stated-owned enterprises shouldered more social welfare responsibilities than private enterprises or foreign joint ventures. It was estimated that one-third of SOEs ran at a deficit (Hsiao, 1995, p.1050). These enterprises often delayed or were simply unable to reimburse health care expenses claimed by their employees or retirees. Therefore many employees in these SOEs became *de facto* uninsured.

Urban residents who worked for state agencies or educational institutions and thus were covered by PFMS were not affected like their counterparts in SOEs. This was because the government still guaranteed that the PFMS ran properly by increasing funding. However, coinsurance was introduced to relieve some of the government's burden. Employees in state agencies were usually required to pay 10% of the total outpatient medical costs and 5% of inpatient medical costs (Ho, 1995, p.1067).

The worst affected populations were those living in rural areas. Along with the abolition of the commune and its replacement by the household responsibility system, the commune welfare fund, which was the key to the CHS, stopped functioning. It was estimated that by 1987 only 5.4% of rural communities maintained their CHS (Liu, et al, 1995, p.1087). Overall only 10% of rural residents had some form of health insurance and most of them were government employees or they lived in wealthy coastal regions where many worked in township and village enterprises. The majority of the rural population had to pay medical expenses out of their own pockets (Liu, 2004b).

Figure 6.1 shows the percentages of urban and rural population uninsured between the end of the 1970s and 2003. The proportion of the urban uninsured population increased from 32% in the late 1970s to 46% in 1993, and up to 58% in 1998, while the rural uninsured population increased from 10% in the late 1970s to 87% in 1993 and to 84% in 1998. The uninsured population was reduced in 2003 as a result of the new insurance schemes but overall about 80% of rural and nearly half of urban populations are still not covered by any insurance scheme (MOH, 2004, p.5).

The efforts to revive and socialise the insurance system

How to reform the health security programmes in line with the new market economy has been the subject of much debate. The government has collaborated with international organisations such as UNICEF and WHO in pilot schemes to restore the CHS in rural areas (Hu, 2004, p.480). In urban areas, many efforts have been made since the early 1980s to contain escalating medical expenditures. For example, co-payment and deductible schemes were introduced to control 'moral hazard', i.e., insured people tended to spend more on health care services. Prepayment methods were also introduced to control 'supplier inducement' because hospitals over-prescribed or over-charged patients. Enterprises usually contracted with certain hospitals on a fixed budget for the provision of services to their employees (Ho, 1995).

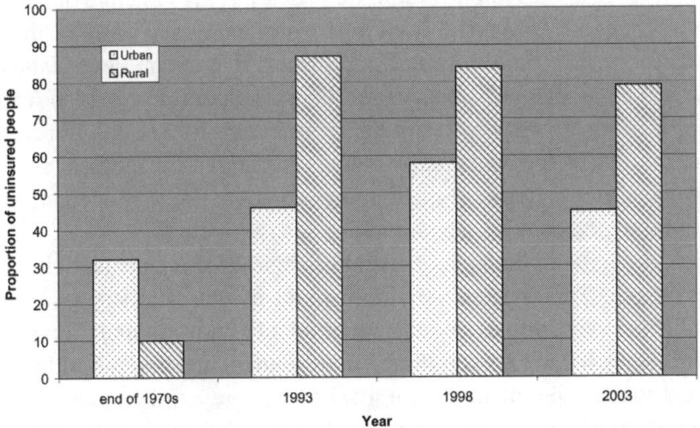

Figure 6.1 Proportion of uninsured people in urban and rural areas 1979-2003 (%)

In 1994, two cities, Zhenjiang of Jiangsu province and Jiujiang of Jiangxi province, were chosen to pilot a systematic reform of the urban health insurance system. The model was extended to 40 cities across the country in 1996. At the end of 1998, a nationwide reform was officially carried out (Liu et al, 2002). The PFMS and LMSS were abolished and replaced by the Basic Health Insurance System (BHIS). The BHIS is administered by the Ministry of Labour and Social Security (MOLSS) and its local agencies. The main features of the BHIS are: a wide access to primary health care; joint premium contributions by employers and employees; and integration of individual medical savings accounts (MSA) and social pooling accounts (SPA) (Liu et al, 2002). The SPA, paid for entirely by employers' contributions, is based on the level of prefecture or city, which enlarges the pooling base and thus reduces the sharing risk. Employers are required to contribute 4 to 6% of each employee's salary, depending upon the individual's age. For those aged 45 and over, the employer's contribution is 6%, whilst for those aged under 45, the contribution is 4%. Retirees do not need to contribute to the MSA. About 70% of the contribution from employers is deposited into the SPA. The remaining 30% goes to the MSA. The employees are required to contribute 2% of their wages to the MSA. Payment for any services first draws funds from the MSAs, followed by a deduction of up to 10% of an employee's salary. After meeting this deduction, the SPA kicks in, coupled with a decreasing co-payment plan ranging from 10% of the total medical expenses under 5,000 *yuan*, 8% for 5,000-10,000 *yuan*, and 2% for over 10,000 *yuan*. The limit on the payment from the SPA is capped at an equivalent of four times an employee's annual salary (Liu et al, 2002).

In 2002 the State Council decided to initiate the new form of CHS (new CHS) in rural areas. Two or three counties were chosen in each province for pilot experiments from 2003. By 2010 the new CHS scheme is intended to cover the entire rural population (Li and Gu, 2004). The new CHS scheme is implemented by the MOH and financed by the central government, local governments and individual households, with each party contributing ten *yuan* per person annually. The scheme is voluntary and usually covers at least a part of the medical costs of the treatment of serious diseases. The fund is pooled and managed at county level. The new CHS is characterised by an emphasis on serious illness and therefore is also referred to as *dabing tongchou*, meaning risk sharing and protection for serious illness. The fund provides 20 to 30% of the costs that a patient is charged for medical services. This means that even after a farmer joins the new CHS, he/she still needs to pay a high proportion of the medical bill (Cao and Fu, 2005).

In China a medical financial assistance fund (MFA) is available for some vulnerable people. This system is administered by the Ministry of Civil Affairs (MOCA) and its local offices. Local governments and voluntary donations from the citizens finance the MFA. The fund is independent and any individual can apply for it, subject to an assessment by the local community and local Agency of Civil Affairs. The scheme has its origins in the early 1990s, when some local governments adopted a policy of providing medical financial assistance for poor people (Sun et al, 2002). In 2002 the State Council of China officially proposed to establish the rural MFA system. Each province was required to start with two or three counties for pilot experiments and gradually to make the scheme cover all rural areas (MOCA, et al. 2003). The vulnerable people who qualify for medical financial assistance are those who do not have any ability to work and have no relatives to support them. They are usually the rural elderly with no offspring to care for them or orphans who are too young to work. Some rural people living in extreme poverty may also qualify for assistance, depending on the criteria set by the local governments. However, the medical assistance only covers about 70% of the costs related to catastrophic illness. Assistance from the fund can also be applied to cover the fees required to join the new CHS. Urban elderly people, who do not have pensions and whose children have very low incomes or are unemployed, can also apply for assistance from local civil affairs agencies (Li and Gu, 2004).

Implementation of the BHIS and new CHS are still ongoing. Although the BHIS is a compulsory scheme for all urban employers and employees, so far, only employees in SOEs and government agencies have joined the new BHIS, whilst most people who are employed or self-employed in private, informal sectors, foreign invested ventures and migrant workers have not been covered. The new CHS system has covered about 100 million rural residents, approximately one eighth of the total rural population. However, with only 30 *yuan* per annum for each person who has joined the scheme, it is far from sufficient in terms of effective insurance and support (Gao, 2005).

Marginalisation in the health sector

Vulnerable social groups

The rapid economic growth has gone side by side with growing disparity both between different socio-economic groups and different regions. Unlike before the reform, when a majority of people could get access to primary health care based on a largely equitable health care system poor people are currently usually uninsured and therefore are effectively excluded from the system.

Most poor people live in rural areas partly due to the government's urban-biased policy that directs resources towards urban areas. Rural poor people are often residents in remote western regions, including a large proportion of China's ethnic minorities. The number of rural poor was estimated to be 26 million in 2000 (People's Daily, 2000). According to a national health service survey coordinated by the MOH in 1998, about 84% of rural residents did not have health insurance with the poor mostly disadvantaged (Figure 6.1).

In urban areas, the number of poor people is small compared to their rural counterparts, but their composition is much more complicated. Because of poor management and severe competition, many SOEs downsize or even go bankrupt. This results in a large number of unemployed people. One study has shown that women, the lower skilled, middle-aged people and those employed by urban collectives have a higher risk of becoming redundant (Appleton et al., 2002). People who lose their jobs usually lose some or all of their welfare benefits, including health insurance. The dependants of these laid-off workers are also affected as they rely on the LMSS providing a 50% refund of their medical costs. Retired people who worked in these debt-stricken or bankrupted enterprises are also at a disadvantage, since they cannot claim any reimbursement for their medical treatment.

There are also many people working in the informal sector, such as retailing, joinery, plumbing, waste collection and recycling, and domestic service. A high proportion of these workers are migrants from rural areas and are part of the mobile population (Goodkind and West, 2002; see also chapters in this volume by Li Zhang and Heather Xiaoquan Zhang). The legacy of urban-rural dualism means that rural migrants do not have urban household registrations and thus cannot claim any benefits from the local government in urban areas. It is estimated that 120-200 million migrants have been working in Chinese towns and cities (State Council, 2006), most of whom undertaking difficult, dirty and dangerous tasks that urban residents are reluctant to do. In addition, they usually live in shabby shelters, have cheap food, and lack access to broader formal social network to provide useful information for health care. Commercial health insurance is usually beyond their means. They cannot apply for rural cooperative insurance because they have left their rural homes. As a consequence they are not covered by any insurance programmes at all.

Yao et al (2004) using household surveys estimated that there were 5.5 to 15 million new urban poor including rural migrants across the country in 1998. According to the 1998 national health service survey (MOH, 1999, p.5), about 58% of the urban population were not covered by any health insurance scheme. However, the percentage of uninsured is even higher among the urban poor. Cheng (2004, p.16) conducted a survey in Wuhan and showed that up to 71% of the urban poor did not have health insurance.

Decline of health care access and utilisation

In general, the accessibility and affordability of healthcare services are determined by the availability of health resources. Rural areas receive only 20% of health resources, but comprise about 64% of total population. Between 1982 and 2001, the number of hospital beds in cities increased from 832 thousand to 1.95 million, a 135% growth, whilst in rural areas the number of hospital beds declined from 1.2 million to 1 million, a 16.7% decrease (Wang, 2004, p.28). With the collapse of the CHS, many barefoot doctors chose to leave the health profession for full time farming because of inadequate compensation and support from the local government. The number of village health stations decreased, as did the staff and beds of middle level facilities. From 1980 to 1989, the number of township clinics decreased by 14.2% and the number of active primary health care workers in rural areas declined by 35.9%. The number of village doctors in practice decreased from 1.8 million to 1.3 million from 1978 to 1985 (Liu et al, 1995). The healthcare input from government into rural sector continued at a low level, accounting for only 15.9% of total government health spending (Wang, 2004, p.25). These figures indicate that health services in rural areas were weakened in comparison to those in urban areas. And today the government still adopts an urban biased policy in spite of the disadvantaged situation in rural areas.

Disparities of health resources at the provincial level are also very pronounced. Due to decentralisation, the local governments play a major role in financing health care services. In 2001, for example, funding from the central government accounted for only 6.5% of total governmental funding in health care (Wang, 2004, p.19). It is therefore not surprising that per capita health expenditure of each province depends almost entirely upon provincial revenue. Rich provinces tend to invest more in health expenditure while poor provinces invest less. In 1998, the highest per capita government health spending was 90 *yuan* in Shanghai, whilst the lowest was only 8.5 *yuan* in Henan, less than one tenth of the former (Wang, 2004, p.20). The quality of healthcare infrastructure and the numbers of health professionals also differ markedly between provinces. In 2000, Beijing boasted the highest ratio of hospital beds per thousand people at 5.6, whilst Guizhou had the lowest ratio at 1.6. Health professionals were highly concentrated in coastal regions and some central provinces. The official statistics in 1999 showed that Beijing had the highest number of doctors per thousand people at 4.8, and Anhui the lowest, at 1.1 (State Council, 2000, p.58).

Health resources also show marked difference at the community level. Table 6.2 presents a summary for health stations in rural villages in 1998. It can be seen that the very poor rural villages were disadvantaged in all indicators. On average, they had the fewest doctors but serve the largest number of rural residents per doctor. In terms of health care facilities, average fixed assets amounted to 4,200 *yuan* in the most deprived villages, which was only about one quarter of fixed assets in the rich villages. Rural residents in poor counties not only received poorer facilities but also suffer from problems in physical access to health care services. In 1998 about one quarter of residents in poor villages had to travel over 30 minutes to reach the closest clinic. In contrast, only one in 50 residents in rich villages had to travel over 30 minutes (MOH, 1999, p.70).

Table 6.2 A descriptive summary of village health stations in 1998

	Total	Rural I[a]	Rural II[a]	Rural III[a,b]	Rural IV[a]
Number of rooms	3	3	3	3	2
Area of rooms (square metre)	57	64	57	58	41
Fixed assets (thousand *yuan*)	15.5	15.8	12.1	21.8[b]	4.2
Number of doctors	1.8	1.6	1.8	1.9	1.4
Number of people under service	904	872	1007	780	1138

[a]Rural areas have been classified into four groups based on the level of development of the economy and social services. I- better-off areas; II-relatively better-off areas; III- relatively poor areas. IV- very poor areas.
[b]It is unclear why the 'fixed assets' were so high in the category of 'Rural III'. This is, perhaps, due to an error in the original survey or sampling biases.
Source: MOH, 1999, p.152.

That people have financial difficulty in seeking health care has become a widespread social problem. According to the 2003 National Health Service Survey 38.2% of people reported that financial difficulties were the major reason for failing to seek medical services. Among those who refused to be admitted to hospital as inpatients against doctors' advice, 70% of them said that they had financial difficulties. More than one third of interviewees tried to avoid using health care services by self-treatment, for example, purchasing medicine from pharmacies (MOH, 2004, p.18). Table 6.3 shows the proportion of patients who requested early discharges due to financial difficulties, residents of poor areas being much more likely to do so. Nearly 80% of patients from the poorest rural areas asked for early discharge for financial reasons, while only 35% of patients in large cities did so (MOH, 1999, p.61).

As a consequence of the problems with accessibility, affordability and availability of health services, the total health utilisation rate has been declining over the last decade, although the total number of people who fall ill has increased. For example, the two-week clinic utilisation rate in 2003 was 11.8% and 13.9% in urban and rural areas respectively, a decline by 27.1% and 15.4% compared to the figures in 1998 (MOH, 2004, p.5).

Moreover, the health service survey in 2003 revealed that those with the lowest incomes had the lowest health care utilisation rate and the largest rate of utilisation decline. (MOH, 2004, p.5). Therefore, it can be concluded that the decline in urban and rural health care utilisation is mainly experienced by low income groups and that lack of access to health care has particularly disadvantaged the most vulnerable.

Table 6.3 Proportion of patients requesting early discharge to the total hospitalised patients (%)

	Total	Large city	Medium city	Small city	Rural I	Rural II	Rural III	Rural IV
Request to be discharged	42.1	30.4	35.1	45.8	37.0	48.4	46.3	48.2
Financial reason for such a request	56.1	35.6	46.8	53.7	56.3	54.1	59.3	79.9

Source: MOH, 1999, p.66.

Inequality in health status

With low socio-economic status and exclusion from the health care system, poor people tend to have a higher morbidity and mortality rate than rich people. According to the 2000 census, life expectancy in the western provinces is 3.5 years lower than the national average of 69.7 years. In Tibet, Qinghai and Xinjiang, in particular, it is 9.9, 7.9 and 5.9 years lower, respectively. The gap between the western provinces and the national average remains unchanged between 1990 and 2000 (Guo and Zhao, 2004, p.10).

The infant mortality rate (IMR) is another significant indicator of health status. The ratio of the IMR between urban and rural areas has remained the same over the last decade, with the IMR in rural areas being three times higher than in urban areas. Studies also show that the disparity between the IMR in eastern coastal provinces and the western inland provinces has widened (Feng and Wang, 2003). In 1990 the ratio of the IMR between the western and coastal regions was 1.80, but increasing to 2.14 in 2000. The IMR in large cities approaches that in the developed countries, for example in Shanghai, it is 5.1 per thousand live births, equivalent to that in Britain. In stark contrast, the IMR in the poorest counties is often still as high as 100 per thousand live births, among the highest in the world (Huang et al. 1997, p.1031). It is quite disturbing that, in the same country, some rural infants are almost 20 times more likely to die before their first birthday than their urban counterparts. It is also a disquieting trend that the inequality in health status between different regions has increased.

The deteriorating financial situation in rural areas has led to less attention being paid to preventative health care. Some surveys suggest that there is a resurgence in some infectious diseases (MOH, 1990; Cook and Dummer, 2004; Dong et al., 2005). The elimination of schistosomiasis was hailed a success story of mass public health campaign in the Cultural Revolution. However, the incidence of schistosomiasis increased from a rate of 540 per 10,000 in 1980 to 788 per 10,000 in 1990. A 2001 study estimated that 865,000 people were infected in the 12 provinces south of the Yangtze River where the disease is endemic (Ross et al. 2001, p.270). TB and hepatitis are still prevalent. People with viral hepatitis account for about 10% of China's 1.3

billion people, and one third of the total number of the people carrying the virus in the world. 4.5 million people carry TB and two million of them remain infectious (Gao, 2005, p.4). Because treatment is not free the situation has not improved (Cook and Dummer, 2004).

In some rural areas HIV/AIDS has become prevalent because deprivation has forced many farmers to sell their blood to make a living. Unregulated and unhygienic blood collection by illegal blood banks up till the second half of the 1990s in a deregulated health system helped fuel an HIV epidemic in several large agricultural provinces, in particular Henan, where many villages are devastated by AIDS. This, together with the use of contaminated blood products by hospitals and other health facilities, has further spread HIV/AIDS, accounting for some 23% of the accumulated reported cases of HIV/AIDS, which presents a rather unusual pattern of HIV transmission in the world (Zhang, 2004). It is estimated that 800,000 to 1,000,000 HIV-positive people live in poor rural areas (Dong et al., 2005, p.573). A higher STD prevalence rate is reported among young rural migrants who have moved into cities for employment. This is because, on the one hand, they are more likely to have casual and commercial sex, and on the other, they tend to have low awareness of the risk and low accessibility to safe sex measures. Moreover, because they are not covered by any insurance schemes, they are less likely to seek health treatment. These migrants may become the bridging population in passing on the infection to the general population, for example, to their wives back in the villages (Smith, 2005).

Poverty leads to poor health, which, in turn, exacerbates poverty. A considerable proportion of people have fallen into a poverty trap due to the heavy financial burdens incurred during serious illness. Surveys have found that 20-30% of rural people living below the poverty line reported the reason as illness and the medical expenses incurred (Hsiao, 1995, p.1053; MOH, 1999, p.18).

Conclusion

Despite remarkable economic growth that China has witnessed since the reforms, disparities between the rich and the poor have widened. With regard to healthcare provision, it is the poor who tend to have no health insurance and therefore it is they who have been marginalised in the new market-oriented healthcare system.

Socio-economic inequality in health is a profound form of social exclusion and marginalisation. Equity in health and health care is an integral component of social development and justice. Health care should not be deemed as a mere private commodity. On the contrary, it should be treated as a public or semi-public good. As a result, the health system should be equitable, allow reasonably equal access and protect the most vulnerable (Liu et al., 1999).

Since the beginning of the economic reforms, World Bank reports have consistently warned that the impact of a more market oriented economy could be particularly detrimental to the vulnerable segments of the population (World Bank, 1984). These warnings have been proved to be correct. China was one of the most egalitarian countries in the world and 'Health for All' was one of the major policy commitments of the government during the first three decades of the People's Republic. But the reforms have given rise to a system that is ruled by the ability to pay. The introduction of market forces into healthcare services has led to the reduction of governmental support and escalating medical costs. The collapse of the CHS and erosion of the LMSS have left most of the rural population and a significant number of urban residents with no health insurance coverage at all. Rural migrants who come to urban areas for employment have been discriminated against due to their rural household registration status. They are not covered by any insurance scheme and usually cannot afford commercial insurance, and thus healthcare services when in need. Meanwhile, the government has long adopted a laissez-faire policy, causing the Chinese to experience increasing inequality in health care access, utilisation, and in standards of health between rich and poor social groups and rich and poor regions.

There are many lessons to be drawn from the experiences of China's healthcare reforms. First, the health sector is different from other economic sectors. Healthcare cannot be considered just as *any* market commodity because it has the character of a public good (Scott et al., 2001). While market forces always drive health providers to improve economic efficiency and may improve quality of services, there is a cost to pay for such a market-oriented health service, and that cost is paid by those marginalised by the new systems. Relying on the free market alone to finance health care inevitably leads to unequal access to health services between rich and poor, between the insured and uninsured.

Secondly, the government should not give up its role in the support of healthcare services. Health policy is one of the most important elements in western societies and should be one of the top priorities of the Chinese government as well. After the SARS outbreak, the government has substantially increased investment in the health sector (Dong et al., 2005). However, financial support alone is not enough. The government must tackle the organisational issue as well and reform the whole health system from surveillance, maternal and child care, to hospital and clinical services (Liu, 2004a). It may not be wise or feasible to go back to a totally government controlled health care system such as existed before the economic reform so there is an urgent need to explore new ways of establishing a mixed system with both public and private institutions meeting the different needs of different social groups.

Thirdly, the government should actively explore new ways of financing the health system, especially to support poor people. The implementation of new social health insurance schemes in urban and rural areas needs to be carefully monitored and the scheme modified if necessary. The current medical financial assistance system is inadequate both in terms of its effectiveness of support and its breadth of coverage. Hu (2004) has suggested that the government increase taxes on tobacco products and use the extra revenue to assist poor people in health care. In addition, the government should encourage non-governmental organisations to get more involved and seek more international collaboration with overseas organisations.

Acknowledgements

I am grateful to Heather Xiaoquan Zhang, who has provided very useful comments and suggestions throughout the writing of this chapter, and Richard Sanders and Kathryn Spry who have proof-read the chapter.

References

Appleton, S.,J. Knight, Song, L and Xia, Q. (2002) 'Labor retrenchment in China, determinants and consequences', *China Economic Review*, vol.13, pp.252–275.

Cao, H. and Fu, J. (2005), 'Twenty years of health care reform', *Southern Weekend* [online], August 4, p.6, available from http://www.nanfangdaily.com.cn/zm/20050804/xw/tb/ 200508040004.asp [accessed 20 October 2005].

Cheng, X. (2004), 'Vulnerable groups and equity in health care', *Medicine and Philosophy*, vol. 25 pp.15-16 (in Chinese).

China Daily. (2001) 'Hospitals found to overcharge patients', 19 September, available from http://www.chinadaily.com.cn/en/doc/2001-09/29/content_86259.htm [accessed 8 August 2005].

China Daily. (2005), 'Medical staff sacked after vagrant dies', May 27 2005, available from http://www2.chinadaily.com.cn/english/doc/2005/05/27/ content_446208.htm, [accessed 8 August 2005].

Cook, I.G. and Dummer, T.J.B., (2004), 'Changing health in China: re-evaluating the epidemiological transition model'. *Health Policy,* vol. 67 pp.329-343.

Dong, Z., Hoven C.W. and Rosenfield, A. (2005), 'Lessons from the past- Poverty and market forces combine to keep rural China unhealthy', *Nature*, vol. 433, pp.573-574.

Feng, X. Tang, S, Bloom, G, Segall, M. and Gu X. (1995) 'Cooperative medical schemes in contemporary rural China' *Social Science and Medicine*, vol. 41 pp.1111-1118.

Feng, Z. and Wang, Y. (2003), 'Regional disparity in infant mortality in China', *International Conference of Medical Geography*, 12-14 July 2003, Manchester University, Manchester.

Gao, J., Tang, S., Tolhust, R. and Rao, K. (2001), 'Changing access to health services in urban China: what implications for equality?' *Health Policy and Planning*, vol.16, pp.302-312.

Gao, Q. (2005), 'To promote health development towards a socialist harmonious society', Ministry of Health, available from http://www.moh.gov.cn/ (in Chinese) [accessed 10 August 2005].

Goodkind, D. and West, L.A. (2002), 'China's floating population: definitions, data and recent findings', *Urban Studies*, vol.39, pp.2237-2250.

Guan, Z., (2005), 'Economic transition and health insurance system reform in urban China', *International Symposium on health care systems in Asia*, 21-22 January, 2005, Hitotsubashi University, Hitotsubashi, Tokyo.

Guo Y. and Zhao, D. (2004), 'Equity of health care services: on the role of the government', *Medicine and Philosophy*, vol. 25, pp.10-12 (in Chinese).

Henderson, G.E., Jin,S., Akin, J., Li, Z., Wang, J., Ma, H., He, Y, Zhang, X, Chang, Y., and Ge K. (1995), 'Distribution of medical insurance in China'. *Social Science and Medicine*, vol. 41, pp. 1119-1130.

Henderson, G.E., Akin, J.S., Hutchinson P.M., Jin S.G, Wang, J.M., Dietrich J., and Mao L.M. (1998), 'Trends in health services utilization in eight provinces in China', 1989-1993, *Social Science & Medicine*, vol. 47, pp. 1957-1971.

Ho, L.S. (1995), 'Market Reforms and China Health-Care System', *Social Science and Medicine*, vol. 41, pp.1065-1072.

Hsiao, W.C.L. (1984) 'Transformation of health care in China', *New England Journal of Medicine*, vol. 310, pp. 932-936.

Hsiao, W.C.L. (1995) 'The Chinese Health Care System: Lessons for Other Nations', *Social Science and Medicine*, vol. 41, pp.1047-1055.

Huang, W., Yu, H., Wang, F and Li, G. (1997) 'Infant mortality among various nationalities in the middle part of Guizhou, China', *Social Science & Medicine*, vol. 45, pp. 1031-1040.

Hu, T. (2004), 'Financing and organization of China's health care', *Bulletin of World Health Organization*, vol. 82, pp. 480-480.

Hu, T. and Ying, X. (2005), The role of private health insurance in China's health care financing, *Wharton Impact Conference: Voluntary health insurance in developing countries*, 15-16 March 2005, University of Pennsylvania, Wharton.

Hua, X. (2004), 'Issues and solutions to health management in the reform era', *Chinese Health Policy* vol.174, pp.27-30 (in Chinese).

Ip, P-K. (2005), 'Developing medical ethics in China's reform era', *Developing World Bioethics*, vol. 5, pp.1471-1487.

Li, G., and Gu, L., (2004) 'On medical security issues for handicapped military veterans', Ministry of Civil Affairs, available from http://www.mca.gov.cn /news/ content/search/20041110111633.html (in Chinese) [accessed 10 August 2005].

Liu, G.G, Zhao, Z., Cai, R., Yamada, T., and Yamada, T. (2002), 'Equity in health care access to: assessing the urban health insurance reform in China', *Social Science and Medicine*, vol. 55, pp.1779-1794.

Liu Y.L. (2004a) 'China's public health system: facing the challenges', *Bulletin of the World Health Organization*, vol. 82, pp.532-538.

Liu, Y.L. (2004b). 'Development of the rural health insurance system in China'. *Health Policy and Planning*, vol.19. pp.159-165.

Liu, Y.L, Hsiao, W.C., Li Q., Liu X.Z., and Ren M. (1995), 'Transformation of China's rural health care financing'. *Social Science and Medicine*. vol. 41, pp. 1085-1093.

Liu, Y.L, Hsiao, W. C., and Eggleston, K. (1999), 'Equity in health and health care: the Chinese experience'. *Social Science and Medicine*. vol. 49, pp. 1349-1356.

Ministry of Civil Affairs, Ministry of Health, and Ministry of Finance (2003) 'Guidelines on Rural Medical Assistance', Ministry of Civil Affairs, available from http://www.mca.gov.cn/artical/content/WJJ_YL/2003122984233.htm (in Chinese) [accessed 9 July 2005].

MOH. (1989), 'Health Statistics Information in China, 1949-88'. Ministry of Health, Beijing (in Chinese).

MOH. (1990), 'China Health Yearbook 1990', Renmin Weisheng Chubanshe, Beijing (in Chinese).

MOH. (1999), 'Reports on the 1998 National Health Service Survey results'. Ministry of Health, Centre for Health Statistics and Information, Beijing (in Chinese).

MOH. (2004), 'Executive Summary on the 2003 National Health Service Survey results' Ministry of Health, Centre for Health Statistics and Information, Beijing (in Chinese).

OECD. (2006), OECD health data 2006, available from http://www.oecd.org/topicstatsportal/0,2647,en_2825_495642_1_1_1_1_1,00.html. [accessed 14 August 2006].

People's Daily. (2000), 'There are further eight million people moving out of poverty in rural China' p. 1, 26 December (in Chinese).

People's Daily. (2005), 'China's health minister slams hospitals for sacrificing public interest for profits', 5 August, available at http://english.people.com.cn/200508/05/eng20050805_ 200418.html [accessed 10 August 2005].

Ross AGP, Sleigh AC, Li YS, Davis GM, Williams GM, Jiang Z, et al. (2001), 'Schistosomiasis in the People's Republic of China: prospects and challenges for the 21st century'. *Clinical Microbiology Reviews*, vol. 14, pp.270–295.

Scott R.D., Solomon, S.I. and McGowan J.E. (2001), 'Applying economic principles to health care', *Emerging Infectious Diseases*, vol. 7, pp. 284-285.

Smith C.J. (2005), 'Social geography of sexually transmitted diseases in China: exploring the role of migration and urbanization', *Asian Pacific Viewpoint*, vol. 46, pp. 65-80.

State Council (2006), *A Research Report on China's Migrant Workers*, Beijing: Yanshi chubanshe.

State Council of China, Committee on Women and Children, (2000), *Statistical data on women and children in the 1990s in China*, State Council: Beijing (in Chinese).

Sun, X., Liang, H, Cheng Y. and Tian, W. (2002) 'Survey of the medical financial assistance schemes of the urban poor in Shanghai' *International Journal of Health Planning and Management*, vol. 17. pp 91-112.

The Economist (2004), 'Where are the patients?' Special report China's health care, 21st August, pp.22-25.

Wang S.G. (2004), 'China's Health System: From Crisis to Opportunity', *The Yale-China Health Journal*, vol. 3, pp. 5-50.

World Bank (1984), *China: the Health Sector*. The World Bank, Washington, DC.

World Health Organization (WHO) (2000), 'The World Health Report 2000-Health systems, improving performance', available at http://www.who.int/whr/2000/en [accessed 10 July 2005].

Xu, F. (1998), 'Expenditure under labour insurance medical service scheme' *China Social Insurance*, vol. 10. pp. 19-20 (in Chinese).

Yao, S., Zhang, Z., and Hanmer, L. (2004), 'Growing inequality and poverty in China'. *China Economic Review*, vol. 15. pp. 145-163.

Zhang, H.X. (2004), 'The gathering storm: AIDS policy in China'. *Journal of International Development*, vol. 16, pp. 1155-1168.

Zhao Y. (2000), *China National Health Expenditure Report in 2000*, unpublished manuscript, China Health Economic Institute: Beijing (in Chinese).

Chapter 7

Institutional Responses to the Changing Patterns of Poverty and Marginalisation in China since 1949[1]

Ka Lin

Introduction

The concepts of marginality, vulnerability and poverty are interwoven in various ways. As Gurung and Kollmair (2005, 16) remarked, in practice, "marginality and poverty are often used as synonyms". This is because the poor are not only disadvantaged in terms of access to resources but also marginalised in social and economic life. Holding a low social status and with only a weak voice in politics and the mass media, people in marginalised groups are likely to fall into the plight of poverty and social exclusion. In this context, research on marginalisation needs to be extended into the broad area of poverty studies. This chapter will deploy such an approach to study the Chinese case, integrating the issues of vulnerability, marginality, poverty and social exclusion.

Since marginality relates to social stratification, its study needs to be conducted within an institutional dimension. This dimension was first explored by Townsend (1971) who argued that poverty was caused not only by resource shortage but by unequal distribution of wealth (see also Wilson 1996, 18-32). From this point of view, it is necessary to examine the influence of institutional factors in generating poverty, especially the relative deprivation caused by social stratification. In particular, it is important to review the changing forms of social structure in transitional China and investigate their impacts on poverty patterns. With this aim, this study will deviate from the popular approach to poverty research in China – which is preoccupied with the issues of measurement and incidence of poverty – and will take an institutional approach.

However, although the institutional study of poverty has been distanced from the issue of social administration – partly as a legacy of social policy itself – this study will make an effort to build up the linkages between institutional factors and state policymaking. This is because in the Chinese socialist regime, institutional change is primarily initiated by the state. And thus, as a result, in order to obtain a full understanding of the characteristics of Chinese poverty, the state's policy

1 This chapter is a partial outcome of a research project funded by the Ministry of Education of the People's Republic of China.

actions need to be examined. Accordingly, this chapter consists of four parts. Firstly, it will provide readers with a national profile of poverty and secondly examine the characteristics of poverty groups. It will then review the state's strategies of poverty elimination, before concluding with an evaluation of recent Chinese experiences in relation to poverty. In so doing, it is designed to help enrich the sociological understanding of the nature of poverty and the possible approaches to poverty reduction.

Changes in the national profile of poverty

Due to the poor facilities and infrastructure of the national economy inherited from the Nationalists in 1949, the newly established Communist regime under Mao Zedong encountered extremely difficult conditions to launch its post-revolution reconstruction plans. The prolonged wars and political unrest had left 'a blank paper' (in Mao's term) for the new regime with regard to its plans for industrialisation and the economic embargo against China imposed by the western powers after the outbreak of the Korean war had disconnected China from international capitalist markets. In these contexts, absolute poverty was widespread and starvation often occurred. Between 1949 and 1977 (apart from the year of 1956, see Xun 2003), people's average calorie intake per day was less than 2000 indicating a general food shortage during that time. Towards the end of this period, one-fourth of the total population remained in poverty. In 1978, the state estimated that 250 million people still lived below the poverty line (Information Office of China's State Council, hereafter IOCSC, 2001).

To ameliorate these harsh conditions, the Communist regime established a collective network as a means of protecting people's basic livelihoods. In villages, the state eradicated private ownership of land by reforms that overthrew the rule of landlords. In their stead, the state encouraged peasants to organise themselves into productive co-operatives and eventually integrated them into a powerful commune system. This state-organised communal system served various economic and social functions. With regard to social welfare, for instance, it ensured meeting the basic needs of the lonely elderly, sick and disabled as well as other vulnerable groups. This system gradually became a network for people's welfare, preventing the majority of the rural population from falling into poverty. In this regard, Guan (2003, 75) has commented that in Maoist China, "rural poverty was not seen as a big problem because income was fairly equal among farmers". To be sure, with low agricultural productivity and little state investment in the agricultural sector, the standard of living of peasants was very low and the means of promoting livelihoods were in seriously short supply. However, it was a collective system that enabled most peasants to subsist and survive.

In cities, through a campaign of nationalisation, China remoulded all private industrial and commercial firms into public ones with either state or collective ownership, eventually employing more than 99% of the urban labour force (National

Bureau of Statistics of China, thereafter NBSC, 1986).[2] Owing to their public nature, these firms undertook certain welfare responsibilities for their employees and their dependents within a framework of enterprise welfare. The workplaces provided various benefits such as pensions, housing, health care and child education for their employees in compensation for their low wages. Moreover, this system also contained the elements of full employment and egalitarian wages, so that the system was characterised by "low wage, high employment, high welfare" (Lee 2001, 61, Chen, N., 2003, 53). For these reasons, urban poverty was not a serious problem in those days. As Mok (1987, 240) commented, the urban poor people "did not have to worry about their living" because the state and collectives practically guaranteed it. Regardless of the collective form of provision, however, the state's direct financial input into welfare support for urban citizens was very limited (except some food subsidies provided by local government). People's living standards were generally low, partly because the profits from production were used mostly for investment in heavy industries rather than in light industries for producing everyday goods.

The condition of poverty changed remarkably in the era of economic reform under Deng Xiaoping, however. During the 1980s, the economic growth stimulated by the reforms contributed to a rapid rise in living standards. In this decade, as statistics have reflected, the per capita annual net income of rural households increased from 133.6 Yuan in 1978 to 397.6 Yuan in 1985, and further to 601.5 Yuan by 1989 (NBSC 2004, 357).[3] In urban society, the wage system was also reformed with the incorporation of an element of company bonus. This component, in Xiao and Wang's (1986, 450) estimation, resulted in a 40% rise in the average wages of urban workers. Consequently, the Engel Coefficient[4] fell from 67.7% in villages and 57.5% in cities in 1978, to 54.8% and 54.5% respectively in 1989 (NBSC 2004, 357). This decline meant that people had more income to purchase goods other than basic food for subsistence. However, although this development gave rise to optimism concerning poverty elimination, the unequal speed of economic growth across regions exacerbated regional poverty.

The problem of regional poverty is not a new one for China, as its large territory includes many mountainous areas and remote regions far away from the industrial and business centres. These areas, mostly located in the central and western regions, have always had difficulties in transportation and access to information, and the harsh ecological conditions severely limited the scope for development even in the days of Mao Zedong. Thus, in 1978, in some inland provinces such as Gansu and Guizhou, the farmers' per capita net incomes were only 64% and 71%, respectively, of farmers' income in Zhejiang province (NBSC 1986, 677). Nevertheless, the accelerated economic growth brought about by the reforms enlarged regional disparities, which,

---

2 In 1979, among 99.67 million urban employees, 76.93 million were working in SOEs, 22.74 million in collective firms, and the remaining 0.32 million were self-employed (NBSC 1986, 124).

3 The exchange rate of Chinese Yuan to US dollar was 1:1.5 in 1979, 1:2.9 in 1985, 1:3.7 in 1989 (Ministry of Commerce of PRC, 2004).

4 Engle coefficient refers to the percentage of expenditure on food in the total consumption expenditure.

in turn, inevitably affected the conditions and patterns of poverty. This is manifested in the fact that the rate of absolute rural poverty in the eastern region declined to 9% in 1988 and 5% in 1995, but in the inland regions, in the corresponding years, the rate fell to 26% and then *increased* again to 31% (Unger 2002, 171). Thus, from the late 1980s to the mid 1990s, regional poverty became a central issue in Chinese poverty studies. In the 1990s, when the eastern regions had a growth rate twice that of their western counterparts (Fang, Zhang and Fan 2004), the condition of regional poverty did not improve, rather it was exacerbated.

While regional poverty remained a tough issue throughout the 1990s, researchers and policymakers became increasingly aware of the emerging relative poverty. This problem was not so serious in the Maoist era, as indicated by a very low Gini-Coefficient (see the chapter by Sanders, Chen and Cao in this volume) at a time when a policy of egalitarian income distribution narrowed the income gaps between social groups. The collective morale and comradely relationships associated with the collectivist ideology of the time also made social stratification a minor issue. However, the growth of market institutions deepened the degree of relative poverty.[5] The Gini-Coefficient, which was only 0.2 in 1978, soared to 0.45 after two decades of reform practices (Fan 1996, Unger 2002, 171). This trend continued in the late 1990s. For example in terms of income share, people in the lowest 20% income group took 9% of the total income in 1990 but only 5.5% in 1998. In contrast, those in the top 20% income group increased their shares markedly over the same period of time, from 38.1% to 52.3% (Guan 2003, 72).

Overall, the above studies demonstrate a change in the patterns of Chinese poverty, from the prevalence of absolute poverty before the reform to more regionally-based poverty, typically from the mid-1980s and 1990s, towards a social stratified relative poverty after the mid-1990s. The successful performance of the Chinese economy contributed significantly to a reduction in the incidence of absolute poverty, but the imbalance in the growth rate between inland and coastal areas made regional poverty a serious problem. However, these regional imbalances were compounded by ever increasing levels of income inequality across social groups *within* different regions. As some surveys made in several cities in the early 2000's have revealed (see Tang 2002, 23), families in the high-income group have a disposable income on average four times higher than ordinary families, and the low-income groups still suffered from factors that raised levels of house prices and the consumptions costs. To the extent that relative poverty reflects the conditions of social stratification and class divisions, it is reasonable to regard the increase of relative poverty at this stage mostly as a consequence of market development.

Changes in the characteristics of the poor groups

Prior to the reforms, poverty was mainly a rural phenomenon. Peasants had a much lower standard of living than urban residents. Comparing their consumption

5 The degree of relative poverty can be measured by the income standard equal to 50% or 60% of the average income of the local people. Besides the income standard, relative poverty can be reflected through indicators of education, housing and health care, etc.

levels, the spending of urban families in 1952 was 2.4 times higher than that of rural households, a ratio remaining almost unchanged until 1979.[6] The reasons for rural poverty included factors such as the lack of capital investment from outside (particularly from the state), the low level of technology in agricultural production and the predominance of agriculture in the rural economy (IOCSC 2001). With regard to institutional factors, some also blamed the commune system for hindering people's work incentives. It is arguable, however, that more emphasis needs be placed on the effects of the state's 'urban-bias policy'. With this bias, the state transferred a large amount of agricultural surplus into the industrial sector (Zhou 1994, Lu 2002), weakening peasants' capacity to increase their production and income (Fang, Zhang and Fan 2004, 308). These factors worked together to create a system of social dualism in which the state left peasants to stand on their own feet with collective support but protected urban workers by generous social welfare schemes. This dualist structure divided Chinese citizens into 'two unequal tiers – the privileged urban and the underprivileged rural' (Fan 2002, 106, also see Li Zhang's chapter in this volume).

This situation changed dramatically subsequent to the reforms of the early 1980s. In the agricultural sector, adoption of the household contract responsibility system gave farmers a large degree of freedom to decide what they wanted to plant for their own interests. The rising prices of agricultural products induced farmers to plant high value-added products and to multiply their production (Bian 2002). The structural adjustment of rural production reflected in the growth of township and village enterprises and the development of non-agricultural work in 'the service sector' now provided peasants with new means of livelihood (Liang, Chen and Gu 2004). Meanwhile increased rural-urban migration took place as more and more farmers looked for better-paid jobs in cities. Consequently, the degree of generalised rural poverty was alleviated. To use some statistical data for illustration, the poor which numbered 250 million in 1978 (equal to 30.7% of the total rural population) was reduced to 125 million (14.8%) in 1985 (Kang 2002). This decrease was achieved in the context of a rise in the poverty line, as defined by the state, from 206 Yuan per annum in 1985 to 300 Yuan in 1990 (IOCSC 2001).[7]

However, it should be noted that this reduction of generalised rural poverty was accompanied by an increase in urban poverty. Whatever measurement was adopted in the definition of poverty (see discussion in Tang 2004), the phenomenon of rising urban poverty gradually became so evident as to attract widespread attention among policy makers and analysts by the end of the 1990s. However, an even more essential aspect of this change was its components. In the past, the urban poor comprised mostly the 'three-no' groups (with no income, no work capacity, and no family support, see Guan 2003, 78) based largely on *personal* factors; but by the start of

6 Taking rural households' spending as 1, the ratio to the urban families' spending was 1:2.7 in 1979 (NBSC, 1986, 646).

7 By 2000, this line was set at 625 yuan a year. With this bottom line, China had 30 million of poor population in 2000. However, in 2001 China used a new standard of 865 yuan as the bottom line, and accounted the poor as 90 millions, equal to 10% of the rural population nationwide (China.com 2004).

the 2000s, the market-generated 'new urban poverty groups' began to predominate, despite the continued existence of the 'three-no' groups. These new poverty groups, according to Wang and Zhao (2003, 109), accounted for around 70-90% of the total urban poor. They included laid-off workers, the unemployed and pensioners who received no (or only partial) benefit from social security schemes (Zhu 2003). Thus, according to Wang and Zhao (2003) it was the unemployed and laid-off workers who accounted for most of this group, although it also comprised temporary workers and chronically low income earners.

In order to demonstrate the relationship between the surge in urban poverty and the reform process, it is important to pay special attention to those laid-off and to the unemployed, comprising, as they do, the majority of the 'new urban poverty groups'. Beginning in the late 1980s, some state-owned enterprises (SOEs) adopted lay-off policies as means of industrial management, but they began to escalate in scale as the process of national economic restructuring accelerated from 1992 onwards. The state accelerated the process of ownership reform by selling off small-size SOEs to private-owners or by merging some SOEs with foreign ventures, generating new dynamics of unemployment. Consequently, between 1998 and 2003, 28 million were laid off as a result of this process (IOCSC 2004b). For these people, job losses meant immediate income loss and a descent into poverty. This jobless condition was created by market forces rather than personal failings and examining urban poverty against this background, the logic of market risk became widely accepted with increased demands for the state to take social responsibility for those made unemployed by introducing new social security schemes and through other social means.

Besides rural and urban poverty, social exclusion – a phenomenon that produces vulnerable groups (Gore et al. 1995; Paugam 1996)[8] – is also a basic issue of poverty studies. In China, the concept of social exclusion has significant implications for understanding the poverty of migrant workers in cities and towns. In pre-reform China, the stringent household registration regime and the communal system of control prevented large-scale labour migration (see Li Zhang's chapter in this volume). In the reform era, rapid industrialisation and urbanisation and the relaxation in rural-urban migration stimulated a large flow of farmers from villages to cities. According to statistics, almost 130 million peasants left the agricultural sector to work as labour migrants between 1978 and 2000 (Nie 2003). In the first half of 2003, as many as 90 million rural migrants left the villages to work in cities (Guo 2005).

Since these people have entered the cities with rural household registration status, they have often been excluded from the major social institutions of urban societies (such as the urban social security system). Consequently they have less social support and are likely to be marginalised (Wang and Zhao 2003). Many scholars (e.g. So, 2003) have reported that most migrant workers earn a living as manual labourers, working in harsh conditions for low (and sometime delayed) payment. They are likely to live on the urban fringe, in housing with poor electricity and water supply. If they get sick, as surveys have disclosed (e.g. Bai 2004), more than half of them will

8 Social exclusion can be seen from various aspects, for instance, as the exclusion from 'participation in decision making and political processes, access to employment and material resources, and integration into common cultural processes' (Madanipour et al. 1998, 22).

not see doctors because their employers will, at best, pay no more than one-twentieth of their health care expenses (see Feng's chapter in this volume). Also, since most of them are employed on a temporary basis, they face a higher risk of unemployment. As some surveys have reported (Bai 2004), more than one-third of migrant workers have experienced unemployment during their stay in cities.

Overall, the economic reforms since the 1980s have reduced the incidence of rural poverty but the development of the market has left urban workers previously protected by their workplaces exposed to high market risk. This is particularly the result of the reform of the SOEs producing a large number of laid-off workers, resulting in a 'semi-proletarianisation of state workers', in So's words (2003, 369). Thus, when Fan (1996) accused the downsizing SOEs of being responsible for the rise in urban poverty, it touched on the burning question of the new market operations endangering workers' livelihoods (see also the chapter by Tang, Dong and Duda in this volume). On the matter of social exclusion, meanwhile, although rural people have entered cities with a hope of better employment and living opportunities, the reality has turned out to be much tougher than they expected. As 'strangers' to urban communities, they are often regarded as outsiders and in many cases, treated unfairly. They get no access to the broader range of social rights available for urban residents, for example, the guarantee of a minimum income and the right to education for their children. Many of them eventually become 'three-nos' (Fan 2002), but nowadays of a different kind – meaning no land (as they have left the village), no workplace (as they are temporary workers only) and no social security (which is available only for urban residents). All these factors, worsening the situation of urban poverty, demand social policy action from the state.

Changes in the state's strategies toward poverty alleviation

In order to fulfil its paternalist obligations and ensure its legitimacy, the state has to use social policy measures to cope with the challenges of poverty. These measures could include, as Townsend (1971) argued, the introduction of social security schemes, the extension of employer benefits to all employees, the imposition of progressive taxes and the development of community services. Silva and Athukorala (1996) have also advocated the important social effects of land redistribution policy and the asset- and/or area-based programmes designed for impoverished areas. To study these effects, it is necessary to be aware of the following points. Firstly, the policy choices made by the state are linked with the state's developmental strategies; secondly, the effect of policy implementation is subject to the characteristics of social institutions; thirdly, policy-making for the purposes of alleviating poverty needs to take into account not only the particularities of poor groups but also those of non-poor groups (Øyen 1996, 11-14), since the latter may shape people's general views on the nature of poverty.

Keeping these points in mind, it is possible to see the evolution of Chinese anti-poverty policies as having taken place in three stages. In the first stage, the communist regime viewed private ownership as the key cause of poverty and therefore, in rural areas, a socialist model of collectivism was adopted as the means of eradicating poverty. The state conducted land reform and established a three-tier system of agricultural production and management comprising the commune, the brigade and the production team. Accordingly, a state-organised collective system was in operation. The 'five guarantee schemes' and a system of cooperative health care became essential components of this system, as they provided the lonely elderly, the disabled, or the sick with a collective guarantee on food, clothing, housing, medical treatment and burial expenses. Thus, the collectives acted as units of social control and welfare provision, together with the state's social assistance at a residual level for particular needy people.

In cities, China founded its economy on the basis of public ownership through nationalising its industrial and commercial sectors. People working in these public firms received protection by means of a state-organised collective system concerned with matters of health care, housing, education and other welfare aspects. An 8-grade wage system effectively prevented relative poverty by narrowing the income gap among wage earners (Kang 2002). In addition, trade unions organised welfare activities and provided aid to their workers, while residential communities offered a range of welfare services to local residents (typically for those out of the labour force). Consequently, the system guaranteed workers' welfare rights endorsed by socialist ideology with an extension to their dependents (and therefore covered almost the entire urban population). For particular needy groups, the state set guidelines for social assistance which was to 'rely on the mass, rely on the collective, self-regeneration through production in the main, supplemented by necessary relief from the state' (Wong 1998, 94). This guideline clearly indicated the state's intent to use collectives as the main actors in the welfare safety net for the majority of people (Mok 1987; Wong 1998).

Nevertheless, starting from the mid-1980s, the functions of this collective-based welfare system faded. Government statistics show that the share of farmers' total household income coming from collectives fell from 66.3% in 1978 to 8.4% in 1985 (NBSC 1986, 673). Simultaneously, the operation of the enterprise welfare system in cities also met with difficulties as many firms began to operate at a loss. As socialist ideas of egalitarianism were replaced with a new set of market values, the spirit of collective welfare was generally eroded. Thus, the state started a new, second stage in its anti-poverty strategies, shifting its orientation from the collective to the state. In 1984, the state initiated a new anti-poverty programme and in 1986, set up a Leading Group of the State Council for the Economic Development of Poverty-Stricken Areas to operate it. State investment in this programme increased during 1986-1992 (Kang 2002), and even more, between 1997 and 2003, with the fund coming from the central budget amounted to 183.8 billion Yuan in total (Li and Wang 2004).

Since anti-poverty strategies are, in nature, likely to be development-orientated their aims often include not only poor relief but also local economic growth. It is a widely accepted view that policies for helping the poor may well misfire if they concentrated only on poor relief without promoting people's own efforts (Mok 1987; Xiao and Wang 1986). Therefore, state relief funds need to be used to construct a 'body to generate its own blood' (*zaoxue*, i.e., to create conditions for development by enhancing people's capacities) rather than a 'blood transfusion' (*shuxue*, i.e., to provide handouts alone) (see Mok 1987). Thus, funds used in this programme were not simply relief payments to individuals but investments to enhance people's capacity for self-reliance and self-help in impoverished areas. Consequently, a large part of the programme's funds were spent on work relief delivered through road construction projects, building irrigation systems and improving the infrastructure of the local economy (Xun 2003). For the same reason, the state banks also used credit funds to assist poverty-stricken households to establish their own businesses.

In particular, it should be noted, this anti-poverty strategy had a strong regional dimension. In the 1980s, poor relief funds were equally distributed to the needy counties in all underdeveloped regions (Xinhua News Agency 2000), but since the 1990s, the state has targeted the programme mostly at the western and central provinces. Li and Wang's (2004) study, for example, has shown that between 1998 and 2001, the amount of state poverty relief funds per capita was 6.53 Yuan in the eastern region, 62.64 Yuan in the central region, but 94.47 Yuan in the western region. Besides, the state managed the establishment of 'friendship' relations between provinces in the developed and underdeveloped regions, such as between Zhejiang and Sichuan and between Jiangsu and Shaanxi.[9] The contracted parties have informal obligations in regard to technological, educational and cultural assistance as forms of cross-regional cooperation, creating new dynamics for regional development. As reported, 5,745 projects have been initiated as a result of partnerships between the eastern and western regions (IOCSC 2001). Over 2.14 billion Yuan of donations and financial support have flowed from eastern to western regions in recent years.

But in the third stage of anti-poverty policy development, both regional poverty and the increased pressure from the labour market have compelled the state to apply redistribution measures to deal with urban poverty. During 1998-2003, laid-off workers increased by 28.18 million (IOCSC 2004b) and this situation led the state's social policy makers to extend unemployment insurance and social assistance. Meanwhile, the growth of market institutions resulted in greater income inequality exacerbating tension between social classes. These problems could not be resolved by the state's development-oriented social policy. Accordingly, the state enacted various policies in the late 1990s, in respect of ensuring the basic livelihood of laid-off workers, demanding the payment of pension benefits for retirees in full (and on time), and allowing those eligible to receive payments of unemployment insurance. Among these measures, the most notable advance with regard to social protection of the worse-off was the establishment of the Minimum Living Standard System for urban residents (see also the chapter by Tang, Dong and Duda in this volume), an important milestone on the road towards state welfare in China.

With regard to migrant workers, the state set the principles for handling these workers as 'treating fairly, guiding rationally, and improving administration and service' (IOCSC 2004b). During the late 1990s, the state abolished numerous old

9 According to the Chinese government's White Paper (IOCSC 2001), the state arranged 'friendship' relations between Beijing and Inner Mongolia; Tianjin and Gansu; Shanghai and Yunnan; Guangdong and Guangxi; Jiangsu and Shaanxi; Zhejiang and Sichuan; Shandong and Xinjiang; Liaoning and Qinghai; Fujian and Ningxia. In addition, the cities of Dalian, Qingdao, Shenzhen and Ningbo are assigned a duty to help Guizhou.

regulations that restricted the movement and settlement of rural people into cities. The state also called on all employers to safeguard these workers with social security programmes on a voluntary basis, although in reality most employers, especially in the informal sector, would not meet this demand. Moreover, as most of these workers remained outside the social insurance schemes (despite state promotion), new efforts were made to monitor and improve their working conditions and provide services for their employment and livelihood. This intent was clearly expressed in the 'National Plan for Training Rural Migrant Workers" drawn up in 2003. In this Plan, the state committed itself to the provision of occupational training for 60 million rural migrant workers between 2003 and 2010. However, so far, the services for these workers are still very limited. For instance, in many cases their children still cannot gain access to the public schools in cities unless they pay a special fee.

To conclude on the Chinese strategies of poverty reduction, three-stage development path has been unfolded. In the first stage, 'the ideological imperative of Marxism (was) instrumental' (Wong 1998, 1), supporting collective welfare. This state-organised collective system created an egalitarian society established on the basis of the working class being the leading political power. The system, despite the problems pointed out by its critics, had some success in reducing poverty and ameliorating marginalisation. In the second stage, the state altered its policy orientation from one of egalitarian collectivism towards one based on development. This reorientation was well displayed through its region-targeted anti-poverty programmes (Zhu 2004) pursued from the 1990s onward.[10] The third stage, starting in the late 1990s, was characterised by state intervention through redistributive policies and the extension of social insurance schemes. During this period, the state increased its social security expenditure from the central budget as much as 5.18 times from 1998 to 2001. Social security spending soared from 98.2 billion Yuan in 2001 to 146.5 billion Yuan in 2004 (IOCSC 2002, 2005). This development of state welfare was originally to facilitate the reform of the state-owned enterprises, but subsequently it had more profound social impact.

Evaluation and conclusion

Firstly, with respect to its patterns, poverty has often been regarded as an outcome of underdevelopment in the national economy (Novak 1996). Therefore, and particularly for neo-liberal observers, economic growth has been seen as the chief means of reducing poverty. The Chinese experience, however, offers us more lessons than this. It shows that it was also possible to alleviate absolute poverty by egalitarian collectivism. Through collective assistance and state egalitarian policy, the basic subsistence of the majority was successfully protected in the Mao period despite the extant conditions of serious resource shortage. Later on, market-oriented development and rapid growth delivered people with more overall resources for

10 In the late 1990s, the state further launched a campaign of 'Developing the West' and in 2000, the state accented this task in the Tenth Five-Year Plan (2001-2005). For undertaking this campaign, the state invested a total 264 million Yuan for its operation between 2000 and 2004 (IOCSC 2005).

living than before, but this development simultaneously worsened regional and urban poverty. In this sense, the Chinese experience has shown the inadequacy of neo-liberal policy prescriptions for poverty reduction through single-minded pursuit of economic growth alone. As Seipel (2003) emphasised, the fight against poverty is not only a matter of wealth creation but is also concerned with mechanisms for wealth redistribution.

Secondly, with regard to institution-building and with an understanding of poverty as 'part of a socially and symbolically created hierarchy' (Øyen 1996, 15), it is necessary to consider poverty in the context of social stratification. In Mao's egalitarian society, class divisions were minimal and the degree of relative poverty was low. The economic reforms saw the emergence of a new form of social stratification, however, creating what has been called 'a new state-mediated class-divided society' (So 2003, 374). This change in social stratification has reduced the power of the working class, making poverty, which was previously a rural problem, an urban problem as well. Urbanisation and marketisation, while blurring the fixed socio-economic boundaries and eroding the spatially and socially urban-rural dualistic structures through encouraging rural-urban migration, have tended to generate new forms of poverty and new marginalised groups including rural migrants. In these ways, this study has illustrated institutional change and its consequences for social stratification. Thus, the Chinese case offers a good example of the interaction between institution-building and state reform policies in their impacts on poverty alleviation.

Thirdly, with regard to the state's role in poverty reduction, when social help was provided mainly through collective and communal means, the state itself was reluctant to engage directly in welfare assistance (Chen, S.H. 2003). Dismantling the collective welfare system induced people to seek help from state agencies (Ngan and Hui 1996), but how effectively these agencies met with their needs still remains unclear. Thus it is important to rethink the merits of collective welfare, keeping in mind the question as to whether or not a new form of collective welfare could be reconstructed. It also raises the question as to the best means of promoting the engagement of civil society agents in poor relief efforts. In recent years there has been a growing influence of NGOs engaged in the state's anti-poverty projects, including the Hope Project (or *xiwang gongcheng*, developing primary schools in poor regions), the Happiness Project (or *xingfu gongcheng,* assisting poor mothers) and the Aid-the-Poor-through-Culture project (or *wenhua fupin gongcheng*, see Zheng 2002). However, these actions still seem inadequate to fill the welfare vacancy caused by the collapse of collective welfare.

Finally, with regard to the forms of state anti-poverty policy, China has adopted a development-oriented strategy in the last two decades. In this policy, the state pays the poor relief funds both directly in the form of poor relief and indirectly through work-relief projects.[11] This strategy has been implemented successfully; today China had achieved the lowest incidence of poverty among the developing

11 Poor people who are involved in the work-relief projects can get the relief payments paid as wages for their work in government-organised projects for improving local facilities and infrastructure.

countries (Xinhua News Agency, 2000). However, this incremental strategy has its limits in resolving the problems of relative poverty and social exclusion. In this context, redistributive policies have been called for, leading to a rapid expansion of state welfare programmes in the late 1990s.[12] As a consequence, it is necessary to consider how best to integrate redistributive policies and developmental policies and how to build up the balance between these two policy dimensions in order to achieve the policy goals both of economic growth and of equity and social cohesion.

This chapter has examined the historical origin and the evolution of patterns of Chinese poverty linking it to the institutional contexts of this evolution. It has discussed the influences of market-oriented development on changing the nature of class, power and social stratification. Revealing these influences is essential for understanding the poverty patterns of any society, since as Schmidt (1995) stated, the degree and form of state intervention are subject to developmental processes, the degree of prosperity in society, the division of labour and the state's responsibility for the poor. Moreover, this study has attempted to understand the conditions for marginalisation in China. Since marginalisation is an outcome of particular forms of social stratification, a study of the latter enriches an understanding of the nature and dynamics of marginalisation. To a certain extent, the causes of marginalisation are similar to the causes generating relative poverty and social exclusion. In this regard, therefore, the study of relative poverty and social exclusion in this chapter has attempted to throw light on the institutional factors for marginalisation and the best possible means of tackling it.

References

Bai, T.L. (2004), 'A Reporter's Observation, The First Light of Early Dawn in regard to Social Security for the Migrant Workers from Villages', *People's Daily*, 30 August 2004.

Bian, Y.J. (2002), 'Chinese Social Stratification and Social Mobility', *Annual Review of Sociology*, Vol. 28, 91-116.

Chen, N.H. (2003), 'Paradigm Shifts in Social Welfare Policy Making in China, Struggling between Economic Efficiency and Social Equality', in Jones-Finer, C. (ed.), *Social Policy Reform in China: Views from Home and Abroad*, Aldershot, Ashgate, pp. 51-68.

Chen, S.Y. (2003), The Context of Social Policy Reform in China, Theoretical, Comparative and Historical Perspectives, in Jones Finer, C. (ed.), *Social Policy Reform in China: Views from Home and Abroad*, Aldershot: Ashgate, pp. 23-36.

China.com (2004), Increased from 30 millions to 90 millions – why the more assistance to give but the more population in poverty, available from http://news.china.com/zh_cn/domestic/945/20040423/11672623.html [Accessed 1 March 2006].

12 For instance in the Minimum Living Standard System, the number of beneficiaries in 2000 was only 4 million nationwide, but reached 22 million by the end of 2004 (IOCSC 2004a, Xinhua News Agency 2005).

Fan, C.C. (2002), 'The Elite, the Natives, and the Outsiders, Migration and Labour Market Segmentation in Urban China', *Annals of the Association of American Geographers*, Vol. 92 (1), 103-124.

Fan, P. (1996), 'Urban Low Income Earners in China – A Sociological Investigation of the Urban Poor in Employment', *Social Sciences in China*, No. 4, 64-77.

Fang, C., Zhang, X. and Fan, S. (2004), 'Urban Poverty and Inequality in the Era of Reforms', in Chen, A., Liu, G.G. and Zhang, K. H. (eds), *Urbanization and Social Welfare in China*, Aldershot, Ashgate, pp. 199-218.

Gore, C. with Figueiredo, J.B. and Rorgers, G. (1995), 'Introduction', in Rorgers, G., Gore, C. and Figueiredo, J. B. (eds), *Social Exclusion, Rhetoric, Reality, Responses*, Geneva, ILO, pp. 1-42.

Guan, X.P. (2003), 'Policies Geared to Tackling Social Inequality and Poverty in China', in Jones Finer, C. (ed.), *Social Policy Reform in China: Views from Home and Abroad*, Aldershot, Ashgate, pp. 69-87.

Guo, Y.-F. (2005), 'Entering the Sphere of Social Protection for Migrant Workers on Health Care', http//society.people.com.cn/GB/1063/3591543.html, [accessed 1 March 2006].

Gurung, G.S. and Kollmair, M. (2005), *Marginality, Concepts and Their Limitations*, IP6 Working Paper No. 4, Zurich, University of Zurich.

Information Office of the State Council, P.R.C. (IOCSC) (2005), *China's Progress in Human Rights in 2004*, available from http://news.xinhuanet.com/zhengfu/2002-11/22/content_638035.htm, [Accessed 1 March 2006].

IOCSC (2001), 'The Development-oriented Poverty Reduction Program for Rural China', available from http://news.xinhuanet.com/zhengfu/2002-11/18/content_633166.htm [Accessed 1 March 2006].

IOCSC (2002), 'Labour and Social Security in China', available from http://news.xinhuanet.com/zhengfu/2002-11/22/content_638035.htm [Accessed 1 March 2006].

IOCSC (2004a), 'China's Social Security and Its Policy', available from http://news.xinhuanet.com/zhengfu/2002-11/22/content_638035.htm [Accessed 1 March 2006].

IOCSC (2004b), 'China's Employment Situation and Policies', http://news.xinhuanet.com/zhengfu/2002-11/22/content_638035.htm [Accessed 1 March 2006].

Kang X.G. (2002) 'The Chinese Poverty and the Strategy of Combating Poverty during the 1990s', The China Information Net of The Poor Relief available from http://www.help-poverty.org.cn/helpweb2/pupinjingcuixia/jcx2-1.htm [Accessed 1 March 2006].

Lee, G.O.M. (2001), 'Labour Policy Reform', in Wong, L. and Flynn, N. (eds), *The Market in Chinese Social Policy*, Basingstoke, Palgrave, pp. 12-37.

Leung, J.C.B. (1995), 'The Political Economy of Unemployment and Unemployment Insurance in the People's Republic of China'. *International Social Work* Vol. 38, 139-149.

Li, S. and Gustsfsson, B. (1996), 'An Estimate of the Extent and Scale of Poverty During the Late 1980s in China', *Social Sciences in China*, No. 6, 24-44.

Li, W. and Wang, S.G. (2004); 'The Distribution of the Poor Relief Fund from the Central Government and the Analysis of Influencing Factors', *The Chinese Rural Economy*, Vol. 8; 44-48.

Liang, Z., Chen, Y.P. and Gu, Y. (2004), 'Rural Industrialization and Internal Migration in China', in Chen, A., Liu, G.G. and Zhang, K.H. (eds), *Urbanization and Social Welfare in China*, Aldershot, Ashgate, pp. 199-218.

Lu, J.C. (2002), 'A Study on the Application of the Theories on the Transferring the Surplus of Agricultural Production', *Forum of Executive Administration* (Ha'erbin), Vol. 9.

Madanipour, A., Cars, G., Allen, J. (eds.), (1998), *Social Exclusion in European Cities, Processes, Experiences and Responses*, London, Routledge.

Ministry of Commerce of PRC (2004), The Exchange Rate of Chinese Yuan to US Dollar since 1979. available from http//gcs.mofcom.gov.cn/aarticle/Nocategory/200405/20040500218170.html. [Accessed 1 March 2006].

Mok, B-H. (1987), Social Welfare in China in an Era of Economic Reform, *International Social Work*, Vol. 30, 237-50.

National Bureau of Statistics of China (NBSC) (1986, 1996, 2004). *China Statistical Yearbook.* Beijing, Zhongguo tongji chubanshe.

Ngan, R. and Hui, S. (1996), 'Economic and Social Development in Hong Kong and Southern China, Implications for Social Work', *International Social Work*, Vol. 39, 83-95.

Nie, R. (2003), 'Research on the Chinese Strategy of Transferring Rudimental Labour out of the Agricultural Sector', *Rural Economy* (Shenyang), Vol. 10, 31.

Novak, M. (1996), 'Concept of Poverty', in Øyen, E. Miller, S.M. and Samad, S.A. (eds.), *Poverty, A Global Review*. Handbook on International Poverty Research, Oslo, Scandinavian University Press, pp. 47-62.

Paugam, S. (1996), 'Poverty and Social Disqualification, A Comparative Analysis of Cumulative Social Disadvantage in Europe', *Journal of European Social Policy,* Vol. 6 (4), 287-303.

Schmidt, S. (1995), 'Social Security in Developing Countries, Basic Tenets and Fields of State Intervention', *International Social Work*, Vol. 38, 7-26.

Seipel, M.M.O. (2003), 'Global Poverty, No Longer an Untouchable Problem', *International Social Work* 46 (2), 191-207.

Shen, H. (2000), 'The Sociological Review of Poverty Studies in China', *Sociological Studies* (in Chinese), No. 2.

Silva, K.T. and Athukorala, K. (1996), 'South Asia, An Overview', in Øyen, E. Miller, S.M. and Samad, S. A. (eds.), *Poverty, A Global Review*. Handbook on International Poverty Research, Oslo, Scandinavian University Press, pp. 65-85.

So, A.Y. (2003), The Changing Pattern of Classes and Class Conflict in China, *Journal of Contemporary Asia*, Vol. 33 (3), 363-376.

Tang, J. (2004), 'An Analysis of the Chinese Condition of Poverty and Poverty Elimination', available from http://www.sociology.cass.cn/shxw/shwt/P020040710270550158392.pdf, [Accessed 1 March 2006].

Tang J. (2002), 'The Origin and Development of Chinese Urban Poverty', *The Chinese Forum of the Party and Executive Personnel* (in Chinese), No. 3, available from http://www.popinfo.gov.cn/popinfo/pop_docrkxx.nsf/v_rkbl/FAF3D9C7826DFB6848256E7C00235BE0 [Accessed 1 March 2006].

Townsend, P. (1971), 'Measures and Explanations of Poverty in High Income and Low Income Countries, The Problems of Operating the Concepts of Development, Class and Poverty', in Townsend, P. (ed.), *The Concept of Poverty*, London, Heinemann, pp. 1-45.

Unger, J. (2002), *The Transformation of Rural China*, London, M.E. Sharpe.

Wang F.-Y. and Zhao, Y-D. (2003) 'Labor Market Construction and Labor Mobility in Urban China', in Jones Finer, C. (ed.), *Social Policy Reform in China: Views from Home and Abroad*, Aldershot, Ashgate, pp. 97-116.

Wang, S.G. (2001), 'Combating Poverty and the State Intervention', in Sun, R.M. et al (eds.), *The Survey Report on the Governmental Behaviors in Social Action of Poor Relief.* Beijing, Zhongguo jingji chubanshe.

Wilson, F. (1996), 'Drawing together Some Regional Perspectives on Poverty', in Øyen, E. 1996, Poverty Research Rethought, in Øyen, E. Miller, S.M. & Samad, S.A. (eds.), *Poverty, A Global Review.* Handbook on International Poverty Research, Oslo, Scandinavian University Press. pp. 18-32.

Wong L.-D. (1998), *Marginalization and Social Welfare in China*, London, Routledge.

Xiao L. and Wang Y. (1986), 'The Welfare System as It Applied to Staff and Workers in China', *International Social Science Journal*, Vol. 109 ,449-458.

Xinhua News Agency (2000), 'China Has Met with People's Basic Need of Food for the Rural Population', available from http://www.gdyunan.gov.cn/news/SSCJNEWS/yunannews_ss_p13_16_11_2000.html [Accessed 1 March 2006].

Xinhua News Agency (2005), 'The Minimum Living Standard System Has Covered Almost All Eligible Applicants', available from http://news.tom.com/1002/20050103-1717761.html, [Accessed 1 March 2006].

Xun J-l (2003) Poor Relief, A Serious Topic, available from http://www.sociology.cass.net.cn/shxw/pkyj/t20030829_0971.htm, [Accessed 1 March 2006].

Zheng, G-C. (2002), 'Poverty Problem and the Development of NGO in Poverty Reduction of China', *China Soft Science* (in Chinese), 2002, Vol. 7. available from http://www.ngocn.org/Article/ShowArticle.asp?ArticleID=396 [Accessed 1 March 2006].

Zhou Q.-R. (1994), 'Chinese Rural Reform, State and the Ownership Transformation'. *Chinese Social Sciences Quarterly* (HK), No. 8.

Zhu, L. (2001), 'The Political Economy of Poverty in the Transitional States', in Sun, R.-M. et al (eds.), *The Survey Report on the Governmental Behaviors in Social Action of Poor Relief.* Beijing, Zhongguo jingji chubanshe.

Zhu, Q.-F. (2003), 'Traits of Urban Vulnerable Groups, Causes of Poverty and the Tackling Policies', available from http://www.sociology.cass.net.cn/shxw/shwt/t20031028_1579.htm, [Accessed 1 March 2006].

Zhu, X-Y (2004), 'New Strategy of Combating Poverty', *Sociological Research* (in Chinese), Vol. 2.

Øyen, E. (1996), Poverty Research Rethought, in Øyen, E. Miller, S.M. & Samad, S. A. (eds.), *Poverty, A Global Review.* Handbook on International Poverty Research, Oslo, Scandinavian University Press, pp. 3-17.

PART 2
Marginalisation in the Era of Globalisation in China

Chapter 8

Globalisation and Marginalisation of Chinese Overseas Contract Workers

Bin Wu

Introduction

As China becomes ever more integrated into the world economy, increasing numbers of Chinese workers have the opportunity to take jobs abroad. However, while considerable attention has been given both to the experiences of skilled or professional workers and to illegal migration (Chin, 2003; Laczko, 2003; Zhang, 2003; Gao, 2004; Liang and Morooka, 2004), little is known about overseas contract workers who go abroad via authorised recruitment agencies to provide labour services for foreign employers for limited periods of time.

Agreements on overseas labour services formed part of the World Trade Organization's (WTO) General Agreement on Trade in Services (GATS) in 2001 at Doha which highlighted the need for the increased liberalisation of movement of peoples to supply labour services across national boundaries (termed GATS Mode 4, OECD 2002: 6). Not limited to skilled workers, in principle Mode 4 covers service suppliers at all skill levels with an emphasis on the forms and nature of temporary movements of workers and the rules governing them. With China's accession to WTO in 2001, unsurprisingly, the provision of overseas labour services has been viewed as a part of China's national strategy of 'opening up to the outside world', a strategy which currently involves hundreds of thousands of Chinese workers going abroad to find employment.

Overseas labour services have widely been recognised as an important means for developing countries such as China not only to earn foreign exchange and utilise labour resources, but also to alleviate unemployment and promote domestic economic growth. As a result, Chinese overseas contract workers have the potential to make significant economic contributions not only to themselves and their families but to their localities and to China generally. However, little is known about the costs to overseas contract workers of finding employment abroad. This chapter focuses on the costs and benefits to overseas contract workers while employed abroad and it argues that those costs and benefits are unevenly distributed. The term *marginalisation* will be used in this chapter to refer to the process whereby the benefits gained by overseas contract workers are not matched by the costs they have to bear.

Marginalisation of Chinese contract workers cannot be separated from changes in the overall labour market system in China. Alongside the national economic transition from plan to the market, the monopoly of state-owned enterprises (hereafter

SOEs) in the provision of overseas labour services has been broken, resulting in the emergence of a new sector servicing the labour market in China comprising brokers specialising in the recruitment, documentation and the posting of contract workers abroad. Many questions arise regarding the impact of globalisation and economic transition on Chinese contract workers. For example, to what extent has an overseas labour service market established in China? Do Chinese contract workers suffer from marginalisation in the processes involved in overseas labour service provision and, if so, to what extent and in what ways? What is the relationship between the marginalisation of Chinese contract workers and the transformation and regulation of the overseas labour service system?

This chapter addresses the above questions through an intensive collection and review of secondary information including governmental documents, published reports and other relevant information supported by two empirical surveys conducted by the author in 2003 and 2004 respectively into the behaviour and experience of Chinese seafarers. By combining questionnaire and semi-structured interviews (Wu, 2004a, 2005; Wu and Liang, 2005), it is possible to glean important insights into the impact of globalisation and marginalisation upon this particular pioneering group of Chinese contract workers.

Globalisation and Marginalisation of Foreign Workers

Globalisation involves, increasingly, international flows not only of capital, finance, commodities, technology and information, but also of labour (Overbeek, 2002; Rowley and Benson, 2000). Currently, there are 81 million workers living outside their countries of origin world-wide and the number is still growing (ILO, 2004). While international migration has become an important element of globalisation, the working conditions, pay and rights of foreign workers vary greatly depending upon skill levels, the industrial sectors involved and the particularities of the sending and host countries respectively. In contrast to managerial and highly skilled workers who are normally welcome world-wide as a key element of the 'knowledge economy', globalisation and labour flexibility have led to the emergence of marginalised immigrant sectors in many host countries. According to Ruths (2003), these immigrant sectors comprise workers doing "undesirable jobs" in "undesirable sectors" (i.e. "3-D" jobs referring to those which are dirty, dangerous and difficult), which "natives no longer wish to take up, [and] have constituted major reasons for the inflow and concentrated employment of foreign workers in these sectors". To cope with the shortage of labour in these sectors, many countries have adopted various Temporary Foreign Worker Programmes (TFWP) for temporary admission, residence and employment of foreign workers (Ruths, 2003).

The structural demand for low and unskilled foreign workers in these sectors can be explained by the dual labour market hypothesis (Berger and Piore, 1980) in which the overall labour market is divided into two segments, with the primary segment open to native workers only, thus confining immigrant workers to the secondary segment. Compared with high and secure pay levels, a high degree of regulation and a long-term perspective in the former, the latter is more likely to be characterised by deregulation, low pay and high labour turnover (Leontaridi, 1998). Whilst native and high-skilled workers in the host countries are prioritised with regard to economic focus and social provision there, low and unskilled migrant workers find themselves at the back of the queue.

All foreign workers are potentially vulnerable to exploitation, but this is particularly true for low or unskilled workers because they "have been utilised in (both) developed and underdeveloped economies as a low cost means of sustaining economic enterprises and sometimes entire sectors that are only marginally viable or competitive" (Taran, 2001). Thus it is not surprising that foreign workers frequently work very long hours with low pay and have limited possibilities to demand benefits or other forms of protection. In order to protect the rights of temporary foreign workers, the International Labour Organization has tried to establish a set of international standards to ensure equal treatment between foreign and native workers in respect of remuneration and other conditions of work and terms of employment (ILO, 2004: 42). Such efforts, however, have yet to lead to any significant progress because 'international standards for the protection of temporary foreign workers' rights in the receiving country are not widely ratified' (Ruths, 2003). As a result, temporary foreign workers are "inherently more vulnerable to deprivation of even their most basic rights than the citizens (and permanent residents) of both sending and receiving countries" (Ruths, 2003). The term *marginality* here refers to the marginal position and vulnerability of the contract workers in foreign/international labour markets, while *marginalisation* refers to the processes, dynamics and consequences leading to the marginality of overseas workers. The former is used to refer to the economic, social and political status of contracted workers in a host country compared with native or highly skilled workers. The latter is employed to link that marginality with the broad background and dynamics related to globalisation and economic and social changes in the home society.

Marginality and marginalisation of overseas contract workers are not new phenomena. Social isolation and exclusion of foreign workers have been recognised by many scholars. For instance, as long ago as 1928, Park described foreign workers as "marginal men" who are "strangers" to the host society. Later, Siu (1952) conceptualised the term 'sojourner' to refer to the overseas worker who "clings to the cultural heritage of his own ethnic group and tends to live in isolation, hindering his assimilation to the society in which he resides". Meanwhile, economic exploitation of contract workers can be traced back to the coolie system employed over two centuries ago. The term 'coolie' was derived from the Chinese phrase *ku li* (meaning 'hard labour'), and was used to describe "any overworked and exploited worker" (Potts, 1990: 63). It was first used to refer to those Chinese workers who were being exported to various parts of Southeast Asia in brutal fashion, the term 'Shanghaied' dating back to the capture of Chinese peasants for export at that time. The working conditions and social situation of these Chinese workers were characterised by a total lack of rights and the absence of rights was experienced not only by those who had been abducted against their will, but also by those who had been inveigled into signing a contract because they had no alternative. Coolies who signed such a document lost every opportunity of defending themselves against exploitation (Potts, 1990: 88).

In spite of fundamental differences from the coolie system of two centuries ago in terms of the economic, social and political regimes involved, questions of forced and/or bonded labour are still issues facing many Chinese workers, to include both rural migrants to urban China and unregulated Chinese workers going abroad (Chan, 2003; Gao, 2004). Today's contract workers worldwide still suffer from marginality as a result of many factors. First, there is an abundant supply of overseas workers and intense competition between recruitment agencies within both the home (sending) and host (receiving) countries. As a result, employers in the relevant labour market segments seek to maintain their small margins by squeezing workers wages in a "bargain basement" fashion (ILO, 2004: 45). Second, while the establishment and involvement of private recruitment agents may be more effective than public recruitment agencies in linking employers in the receiving country with overseas workers in the sending country, they may be more difficult to regulate, resulting in misinformation, overcharging and low payment (Ruths, 2003). Finally, but no less important, it is difficult for international labour standards to adequately protect foreign workers partly because "the sending country does not have any legal jurisdiction outside its territory" and partly because the host county is "often reluctant to assume full responsibilities unless migrant workers are permanent residents or become citizens" (Ruths, 2003).

While overwhelming attention is paid to the marginality of contract workers in receiving countries, few scholars have written about the linkages between that marginality and the processes and management of overseas labour services in the sending countries (Xiang, 2003). While Huang (1996) explored the impacts of China's economic reform on emigration pressure and the overseas labour service, this chapter attempts to go further by examining the marginality of Chinese contract workers in the context of changes in China's overseas labour service system.

The Transformation of the Overseas Labour Service System in China

Globalisation is a double-edged sword for Chinese workers. On the one hand, it has brought more working opportunities for them to earn foreign exchange in the overseas labour market and to reduce the pressure of unemployment in China. One the other hand, like many foreign workers overseas, Chinese workers find themselves vulnerable and marginalised as soon as they enter the overseas labour service process.

The term *overseas labour service process* in this chapter refers to a process of recruiting, managing, and controlling contract workers to fulfil a labour service contract which is approved by the sending governmental or otherwise authorised institution. According to this definition, an overseas labour service system normally contains the following elements:

- A labour service contract, which has been negotiated and agreed by both sending and receiving operators (e.g. relevant departments, organisations or companies). This may be differentiated from many overseas labour service contracts which are negotiated and signed between migrant workers and overseas employers or their representatives directly.

- A triangular relation involving the contract workers, the recruitment agencies in the sending country and the overseas employers.
- Government involvement. An overseas labour service involves not only individual economic activities or business operations, but policy intervention by the government of the sending country to fulfil its economic, social or political objectives.
- A limited term contract and the circulation of contracted workers, to be differentiated from the processes associated with permanent migration.

China's overseas labour service system has seen fundamental changes since 1949 when the Communist Party took power. In the 1950s, it was used to further the government's broad international political objectives whereby large numbers of Chinese workers were sent to the former Soviet Union and Eastern European countries to combat labour shortages there. During the period of the 1960s and 1970s, many developing countries in Asia, Africa and Latin America became the destinations of contract workers in order to implement the government's international aid programmes (Skeldon, 1996).

From the 1980s onwards, however, overseas labour services have no longer been viewed in China purely as a means of promoting national political tasks. Rather they have been used as a means whereby important *economic* objectives can be promoted, to include both the earning of foreign exchange and the stimulation of local economic development through remittances. Overseas labour services have taken place through two major channels: through overseas contracted engineering projects (e.g. roads, bridges, stadiums and power stations) and through contracted labour services (Xiang, 2003). In the 1980s, the former predominated and the large state-owned construction companies played leading roles in the recruitment of labour to fulfil the contracted projects abroad. Since the 1990s, however, contracted labour services have predominated, with the newly developing labour brokers becoming the dominant channel for Chinese workers to work abroad (Wang, 1995; Huang, 1996).

The overseas labour service system has become an important part of China's 'opening to the outside world', a strategy which has been encouraged by the Chinese government at national and local levels. The number of contract workers working abroad, according to official statistics, has rapidly increased from only 52,000 in 1990 to 253,000 in 2000, a five-fold increase within ten years; by 2004, the total of Chinese contracted workers in abroad had reached over 532,000 compared with only 67,000 in 1990 (Table 8.1). The major destination for Chinese overseas contract workers is (non-Chinese) Asia whose share of the total has increased from 47% to 72% during the period. They are concentrated in textile and garment manufacturing (38%), the construction industry (26%) and agriculture (14%) and the vast majority are low or unskilled workers (CHINCA, 2005a).

Table 8.1 Number of Chinese overseas contract workers in selected years 1987-2004

Year	No. of sent workers	Total workers abroad
1987	--	63,200
1990	52,366	67,000
1995	194,258	264,535
2000	252,575	425,687
2004*	210,000	532,000

*from January to November 2004.
Source: China International Contract Association, 2005a.

The management of overseas labour services in China currently involves three different elements (MOFCOM, 2004). Firstly, special licences to recruitment agencies are issued by authorities on behalf of the central government. Without a central government licence, in principle, neither company nor individual is allowed to be involved in overseas labour services. Secondly, a deposit is paid to the government for the purposes of monitoring the process and to cover any other costs. Thirdly, full responsibility for the training and managing of the overseas contract workers is devolved to the recruitment agencies. This means that a recruitment agency is more than a labour broker, but also a genuine part *employer*, taking responsibility for controlling and managing contract workers abroad. In this regard, the foreign employer is better conceptualised as a *partner* of the Chinese recruitment agency, supervising and ensuring that Chinese workers follow the service contract. Reflecting such a complex situation, there are, in theory, three contracts signed between the foreign client, the Chinese recruitment agency and the contract workers simultaneously. In practice, however, the contract between the foreign employer and the Chinese licensed recruitment agency is the only one that matters in that it defines terms for the period of employment, wages, bonuses, working hours, the sharing of transportation costs, accommodation arrangements, working conditions and insurance. Based upon this document, the recruitment agency is then able to go into the domestic labour market to recruit qualified workers and sign service contracts. Under normal circumstances, therefore, the foreign employer has little or no involvement in the process of selection and recruitment of workers while the workers themselves have little opportunity to see the original contract between the recruitment agency and the foreign employer. The 'triangular contract' remains so in theory only.

The above policies were initially established and implemented in the 1980s through the Ministry of Foreign Trade and International Economic Cooperation (now part of the Ministry of Commerce, hereafter MOFCOM), which had previously controlled and managed the SOEs with overseas project contracts when most of the contract workers were actually their employees. But as part of China's economic reform, with SOEs becoming increasingly independent of the government, MOFCOM began to relinquish the control of SOE enterprises and took increasing responsibility for regulating the overseas labour service system generally. In practice, the local branch of MOFCOM took responsibility for the overall regulation of the licensed agencies while the China International Contractor Association (CHINCA) took charge of managing and coordinating them from the perspective of their sectoral division (e.g. construction, catering, seafaring, fishing etc.). The tentacles of China's overseas labour service system have been extended overseas through the business sections of Chinese Embassies in host countries, which are responsible for the collection of market information, the verification of proposed projects, the monitoring of labour contract implementation and the handling of labour abuse issues or emerging events.

The monopoly of SOEs in overseas labour service provision was broken in the early 1990s when the Ministry of Labour (now Ministry of Labour and Social Security, hereafter MOLSS) began to involve itself in overseas labour services (Huang, 1996; China Labour Market – hereafter CLM, 2005a). Similar to its counterpart, MOFCOM, MOLSS began to issue licences to qualified labour brokers and managed deposits collected from the licensed agencies. The two government departments today, however, have different emphases on and approaches to the regulation of overseas labour services (Xie, 2004) reflected in their different requirements for issuing licences to recruitment agencies (Table 8.2). For instance, MOFCOM views overseas labour services within the context of international economic cooperation, while MOLSS' emphasis is on the quantity and quality of overseas employment *per se*. The former is favoured by the SOEs because of their marketing experience and the business scale while the latter has removed constraints on non-SOE agency registration and is thus favoured by them. As a result, we have witnessed the emergence of two regulatory systems headed by two different government ministries. In Shanghai, for instance, there are 28 recruitment agencies registered by MOFCOM while 23 have been licensed by MOLSS (CLM, 2005b).

Table 8.2 Comparison of recruitment agencies registered in different ministries

Ministry	MOFCOM	MOLSS
Objective	International economic cooperation	Labour broker for overseas employment
Minimum Requirements	3 year experience; minimum scale: 300 workers	No experience required except basic qualification of staff
Ownership	All SOEs until 2004	No constraints, ¾ are non-SOE
Deposit to Authority	1 million Yuan	Half million Yuan

Source: CLM, 2005a.

As the Chinese economy has increasingly opened its doors to the outside world, the provision of overseas labour services has become an emerging industry and a large number of labour brokers have been established in China. Not limited to MOFCOM and MOLSS, many labour brokers have gained licences from other ministries to include the Ministries of Education, Public Security and Foreign Affairs. Most of them are allied with MOFCOM and MOLSS in order to ensure that all licensed agencies complete valid procedures associated with recruitment and documentation. However, the regulatory system is not unified and is inconsistent in process and principle. Moreover, there is no trade union or similar organisation involved in the process, a critical institutional absence in the current circumstances.

Marginality of Chinese Contract Workers

While the impressive growth of the Chinese overseas labour service has brought more and more job opportunities for Chinese employment abroad, not all contract workers enjoy their working experience. Rather, many feel isolated, vulnerable and marginalised.

The marginality of Chinese workers is rooted in the overseas labour service process. According to current regulations, a contract worker needs to pay the recruitment agency a deposit of up to 20% of the total predicted salary for the purpose of ensuring the completion of the signed labour contract. It can be refunded if both the foreign client and the recruitment agency are satisfied with the worker's performance abroad. In addition, s/he is also required to pay the agency up to 25% of his/her total income as service charges. The above costs do not include other expenditures such as the costs of training, a health examination, passport, visa and certification. Taking a two year contract for a job paying 100,000 RMB (or US$12,000) as an example, therefore, it is possible for contract workers to pay to the recruitment agency as much as 45,000 RMB in advance before they gain all the valid documentations they need to start their journeys abroad. Chinese contract workers in Israel, according to Ellman and Laacher (2003), are often the worst affected compared with other nationalities. While a Chinese construction worker pays US$6,000-$10,000 to come to Israel (including $4,000 deposit, $1,500 airfare and $4,000 to mediators, employers and contacts), this is in contrast to only $5,000 paid by a Filipino home nurse (Kav LaOved, 2002). Clearly, it is the contract workers, rather than recruitment agencies, who take the economic risks before they can earn money in the overseas labour market. Yet to get access to that market, most if not all contracted workers have to borrow from their relatives and friends. Although the Chinese government has recently abolished the personal deposit and introduced a form of insurance instead, the principle behind such a policy is problematic in that the recruitment agency and contract workers are unequally treated, the former secures the profit while the latter takes the risk.

The vulnerability of Chinese overseas contract workers is also related to the long chain between them and the foreign clients. As stated above, in theory the system involves a 'triangular contract' between the foreign client, the recruitment agency and the contract worker. In practice, the foreign client is not the ultimate employer of the Chinese contract workers: there is neither any negotiation between Chinese workers and foreign employers nor is there a signed contract between them in most cases. Inevitably, there are many labour brokers involved in the process who are sharing the benefits, leading to an increase in the total costs of the recruitment process and a decline in the income of contract workers. Labour brokers are more likely those individuals or small firms who are registered locally as a labour consultant or relevant company to provide any kind of information related to overseas employment. Although alliances between unlicensed labour brokers and licensed agencies are not allowed, this cannot be prohibited in practice partly because licensed agencies do not always have foreign clients on their books while unlicensed agents may represent a number of desirable potential contract workers who trust them and are willing to pay them a premium. Frequently, contract workers find that working conditions and pay at their destination are totally different from what they were led to believe at home, and in some extreme cases, there is no job at all. Taking into account the complexity of the overseas labour market environment and the limited information available, unsurprisingly, it is very difficult for a Chinese worker to determine what exactly a real job abroad entails and whether it is worth borrowing a large amount of money to secure it (Wu, N. 2004).

Driven by strong demand for overseas employment, generating high profits at little risk for agencies, international labour brokerage has become a growing industry in China (Hong Kong Liaison Office, hereafter HKLO, 2004; Li, 2004). Lacking unified national regulation and coordination, together with intense competition between agencies, however, has led to the degradation of wages and working conditions of Chinese overseas contract workers. For example, in the early 1980s a contract worker could earn 150,000 Japanese yen per month (120,000 yen to the contract worker and 30,000 yen to the recruitment agency), which is in stark contrast to the 80,000 yen per month or less he/she could earn in the early 2000s (60,000 yen to the worker and 20,000 yen to the agency) (Zha, 2001; Wang, 2003). The major explanation for this, according to the China International Contractors Association (CHICA, 2005a), is related to the lack of discipline and unified regulation in China, which has resulted in a vicious circle of decline both of agents' profits and workers' wages.

Frequently heavily burdened with debt as a result of securing their overseas jobs, Chinese contract workers are particularly vulnerable to any changes in the host countries or in international markets. The removal of textile and garment quotas world-wide with the final abandonment of the Multi-Fibre Arrangement in 2005, for instance, has threatened thousands of Chinese contract workers who have gone aboard and have yet to earn enough money to pay off their loans. Unsurprisingly, this has caused industrial relation tensions between contract workers, recruitment agencies and foreign employers (see CHICA, 2004, 2005b, 2005c). To pay back the borrowed money, many of them have had to overstay in the host country, a change of their status from legal to illegal migration, in order to continue to work aboard.

Because there is no effective measure to protect contract workers, frequent incidents of labour abuses are inevitable (CLM, 2005a; ITGLWF, 2005; Ma, 2005; Wu, N., 2004). From September 2002 to the end of 2004, the Complaints Centre of the China International Contractors Association received 129 complaints, involving

1598 contract workers (CHICA 2005b). The above figures, however, are merely the tip of the iceberg because this Centre only deals with cases related to the licensed agencies registered within CHICA.

The marginality of Chinese contract workers is illustrated by the case reported below which exposes some institutional issues behind the poor working conditions of many Chinese construction workers abroad (LCR, 2003).

> The case reported involves an agreement between an Israeli building contractor (A. Dori) and a Chinese contractor, to bring Chinese workers to Israel to build various phases of buildings for the Dori Company. The Chinese contractor and the Chinese workers signed labour contracts in China, the remuneration for two years work in Israel was to be paid when the workers returned to China [they were to receive a salary of about US$150 a month instead of the Israeli monthly minimum wage, which is about US$650].... This arrangement was illegal under Israeli law, which required the Israeli company receiving the work to be the employer and obtain a work permit from the government for each overseas worker. In addition, Israeli law compels an employer to pay the employee a minimum wage in Israel. To avoid this illegality the Chinese contractor told each of its employees to sign a labour contract with the Israeli contractor, who paid their salary and obtained work permits for them. However, the workers did not receive their salary; it was transferred by the Israeli contractor to the Israeli bank account of each overseas worker and then transferred to the bank account of the Chinese contractor. Such transfer was possible because the Chinese contractor ordered its workers to sign a power of attorney by which it controlled the bank accounts of the contract workers. As a result, when the Israeli contractor transferred the worker's wages to his Israeli bank account, the Chinese contractor immediately transferred this money from the worker's account to its account; therefore, in reality the worker did not receive any wage. The Chinese contractor gave each worker a small monthly allowance while they were in Israel – about 10% of the actual payment – prepared food for them and supervised their work. After about a year of this arrangement a local non-profit organisation (NPO) informed the workers of their rights and some of them began a strike, which received extensive media coverage. These workers were threatened by the Chinese contractor and received letters from a Chinese court (in their home city) and the police of this city informing them that the strike was illegal and they would be arrested and sentenced to prison upon their return to China. The NPO filed a case for these workers in the Israeli Labour Court to compel the Israeli contractor to pay them the minimum wage for the entire period they worked in Israel for the Dori Company.

This is a typical case which highlights the manner in which the Chinese contracting agency remains the effective employer of Chinese contract workers abroad. Regardless of labour standards in the host country, the Chinese authorities and recruitment agencies apply Chinese practices to the contract workers, which, more often than not, impact negatively on the conditions of overseas Chinese workers. And this is the reason why Chinese contract workers are not allowed to contact with local organisations or trade unions in host countries. It is not because the latter may not be able to help the Chinese workers; rather it is because the Chinese authorities do not want to raise the prospect of political debates over labour standards in China. Instead, contract workers are asked to contact the Chinese embassy in the host country or the Chinese contracting agency to seek for help, which, in most cases, are ineffective in addressing the issues.

To conclude, the evidence presented here points to two key factors that have contributed to the marginality of Chinese contract workers. First, the lack of an open labour market for foreign employers to recruit Chinese contract workers directly has made it impossible for Chinese contract workers to be treated equally with other nationalities in the host countries even if the foreign employers intended to do so. Second, the lack of political representation within a national debate has inevitably made Chinese contract workers vulnerable because the current fragmented regulatory system has given power to recruitment agencies to take a large amount of service charges from them with little risk and costs. Such an unbalanced and uneven distribution of benefits and costs has encouraged not only private labour brokers to join the competition in the provision of overseas labour services but also more government departments to share the powers and benefits. Such 'competition', however, does not necessarily lead to any improvement in overseas labour services, but instead has resulted in a deterioration of the working conditions of contract workers.

Bearing in mind the problems discussed above, the next section will bring the case of Chinese seafarers to the fore and examine the marginality of Chinese contract workers in the international labour market to explore the linkages between the marginalisation of Chinese workers and the opening up of the labour market for foreign employers in China.

Marginalisation and Transformation of Chinese Seafarers

The marginality of Chinese contract workers cannot be understood in isolation from the establishment and development of an overseas labour service market in China. In this regard, a good example is Chinese seafarers, a pioneering group of Chinese contract workers. There is a long history of Chinese seafarers participating in the international shipping business which can be traced back over 150 years (Benton and Pieke, 1998). In the first half of 20th century China was the largest supplier of seafarers in the world. This supply was interrupted during the period of 1950s to 1970s, but since the 1980s China reopened its doors to the outside world, leading to a strong growth of Chinese seafarer supply, from 9,733 in 1992 to over 40,000 in 2004 (CHINCA, 2004).

There are many reasons why Chinese seafarers are perceived as a good case to illustrate the themes of this chapter. Firstly, accounting for nearly 10% of the national total of overseas contract workers, Chinese seafarers are often viewed as a flagship of the overseas labour service because seafaring, like nursing, requires special training and certificates. Secondly, China has maintained a large national fleet (the fourth largest in the world) and the majority of vessels are controlled by SOE shipping companies. This offers opportunities to observe the impact of SOE companies on the nature of employment and working conditions of foreign employers (Wu, 2005). Finally, a global labour market has been established for the international shipping industry since the late 1970s, which has allowed shipowners or managers to recruit qualified and cheaper seafarers worldwide regardless of the constraints of host country regulations (ILO and SIRC, 2004). This makes it possible to compare and contrast the working conditions of Chinese contract workers with those of other nationalities. Today, about two thirds of the world's seafaring labour force work for foreign ships. Chinese seafarers share about 5% of the global labour market, far behind the Philippines (42%), and trailing Ukraine (7%) and India (7%) (Wu and Sampson, 2005). The potential growth of Chinese seafarers' market share, however, is enormous given China's huge labour supply, the large size of its seafaring population and the strength of its maritime education and training infrastructure (Wu, 2004a, Wu and Morris, 2006).

As a major supplier to the global labour market, Chinese seafarers are much cheaper than other nationalities (ISF, 2004). If the wage costs of an Indian chief officer are represented by a figure of 100%, ship-owners would pay 2.87 times more to the Norwegian seafarer but just 63% to the Chinese, even lower than to the Filipino seafarer. With regard to able seamen's remuneration, Chinese ratings (able seamen) earn only two thirds of Indian ratings. As a result, Chinese seafarers fall to the bottom of the global seafaring market in terms of pay. The difference in crewing costs between Chinese and Indian seafarers is in contrast to the gap in GDP per capita (in purchasing power terms) between the two countries, which is approximately USD$5,000 for China and US$2,900 for India (CIA, 2004).

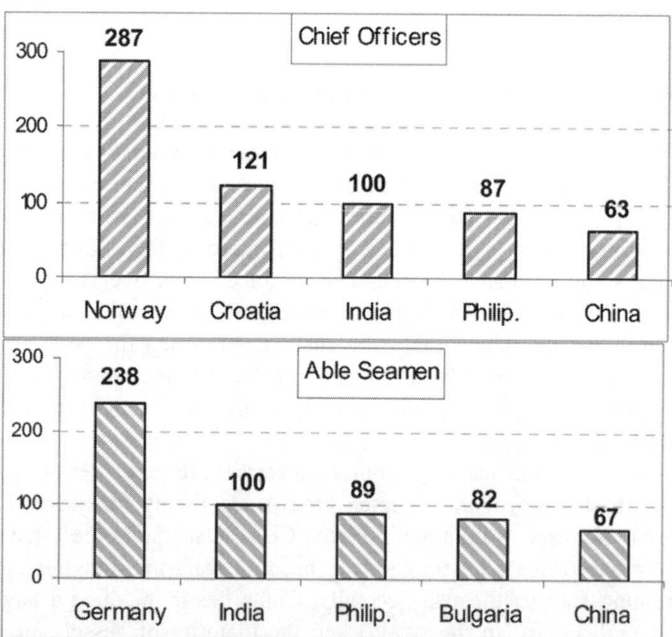

Figure 8.1 Comparative wage costs of seafarers by nationality and rank in 2002 (%)

The income gap shown in Figure 8.1 is the difference in costs for ship owners or managers. The actual income of Chinese seafarers is even less than Figure 8.1 indicates, however, because the agencies supplying the Chinese crews can take a proportion of the Chinese seafarers' wages as service charges, a situation quite different from that experienced by other nationalities who can gain full payment directly from foreign shipowners. Taking into account long chains between Chinese seafarers and the foreign shipowner, it was quite normal for 30-40% of seafarer salaries to be taken by recruitment agencies. Service charges, however, vary greatly agency by agency and case by case, depending upon many factors such as the number of labour brokers involved and the rank, experience and skill of the seafarers. In order to understand the nature and working conditions of Chinese contract seafarers in the global labour market, two field trips have been undertaken by the author in recent years. One was taken in the early 2003 at the anchorage area of the Hong Kong Port (Hong Kong survey thereafter) where I boarded nearly 50 ships with Chinese crews for both questionnaire survey and in-depth interviews (Wu, 2004a). The other was held in several recruitment agencies and labour brokers in Beijing and Dalian in Northeast China (China survey thereafter) in late 2004 when those seafarers, who were going to be sent to foreign ships to fulfil their labour contracts, were invited to participate in either questionnaire survey or interviews (Wu, 2005; Wu and Liang, 2005). Below is an interview quote taken in the Hong Kong survey from a third officer who was on board a foreign ship:

> I am a 3rd officer and have had five years of experience working with multinational crews in foreign vessels, Now I earn US$750 per month, less than half of my Filipinos colleagues. Comparing my skills with my colleagues from other Asian countries (e.g. the Philippines, Indonesia, India, Bangladesh, Burma), I feel it is unfair for Chinese seafarers to receive such low payment. More than the income itself, why should Chinese seafarers be so much 'cheaper' in the global labour market despite China becoming increasingly powerful in the world?

The poor working conditions of Chinese seafarers in the global labour market reflect not only the incomplete establishment and regulation of the Chinese seafaring labour market but also the lack of independent trade unions to protect the interests of Chinese seafarers. Another quotation also taken from the Hong Kong survey from a Chinese crew member amplifies this point:

> The big issue facing Chinese seafarers onboard foreign ships is the lack of an organisation to protect us. For instance, if any conflict happens with the shipping company, Filipinos may ask for their Seamen Union to provide legal assistance or submit their complaints to the International Transport Workers Federation (ITF). By contrast, we can do nothing because we are told to make no contact with the ITF, and cause no argument with the shipping company. Being at the bottom of the global seafarers in both income and political rights, we feel really vulnerable and frightened of making any minor mistakes as soon as we go onboard a ship.

This marginality of Chinese seafarers in the global labour market is related to the recent transformation of China's seafaring employment and management system. Before the 1990s, almost all Chinese ocean seafarers were permanently employed by SOE shipping companies and a few of them were sent to foreign ships to fulfil labour service contracts. However, alongside similar developments in other labour sectors in the 1990s discussed above, the monopoly of the SOE shipping companies for seafarer supply was broken as many crew agencies were established outside the shipping sector. In Dalian, for instance, there are currently over a hundred of labour brokers involved in the seafarer recruitment and sending business (interview with a private labour broker in the China survey).

Compared with SOE shipping companies, however, crew agencies are varied in nature (state owned or private), in scale (from a one person agent to a nationwide recruitment network), in regulatory status (licensed or un-licensed) and in marketing strategy (from information providers to effective employers). Large, state-owned crew agencies may keep a large number of seafarers through long term job contracts (5 years or longer, called "agency-owned" seafarers) similar to SOE shipping company's employees in terms of job security, welfare and career development opportunities. Seafarers hired by newly established, private, small, often unlicensed agencies not owning their own ships, however, face a very different state-of-affairs.

The establishment and development of such crew agencies have resulted in an emergence of 'free seamen' (*shehui chuanyuan*), a new group of Chinese seafarers whose primary employment target is the global labour market (Wu, 2004a, 2004b). In contrast to SOE employees and agency-owned seafarers, free seamen have no long-term relationships with Chinese shipping companies or crew agencies, but instead they are given short-term sailing contracts which enable them to work for foreign companies. However, free seamen have more bargaining power than the other two classes of seafarers for two reasons. First, the service charges for free seamen, according to current regulations, can be as low as 12.5% of their total income, just half that of SOE employees. Second, free seamen can contact and negotiate with many crew agencies and select the best offer. Thus, driven by the prospects of a higher income and more freedom to select suitable crew agencies and foreign employers, more and more Chinese seafarers have left SOE companies or state-owned crew agencies and become free seamen. According to the China Maritime Service Centre (CMSC), a semi-government organisation responsible for the registration of 'free seamen' nationwide, the number of the registered free seamen has rapidly grown from 4,000 each year in 2000 to approximately 20,000 in 2004 (Wu, 2005). Despite growth in their numbers, however, the marginality of overseas seafarers has not changed in any substantial way.

Table 8.3 offers an insight into the scale and extent of the seafaring labour market in China. This indicates that although SOE shipping companies are still the largest employer for Chinese seafarers, crew agencies have become an important channel for seafaring employment accounting for about 30% of the sample, with only 10% agency-owned, 20% being free seamen. The overseas seafaring labour market in China is obviously very important in that it provides a large percentage (27%) of working opportunities for SOE seafarers. But the existence of a large seafaring labour market sector in China is very important to foreign ship owners and managers who recruit three quarters or more of China's agency-owned seafarers and free seamen, and over one quarter of SOE seafarers.

Table 8.3 Recruitment of the sample by employment division (2003)

Employment	Sample distribution		Ship owner (%)	
	No.	%	National	Foreign
SOE shipping	348	70.7	72.7	27.3
Agency-owned	49	10.0	16.3	83.7
Free seamen	95	19.3	24.2	75.8
Total	492	100	57.8	42.3

Source: The Hong Kong survey, see Wu, 2004b.
Notes: For sample distribution, column as 100%; for ship owners, row as 100%.

Under the current system, foreign employers are not allowed to contact and sign a contract with seafarers directly. Instead, licensed crew agencies are in charge of negotiating and signing contracts with foreign employers in the first instance and then discussing and signing further contracts with individual seafarers (in the case of free seamen) or their bosses (in the case of SOE or agency-owned seafarers). By 2004, 60 crew agencies had been registered by the China Co-ordination of Overseas Seamen Employment (COSE) which provides an institutional base to deal with the business of supplying seafarers overseas. But it is notable that while all the licensed agencies were state-owned by 2004, not all were specialist seafaring agencies or had expertise in seafaring labour provision. Under those licensed agencies, there is a network composed of countless formal and informal crew agents. Due to the complexity of seafarer employment and contract processing, unsurprisingly, working conditions and pay amongst Chinese seafarers vary greatly. For example, two ABs (ratings) were working on the same foreign ship through crewing agencies. One received US$580 per month from his company, another only $430 per month. Such a difference was related not to their seafaring experience, nor to their social welfare, because both were similar. What was different, according to them, was that the former had only one crewing agency taking a percentage of the wage, whereas the latter had two (Wu, 2004a).

During the survey many seafarers expressed concerns about the current system. Not only did they report having to pay large amounts to intermediaries in this process, resulting in a reduction of their wage packets, but they felt the system constrained their career development and their opportunities to build relationships with foreign companies. The quote below taken in the China survey from a chief engineer is illustrative:

> Many free seamen like me hope that we can be recruited by foreign shipowners directly because the latter would take care of my performance and appreciate any contribution I may make. This also encourages me to do my best aboard because I know for whom I am working. In the current situation, however, there is a long chain between shipowner, ship managers, crew agencies, and seafarers. As a result, the quality of my services for foreign

> ships is rarely assessed by the crew agency whose assessment is based upon the report from ship managers. The shorter the chain, the better seafarers work for […] In addition, direct recruitment by foreign shipowners can save a lot of my time in job searching and interviewing because I can inform the company how long I want to stay at home when I leave the ship. In reality, unfortunately, I have to spend an awful lot of time on job searching from the first day of my holiday. So being a free seaman is not really as free as it sounds.

The above quotation represents the opinion expressed by a large number of Chinese seafarers within the sample. When respondents were asked to express their preference in recruiting style, our survey showed that over 70% favoured direct recruitment by foreign companies or their representatives in China, while less than 30% wanted to retain the current system recruiting via shipping companies or crew agencies (Wu, 2005). Table 8.4 indicates that recruitment preference is, however, significantly related to rank. Senior officers were more likely to be interested in direct recruitment than ratings.

Table 8.4 Preference of recruitment style by selected categories

Categories	No.	Indirect (%)	Direct (%)
Senior	44	18.2	81.8
Junior	87	23.0	77.0
Ratings	81	40.7	59.3
Total	**212**	**28.8**	**71.2**

Source: The China survey, see Wu, 2005.

The case of Chinese seafarers thus confirms that the closed nature of the Chinese labour market to foreign employers is one of the important factors contributing to the marginality of Chinese seafarers in the global labour market. And while we have witnessed the establishment and development of the seafaring labour market in China resulting in a transformation of Chinese seafarer employment from SOE employees to free seamen, the case of Chinese seafarers seems to indicate the general case that Chinese contract workers may be more vulnerable and marginal than other nationalities in the international labour market due to the restrictions imposed by the Chinese authorities and the domestic recruitment agencies. A challenging issue facing the Chinese authorities is how to reduce the control of SOE shipping companies over seafaring employment overseas. SOE shipping companies have impeded the process of opening the labour market to foreign employers with the price being paid by Chinese seafarers.

Conclusions

This chapter has attempted to reveal linkages between globalisation and the marginalisation of Chinese contract workers in overseas labour service provision, a newly-emerging industry in China and comes to a number of conclusions.

Firstly, Chinese contract workers are even more vulnerable than other nationalities in the international labour market. This is not only because that they have to pay a large amount of money in deposits and service charges to gain job opportunities abroad, but also because they have to bear all the economic risks while labour brokers and licensed agencies enjoy the profits.

Secondly, the marginality of Chinese contract workers is rooted in the overseas labour service system which originated in the planned economy of the Mao period and which, despite modifications, still favours state ownership. SOE companies and agencies, acting as effective employers of contract workers rather than mere brokers, still predominate. As a result, Chinese recruitment agencies can determine how much to pay to Chinese workers based upon domestic pay levels rather than those in the host countries. In addition, recruitment agencies also take charge of managing Chinese contract workers abroad to ensure the completion of the labour contract and the return home of the workers in due course.

Thirdly, the marginalisation of Chinese contract workers is related to both the incomplete development of an open labour market in China and the lack of political power of Chinese contract workers. The SOE companies and agencies in the labour service still have a monopoly over supply and potential foreign companies cannot contract and employ Chinese workers directly. At the same time, Chinese workers are powerless either to establish their own trade unions or to be allowed to join international or local trade unions in host countries. Under such an institutional framework, the growing numbers of private labour brokers and government departments have simply got in on the act, joining the competition to share the market benefits, rather than seeking to improve the overseas labour service system or the working conditions and welfare of Chinese workers.

Finally, the case of Chinese seafarers indicates that a fundamental change of the regulation system is necessary to allow foreign employers to recruit Chinese workers directly and to ensure there is the appropriate connection between Chinese and international labour standards. In the recent years of transition, we have witnessed increasing competition between private labour brokers and SOE agencies, and the transformation of seafaring employment from SOE employees to freelance seafarers. It is now high time to improve both the regulatory system and labour standards. A good start would be to rethink the practical implications of the theoretically 'triangular' relationship between agencies, overseas employers and contract workers to ensure the interests of the latter are more central to the system, rather than an afterthought, as is the case at present.

Acknowledgement

Special thanks are given to Heather Xiaoquan Zhang and Richard Sanders for their constructive comments and suggestions on this chapter.

References

Benton, G. and Pieke, F. (eds.) (1998), *The Chinese in Europe*, Hampshire: Macmillan.

Berger, S. and Piore, M. (1980), *Dualism and Discontinuity in Industrial Societies*, Cambridge: Cambridge University Press.

Central Intelligence Agency (CIA) (2004). *The World Factbook 2004*. Online: www.cia.gov/cia/publications/factbook/, retrieved 15 June 2006.

Chan, A. (2003), 'A "Race to the Bottom": Globalization and China's Labour Standards'. *China Perspectives*, Vol. 46, pp. 41-49.

Chin, J.K. (2003), 'Reducing irregular migration from China', *International Migration*, Vol. 41(3), pp. 49-72. Special Issue 1.

China International Contract Association (CHINCA, 2004), 'A case of labour abuse in Malaysian foreign labour market', *International Project Contracting and Labour Service* (in Chinese), Issue 10.

China International Contract Association (CHINCA, 2005a), *China's International Labour Cooperation: Annual Report 2004* (in Chinese). Online: www.chinca.org, retrieved 6 February 2006.

China International Contract Association (CHINCA, 2005b), 'Protection of contracted workers' rights', *International Project Contracting and Labour Service* (in Chinese): Issue 3.

China International Contract Association (CHINCA, 2005c), Cases of Labour Appeals, online: chinca.mofcom.gov.cn/zhongyts/zhongyts.html, retrieved 6 February 2006.

China Labour Market (CLM) (2005a), 'Bewaring four types of forged overseas employment'. Online: http://www.lm.gov.cn/, retrieved 8 November 2005.

China Labour Market (CLM) (2005b), 'About overseas employment this year'. Online: www.lm.gov.cn/gb/employment/2005-06/16/content_76864.htm, Retrieved 8 November 2005.

Ellman, M. and Laacher, S. (2003). *Migrant Workers in Israel: A Contemporary Form of Slavery*, joint publication by The EURO-Mediterranean Human Rights Networks & The International Federation for Human Rights, Copenhagen & Paris, June.

Gao, Y (2004), *Chinese Migrants and Forced Labour in Europe*, Working Paper 32, July, Geneva: International Labour Office.

Hong Kong Liaison Office (HKLO) (2004), *Labour Export from China: A Growth Industry*, online: www.ihlo.org/focus/150.htm, retrieved 6 February 2006.

Huang, Y. P. (1996), Economic Reform and Emigration Pressures in China, A Report Prepared for ILO Regional Office, Bangkok, online: www.ilo.org/public/english/region/asro/bangkok/paper/china.htm, retrieved 10 January 2006.

International Labour Office (ILO) (2004), *Towards a fair deal for contracted workers in the global economy*, ILO, 92nd Session. Geneva: ILO.

International Labour Office and the Seafarers International Research Centre (ILO and SIRC, 2004), *The Global Seafarer: Living and Working Conditions in a Globalized Industry*, Geneva: ILO.

International Shipping Federation (ISF) (2004), *The ISF Year 2003*, London: ISF.

International Textile, Garment and Leather Workers' Federation (ITGLWF) (2005), 'Contracted Labour: Too Much Task Kills the Workers', online: www.itglwf.org, retrieved 10 January 2006.

Kav LaOved (2002), *Annual Report 2002*, online: //www.kavlaoved.org.il/word/2002_report.doc, retrieved 10 January 2006.

Labour Court Reports (LCR) (2003), *Xue Bin and others v. A. Dori Building Company*, Published in LCR, Vol 38, pp. 650 – 720, March 20, online: http://isllss.haifa.ac.il/Dori%20case%202003.rtf, retrieved 10 January 2006.

Laczko, F. (2003), 'Introduction: understanding migration between China and Europe', *International Migration* Vol. 41 (3), pp. 5-19. Special Issue 1.

Leontaridi, M.R. (1998), 'Segmented labour markets: theory and evidence', *Journal of Economic Survey*, Vol. 12 (1), pp. 63-101.

Liang, Z. and Morooka, H. (2004), 'Recent trends of emigration from China: 1982-2000', *International Migration*, Vol. 42 (3), pp. 145-164.

Li, M.H. (2004), 'Labour brokerage in China today: formal and informal dimensions', *Duishurg Working Papers on East Asian Studies,* No. 58, Institute for East Asian Studies, University of Duishurg-Essen, Germany.

Ma, Y. (2005), 'International trade, competitive capacity and labour standards in China' (in Chinese) online: www.caitec.org.cn/xsyjbg/050406001.htm, retrieved 10 January 2006.

Ministry of Foreign Trade and Economic Cooperation (MOFTEC) (2004), 'Policies and Management Systems of China's Labour Export' (in Chinese), online: www.china-labor.net/zcfg/, retrieved 6 February 2006.

Organisation for Economic Co-operation and Development (OECD, 2002), *Service Providers on the Move: A Closer Look at Labour Mobility and the GATS*, OECD Working Party of the Trade Committee, online: www.olis.oecd.org/olis/2001doc.nsf/LinkTo/td-tc-wp(2001)26-final, retrieved 6 February 2006.

Overbeek, H. (2002), 'Neo-liberalism and the Regulation of Global Labour Mobility', *The Annals of the American Academy*, Vol. 581, pp. 74-90.

Park. R.E. (1928), 'Human Migration and the marginal man', *The American Journal of Sociology*, Vol. 33 (6), 881-893.

Potts, L. (1990), *The world labour market: a history of migration*; translated by Terry Bond. London and Atlantic Highlands, N.J: Zed Books.

Rowley, C. and Benson, J. (2000), 'Global labour? issues and themes', *Asia Pacific Business Review—Globalisation and Labour in the Asia Pacific Region* (special issue), Vol. 6(3&4), pp. 1-14.

Ruths, M. (2003), 'Temporary foreign worker programmes: policies, adverse consequences and the need to make them work', *Perspectives on Labour Migration*, No 6, Geneva: International Labour Office.

Skeldon, R. (1996), 'Emigration from China', *Journal of International Affairs*, Vol. 49, pp. 434-455.

Siu, D.C.P (1952), 'The sojourner', *The American Journal of Sociology*, Vol. 58, pp. 34-44.

Taran, P.A. (2001), 'Human rights of migrants: challenges of the new decade', *International Migration*, Vol. 38(6), pp. 7-51. Special Issue 2.

Xia, G.X. (2004), 'An analysis of Malaysian foreign labour market', *International Project Contracting and Labour Service* (in Chinese), Issue 7.

Wang, S.G. (1995), 'China's export of labour and its management', *Issue - Migration and the Family* Vol. 4 (2/3), pp. 429-447.

Wang, X.H. (2003), 'Review and prospect to international labour service', *International Economic Cooperation,* (in Chinese), Issue 1.

Wu, B. (2004a), 'Participation in the global labour market: experience and responses of Chinese seafarers', *Maritime Policy and Management*, Vol. 31(1), pp. 69-72.

Wu, B. (2004b), '"Transgration" of Chinese seafarers in economic transition: an institutional perspective on labour mobility. *Cardiff School of Social Sciences Working Papers Series*, 64, Cardiff University, Online: http://www.cf.ac.uk/socsi/publications/workingpapers/

Wu, B. (2005), 'Chinese seafarers in transition: trends and evidence', *Proceedings of SIRC International Symposium*, 6th to 7th July, Cardiff: SIRC.

Wu, B. and Liang, T. (2005), 'China walls: barriers against Chinese seafarers' entrance to the global labour market', *Lloyd's Shipping Economist*, March Issue, pp. 10-12.

Wu, B. and Sampson, H. (2005), 'Reconsidering the cargo sector and seafarer labour market: A 21st century profile of global seafarers", *Ocean Yearbook*, Vol. 19, pp. 357-380.

Wu, B. and Morris, J. (2006), 'A life on the ocean wave: the 'post socialist' careers of Chinese, Russian and Eastern European seafarers', *International Journal of Human Resource Management*, Vol. 17(1), pp. 25-48.

Wu, N. (2004), "108 Chinese workers cheated to Malaysia", online: //www.china.org.cn/english/2004/May/95995.htm, retrieved 6 February 2006.

Xiang, B. (2003), 'Emigration from China: A sending country perspective', *International Migration*, Vol. 41 (3), pp. 21-48. Special Issue 1.

Zha, D.J. (2001), *Chinese contracted workers in Japan: policies, institution and civil society*, online: //216.239.59.104/search?q=cache:nARHUFTF1gUJ:gsti.miis.edu/. retrieved 6 February 2006.

Zhang, G.C. (2003), 'Migration of highly skilled Chinese to Europe: trends and perspective', *International Migration,* Vol. 41 (3), pp. 73-97. Special Issue 1.

Chapter 9

The World Trade Organization and Chinese Farmers: Implications for Agricultural Crisis and Marginalisation

John Q. Tian

Introduction

The readmission of China to the World Trade Organization (WTO) at the end of 2001 was a historic event for both China and the rest of the world and China's consequent commitments with regard to market access and rule-based issues were sweeping and highly controversial. These commitments sparked a fierce debate within China which, in the mid-2000s, is still ongoing over the possible impacts on the Chinese economy and how China can best cope with the new challenges and opportunities as it becomes increasingly intertwined with the global economy. For supporters of China's membership, WTO accession further integrates China into the world economy and the more open and stable trading arrangements consequent upon this attracts more foreign investment and boosts economic growth. In addition, WTO membership, it is argued, also helps secure reforms already in place and speeds up new ones as China commits itself to open ever more areas of business previously closed or protected from foreign involvement such as agriculture and banking services.

For critics, this optimism about the economic benefits of China's WTO accession is misplaced. They believe China's WTO membership requires it to go through painful structural changes that will, in both the short *and long run* inevitably produce more losers than winners. Of particular concern is the potential impact of China's far-reaching commitments regarding market access on its fragile agricultural sector and farmers' income growth. It was feared that as part of China's WTO commitments, substantial tariff reductions and minimum access opportunities under the tariff-rate quota (TRQ) system and the weakening of other mechanisms of state control and support would bring surging imports of cheap agricultural products, further undermining the livelihoods of the Chinese farmers. A sharp fall in farmers' income and sweeping structural changes in the agricultural sector would, it was feared, only exacerbate China's agrarian crisis (*sannong wenti – nongye*, *nongcun*, *nongmin* – difficulties facing agriculture, rural areas, and farmers). These concerns over the potential negative impacts on farmers' income and structural adjustments accentuated the urgency for the Chinese government to revamp its policy towards agriculture and to restructure rural institutions of governance that impose heavy burdens on Chinese farmers and undercut China's only limited support for agriculture.

This chapter is intended to contribute to the debate over rural marginalisation through a reassessment of the impact of WTO entry to date on China's agriculture and its farmers. While initial assessment of China's WTO entry has been largely positive and many of the much feared disruptions have been either absent or minimal, it is still too early to be complacent and it would be irresponsible to ignore many of the existing problems as well as formidable challenges lying ahead. The widening income disparity and multifarious inequalities between urban and rural residents point to persistent institutional barriers and structural constraints that continue to marginalise Chinese farmers. They still face discrimination in terms of access to the provision of public goods like health care, education and equal opportunity in employment and equitable pay. While farmers' financial burdens have been alleviated somewhat as a result of the tax-for-fee reforms (*shuifei gaige*) (see later this chapter for elaboration), subsequent reduction and eventual abolition of agricultural taxes, new disputes over land rights and compensation are on the rise. The continuing plight of Chinese farmers is reflected in the increasing number of farmers' protests, petition movements and sporadic riots (see the chapter by Sanders, Chen and Cao in this volume).

This chapter revisits some of the initial anxieties, policy changes and continuing challenges facing Chinese agriculture and farmers. First, I review China's original commitments to the WTO regarding agriculture and some of the concerns regarding the likely impact on Chinese agriculture and farmers; then I evaluate how China has fared in the years since WTO entry and the policy changes and institutional reforms that have been put into place to cope with the challenges from WTO; in conclusion, I analyse the simmering new crises in the institutions of rural governance and the implications for marginalisation of Chinese farmers.

WTO and Chinese Agriculture

China has made extensive commitments over market access to its agricultural sector upon WTO accession. These commitments encompass areas of tariff reduction and minimum access opportunities under a tariff-rate quota system, the end of state monopoly over trade of agricultural products, limits on domestic support and export subsidies for agricultural products.

First, China agreed to reduce the average statutory tariff rate for agricultural products from 22.5% to 17.5% by January 2004. By 2005, it was further lowered to 15.35%. For U.S. priority agricultural products, the tariff rate was reduced from 31% to 14%, and, at the same time, the restrictions on the import of wheat from the northwest areas of the United States that might have TCK (Tilletia Controversa Kuhn) spores were eliminated. China has made commitments to important changes with regard to non-tariff barriers and agreed to replace its import quota and licensing system with a TRQ system. The introduction of such a system brings the quota tariff rate for major agricultural commodities, such as wheat, corn, rice, and cotton down to an extremely low tariff rate of 1% for a substantial fixed quantity of imports and to no more than 10% for partially processed grain products (Wang 2002, 87-88; Lardy 2002, 75-79).

Imports of major grain products above the quota levels initially faced a higher tariff of 76% but this was reduced to 65% in 2004. For cotton, the above-quota tariff was 54.4% initially, subsequently reduced to 40% in 2004. There was no tariff quota for soybeans, and the import duty was set at only 3% (Johnson 2001, 402-4).

Furthermore, China agreed to eliminate the monopoly that the state trading companies previously had over trade in priority agricultural commodities such as grains, cotton, and soybean oil. Under the agreement, only a part of the TRQ for each grain is now reserved for state-owned trading companies while the rest is made available to private and/or foreign grain traders. Given the importance of the government monopoly in the control of prices farmers receive for their grain, the ending of this monopoly over imports of important agricultural commodities has the potential to undermine the effectiveness of the government's agricultural policies, including pricing, marketing and distribution (Schmidhuber 2001, 21-51).

In addition, China agreed to severe limits to its domestic subsidies for agriculture. From 1996 to 2000, China's aggregate measurement of support (AMS) was between 4.9-8.8% of its annual agricultural output. Out of this, about 30-50% or roughly 3.5% of agricultural output (since 1998 between 50-70 billion yuan) goes on price support, which, according to the Agricultural Agreement, is included in the AMS and is thus subject to limitations. In China's accession agreement, the amount of China's domestic agricultural support subsidies ("amber box") was set at 8.5% – half-way between the levels for developed countries (10%) and developing countries (5%) (Lardy 2002, 92, 156-7).

Legitimate farm supports under the WTO Agricultural Agreement are called "green box" measures. They include direct payments to farmers, domestic food aid, income insurance, insect control, safety net support payments, research and technical support and environmental protection. Currently, China's "green box" supports are still very limited and mostly in the form of research and technological support, food security reserve funds, disaster relief funds, ecological preservation and environmental protection. In addition, China agreed to eliminate subsidies for agricultural export. This commitment far exceeds those made by other WTO members (Lardy 2002, 92; Gilmour and Brink 2001, 150; Ma and Lan 2002).

Of all the promises China made in its agreement to join the WTO, its agricultural commitments were the most contentious. Substantial tariff reductions, minimum access under the TRQ and the end of the state subsidies for agricultural export would make China, it was argued, one of the world's most open countries for food imports. At the time, there were widespread concerns about China's food security. Given the size of its population, historical experience with embargos and the current geopolitical situation, it was (and still is) seen as vital for China to ensure a stable supply of major agricultural products essential to its people. Therefore, China has always been concerned about the possibility of over-dependence on foreign food supplies to feed its huge population. This concern was only heightened by the publication of Lester Brown's book in 1995, *Who Will Feed China?* This sensitivity over food security led to an explicit government policy of limiting key agricultural imports to within 5% of its food needs. This was reflected in the quota established in the U.S.-China bilateral agreement in November 1999 which was roughly in line with the Chinese government policy goals (Ma 1999, 45-54; Crook 1999, 55-73).

However, concerns over food security have eased somewhat partly due to the TRQ limits of imports to about 5% of China's food needs. Also for the first two years after its WTO accession, China imported relatively small amounts of grain, much less than its quota for the first two years. Indeed, China even incurred a surplus of US$3.88 billion and US$2.5 billion in overall agricultural trade in 2002 and 2003. More importantly, since 1995, ironically the year Lester Brown's book was published, China has had several years of continuously good harvests that have resulted in a historical transition for China from the long-standing shortage of supply of major agricultural products to "balances in aggregate and surpluses in years of good harvests" (Chen 2002: 3; Liang 2002).

WTO and Chinese Farmers: Implication for Marginalisation

However, the surpluses of agricultural products have created problems of a new kind. Excess supply leads to a decline in prices, which in turn depresses income growth for farmers. The situation improved somewhat from late 2003 and 2004 when the prices of grain rebounded by about 30% due to a sharp fall in grain production. In 2003 land cultivated for grain production fell to about 65.2% of all agricultural land from 80.3% in 1978 and grain production fell to 430.7 million tons only, the lowest amount in 10 years. The subsequent increases in grain prices and strong demand created new incentives for farmers to increase grain production. Reinforced with a series of policies by the central government to reduce agricultural taxes and raise subsidies, grain production reached more than 469 million tons in 2004, an increase of about 9% than in 2003 (People's Daily, 2004a; ZGNW, 2005a). But it may be too early to be overly optimistic and the overall picture for Chinese agriculture is still mixed. While increased grain production and extended policy subsidies all contributed to income growth for Chinese farmers in 2004, it is doubtful the pulling impact of policy stimuli is sustainable over time. Besides, Chinese agricultural trade also turned from a surplus for 2002 and 2003 to a deficit of $4.64 billion in 2004. The deficit incurred in 2004 was due largely to the imports of more than 7.60 million tons of wheat and more than 1.79 million tons of cotton. While most of the imported wheat was used to increase stocks, many fear that it may be the beginning of the widely expected surge of agricultural imports following China's WTO entry (Cheng 2005; Han 2005). Therefore, even in the mid 2000s, concerns over employment pressure, farmers' income growth, challenges of structural adjustment, and signs of growing instability of rural areas still remain at the core of the debate over China's agrarian crises.

Given the number of people employed in agriculture, many have predicted that China would face severe employment pressures. In 2003, around 312.6 million people, about 49.1% of the total national labour force were still employed in agriculture. At the time of China's WTO entry, it was estimated that about half of this number was not productively employed (Wang 2002; Pan 2001, 40-41).[1] While these statistics

1 According to one estimate, Chinese agriculture at current technology only needs a labour force of 130 million and therefore over 200 million or 60% of the employment in agriculture now is redundant (Wang, J. 2002).

may overestimate the farming population, there is no doubt that a substantial number of them are redundant. This large amount of surplus labour has already fuelled a massive flow of migrant workers that is estimated to be between 120 million to 200 million (State Council, 2006). A more competitive economic environment following China's WTO entry could only intensify this migration process.

Table 9.1 Farmers' income growth (1980-2004) and distributional disparities (1980-2000)

Year	Per Capita Annual Income (*Yuan*)	Nominal Growth Rate (%)	Net Income Growth Rate (%)	Overall Gini Coefficient	Provincial Gini Coefficient
1980	191.3	--	--	0.238	0.14
1981	223.4	16.8	14.5	0.239	0.13
1982	270.1	20.9	18.5	0.232	0.13
1983	309.8	14.7	13.3	0.246	0.14
1984	355.3	14.7	11.3	0.258	0.15
1985	397.6	11.9	4.0	0.264	0.15
1986	423.8	6.6	0.4	0.288	0.18
1987	462.6	9.2	2.7	0.292	0.18
1988	544.9	17.8	0.3	0.301	0.19
1989	601.5	10.4	-7.5	0.300	0.19
1990	686.3	14.1	9.2	0.310	0.20
1991	708.6	3.2	0.9	0.307	0.20
1992	784.0	10.6	5.7	0.314	0.21
1993	921.6	17.6	3.4	0.320	0.22
1994	1221.0	32.5	7.4	0.330	0.22
1995	1577.7	28.9	10.0	0.340	0.23
1996	1926.1	22.1	13.1	0.394	0.28
1997	2090.1	8.5	5.6	0.408	0.30
1998	2162.0	3.4	4.3	0.414	0.30
1999	2210.3	2.2	3.1	0.418	0.31
2000	2253.4	1.9	2.1	0.421	0.31
2001	2366.4	5.0	4.2	--	--
2002	2475.6	4.6	4.8	--	--
2003	2622.2	5.9	4.3	--	--
2004	2936.4	11.9	6.8	--	--

Sources: National Bureau of Statistics of China, *China Statistical Yearbook 2000, 2003, 2004*, 2005, 312, 344, 357; 335. Lu and Wang (2001),19; for 2001 data, see Niu; for 2002 data, see *ZGNW*, 2003b; for 2003 data, see *People's Daily* (2004c).

Initial estimates of potential employment loss in agriculture following China's WTO entry varied between 11 to 25 million (Lardy 2002, 109-110; Ma and Lan 2002). With the ability of township and village enterprises (hereafter TVEs) to absorb rural labour declining, many feared that it would be difficult to find alternative employment opportunities for the redundant farming workforce (Park 2001), especially at a time of surging urban unemployment and increasing labour unrest in a number of Chinese cities (New York Times 2001). Concerns over employment pressures have been eased somewhat recently by a surprising labour shortage of migrant workers in the booming Pearl River Delta. But many regard this as a temporary phenomenon that results from a combination of harsh working conditions and stagnant wages for migrant workers in the region and new government initiatives to support agriculture back home.

In addition to employment pressures, many have worried that China's WTO accession might depress farmers' income growth at the time when farmers' incomes have already fallen substantially, decreasing every year from 1996 to 2000. As Table 9.1 shows, while income growth has rebounded in 2001, 2002 and 2003, it remains below 5% at a time when average per capita incomes in China are rising twice as fast.

Slow income growth for farmers has led to widening income disparities between rural and urban residents (Tian 2001). According to the former director of China's National Bureau of Statistics, Qiu Xiaohua, the real ratio of urban-rural income disparities in 2001 was about 6:1.[2] One of the main reasons for the slow rate of growth of farmers' incomes has been the declining gains from agricultural production. After a short period of sporadic but substantial grain imports in the mid-1990s, China began to produce considerable amounts of cereal in excess of domestic consumption. Bumper harvests and subsequent high domestic cereal stocks occurred at a time of profound changes in the consumption structure of both urban and rural residents. One of the chief changes has been the decrease of the Engel coefficient and the associated decline in the income elasticity of demand for food (see chapter in this volume by Ka Lin). Since the beginning of the reforms, the Engel coefficients of urban and rural households in China have fallen from 57.5 and 67.7% in 1978 to 37.7 and 46.2 respectively in 2002 (see Table 9.2). According to one study, for urban residents, income elasticity of demand for food has fallen from around 1.0 in the early 1980s to around 0.5 in 1996 and thereafter dropped even more sharply, falling to 0.22 in 1999. For rural residents, it dropped from above 1.0 in the 1980s to 0.58 in 1999 (Zhou 2001, 25-29; Chen 2002, 14).[3]

---

2 According to a figure released by the government, the ratio of rural and urban income rose to 1:3.24 in 2003 (People's Daily 2003). However, according to Qiu Xiaohua, about 40% of rural residents' income is in-kind and cash income is only about 1800 *yuan* a year, or about 150 *yuan* a month. After deducing costs on agricultural inputs, rural per capita disposable income (PDI) is only about 120 *yuan* a month; while at the same time, urban PDI is about 600 *yuan*. If we add various urban social welfare benefits, the ratio of real urban-rural PDI gap is about 6:1 (Chinese Youth Daily 2002).

3 The Engel coefficient is an indicator reflecting the proportion of income that goes into the consumption of food. Income elasticity of demand is the ratio of proportional increase in quantity demanded to proportional increase in income, with all prices held constant.

Table 9.2 Engel coefficients for rural and urban households (selected years 1980-2004)

Year	Rural Residents	Urban Residents	Year	Rural Residents	Urban Residents
1980	61.8	56.9	1996	56.3	48.8
1985	57.8	53.3	1997	55.1	46.6
1989	54.8	54.5	1998	53.4	44.7
1990	58.8	54.2	1999	52.6	42.1
1991	57.6	53.8	2000	49.1	39.4
1992	57.6	53.0	2001	47.7	38.2
1993	58.1	50.3	2002	46.2	37.7
1994	58.9	50.0	2003	45.6	37.1
1995	58.6	50.1	2004	47.2	37.7

Source: National Bureau of Statistics of China, China Statistical Yearbook 2005, 335.

This means that the traditional method of raising farmers' incomes through increasing urban and rural food consumption has become less important. The resulting excess of supply over demand for most farm produce has led to difficulties in sales and falling prices, which, in turn, has depressed farmers' income growth. From 1997 to 1999, prices of major agricultural produce relative to the prior year (indexed at 100) were 95.5, 92, and 87.8 respectively (Central Research Office and Ministry of Agriculture 2001, 4). In response, the government allocated special funds to state-owned and other authorised grain enterprises to monopolise grain purchases at a state protected price and then sell grain at a price above the purchasing price in order to make a profit. This policy was designed to stop grain prices falling in order to protect farmers' interests. However, according to Dewen Wang (2001, 215-16), since the monopoly was not complete and the market price often fell below the protected and quota prices, the state grain enterprises were unwilling to sell grains at the market-clearing price at a loss. This resulted in overstocking and the reported refusal of state grain stations to purchase farmers' grain at the protected price. Many feared that with China's WTO accession, high quality cheap imports (often heavily subsidised by the exporting countries) would drive down domestic grain price, thus further eroding farmers' income growth.

Fortunately, this hypothetical situation has not yet materialised. On the contrary, in 2004 farmers' income saw the fastest growth since 1997 as the result of a series of government policies to boost farmers' incomes. These policies included a gradual phasing out of the agricultural tax, programmes to cut the cost of electricity for rural residents, a campaign "to help migrant workers claim back wages, assistance for the education of migrant workers' children, and a potentially substantial programme to provide welfare for rural residents who have followed the government's birth-control programme." (Yang 2005, 21) By January 2005, about 33.1 billion yuan, nearly 98.4% of the arrears owed to migrant workers before 2003 were paid. Also, over 29 provinces began to provide direct subsidies to farmers for grain production. The total amount of direct subsidy payments amounted to 11.6 billion yuan in 2004. In addition, the central government also provided 2.85 billion yuan to subsidise the use of improved seeds in 13 major grain-producing provinces and another 70 million yuan to subsidise the purchase of farm equipment (Xinhuanet 2005a; 2005b). Together with a booming economy, recovering agricultural prices and increasing subsidies to farmers, these pro-rural policies have led to the fastest income growth for farmers since 1997. In 2004 farmers' income grew by 6.8% (People's Daily 2004a).

But it is not yet time for euphoria because the sudden surge in farmers' income growth may turn out to be only temporary. With many of the challenges facing Chinese agricultural still remaining, it is not clear how to sustain growth of farmers' income once the short-term policy stimuli, especially once the impact of the cancellation of agricultural taxes has tapered off.

And while the impact of the WTO entry on employment and farmers' income growth has been more benign than expected, many of the structural challenges facing Chinese agriculture still remain. A predominantly rural society with most of its labour employed in agriculture needs to be transformed into a much more urban society with the majority of workers employed in manufacturing and services. In 2004, among China's population of nearly 1.3 billion, those living in rural areas fell to 58.2% from over 82.1% in 1978.

Figure 9.1 Agriculture in the Chinese economy, 1978-2004
Source: China Statistical Yearbook 2005, 52, 93, 118.
Note: Agricultural labour includes those engaged in both grain and non-grain production.

According to Lardy (2002, 114), since the early 1990s, around 4 million jobs each year have been shed in agriculture while many of those remaining have shifted out of grain production. As currently defined, "rural" also includes rural migrant workers in urban areas even though many of them are working there on a long-term basis. Therefore, according to another study, over a third (34.2%) of the rural labour force is no longer employed in farming activities (Hussain 2002, 23). Clearly, China's WTO accession only reinforces the urbanisation process, increasing pressures on government to readjust its policies to facilitate this transformation.

Structural changes will also have to occur on the agricultural production side. Most Chinese farms are barely large enough to provide even for the needs of the families working on them. In 2000, the average size of farmland per household dropped to 1.15 mu (about 0.077 hectares), less than 25% of the global average. There is no way that these small farmers are able to compete successfully with multinational agribusiness groups. Given its acute shortage of arable land and worsening water supply situation in major grain-growing areas, China has no comparative advantage in the production of land – and water-intensive crops such as grain. Some economists even claim that imports of grain are the equivalent to imports of land and water (Lin 2001, 405-408). Therefore, WTO entry is likely to push China through an adjustment process in the patterns of both agricultural production and trade to areas more in line with the country's comparative advantage, to include the production of fruits, organic vegetables, flowers and other labour-intensive crops. Indeed, largely in response to relative price changes, farmers have already been moving out of land-intensive crops, such as grains and oilseeds, and into more labour-intensive production of vegetables and horticultural crops (Lardy 2002, 114; Huang et al. 2001, 397-401; Liu 2001). From around the mid-1990s, farmers in Shandong and Hebei provinces began to move from traditional grain crops to growing vegetables and other specialty agricultural products for export to South Korea and Japan.

The road to this necessary structural adjustment, however, is a rocky one. By 2000, China was providing 40% of Japan's imports of fresh vegetables. But in response to pressures from farmers, the South Korean government imposed punitive tariffs on imports of Chinese garlic in 2000, and then in April 2001 the Japanese government imposed similar tariffs on Chinese imports of shiitake mushrooms, green onions, and rushes used to make tatami mats. By September of that year, Japanese imports of Chinese mushrooms, onions, and rushes dropped by 51%, 74%, and 61% respectively. Both incidents touched off trade wars when China retaliated by imposing punitive tariffs on Korean and Japanese imports (Lardy 2002, 169-170; Asia Times, 2001a, 2001b; ZGNW, 2002; Chinaonline, 2001). In 2004, the U.S. imposed punitive tariffs ranging from 55.2% to 112.8% on Chinese shrimps after the Commerce Department ruled that Chinese firms were dumping shrimps on the U.S. market (Chinese Ministry of Commerce 2005). In addition, Chinese agricultural exports, especially poultry products, were severely affected by SARS in 2003 and more recently by the ongoing avian flu. The U.S., Japan, and the EU have also increasingly resorted to sanitary regulations ("green barriers") to restrict China's agricultural imports and, more recently, re-imposed trade restrictions on Chinese textile and clothing imports. Partly because of these trade barriers, the expected export increases in areas where China has a comparative advantage have yet to be realised. Indeed, if protectionist measures like these expand, despite China's membership of the WTO, the process of adjustment in Chinese agriculture will be much more difficult (Wu 2003).

Agrarian Crises, Institutional Change and New Sources of Marginalisation

An immediate impact of China's WTO entry has been the increasing pressure put on the government to tackle the growing agrarian crises and to restructure local institutions of governance. Even before China's WTO accession, state-farmer relations were strained. The old problems of excessive taxation, illicit fees, charges and fines caused widespread discontent and growing instability in rural areas (Bernstein and Lu 2003; Far Eastern Economic Review 2001). From 1996 to 1997, approximately 380,000 farmers took part in various protests. During the first half of 1998, according to Jonathan Unger's study, a total of 3,200 incidents of collective action occurred in rural China and 7,400 casualties were officially reported, including more than 1,200 local officials and police wounded (Unger 2002, 213; O'Brien 2002, 141). In 2002, there were more than 37,500 cases of public protests in rural areas involving more than 12 million people (Cheng Ming 2003). In 2003, nearly 60,000 public protests were reported and in 2004 some 74,000 mass protests involving more than 3.7 million people were reported in various places (The Economist 2005). In November 2004, 100,000 farmers in Sichuan seized Hanyuan County government offices to stop the work of a dam project for days and 10,000 paramilitary troops had to be called in to quell the unrest. A month later tens of thousands of angry people swarmed the central square of Wanzhou, Sichuan to protest against the beating of a porter by an official (Kahn 2004). Many remain worried that China's WTO entry and its aftermath may exacerbate the problem of public unrest, especially among farmers in the grain-growing regions in the interior (central and western) provinces where rural industrialisation remains too underdeveloped to provide alternative sources of employment and income for farmers.

Thus WTO accession has increased pressures to reform the existing tax system and, consequently, to restructure local governance institutions that impose heavy financial burdens on farmers and undercut China's already limited support for agriculture. Ever since the 1990s, the government has held a series of national conferences on agriculture and issued numerous decrees instructing local governments to reduce farmers' burdens with dismal results. This failure to reverse the deteriorating situation regarding farmers' burdens has raised serious doubts about the effectiveness of central government policies. This potentially explosive situation and the challenges posed by China's WTO accession has led the central government to adopt local initiatives to reform the institutions of governance at the local level. Politically, the central government has promoted village democratic elections in order to increase the transparency of village government and curb corruption by local officials. Economically, the government has expanded the tax-for-fee reforms intended to reduce farmers' financial burdens.

While it is too early to draw definitive conclusions about the merits and problems of village elections, tentative evidence suggests they have been reasonably effective in increasing village's financial transparency and curbing the abuses of power and corruption by local officials. For example, Oi and Rozelle found that even before WTO entry some villages had implemented the "ten opens" demand for publicly posted detailed accounting of village expenditures; in others, the tiliu amounts (see below) are now openly posted. Some village committees have acquired veto power on the general use of village resources (Oi and Rozelle 2000).[4] To the extent this is true and if these practices can be expanded, they may have the potential to improve the tenuous relations between local governments and farmers, transforming local institutions of governance and promoting rural stability.

Another major experiment has been the tax-for-fee reform. Initially started in Anhui province and later extended across the country, this reform, as a method of reducing farmers' burdens, has become especially important in the light of China's WTO accession and of the concerns over its impact on the already stagnant rural incomes. As mentioned earlier, China's agricultural subsidies at the time of the WTO entry were very low and if one takes account of the various taxes, fees and charges that farmers had to bear, real farm subsidies in China were negative. Given the number of rural households and the difficulties for the government in administering direct transfer payments and other "green box" measures, the only viable option for farm support has been to reduce the financial burdens on farmers. But the government has tried to do this for many years with little success.

Hailed as a third revolution (after land reform and the household responsibility system), tax-for-fee reform, in essence, aims to replace various taxes, fees and charges with a simplified tax system. In Anhui, where it began in 1993, initially only two taxes remained after the reform: a 7% agricultural tax (or an equivalent tax on specialty agricultural products) and an agricultural tax plus (nongye fujia shui) which was set at no more than 20% of the agricultural tax. With the two combined, the overall tax was about 8.4%. Slaughter taxes, i.e. "expenses" (tongchou) imposed and used by local governments and rural education fees (funding for rural education taken over by higher levels of government) were abolished with "volunteer" labour being phased out over three years. Construction of water control projects, bridges, roads, and other public projects were to be decided by villagers' general meetings on a case-by-case basis. Tiliu, an elastic "deduction" that households have to pay for using land and other facilities belonging to the collective will be collected as the agricultural tax together with no more than 20% of the prior agricultural tax, to be used to maintain the continuous functioning of the village government and to pay for those rural residents without other forms of support (wubaohu). The new tax system is much simplified and has reduced farmers' financial burdens in many areas. With the expansion of this reform across the country and with various schemes to cut agricultural taxes and abolish taxes on special agricultural products (nongye techan shui excluding taxes on tobacco) later, farmers' financial burdens were reduced by about 33% nationwide (People's Daily, 2004b).

With pressures building up to defuse the agrarian crisis following China's WTO entry, the tax-for-fee reform soon built up a momentum of its own. In March 2003,

4 See also other articles in this special issue of *The China Quarterly*, no.162: Elections and Democracy in Greater China (June 2000).

the newly-elected Premier Wen Jiabao recognised the agrarian crisis as the main challenge for his tenure and in 2004 he declared at the National People's Congress (NPC) that China would reduce agricultural taxes at an average rate of one percentage point every year with the ultimate aim of abolishing them altogether within five years. But a year later at the 2005 NPC annual meeting, Wen proposed a complete abolition of agricultural taxes in 2006. By October 2005, 28 provinces, autonomous regions and provincial-level municipalities had decided to abolish agricultural taxes. In the remaining Shandong, Yunnan and Hebei provinces, tax rates dropped to 2%. This meant that in 2005, more than 800 million farmers were exempted from agricultural taxes worth more than 22 billion yuan (Qiao 2005, 12-14; People's Daily, 2005; ZGNW, 2005b). Also, as mentioned before, starting from 2004, over 29 provinces began to provide direct subsidies to farmers for grain production. In addition, the central government allocated 2.85 billion yuan to subsidise the use of improved seeds in 13 major grain-producing provinces and another 70 million yuan to subsidise the purchase of farm equipment (People's Daily, 2005).[5]

The twin reforms of village elections and tax-for-fee changes have the potential to stabilise rural areas by transforming local institutions of governance. But they have also created new problems and/or exacerbated existing ones that may well change the way the government works at local level. For example, while the tax-for-fee reform has drastically reduced farmers' burdens, it has also precipitated severe budget crises at the local level that threaten the continuous functioning of many local governments, especially in poor agricultural regions. According to various reports, since the late 1990s the total accumulated debt at the township level across the country was estimated to be in the range of 200 - 400 billion yuan, an average of more than four million yuan for each township (Development Research Centre 2002; Lian 2002; Liu 2002; Zhu and Ye 2005). Recent reports have estimated that the combined government debt at the township and village levels could be as high as 500 billion yuan and at the county and township levels as high as 1,000 billion yuan, far beyond the 400 billion yuan acknowledged by the Ministry of Finance (ZGNW, 2004a; Economic Reference News, 2005). As a result, many township and village governments do not even have funds to pay their employees and teachers.

For many years, scholars and the central government have blamed local governments for the problems in the countryside and have argued for strengthening the capacity of the state to enhance its ability to extract more financial resources. Neglected is the spending end of the equation, especially the "downward trend of dividing expenditure responsibilities among levels of government" (Lee 2000, 1022). Through the 1994 tax assignment reform and the 1996 reform of "off-budget" revenues, "central government had augmented its tax base and modified the rules of the game in order to raise the central share of national budgetary revenues, and at the same time transferred expenditure responsibility downwards to lower-level governments" ("shouru yu zeren weiyi" xianxiang) (Lee 2000, 1021).

5 According to the Minister of Finance, direct subsidies are expected to increase in 2005 by13.8% to about 13 billion *yuan* and subsidies for purchasing farm equipment are expected to double that of last year to reach 140 million *yuan* (People's Daily, 2005).

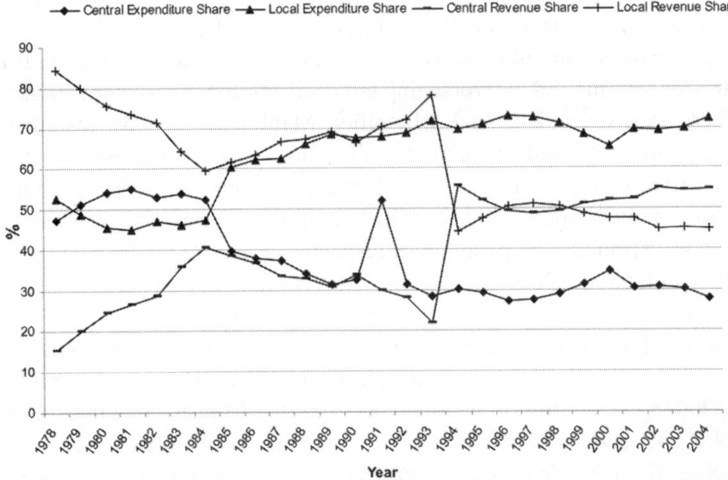

Figure 9.2 Central and local government share of revenue and expenditure, 1978-2004

Source: *China Statistical Yearbook 2005*, 276.

As the central government transfers more and more of its obligations to local governments, including expenditures on education, health, family planning, pension and social welfare funds, price subsidies and fixed capital investment, local budgets – especially those in the poor agrarian regions – become increasingly squeezed between the "centralisation of revenues and the simultaneous decentralisation of expenditure responsibilities" (caiquan shangshou, shiquan xiayi). Often, the central government sponsors various programmes without matching funds and these unfunded mandates simply translate into various fees and charges on the farmers.

Thus the recurrent agrarian crises in China can be traced to an imbalance between resource extraction and obligations of service deliveries (caiquan yu shiquan de bu tongyi) (Lee 2000, 1009, 1023; Cao 2000). For example, although overstaffing of local bureaucracies does exist, the largest item in local budget outlays is education, which, on average, constitutes about half of local budgets. In many of the poor interior regions, it is somewhere between 70 and 80% of local budgets (South Farmers' News, 2002). In a township in Anhui province, it is as high as 93.1% (Zhao 2001, 50; Zhu 2001, 12-16). Part of the education expense comes from local obligations to implement central government sponsored programmes promoting nine-year compulsory education (pujiu dabiao). While the central government promulgated a law on compulsory education in 1986 and another law on education in 1995, its share of expenditures on compulsory education by 2002 was only about 2% compared with 78% by township governments, 9% by county governments and 11% by provincial governments (Economic Reference News, 2002; ZGNW, 2003a).

While the central government funding rose to 8% in 2004, it is still far from enough to ease the financial pressure felt by local governments (Lu 2005, 29).

Given the cancellation of rural education fees and other ad hoc charges as part of the tax-for-fee reforms and the worsening township budget crises, many rural schools have experienced severe financial difficulties. Many teachers have resigned either because they are underpaid or not paid at all. This, in turn, has caused deterioration in the quality of education in many rural areas. In response, the State Council has decided to put the responsibility of rural compulsory education on county-level governments, especially the payment of teachers' salaries (Xie 2002; State Council 2002; Duowei Newsnet 2003). But country government budgets are not necessarily any healthier, especially in the poor agrarian regions in the interior. For example, by the end of 2003 the total debt burden for the county level governments alone in Anhui stood at 18.1 billion yuan with an average of 229 million yuan for each county (ZGNW 2004b). According to a researcher from the Ministry of Finance, in 1998 and 1999, 31.8% and 35.5% of county level government budgets nationwide were in the red (Xue 2002). While the central government and provincial level governments have promised more financial transfers to help cover the costs, these transfers are more likely to be handled in an ad hoc manner rather than being based on a clear division and institutionalisation of rights and responsibilities between the different levels of governments.

Consequently, cancellation of agricultural taxes and various fees and funds has led to increasing pressures to restructure local governance institutions in order to reduce the number of employees. Since 1998, more than 7,400 townships have either been eliminated or merged. In 2005 alone, more than 1,600 townships have been eliminated. However, this task is very challenging in the poor agricultural regions in the interior. With limited alternative employment opportunities and continuing pressure from higher-level governments to find employment for college graduates and demobilised military officers, cutting the number of personnel at the township and county levels turns out to be much more difficult than reducing the number of administrative units. Between 2000 and 2003 the central government decided to provide subsidies as an incentive to local governments based on the number of townships reduced and personnel cut. For each township eliminated, the subsidy was 400,000 yuan. For each person got rid of, it was 3,000 yuan (Economic Daily 2005).

But the focus on streamlining local governments diverts attention away from another important issue: the provision of public goods. Due to years of neglect and lack of funding, rural infrastructure like irrigation, flood control, the public health system and education has deteriorated greatly. The seriousness of the decay is partly reflected in the repeated ravages of disastrous floods in recent years, the ongoing spread of avian flu, the AIDS epidemic and overcrowded rural schools. The deepening budget crisis at the local level and the low morale of officials caught in the restructuring of the local administrations only makes the situation worse. Besides, the local budget crises have pushed local officials to frantically seek new sources of revenue especially through the sale of land to developers and investors. The taking of land without proper compensation to farmers has become the main cause of a new wave of disputes and even violent clashes between local officials and farmers in rural China. Throughout 2005 mass protests and riots were frequently reported. In mid-December 2005, thousands of farmers in Shanwei, Guangdong protested and clashed with police over disputes on land compensation and several villagers were shot dead (French 2005; Kahn 2005). On January 15, 2006 another major violent confrontation between police and rural protestors over land dispute occurred in Zhongshan, Guangdong where more than 30 villagers were reportedly wounded by police (World Journal 2006; The New York Times 2006). Finally, lack of funding at the local level has pushed up the tuition fees at schools and the costs of medical treatment. The growing costs of education and health care have become new sources of inequality and marginalisation for Chinese farmers. With tuition fees rising to thousands of yuan a year, a four year college education can cost an average farming family more than ten years of total income (ZGNW 2005c). Also, with the collapse of socialised medical services in the countryside and the staggering cost of health care, farmers often have to face a difficult choice between health and poverty. While the government is experimenting with new health insurance schemes, the premium are frequently still too high for rural residents and about 79% of them remain uninsured. The lack of adequate health care in much of the rural areas "has sown deep resentment among peasantry while helping to spread infectious diseases like hepatitis and tuberculosis and making the country – and the world – more vulnerable to epidemics like severe acute respiratory syndrome or SARS, and possibly bird flu" (French 2006). With access contingent on ability to pay, the rising costs of education and the misfortunes associated with serious illness have become the new causes of a resurgence of rural poverty and marginalisation. Despite promises to help, government assistance remains limited and slow to come, much to the chagrin of China's poor farmers.

Conclusion

More than five years after its entry into the WTO, Chinese agriculture and farmers have fared better than expected and the many feared disruptions have not occurred due to a combination of a favourable international market situation, various policy measures and institutional changes. Paradoxically, it could be argued that it has been the many challenges that WTO membership brought about that has prompted the Chinese government to revamp many of its policies towards agriculture and to restructure rural institutions of governance that had imposed heavy burdens on Chinese farmers. In 2004 and 2005, the central government twice issued an all-important "Document No.1" (*yihao wenjian*) that emphasised the importance of increasing food production and farmers' incomes through the strengthening of overall agricultural production capacity, improving infrastructure and the use of science and technology. The 2005 Document No 1 also called for holistic and coordinated development between urban and rural areas (*chengxiang tongchou fazhan*).

While these policies may have helped avert a pending crisis in China's rural areas, many of the challenges facing Chinese agriculture and farmers still remain. First, the stimulating effect of abolition of agricultural tax on farmers' income growth could turn out to be only temporary: indeed the recent increase in farmers' income has already been threatened by higher prices of production materials like fuel and fertiliser. It is also unrealistic to expect grain price to remain high as happened in 2004 when a drop in grain production in previous years led to rebound in price. Indeed, bumper harvests and increased imports in 2004 caused a slight fall in the grain price in 2005. And, to date, it is still unclear how to sustain farmers' income growth once the effect of the cancellation of agricultural tax tapers off. Meanwhile, as an increasingly important source of rural household income, wages for migrant workers in cities remain low and stagnant despite long hours and harsh working conditions. Notwithstanding the rhetoric, discrimination against migrant workers remains persistent and widespread (China Today 2005). Finally, the deteriorating situation in terms of the provision of public goods in China's rural areas and the rising costs of education and health care are already eating away some of the recent increases in farmers' income.

More importantly, efforts to restructure power and authority in rural China have precipitated a debt crisis that threatens the fiscal viability of many local governments, especially those in poor regions. This has, in turn, exposed a deep structural problem of the Chinese political economy in the discrepancy between extraction demands and service obligations. On the one hand, local officials are continuously subjected by the cadre evaluation system to certain performance criteria that requires them to be proactive (Whiting 2001, 100-118). On the other hand, their ability to live up to these criteria is increasingly restrained by the political and fiscal constraints resulting from recentralisation of financial resources and the twin reforms of village election, tax-for-fee reform and more recently the abolition of agricultural taxes. Consequently, as Prasenjit Duara describes an early period of state building in north China and its impact on the weakening of local authority, "the symbolic and material rewards of a career in public office were gradually being outweighed by the increasingly onerous nature of the tasks involved." (Duara 1988, 218). Similar to Duara's account, the plight of many local officials is so unenviable that there are already reports of local officials who choose to relinquish their leadership positions (Rural News 2002).[6] The vacuum of power and authority caused by local governance crisis may leave the Chinese countryside increasingly unstable. Recent reports of mass protests and sporadic riots and violent crackdown by the state at various places may be an indication that order is already yielding to lawlessness in some rural areas (Eckholm 2002). This may in turn undercut the potential of rural development, leading to further marginalisation of Chinese farmers. Therefore, it is arguable that even though the much feared disruptions following China's WTO entry on the country's agriculture have not come about in the last few years, many of the challenges facing Chinese agriculture will remain for the foreseeable future.

6 Interview by author, summer of 2003 and fall of 2006. See also (Rural News, 2002).

References

Asia Times (2001a), 'Dispute marks China's first day in WTO,' <www.atimes.com>, retrieved on 2001, 12, 12.

Asia Times (2001b), 'Tit-for-Tat Stays Like That,' <www.atimes.com>, retrieved on 2001,12,13.

Bernstein, T. and Lu, X. (2003), *Taxation Without Representation in Contemporary Rural China* (Cambridge, U.K.: Cambridge University Press).

Brown, L. (1995), *Who Will Feed China? Wake-Up Call for a Small Planet* (New York: W.W.Norton).

Cao, J. (2000), *China by the Yellow River: a scholar's observation and analysis of rural society* (Shanghai: Shanghai wenyi chubanshe) (in Chinese).

Central Research Office and Ministry of Agriculture (2001), "An empirical study of farmers' income during the ninth five-year plan," Issues of Agricultural Economy, no.7, 2 (in Chinese).

Chen, X. (2002), 'China's agricultural development and policy readjustment after its accession to WTO', paper presented at World Bank Panel "WTO Accession, Policy Reform and Poverty Reduction," December 14.

Cheng, G. (2005), 'Chinese agriculture in the world trading system,' <www.aweb. com. cn/2005/3/21/ 1256191.htm> (in Chinese), retrieved on 2005,3,21.

Cheng Ming, (2003), 'Hu warns: corruption pushes people to revolution,' no.306, (April): 9.

China Today (2005), 'Rural workers tell their own stories,' (May): 58-60.

Chinaonline, (2001), 'Sino-Japan trade spat hurts Chinese Ag exports,' <www. Chinaonline.com>, retrieved on 2001,11,1.

Chinese Youth Daily (2002), 'Chengxiang jumin shouru guoda zhide jingti,' (Widening urban-rural income gap calls attention), <www.aweb.com.cn/2002/11/2/2002112 11010 9.htm>, retrieved on 2002,11,2.

Crook, F. (1999), 'An analysis of China's food grain security policy', in OECD, *Agriculture in China and OECD Countries: Past Policies and Future Challenges*, 55-73. (Paris: OECD).

Development Research Centre, State Council, (2002), 'Research report on township budget deficits and debts,' <www.aweb.com.cn/2002/11/1/200211182716.htm> (in Chinese), retrieved on 2002, 11,1.

Duara, P. (1988), *Culture, Power, and the State: Rural North China, 1900-1942* (Stanford: Stanford University Press).

Duowei Newsnet (2003), '"Dalu nongcun jiaoshi xindi liushi duoxuexiao wufa kaike" (Many rural schools stop classes as rural teachers leave because of low pay), <www.chinesenewsnet.com>, retrieved on 2003,4,11.

Eckholm, E. (2002), 'Order yielding to lawlessness in rural China', The New York York Times, online. (May 29).

Economic Daily (2005), 'Zhongyang caizheng chuzi huanjie xianxiang caizheng kunnan" (Central government budget to help alleviate county and township financial difficulties), June 8, 2005, <http://news.aweb.com.cn/2005/6/8/9201815. htm>, retrieved on 2005,6,8.

Economic Reference News (2002), 'Nongcun yiwu jiaoyu caiquan yu shiquan bu duicheng' (Compulsory education in rural areas: the imbalance between financial resources and service obligations), <www.aweb. com.cn/2002/8/5/200285151937.htm>, retrieved on 2002,8,5.

Economic Reference News (2005), 'Zhongguo xianxiang zhengfu zhaiwu tupo 1 wanyi, fuzhai jianguan yigai poti' (Chinese government debt at the county and township level reaches 1,000 billion yuan. It's time to tighten supervision and regulation), March 23, 2005, <http://news.aweb.com.cn/2005/3/23/8021189.htm>, retrieved on 2005,3,23.

Far Eastern Economic Review (2001), 'Agriculture: how to build a rebellion,' September 29, online.

French, H. (2005), '20 reported killed as Chinese unrest escalates', *The New York Times*, online (December 9).

French, H. (2006), 'Wealth grows, but health care withers in China', *The New York Times*, online (January 14).

Glimour, B. and Brink, L. (2001), 'China in the WTO: implications for international trade and policy making in agriculture', OECD, China's Agriculture in the International Trading System, 71-88. (Paris: OECD).

Han, J. (2005), 'Directions of international trade and its impact on Chinese agriculture,' a speech at the Forum on Development Strategy of Chinese Agriculture, Tsinghua University, <www.aweb.com.cn/news/2005/4/28/13352863.htm> (in Chinese), retrieved on 2005,4,28.

Huang, J. et al. (2001), 'WTO and agriculture: radical reforms or the continuation of gradual transition', *China Economic Review*,11: 4 (Winter):397-401.

Hussain, A. (2002), 'Coping and adapting to job losses and declines in farm earnings', paper presented at World Bank Panel "WTO Accession, Policy Reform and Poverty Reduction," December 14.

Johnson, G. (2001), 'The WTO and agriculture in China', China Economic Review, 11, no. 4 (Winter): 402-04.

Kahn, J. (2004), 'China's "haves" stir the "have nots" to violence', *The New York Times*, online (December 31).

Kahn, J. (2005), 'Police fire on protestors in China, killing several', The New York Times, online (December 9).

Lardy, N. (2002), 'Integrating China into the Global Economy' (Washington, D.C.: Brookings Institution Press).

Lee, P. (2000), 'Into the trap of strengthening state capacity: China's tax assignment reform', *The China Quarterly*, no.164 (December):1007-24.

Lian, J. (2002), 'Local governments' budget crisis in mainland China,' *Commercial Times*, (Taipei), online, (August 12) (in Chinese).

Liang, C. (2002), 'Chinese agriculture after WTO entry,' *South China daily*, (November 13).

Lin, J.Y. (2001), 'WTO accession and China's agriculture', *China Economic Review*, 11, no.4 (Winter):405-8.

Liu, X. (2001), 'Four strategies to ensure growth of farmers' income,' *Economic Daily*, online, (October 26) (in Chinese).

Liu, Z. (2002), 'The cause and policy response to township budget deficits,' *Economic Daily*, online, (July 9) (in Chinese).

Lu, R. (2005), 'When will Chinese children enjoy free compulsory education?' *China Today*, (June):29.

Lu, Y. and Wang Z. (2001) 'An empirical analysis of disparities in farmers' income and distribution,' Chinese Rural Economy, no.6, 19.

Ma, X. (1999), 'China's policies on self-sufficiency of grain and food security', OECD, *Agriculture in China and OECD Countries: Past Policies and Future Challenges*, 45-54. (Paris: OECD).

Ma, X. and Lan H. (2002), 'A study of China's agricultural subsidy policy after WTO entry,' *Journal of Agricultural Economy*, no.2:10 (in Chinese).

Ministry of Commerce of the PRC (2005), 'Analysis of Sino-US agricultural trade in 2004,' <http://finance.aweb.com.cn/2005/4/14/8131933.htm> (in Chinese), retrieved on 2005,4,14.

New York Times (2001), 'Leaner factories, fewer workers bring more labour unrest in China,' (March 19), online.

New York Times (2006), 'China Seals off Villages after Protest Violence,' (January 16), online.

Niu, R. (2002), 'Farmers' income and dual structure policy,' <www.aweb.com.cn/2002/ 12/23/2002122394910.htm>, retrieved on 2002,12,23.

O'Brien, K. (2002), 'Collective action in the Chinese countryside' (Review Essay) *The China Journal*. no.48 (July):139-154.

Oi, J. and Rozelle S. (2000), 'Elections and power: the locus of decision-making in the Chinese villages', *The China Quarterly*, no.162 (June): 513-39. Special Issue: Elections and Democracy in Greater China.

Pan, W. (2001), 'Prospect of transferring redundant rural labour in China,' Liaowang Newsweek, no.13, (March 26): 40-41 (in Chinese).

Park, A. (2001), 'Trade integration and the prospects for rural enterprise development in China', in OECD, China's Agriculture in the International Trading System, 186-96. (Paris: OECD).

People's Daily (2003), 'Dangqian zhongguo de nongcun jingji he nongcun zhengce' (Current Chinese rural economy and policy), February 9, <www.peopledaily.com.cn/ GB/jingji/1037/ 2327776.html>, retrieved on 2003,2,9.

People's Daily (2004a), '2004 Zhongguo nongmin shouhuo xiyue' (2004 Chinese farmers harvest happiness), overseas edition, December 13, <www.aweb.com.cn/2004/12/13/10322533. htm>, retrieved on 2004,12,13.

People's Daily (2004b), 'Nianzhong nongcun jingji shuping: Nongmin Shouru jiaoda fudu zengzhang' (End of year comment on rural economy: great income growth of farmers' income), <www.aweb.com.cn/2004/12/27/8532166.htm>, retrieved on 2004,12,27.

People's Daily (2004c), 'Dangqian zhongguo de nongcun jingji he nongcun zhengce' (Current Chinese rural economy and policy), February 9, <www.peopledaily.com.cn/ GB/jingji/1037/2327776.html>, retrieved on 2006,2,9.

People's Daily (2005), 'Jinnian 8 yi nongmin jiang mianzheng nongye shui' (800 million farmers will be exempted of agricultural taxes in 2005), June 29, 2005,

<http://politics.people. com.cn/GB/1027/3503943.html>, retrieved on 2005,6, 29.

Qiao, T. (2005), 'Sharing economic fruits with 900 million farmers', Special Report, China Today. 54:5 (May):12-14.

Rural News, (Nongcun xinbao) (2002), 'Jiceng diaocha: xiangcun ganbu dui shuifei gaige "sampan" "sanpa"' (Local survey: township and village officials' "three hopes and fears"), <www.aweb.com.cn/2002/5/26/200252693639.htm>, retrieved on 2002,5,26.

Schmidhuber, J. (2001), 'Changes in China's agricultural trade policy regime: impacts on agricultural production, consumption, prices, and trade', in OECD, *China's Agriculture in the International Trading System*, 21-51 (Paris: OECD).

South Farmers' News (2002), 'Nongmin zenshou xiancong jianshui rushou'(Tax reduction to boost peasant income), March 29, 2002.

State Council (2002), 'To ensure smooth of the new management system of rural compulsory education,' <www.aweb.com.cn/2002/5/17/200251783822.htm> (in Chinese), retrieved on 2002,5,17.

State Council (2006) A Research Report on China's Migrant Workers, Beijing: Yanshi chubanshe (in Chinese).

The Economist, (2005), 'The Cauldron Boils,' (September 29), online.

Tian, Q. (2001), 'China's new urban-rural divide and pitfalls for the Chinese economy', *Canadian Journal of Development Studies* 22:1,165-90.

Unger, J. (2002), *The Transformation of Rural China* (Armonk: M.E. Sharpe).

Wang, D. (2001), 'China's grain economy toward trade integration: policy adjustment and trade implications', in OECD, China's Agriculture in the International Trading System, 208-28. (Paris: OECD).

Wang, J. (2002), 'The causes of the agrarian crisis,' <www.aweb.com.cn/2002/9/29/2002929104034.htm> (in Chinese), retrieved 2002,9,29.

Wang, X. (2002), 'The WTO challenge to agriculture', in Ross Garnaut and Ligang Song, eds., China 2002: WTO Entry and World Recession. (The Australian National University, Asia Pacific Press), 81-95.

Whiting, S. (2001), *Power and Wealth in Rural China: the political economy of institutional change*. (Cambridge, U.K.: Cambridge University Press).

World Journal, (2006), 'Violent clash over land dispute and more than 30 were wounded,' (January 15) online.

Wu, X. (2003), 'Green barriers block China's agricultural exports,' *Economic Daily*, online, (January 1) (in Chinese).

Xie, Y. (2002), 'Rural compulsory education: the central government owes too much,' <www.aweb.com.cn/2002/12/18/ 2002121884651.htm> (in Chinese).

Xinhuanet (2005a), 'Gedi qingqian gongcheng kuan he mingong gongzi shijian biao' (Timetable for paying back arrears of construction projects and back wages for migrant workers), <http://news.xinhuanet.com/banyt/2005/01/21/content_2491549.htm>, retrieved on 2005,1,21.

Xinhuanet (2005b), 'Qunian 29 ge shengfen yue liu yi nongmin xiangshou liangshi zhibu' (About 600 million farmers in 29 provinces benefit from direct subsidies in grain production last year), <http://news.aweb.com.cn/2005/2/11/0083087.htm>, retrieved on 2005,2,11.

Xue, X. (2002), 'Central budget should increase support for rural basic education: interview with Su Ming,' *Economic Daily*, online, (October 8) (in Chinese).

Yang, D. (2005), 'China's Looming Labor Shortage', *Far Eastern Economic Review*, (January / February), 168:2, 19-24.

Zhao, Y. (2001), 'Tax-for-fee reform in the countryside: another major institutional Innovation since household responsibility system,' *Chinese Rural Economy*, no.6, 45-51, (in Chinese).

Zhongguo nongwang (*ZGNW*) (2002), 'Shijie shucai shichang qianjing yu woguo chukou zhengce' (Prospect of the world vegetables market and our export policy), <www.aweb.com.cn/2002/11/22/2002112284849.htm>, retrieved on 2002,11,22.

Zhongguo nongwang (*ZGNW*) (2003a), 'Nongcun jiaoyu: loudou jingji xia de "jiandaocha,"' (Rural education: the "scissor situation" under a "filter economy"), <www.aweb.com.cn/2003/2/22/2003222 105807.htm>, retrieved on 2003,2,22.

Zhongguo nongwang (*ZGNW*) (2003b), <www.aweb.com.cn/2003/3/10/200331083 123.htm>, retrieved on 2003,3,10.

Zhongguo nongwang (*ZGNW*) (2004a), 'Xiangzhen jiceng caizheng fuzhai 5000 yi, tizhi gaige hushing rijing poqie,' (Local government debt at 500 billion *yuan*, institutional reform urged), <www.aweb.come.cn/2004/4/4/200444103913.htm>, retrieved on 2004,4,4.

Zhongguo nongwang (*ZGNW*) (2004b), 'Guanyu Anhui xianxiang caizheng qingkuang de diaocha,' (A survey of county and township finance in Anhui), <http://news.aweb.com.cn/2004/7/31/2004 731112716.htm>, retrieved on 2004,7,31.

Zhongguo nongwang (*ZGNW*) (2005a), 'Zongguo jingji jinru zuihao fazhan shiqi' (Chinese economy enters the best period of development), <http://news.aweb.com.cn/ 2005/1/31/10093 366.htm>, retrieved on 2005, 1, 31.

Zhongguo nongwang (*ZGNW*) (2005b), 'Zhongguo zhengfu chengxian zhongnong' chengnuo'(Chinese government deliver what it promised to hundreds of millions of farmers), <www.aweb.com.cn/2005/10/11/930520.htm>, retrieved on 2005,10,11.

Zhongguo nongwang (*ZGNW*) (2005c), 'Nongmin Peiyang yige daxuesheng xu 18 nian de shouru,'(A four year college education costs farmer 18 years of income), <http://news.aweb.com.cn/2005/12/ 19/8243750.htm>, retrieved on 2005,12,19.

Zhou, H. (2001), 'A study of the impact of urban-rural food demand on farmers' income from food production,' *Chinese Rural Economy*, no.6, 25-29 (in Chinese).

Zhu, B. (2001), 'Tax-for-fee reform: progress, difficulties and analysis,' *Chinese Rural Economy*, no.2, 12-16, (in Chinese).

Zhu, M. and Ye Z. (2005), 'Three problems troubling tax-for-fee reforms,' *People's Daily*, online, (June 8), <http://theory.people.com.cn/GB/40764/48184/3450846.html>.

Chapter 10

China, the World Trade Organization and the End of the Agreement on Textiles and Clothing: Impacts on Workers[1]

Markus Eberhardt and John Thoburn

Introduction

China is the world's most important exporter of textiles and clothing (T&C). For three decades, its exports of these products, like most developing countries, were restricted in the world's largest markets – the US and the EU – by the system of export quotas under the Multi-Fibre Arrangement (MFA) and its successor, the Agreement on Textiles and Clothing (ATC). Despite these restrictions, China's exports of both clothing and textiles over the period 1990-2001 grew at more than double the rate of world exports of those products, and faster than world trade as a whole (WTO 2002). At the beginning of 2005 the ATC and the system of MFA[2] export quotas came to an end, and clothing and textile trade has been 'integrated' into the normal rules of the World Trade Organization.[3] Developing countries now have the opportunity to expand their exports to markets formerly restricted by quota.

China will still be faced with some restrictions on its exports both to the US and the EU until around 2008 under bilateral trade agreements. Nevertheless, it has been predicted that China will be the main beneficiary from the ending of ATC/MFA export quotas, with its market share in both the US and the EU rising substantially, especially in clothing (Nordås 2004). China is currently widely seen as a threat to the many developing countries that expanded clothing and (to a lesser extent) textile

---

1 The survey of secondary sources on which this chapter is mainly based was undertaken as part of the project 'Globalisation, Production and Poverty' (R7623), 2000-2003, financed by a research grant from the UK Department for International Development (DfID). For more information on the project, see www.gapresearch.org/production/globprodpov.html. DfID supports policies, programmes and projects to promote international development. DfID provided funds for this study as part of that objective, but the views and opinions expressed are those of the authors alone. The project also included fieldwork on textiles and garments in China by Eberhardt and Thoburn in the summer of 2002.

2 Strictly speaking, the MFA ceased to exist after 1994 when the ATC came into effect. However, virtually everyone in the industry still refers to the MFA, and we follow that practice here.

3 Non-WTO members can continue to have MFA quotas imposed on them after the start of 2005, as has happened in the case of Vietnam's export to the US.

exports on the basis of possessing under-utilised MFA export quotas. The 'quota hopping' foreign investment that such developing countries attracted may well, it is feared, relocate to China as global buyers take the opportunity to rationalise their sourcing (Nadvi and Thoburn 2004).

In the face of such past, and predicted future, successes, at first sight it may seem odd to discuss China's clothing and textile industries in terms of marginalisation. Yet two dimensions justify such discussion. First, while much of current discussion on the end of the MFA focuses on the impact on workers in countries whose T&C industries are vulnerable, workers in 'winner' countries like China are vulnerable too as the T&C industries consolidate into fewer larger factories (AccountAbility 2005, p. 4). In China's particular case, the clothing and (especially) textile industries also have been restructuring under the country's economic reforms, particularly since the mid-1990s (Moore 2002: ch 5): there have been substantial job losses, and much restructuring remains to be done. Second, China achieved its export successes in the 1980s and 1990s while keeping its domestic economy heavily protected from import competition. As part of its agreement on joining the WTO in 2001, China has undertaken major cuts in tariffs, including those on textile and clothing. Increased import competition will intensify the urgency of economic reform, again with potential social costs.

This chapter offers some thoughts, based both on Chinese and English sources, on the past and possible future social costs of China's export successes and of its trade liberalisation under the WTO, with the T&C industries as the focus. It does so by focusing on the processes of economic reform of the clothing and textile industries in the late 1990s in *preparation* for WTO membership and considers the employment and social implications of that restructuring.

The restructuring of China's clothing and textile industries

The Chinese textile and clothing industries have faced many problems in their pursuit of international competitiveness over the years. At the beginning of the 1990s only some 1% of China's textile machinery met international standards (*China Economic Review*, June 2000). The *China-Britain Trade Review* reported that in 1996 the textile industry had a production capacity of 41 million spindles, with market demand standing at the equivalent of only 20 million (CBTR February 1997). In addition, state enterprises were burdened by the costs of providing education, medical and other charges as well as redundancy benefits (OETH 1999). A further problem area related to modern business techniques and production patterns/characteristics: China lacked abilities in marketing and in managing small-batch flexible production and greater varieties of product.

When China was rapidly expanding its textile and garment exports in the 1980s it was able to sell without strong reference to production costs. Losses to foreign trading corporations and to the state owned enterprises that then dominated the industry were subsidised by government. As China's foreign trade reforms preceded, prices received by enterprises increasingly mirrored international prices, and as enterprises became responsible for their own profits and losses, the need for enterprise reform became urgent (Moore 2002, ch.5). However, even though the problem areas mentioned above had been clearly identified during the early 1990s, few concrete measures were taken, although the share of state owned enterprises in total production had been much reduced.[4] Production competitiveness to some extent still relied on increased scale of output, in connection with a low-quality, low-price strategy – although, as Moore (2002, ch.2) showed, the MFA/ATC quota restrictions on Chinese textile and clothing exports generated strong counter-pressure to restrict output and upgrade products. Government recognised the urgency of structural reform in order to guarantee the sustainability of the sector, especially after entry into WTO, and a restructuring plan for the sector finally started in 1997.

By the turn of the millennium, the *China Economic Review* reported the Chinese textile industry to be "top of the Chinese government's restructuring list." (June 2000). A first wave of restructuring efforts had centred on the issues of obsolete technology and overcapacity in the sector. In order to achieve this aim, it was planned to close down the most inefficient mills, start to replace outdated technology with high-tech machinery and reduce the number of spindles by about 25%. The first of these aims was said to have been implemented with vigour, resulting in a substantial reduction of work force (discussed later). By the year 2000, 134 bankruptcies and 217 mergers were reported to have taken place within the large-scale textile production sector. Reduction of spindles was also pursued in accordance to plan, with some sources even reporting the physical destruction of spindles by steamroller in order to prevent them from being sold and re-deployed in other areas (*China Economic Review* April 1998). The reduction of spindles amounted to 5.1 million in 1998 and 4.4 million in 1999, suggesting that the target of 10 million was successfully reached by the end of 2000.

It was also planned to change the geographical structure of the industry, by reducing the processing capacity mainly located in large cities and strengthening production in central and western China. This was said to have been achieved, at least to some extent, with a significant number of enterprises moving to low wage provinces such as Jiangxi, Shanxi or Xinjiang:

> The development of a textile industry in the western part of China has advantages such as good supply of textile raw materials, low cost of labour, and an industrial base after decades of development. Besides, due to its traditionally economic and cultural relations with neighbouring countries as well as a clear complementation in resources and technology, western China has superior conditions for border trade of textiles. However, there are also some distinct disadvantages. Most textile enterprises in western China are state-owned enterprises (hereafter SOEs), lacking strong innovating capacity or market adaptability. In addition the economic system lacks vitality in a highly market-depending industry such as textiles. With a view to the industrial and product structures, western China mainly focuses on the primary processing of cotton and wool textiles. Due to a sharp gap between

---

4 Moore notes that the share of SOEs in China's total textile output had fallen from almost 90% in the 1970s to 54% in 1991, and then to 29% in 1995. In garments, township and village enterprises produced 60% of garment output from 1991 to 1995. Foreign invested enterprises accounted for 24% of textile exports in 1994 and about a third of garments in the late 1990s (Moore 2002: 76-7, 160).

> the West and seaboard provinces in additional factors of production (capital, technology, management skills and information access), garments have low technical content and added value. (CNTEX, August 2001)

These plans and achievements of the first restructuring phase needed to be regarded with some scepticism, however. No doubt over-capacity and waste of resources were reduced, but there is some doubt whether this was carried out in the most sensible fashion. One source noted that "experience shows that the government, not managers, controls the process of merging SOEs so state interests rather than business interests are at the heart of the matter." (*China Economic Review*, June 1998). The same source questioned the viability of the restructuring process given the social implications: "The ability to find employment for laid off workers is a fundamental requirement of SOE reform. This would necessitate an annual [GDP] growth rate of around 8% – if this is not achieved, the pace of reform would have to slow down." The European Organisation for Textiles and Clothing (OETH) had similar reservations about whether the government would be able to carry out the closure of enterprises and laying-off of workers as envisaged (OETH 1999).

Further difficulties for the sector arose from the internal competition with a growing number of unregistered small textile mills. These low cost, low quality, low product price producers threatened to undermine the success of the restructuring programme, as they challenged the market positions of large- and medium-scale enterprises, competing with them for acquisition of raw materials. This had the potential to lead to "chaos in the already saturated cotton yarn and cotton fabric market" (CNTEX August 2001).

In early 2000, the Chinese State Textile Bureau announced that the campaign to eliminate surplus production capacity was coming to an end, and that the second phase of restructuring would now shift to focus on technical 'modifications'. 20 billion Yuan (US$2.4 billion) were planned to be allocated to various enterprises to upgrade textile technologies (interest-free contribution by the government), and an additional 14 billion Yuan (US$1.7 billion) was planned to be available in the form of preferential bank loans (*China Economic News* 13 March 2000). Furthermore, in early 2001 the State Development Planning Commission and the State Economic and Trade Commission compiled a catalogue of 'Priority Industries, Products and Technologies', covering 28 areas and 526 products, technologies and projects. The areas identified were to receive special treatment (e.g. exemption from import duties and VAT for imported equipment and technology) in order to foster them as spearheads of Chinese industrial development. The textile and associated industries featured prominently in this catalogue. Special attention was given to product innovation in natural and chemical fibres (including compound materials, and multi-purpose and differentiated chemical fibres), manufacture of special textiles for industrial use and improvements in textile machinery manufacture identified as priority goals (*China Economic News* Supplement 12 March 2001).

The development of T&C within Chinese industry was also given special attention in the government's 10th Economic Five-Year Plan, 2001-2006. Development goals included a sectoral growth rate of 6.5% per annum, based on a 15% rise in processing quantity of textile fibres, a 40% increase in productivity per worker and an export volume of US$70-75 billion (an increase of 40% over 2000 levels). In addition, the development of 'non-traditional' textiles for industrial and household use was made the focus of future development. These goals were accompanied by an emphasis on technology development and water- and power-saving measures (CNTEX June 2001). In general, there were five key areas of reform emphasised in the new Plan:

- *Product development:* increase in product quality, variety and sophistication.
- *Enterprise development:* Develop organisational structure in accordance with market demands; within enterprises strengthen R&D, marketing and service; create flexibility in terms of rapid reaction to changing market demands.
- *Regional production clusters:* Make active use of regional comparative advantages between different parts of the country (especially western provinces and seaboard) and encourage intraregional production networks and trade.
- *SOE reform:* Deepen the reforms carried out in the first phase of restructuring; adopt various strategies to alter the capital structure of SOEs: float on the stock market, enter into joint venture contracts, etc.
- *'Informationalisation':* Improve the rapid flow of information between different sections of the production chain and between producers and consumers by means of information technology.
(Adapted from CNTEX June 2001)

These recommendations showed an understanding that in order to continue to compete on the global market, the Chinese textile industry had to move away from production of cheap textiles and garments with little variety, and turn towards more sophisticated products, including industrial textiles. This move was to be accompanied by increased forward and backward linkages within the sector and the adoption of modern management and marketing strategies (e.g. increased branding of products), against a background of differential development in different regions of the country. The recommendation was to concentrate production focused on the domestic market in central and western provinces, while the eastern seaboard provinces had to emphasise quality-export production (Shi 2000).

The implementation of these plans hinged on a number of factors, but most importantly the availability of capital to carry out continued technological upgrading, intensified R&D, and training of textile production personnel, in addition to the financial requirements of 'informationalisation' and managerial training (including business management and marketing). Even though the term 'informationalisation' seems vague, there were signs that significant achievements had been made on this front, with a large number of private and public/institutional information 'hubs' for trading in T&C inputs and outputs available online. A further important factor in the realisation of reforms in the T&C sector was the extent to which decisions were based on unbiased economic/business analysis, rather than political favouritism or other directly unproductive profit-seeking activities (Shi 2000).

Profitability

After annual deficits for almost a decade, the textile sector emerged for the first time into profit in June 1999 (*China Economic Review*, October 1999). The sector's profitability was finally turned around after a series of serious restructuring measures detailed in the previous section, and major debt owed by SOEs being written off by the government – 12 billion Yuan in the third and fourth quarters of 1998 (*China Economic Review* March 1999).

This information needed to be treated with caution, however, as in autumn 1998, the state-run China Economic News service still detailed a number of reasons for sustained loss in the textile industry. Firstly, constraints on the international market due to the East Asian crisis had led to slightly reduced exports, but had more serious implications for the raw material supply for China's industry, as cotton prices slumped, and some of the crisis nations 'dumped' chemical fibre raw materials on the international market, thus forcing down the prices of domestically produced goods. Secondly, the domestic consumer market was said to have been negatively affected as well. Thirdly, structural factors within the T&C industry, most notably overcapacity and excess labour, were still blamed for holding back the development of the sector.

Data on the profitability of the textile and garment sectors in 2000 is presented in Table 10.1. This information suggests that the textile industry as a whole recovered from the deficit era of the 1990s, with total profits exceeding total losses by a margin of roughly 9 billion Yuan. The percentage changes however show that this recovery was toward the end of the period as the losses accumulated by deficit enterprises halved between 1999 and 2000, while profits increased very significantly in this period. Somewhat surprisingly, the clothing industry's deficit enterprises added 18% in value to their losses in the period studied – however, the clothing industry's profitability was still positive by a margin of more than 6 billion Yuan in 2000.

Table 10.1 Textile and clothing industry profitability in 2000

	Total textile industry	Chemical fibre industry	Garment industry
Total profits (in Yuan bn)	13.89	6.25	8.04
Change from 1999	41.1%	34.0%	57.7%
Total losses from deficit enterprises (in Yuan bn)	4.57	0.93	1.32
Change from 1999	-45.5%	-50.0%	18.1%

Source: CNTEX Feb 2001.

The employment implications of restructuring in the textile and clothing industry

The restructuring of the textile and clothing industries in the 1990s in China had major effects on employment. Available employment figures for the T&C sector in China vary considerably, however. There are two things to note prior to examining them in some more detail. Firstly, industrial statistics in China are generally subject to considerable doubt as to their accuracy in collation and presentation. Although quality of statistics and collection of data are thought to have improved rapidly, there is a serious problem when looking at historical developments given the differences in data quality – until most recently, statistics were limited to a focus on ownership structures, favouring the state-owned enterprise section of industry. In defence of Chinese statisticians one might add that it does represent a formidable challenge to cover this vast economy in transition in terms of industrial data collection. Secondly, and related to the above point, with regard to employment figures in T&C there is a good reason why one should be cautious in accepting the more recent official figures presented in the China Statistical Yearbooks. As the sector was the focus of increased restructuring efforts in the second half of the 1990s, a decline in the work force could be interpreted as wishful ideological thinking rather than actual reality of the progress of the reforms.

Two sets of information exist for past employment in the sector. The data presented in Table 10.2 are taken from various editions of the China Statistical Yearbook. Based on this information, one can detect slightly differential developments in textiles and garments. Throughout the 1990s textile employment more than halved from 7.6 million in 1991 to 3.5 million in 1999. The most significant dip took place in 1997/98, when almost two million employees were shed in the sector. Employment in clothing also declined significantly over the 10 year period studied, however at a much reduced rate. While hovering at around 1.7 million between 1991 and 1996, employment declined by roughly 28% towards the end of the 1990s. Both developments can be seen to reflect the impact of enterprise reform and restructuring pushed by the government from 1997/98. These figures have to be compared with overall employment in the Chinese industrial sector. The latter displays a similar movement to the clothing industry employment, with numbers of employees relatively stable around 65 million until the end of 1996, before declining by almost 20 million in the space of three years. As a result, the share of textile employment in total industrial employment declined from 11.5% in 1991 to 8% in 2000, while the share of clothing employment remained stable at under 3% (all data based on China Statistical Yearbooks 1996-2001).

The second set of employment figures is taken from a study by Szirmai et al (2001), whose findings are presented in Figure 10.1. Their adjusted time series data is based on a 1995 census of industrial activities in China. "[T]he census has the major advantage that the data on employment and output derive from one and the same source, the enterprises." It arrives at a "figure for persons engaged in industry, which is no less than 37.4 million higher than figures in all other available sources." (Szirmai et al 2001). It is thus not surprising that the magnitudes of employment figures are far more substantial than in the data presented above.

Textile employment peaked in 1991 with 9.6 million workers, subsequently falling (in exception of 1994) at an accelerating speed to arrive at 6.4 million in 1999. It is interesting to note that the size of this reduction (3.2 million) is very roughly comparable to the reduction in the China Statistical Yearbook figures (4 million). The share of total industrial employment underlines this similarity: from about 12% in 1991, the share of workers in textiles fell to 9% in 1999, representing a slightly less pronounced reduction than in the Statistical Yearbooks (11.5% to 8%). For clothing employment, the general trend of the data equally supports the findings presented earlier.

Table 10.2 Number of staff and workers in the textile industry (1991-2000)

	1991	1992	1993	1994	1995	1996	1997	1998	1999	2000
Textiles employment 10,000 workers	756	743	684	691	673	634	596	393	353	327
Clothing employment 10,000 workers	172	174	164	181	175	168	162	127	122	120
Total industrial employment 10,000 workers	6,551	6,621	6,626	6,580	6,610	6,450	6,215	4,753	4,428	4,102
Share of textile industry in total industrial employment	11.5%	11.2%	10.3%	10.5%	10.2%	9.8%	9.6%	8.3%	8.0%	8.0%
Share of clothing industry in total industrial employment	2.6%	2.6%	2.5%	2.8%	2.6%	2.6%	2.6%	2.7%	2.8%	2.9%

Sources: China Statistical Yearbooks 1996-2001.

One can make several comments on this development. The stable employment for the clothing sector could be said to have been based on the relative efficiency of the sector in comparison to the textile sector, which meant that textiles had to shed significantly more workers than clothing production. The labour-intensive nature of clothing production allowed only limited scope in the increase of productivity (although some progress had been made with the introduction of computerised cutting). On the other hand, the more capital-intensive textile industry had more scope for productivity increase, which could also be read into the massive reduction of textile employees vis-à-vis rising output figures presented above. It is erroneous, though, to assume that the Chinese textile industry caught up significantly in terms of productivity. These matters will be discussed in some more detail below. However, with regards to the clothing industry, the generally positive tenor of comments which can be found throughout the literature at the time seems to support the above interpretation of a relatively appropriate sector size with international competitiveness.

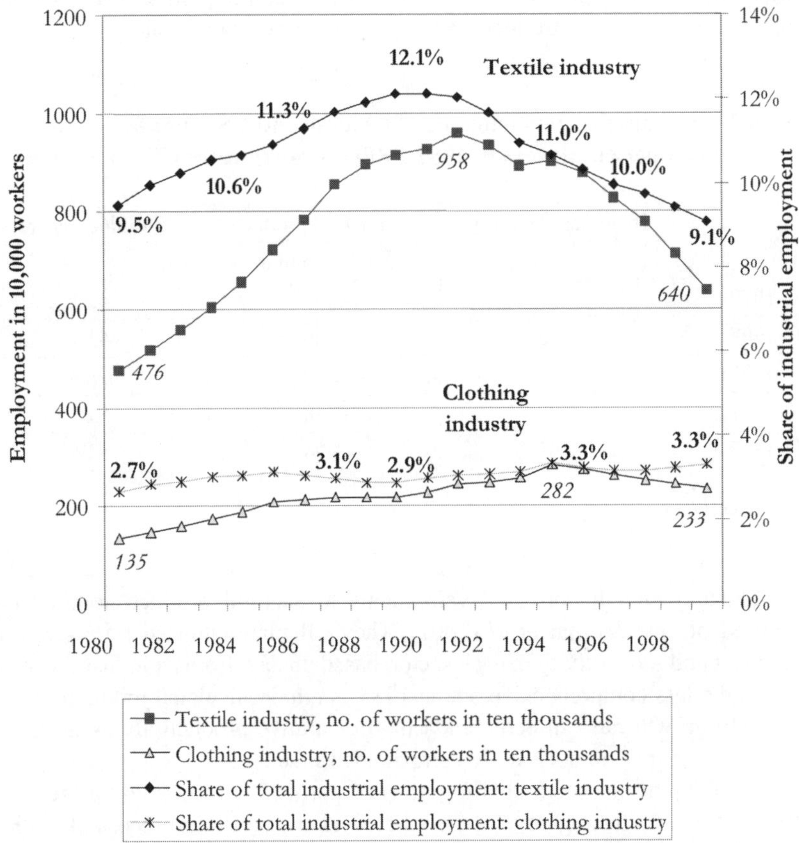

Figure 10.1 Employment in textiles and clothing
Source: Szirmai et al (2001).

Productivity growth

The restructuring of the textile and clothing industries in the late 1990s was associated with rising labour productivity, especially in clothing. Wu (2001) measured the value-added developments in comparison to the United States, in order to see whether China was catching up with industrialised nations in terms of productivity or not. Table 10.3 shows Wu's results for annual growth rates of Gross Value Added (GVA) per employee in total manufacturing, textile and clothing production respectively. A positive rate means that productivity grew faster than US productivity, i.e. China was 'catching up'. A negative rate should be interpreted as China falling further behind in terms of productivity. Wu's results show clear evidence of a catch-up process for the whole of Chinese industry, but that this had not materialised until the intensification/deepening of market-oriented reforms in the 1990s, after a long period of stagnation between 1958 and 1990. A similar conclusion can be made for the T&C sector developments, but with productivity performance in clothing much stronger than in textiles, and indeed much stronger than in manufacturing as a whole.

Table 10.3 Comparative performance of Chinese and US manufacturing: GVA per employees in 1987 PPPs – growth rates (China vs. US)

	Total manufacturing	Textile mill products	Clothing apparel
		Annual growth in %	
1952-1978	1.52	-2.53	4.61
1978-1987	-0.45	-7.69	-4.04
1987-1997	5.77	5.07	15.18
1978-1997	2.78	-1.18	5.63
1952-1997	2.05	-1.96	5.04

Source: Wu (2001).

A second study into historical developments in sectoral productivity in China was carried out by Szirmai *et al* (2001). They calculate adjusted time series for employment and productivity in each sector, based on data from an industrial census in 1995 and a less comprehensive one in 1985. As they calculated productivity and productivity growth rates directly, and not comparative productivity as in the Wu approach, the figures are not readily comparable to the latter.

Figure 10.2 plots the sectoral GVA and GVA per worker employed for the period of 1984 to 1999. A striking development here was the catch-up process of clothing productivity per worker with that of the textile sector, while the rise in labour productivity in both textiles and clothing compared to the 1980s was considerable.

Social implications of employment restructuring

One result of rationalisation in China's industrial sector was social unrest. *The China Economic Review* reported in February 2001 that workers from the Guiyang Textile Factory in Guizhou province in south-western China (one of the poorest and most infrastructure-weak provinces in the country) had clashed with police. This occurred after it emerged that 1,500 workers would be laid off as a result of restructuring. Accounts like these are hard to come by, and may be only the tip of the iceberg. Unrest in China's oil-industry, reported in the British press gives some insights into the current situation in China's industry, and the situation probably did not differ greatly from that in textiles. At the start of the new millennium, tens of thousands of workers in SOEs were reported to be on strike in the Chinese industrial heartland of the north-east. Reform was pushed by officials, stating that WTO-entry was forcing them to reduce the work force in order to cope with competition on the world market. Social security systems in China required that "most laid-off workers stay on a company's books, and rely on it for housing and welfare". However, many companies were unable to continue paying the monthly allowances of a meagre 180 Yuan. "The Chinese government expects a further 20 million jobs to be lost across the country as a result of joining the World Trade Organization." (The Guardian, 21 March 2002).

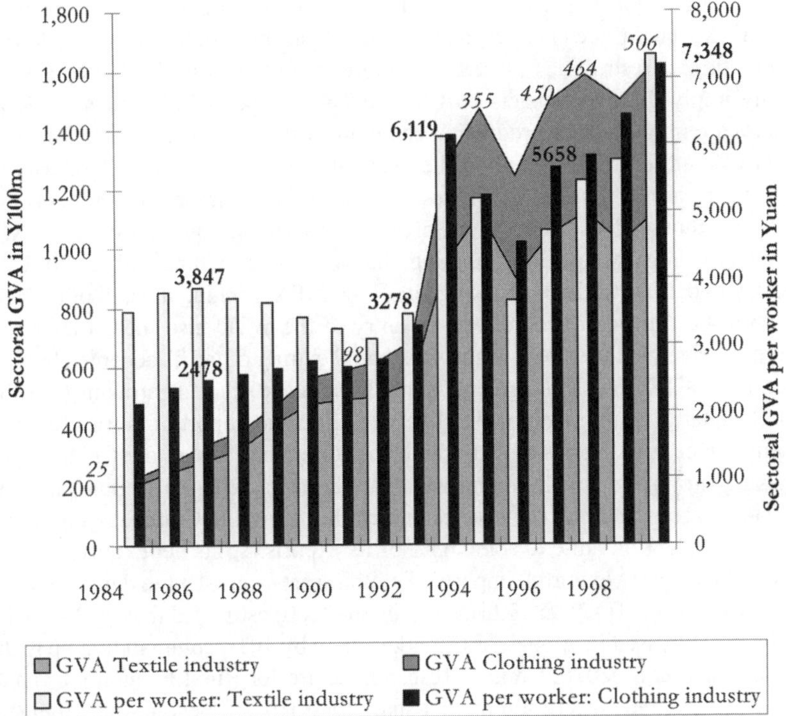

Figure 10.2 Gross value added in T&C
Source: Szirmai et al (2001).

Cook and Jolly (2000), in a qualitative study of 93 workers laid off from mainly state and collectively owned enterprises in China, chronicled the impact on workers retrenched following restructuring, although their findings were not specific to the T&C sectors. Laid-off workers did not necessarily fall into poverty but they suffered from great loss of status and value. Social networks of family and friends were used for support, and great stress was put on continuation of educational provision for children so as to avoid poverty being passed to the next generation. Many laid-off workers were among the least educated of their former work colleagues.

Impacts of the ending of the ATC and of WTO membership

As noted earlier, it is widely believed that the ending of the ATC from the start of 2005, and the consequent integration of textiles and clothing into the normal WTO rules, will be of major benefit to China's T&C exporters. An influential WTO study (Nordås 2004) has estimated that the market share of Chinese clothing exports in total EU clothing imports will rise from 18% to 29%, and in the US from 16% to 50%. Virtually all other exporters to those markets will see their shares fall, except for India. Similar, though much smaller, increases are predicted to occur in China's share of the EU and US textiles market. While these estimates are based on the effects of expected price changes, and do not take account of any wage rises within China or further restrictions placed on imports from China in the EU or US, they certainly imply that the impacts on Chinese T&C output will be positive. Export prospects are important for production and employment in textiles and garments, as exports account for around a half of the total value of output (Moore 2002: 61).

There are also a number of Chinese estimates of the impact of the end of the MFA/ATC, though these tend to be presented as studies of the effects of WTO membership. Legally speaking, joining the WTO – as China did in 2001 – is necessary to participate in the phasing out of the MFA. Linking the end of the MFA/ATC with the analysis of the effects of entry to the WTO also means taking into account in principle the impact of the substantial cutting of tariffs accepted by China as part of its WTO accession agreement, not least in textiles and garments (see Table 10.4). Such tariff cutting would be unlikely to affect the import of fabrics for export garments, since such fabrics already can be imported duty free under China's export processing arrangements (Lemoine and Unal-Kesenci, 2004). It could, however, affect the domestic market for textiles and clothing. While China already imports textiles equivalent in value to some 63% of its exports (so its net exports are much smaller than its gross exports), imports of clothing are equivalent to a mere 3% of its garment exports (WTO 2003). Zhi Wang (in Shi 2000) estimated that by 2005 China would have increased its global T&C market share by 10%, commanding up to 30% of the US market by 2010. China's Research Centre for Rural Economy arrived at a more conservative 20% of US market share for 2010 and beyond in a 1999 study (Research Centre for Rural Economy, CICC 1999). Interestingly, these are both less optimistic than the WTO study by Nordås (2004).

Shi (2000) presented a 1996 study, comparing the WTO entry versus non-entry scenarios, based on differential GDP growth rates prior to WTO entry (8% per annum during 1996-2000 for model A – the non-WTO scenario, 9% for model B – the WTO scenario). The study calculated that Chinese annual exports of T&C would rise from US$50 billion in value in 2000 to US$63 billion in 2005 and US$82 billion in 2010 (thus a 64% increase) without WTO-membership, and from US$60 billion in 2000 to US$80 billion in 2005 and US$108 billion in 2010 (an 80% rise) in the alternative case. Consequently, China was said to lose significantly if it were to be excluded from WTO-membership. It is worth noting that actual export value in 2000 was US$52 billion, representing a strong recovery from the meagre post-Asian-crisis years, which naturally could not be anticipated by the above study.

Table 10.4 Estimated reduction in trade protection in China: tariff and NTB protection rates in China after its WTO accession (%)

	2000	2001	2002	2003	2004	2005-2010	Rate of reduction	Initial NTB
Apparel	32.1	28.5	24.9	21.4	17.9	17.9	44.3	
Electronics	11.6	9	6.3	3.7	3	3	74.5	7.8
Motor vehicles and parts	33.3	29.2	25.1	21.1	18.4	18.4	44.7	26.3
Textiles	25.4	22	18.5	15.2	12.4	12.4	51.2	7

Source: Ma & Wang (2001).

The most comprehensive study of the likely impact of WTO-entry on China's economy was carried out by Chinese academics Jun Ma and Zhi Wang (Ma and Wang 2001). Based on a set of reasonable assumptions (concerning tariff reductions, MFA quota phase-out, FDI increase) they employed a general equilibrium model to estimate the developments of China's industrial sectors in 2005. They concluded that WTO accession and related growth in foreign direct investment would bring about an additional 0.45% of annual real GDP growth between 2001 and 2005. The estimated 6.7% rise in overall exports would outweigh a 5.2% increase in imports, thus further strengthening China's positive balance of trade. These figures gain in significance if compared to the predicted performance of Taiwan and Hong Kong, both with less than one tenth of a percentage point gain in real GDP growth and negative balance of trade effects as a result of China's WTO entry.

In their sector-specific analysis, they painted an optimistic picture of the prospects both for China's textile and its clothing industries. This is despite the lower protective measures in place to safeguard China's domestic market from an influx of foreign T&C products, as a result of WTO stipulations (see Table 10.4). The electronics and motor vehicle sectors are presented in the following tables to provide some means of comparison to other sectors in the Chinese economy. The auto industry is said to be one of the losers of future developments in a WTO environment, while the electronics sector was, according to Shi (2000), believed to overtake the T&C sector as prime export earner by 2010.

The results for the 2001 Ma & Wang study into sectoral production changes are presented in Table 10.5. The apparel/clothing industry was estimated to have increased production by over 60% by 2005, in comparison to the non-entry scenario, while the impact on the textile industry was much lower, with roughly 13%. These figures were surprising, especially in the case of the rise in apparel/clothing output, given the discussion of the characteristics of the MFA phase-out, which virtually postponed the liberalisation of clothing categories until the very end of the re-integration process in 2005.

Table 10.5 Percentage change in production by 2005*

	HK	Taiwan	China
Apparel	-9.9	-6	60.6
Electronics	6.3	1.5	26
Motor vehicles & parts	-2	-7.9	-5.4
Textiles	0.6	9.9	13.4

Note: * comparison to non-entry scenario
Source: Ma & Wang (2001).

A further source for the benefits of WTO-entry presented both textiles and clothing/apparel industrial sectors as major long-term job-creators. Egan and Steinhoff (2001) reported that China's State Council Development Research Centre has optimistically projected that its exports of textiles would double between 1998 and 2005, creating 2.85 million jobs in textiles (a 23.5% increase) and 2.61 million jobs in apparel (a 52.3% increase).

While all these estimates were optimistic about China's T&C sector development under WTO entry and the end of the MFA/ATC, there were also some sceptical voices. Firstly, there were doubts as to whether there would ever be free, fair and equal trade in the global textiles and clothing industry (Shi 2000). This appears to be borne out by the existence of the bilateral agreement with the US to the end of 2008, and a similar agreement with the EU.

The second category of doubts about a rapid increase in Chinese T&C exports was focused on the structure and competitiveness of the domestic industry. Analysts believed that the restructuring process was incomplete and that most enterprises were ill-prepared for the stiff wind of competition on the international market. Some enterprises which under the quota regime engaged in foreign trade did not represent the most suitable, i.e. most competitive enterprises, and were therefore said to have developed a dependency on quota allocation, often carried out based on political favouritism and cronyism, rather than competitiveness. Once quotas were abolished, it was feared they would be unable to cope with the 'sudden' competition, and it was certainly questionable as to whether they would be able to significantly increase their competitiveness in the short run. Those enterprises previously prevented from external trade through the quota allocation system, on the other hand, faced problems of a different nature. While their productivity was comparable to foreign competitors, they lacked the experience of marketing on a global scale, the trained staff and the established client channels to achieve significant export volumes in the short run.

Analysts from the Chinese Textile Institute furthermore argued that "it is quite likely that [after quota abolition] there will be fierce competition among Chinese textile export enterprises, especially the 20,000 currently without quota allocation. If the state cannot give appropriate guidance, the export price will be severely affected. In this situation, even if the export quantity can increase significantly, the export value may drop, leading to a decline in export profits" (CNTEX November 2001).

A third group of arguments centred around the 'dangers' of increased imports as a result of WTO membership, and their impact on the T&C industry. There was a pronounced worry among experts that the increase in imports of especially medium- and high-grade, as well as famous-brand textiles and garments would have a significant impact on Chinese products. In particular, the development of chemical fibres, textile machinery and some other textile-related sectors, which were relatively weak compared with their foreign counterparts, were expected to suffer (CNTEX November 2001).

Finally, a further group of arguments concerned the T&C trade patterns in a post-quota world. OETH pointed to the increased trading activities between the US and nearby suppliers in the Caribbean, suggesting that the US market would be supplied from these producers closer to home. "This implies that the relative pressure on Europe of Asian textile and clothing imports is likely to increase, especially as clothing prices are higher in the EU than in the US. But the EU does not expect its own consumption to grow fast. Estimates suggest a moderate increase in consumption of only 1.5% per annum (1995-2005)" (OETH 1999). Future Chinese exports to traditional import markets such as the EU and US were thus likely to be constrained by saturation/slow growth and by firmly established trading relations.

Shi (2000) voiced his grave concern over the ability of the post-2005 textiles and clothing world market to absorb an expected increase of output on behalf of all producer countries. The logical consequence of this 'fallacy of composition' would be a price war between China and other textile producers, where each side would try to oust the opponents by offering yet even lower prices. The most competitive nations would then emerge as victors, or rather *survivors* of this conflict, while the T&C industry of the defeated nations would be forced to close down. Given this scenario, Shi was far from certain whether China will be among the victorious few.

In summary, pessimistic views on China's T&C development at the start of the twenty-first century over the next decade were cautious about possible production and export gains. While not trying to quantify future gains, which would probably still result in a positive impact for the decade ahead, various arguments such as continued restrictions in access to import markets, inherent structural problems and lack of competitiveness, and import effects were presented in order to bring overly optimistic predictions into perspective. There were also dangers stressed by Nolan (2001) of foreign takeovers of domestic enterprises, which Shi (2000), for example, thought could happen in the Chinese man-made fibre industry.

Conclusions

'Marginalisation' is by no means an obvious lens through which to view the impacts of the development of two of China's highly successful export industries, textiles and clothing. Yet we have shown that there were considerable social costs incurred in the late 1990s. These resulted from the restructuring of enterprises in the state owned sector to make them competitive, both as potential exporters and in order to compete against future imports once China had reduced its import barriers under its agreement to join the WTO. The restructuring hit textiles particularly hard and some three million jobs were lost in the sector in the 1990s.

Working mainly with Chinese and other secondary sources published at the time, this chapter has looked, then, at the process through which China reformed its textile and clothing industries in the late 1990s as it moved towards greater international competitiveness and has shown the drastic implications for employment of this restructuring. Estimates for the impacts of the end of the Agreement on Textiles and Clothing from January 2005 generally were optimistic in terms of market shares for China and the impact on production and employment. However, in a situation where individual companies' exports are not constrained by their access to MFA quotas, it is likely that the post-MFA/ATC situation will see global buyers consolidating their purchases on a smaller number of suppliers in China, even if their total purchases from China expand. It is too soon to observe the impacts of this likely process, but it threatens the jobs of workers in particular firms and regions even if employment in the industry as a whole expands. Workers who lose their jobs from SOEs in addition face the problem that they lose their social (housing, medical, pension) benefits if the enterprises close, in the absence of well developed state provision of such benefits (see also the chapter by Tang, Dong and Duda in this volume). Optimistic estimates of the probable job creation in textiles and clothing have been subject to the criticism that they failed to take full account of the effects on employment of intensified import competition in the Chinese domestic market as China reduces its import barriers under its WTO accession agreement. Other research at the time (Cook and Jolly 2000) additionally suggested that less educated and older workers were the most likely to suffer from retrenchment by firms that restructure to remain competitive, and such workers faced a greater probability of being marginalised in China's economy and society than younger and better educated workers.

References

AccountAbility (2005), Managing the Transition to a Responsible Global Textiles and Garment Industry: An Integrated Study of Research by Accountability, Business for Social Responsibility, and the World Bank for the MFA Forum http://www.accountability.org.uk/uploadstore/cms/docs/Managing%20the%20Transition%20(2).pdf, retrieved 2 June 2006.

China-Britain Trade Review (CBTR) (various editions). London: China-Britain Business Council.

China Economic News (various editions). Beijing: External Division of the Economic Daily newspaper.

China Economic Review (various editions). London: Alain Charles Publishing Ltd. (note: not to be confused with the US academic journal of the same name – see for example entry under Wu below).

CICC (1999) Proceedings – The China International Cotton Conference. United Nations Food and Agriculture Organization. http://www.fao.org/waicent/faoinfo/economic/ESC/esce/escr/cotton/China-e/cov_toc.htm: L Zhu (Deputy Director, Industry Administration Department, China Textile Industry Bureau): Developments in textiles consumption and trade in China, retrieved 6 June 2006.

Cook, S. and S. Jolly (2000), *Unemployment, Poverty and Gender in Urban China: Perceptions and Experiences of Laid Off Workers in Three Chinese Cities*, Institute of Development Studies, University of Sussex, Research Report 50.

CNTEX (various editions) News. China Textile Network Information Technology Co. Ltd. http://www.cntextile.com/cntex/english2/news/e_news.asp?Page=1

Egan, S, and D Steinhoff (2000), 'China's WTO entry: Who wins? Who loses?' *Apparel Industry Magazine*, March 2000.

The Guardian newspaper (various editions), London.

Lemoine, F, and D. Unal-Kesenci (2004), 'Assembly trade and technology transfer: the case of China', *World Development*, vol.32, no.5.

Ma, J. and Z. Wang (2001) Winners and Losers of China's WTO entry. *The China Business Review*, March-April 2001. Washington: US-China Business Council.

Moore, T.G. (2002), *China in the World Market: Chinese Industry and International Sources of Reform in the Post-Mao Era*, Cambridge: Cambridge University Press.

Nadvi, K and J.T. Thoburn, with Bui Tat Thang, Nguyen Thi Thanh Ha, Nguyen Thi Hoa and Dao Hong Le (2004), 'Challenges to Vietnamese firms in the world garment and textile value chain, and the implications for alleviating poverty', *Journal of the Asia Pacific Economy*, vol.9, no.2.

National Bureau of Statistics of China (various editions) *China Statistical Yearbook*. http://www.stats.gov.cn/sjjw/ndsj/index.htm.

Nolan, P. (2001) *China and the Global Economy*. Basingstoke: Palgrave.

Nordås, H.K. (2004), *The Global Textile and Clothing Industry Post the Agreement on Textiles and Clothing*, Geneva: WTO (www.wto.org).

OETH (1999) PR China – Textile and Clothing Sector and Its Export Potentials. Brussels: L'Observatoire Europeen du Textile et de l'Habillement.

OETH (2000) *Phase III of the Agreement on Textiles and Clothing – Identifying Areas for Reform: Final Report*. L'Observatoire Europeen du Textile et de l'Habillement. http://www.dfid.gov.uk/AboutDFID/files/itd/atc.pdf, retrieved 9 January 2006.

Shi, Y. (2000) WTO yu Zhongguo fangzhi gongye (WTO and China's Textile Industry), In: Yu, Yongding, Zheng, Bingwen (eds.) Zhongguo 'rushi' yanjiu baogao: jinru WTO de zhongguo chanye (*Research Report on China's Entry into WTO*). Beijing: Shehui kexue wenxian chubanshe.

Szirmai, A., M Bai and R Ren (2001) 'Labour Productivity Trends in Chinese Manufacturing, 1980-1999'. Paper presented the International Conference on the Chinese Economy 'Achieving Growth with Equity', 4-6 July 2001, Beijing. http://fp.tm.tue.nl/ecis/ (working papers 2001/10), retrieved 8 April 2006.

Wang, Z. (1999) 'The Impact of China's WTO Entry on the World Labour-intensive Export Market: A Recursive Dynamic CGE Analysis', *World Economy* 22 (3), pp.379-405.

WTO (annual), *International Trade Statistics 2002, 2003*, Geneva: WTO (www.wto.org).

Wu, H. (2001) 'China's comparative labour productivity performance in manufacturing, 1952-1997 – Catching up or falling behind?' *China Economic Review*, Vol. 12, pp.162-189.

Chapter 11

Conceptualising the Links: Migration, Health and Sustainable Livelihoods in China

Heather Xiaoquan Zhang

Introduction

This chapter tackles an important but much overlooked issue in rural-urban migration in China, that is, health and its relationship to sustainable livelihoods of rural migrants and their families. It is not a systematic investigation into the structural barriers to the health of migrants, nor a discussion of the impact and implications of such barriers for this large group in terms of their livelihoods and the sustainability of those livelihoods. Instead, the chapter identifies missing links between the core notions of our conception of livelihood, its diversification strategies and its components from a health and well-being perspective. It further develops a conceptual framework for understanding the main factors that affect livelihood and its sustainability in such a way that may help inform future empirical research and policy domains in respect of achieving broader and holistic sustainable human development goals in China and beyond.

An Early Experience

In the summer of 1996 my aunt in Beijing was moving house and hired a removal company, *Likang*, which sent over four migrant workers to do the job. *Likang* set strict rules for its workers. For example, it forbade them from accepting anything but the agreed payment from the customer and any employee who did not follow this to the letter would be fined or fired. As a consequence, the migrant workers did not dare even to drink a glass of water when offered one. In the heat of mid-summer, they had to carry heavy furniture by hand through the narrow corridors and staircases in the old apartments of Beijing. If they accidentally damaged the furniture and the customer complained, the compensation would come from their meagre wages. This increased the physical demands of their job since they had to manoeuvre large pieces of furniture on their backs or shoulders within very confined and awkward spaces.

It was an extremely hot day, one of the men was about to faint, and had to leave early (without pay, I assumed). It was not until the rest of the team finished loading the truck that the migrant removers took a break, allowing me an opportunity to chat with them and gain a glimpse of their precarious livelihoods – precarious in all the term's conceivable senses. One told me that they were unable to work in the occupation for long because their "body couldn't withstand it" (*shenti shoubuliao*). Referring to his co-worker who had to leave earlier, he commented, "I wouldn't be surprised if he could not carry on anymore. He has to leave for home [in his village]". He also told me stories about his co-workers who suffered from injuries or ill health and I was surprised to learn that the span of their working life in the removal business could be as short as 4-5 years.

Interrogating Assumptions

This rather brief encounter with migrant removal workers in Beijing marked the beginning of my curiosity about what would happen to them after a few years' working in urban areas and the impact, if they fell victim to ill health, on their families and communities in the villages. I started wondering whether their cash-earning jobs in towns and cities would, in the longer term, necessarily lead to better lives for themselves and their families. I also started interrogating the often taken-for-granted assumptions that rural people will necessarily benefit merely because they are allowed greater physical mobility and are less restrained in finding employment in urban areas. Some other related questions that have since come to my mind include: Would the cash incomes be sustainable if the health of the migrant workers were adversely affected or even permanently ruined? Should migrant workers be solely responsible for their health risks and problems, perceived as the outcomes of their individual health behaviour only? Or are there institutional issues and wider economic and political interests and power involved? What are the relationships between migration, health, livelihoods and sustainability? As well as a larger question: what are the implications of all this for China's development, particularly with respect to poverty reduction, livelihood sustainability, equity and well-being?

The above issues and problems have intensified since the mid-1990s and this chapter presents some ideas on migration and health in China based on a critical reading of existing literature, particularly that of the 'livelihoods approach', which has attracted growing attention in academic and policy arenas since the 1990s. It is an attempt to identify appropriate conceptual tools for furthering our understanding of rural-urban migration and its related issues of livelihoods, health, sustainability and well-being in China and beyond, exploring links between these different dimensions based on a systematic review of current and often disparate bodies of research. In so doing, the chapter is designed to draw the attention of academic and policy domains to the issues raised, as well as to provoke critical thinking and reflection on China's predominant ideologies governing development agendas and practices, and their impact on achieving the broader human development goals of equity, sustainability and well-being. Following this introduction, the chapter discusses the changing status of rural migrants in China in the context of transition, globalisation and shifting social stratification. It points to an urgent need to identify suitable conceptual tools for investigating the many new issues in conjunction with rural-urban migration in the country and argues that the sustainable livelihoods approach is potentially useful to accomplish the task. The chapter then proceeds to examine the sustainable livelihoods framework and identifies its main strengths and weaknesses. It explores the possibility of building a linkage between migration, health, sustainability and livelihoods and of conceptualising ways in which the livelihood framework can be strengthened to enable us to broaden our interrogation and investigate these challenging issues in connection with institutional arrangements and power relations. Finally the chapter draws tentative conclusions by summarising the key arguments and suggesting possibilities of applying this enhanced approach to the analysis of migration and health in China.

Examining the Context – the Shifting Situations of Rural Migrants in China

Erosion of the Household Registration System

Although rural-urban migration is very common in many developing countries, large-scale rural-urban migration has been a quite recent phenomenon in China. For the first three decades of the People's Republic (1949-1979), China was able to prevent most rural-urban migration by introducing and consolidating a centrally planned economic system. This development model placed overwhelming stress on urban-centred heavy industry at the expense of agriculture. One of the key measures adopted to guarantee the state's systemic squeeze of rural surpluses for the expansion of capital-intensive heavy industry was the establishment of a population control mechanism, known as the household registration system, or *hukou* (see also Yi Zhang's chapter in this volume). The regime functioned to minimise consumption and maximise accumulation for industrialisation through rationing in towns, state monopolisation of the markets for goods and services and the virtual elimination of a non-state labour market (Mallee, 1995; Zhang, 1999a). Current literature agrees that the *hukou* regime constituted a serious structural constraint for rural people in terms of geographical, occupational and social mobility, limiting their employment opportunities and life chances. This industrialisation model, therefore, is construed as serving to reinforce a spatial and social hierarchy, dichotomising urban and rural spaces into the core and periphery in respect of development and quality of life (Christiansen, 1990; Davin, 1999; Mallee, 2000; Murphy, 2002).

Since the post-Mao reforms, however, this system has been substantially eroded and the country has witnessed unprecedented population mobility in its recent development history (Croll, 1997; Mallee, 1995; Zhang, 1999b). This is partly shown in the phenomenon of rapid urbanisation. At the beginning of the reforms, the proportion in the country's total population living in rural areas was more than 80%. By the early twenty-first century, it had fallen to 64% (National Statistics Bureau of China, 2001). Although it is difficult to obtain accurate data on the exact size of the mobile population, the Chinese official sources estimate that the scale of rural-urban migration has reached 120-200 million (State Council, 2006). Thus far, much has been documented about the ways in which the *hukou* system operated to control population mobility and the ways in which it has been seriously undermined by both market forces and the actions of rural migrants in seeking economic opportunities (cf. Christiansen, 1990; Mallee, 1995, 2000; Murphy, 2002). Indeed, spontaneous rural migrants at the earlier stage of the reforms were seen by many Chinese scholars as "pioneers" in a "new revolution",[1] playing out their agency, contesting the socio-economic and political boundaries demarcated for them by the state and challenging the structural rural-urban cleavage through actively participating in the newly emerging non-state market (Zhou, 1996; Zhang, 1999b).

Globalisation, Commercialisation and Emerging Social Stratification

By the beginning of the twenty-first century, however, this large and expanding group has been increasingly perceived as "marginalised", "deprived" and "socially excluded" (cf. Li, 2004; Wu, 2004). This is partly due to the more recent changes in the labour market and the related pay structure of the country in an age of intensifying globalisation. As the Chinese economy is increasingly integrated within global markets, highlighted in particular by China's WTO accession in 2001, knowledge, education and skills are increasingly demanded with professionals, technical and managerial personnel and skilled labour commanding much higher pay than non-skilled labour (Guan, 2001; Yang and Xin, 2002), a category into which the majority of rural migrants have fallen (Chan, 1999; Li, 2004). This process, combined with ever growing competition in the international marketplace and thc ruthless pursuit of even cheaper labour in order to maximise profits by both global and domestic capital in the non-skilled sector, has seen wages of rural migrant workers remain stagnant at best for the past couple of decades (Ngai, 2005).[2] The heavy pressure exerted on the jobs market by the country's huge population and its relatively young structure further compounds this. Chinese academics estimate that there are around 15 million people reaching job-seeking age in the country each year, the majority being from rural areas (Li, Q. 2002, p. 59). In such circumstances, much of the earlier "comparative advantages" of rural migrants, who possess little more than abundant cheap labour power, have largely disappeared. The situation has been further exacerbated by a considerable rise in relative poverty and by enlarged gaps between both urban-rural areas and coastal-inland regions in terms of income and social-cultural development (Bhalla, Yao and Zhang, 2003; Yang and Xin, 2002; Zhang, 2004). The worsening inequalities have functioned as a push factor for ever-increasing rural-urban migration. As a consequence, rural migrants are faced with greater competition and growing difficulties in the urban labour market but decreased

---

1 A "revolution" in a sense of both striving for greater individual liberty and nation-building in that rural migrant workers were deemed as effectively contributing to China's rapid economic growth, urbanisation and industrialisation.

2 Although it is difficult to generalise the growing income gaps between professional, managerial and technical personnel and unskilled labour, particularly rural migrants, some personal experiences/contextual knowledge may provide a glimpse of such differences. For example, some of my own acquaintances/friends in their late 20s or early 30s had self-financed their master's degrees in the UK in business or management studies. On completion of their studies abroad, the sought-after employer back home are often foreign-invested or foreign-owned firms (*waiqi*). As far as I am aware, the starting salary for these young managerial staff ranges from 7,000-9,000RMB per month, in contrast with an average monthly wage of between 500-800RMB for rural migrants, which has remained largely unchanged for the past decade or so.

leverage in negotiating their citizenship rights, including rights to employment and residence, equal and on-time pay, decent working and living conditions, fair treatment in housing, healthcare and children's education and so forth. All this has caused concerns that many members of this group may well be turned into a new urban "underclass" in China's changed social stratification (Li, 2004; Wu, 2004).

The vulnerability of rural migrants has been aggravated by growing threats from the many emerging health hazards and infectious diseases, such as tuberculosis (TB), Severe Acute Respiratory Syndrome (SARS), sexually transmitted infections (STIs) and HIV/AIDS (Dong, Hoven and Rosenfield, 2005; Zhang, 2004; Zhang and Lin, 2002; see also the chapters by Cook and Dummer, and by Feng in this volume), together with a sharp rise in mental health problems during the transition period (cf. Dennis, 2004). The market reforms have brought rapid and drastic social-economic changes, created winners and losers in an inadequately regulated market, seen *de facto* privatisation of many social services, particularly healthcare, which has rendered rural migrants unable to access such services, and continued discrimination against and exclusion of rural migrants in most aspects of urban lives.

The newly emerging social stratification since the mid-1990s, combined with the very magnitude of internal migration witnessed in present-day China, necessitates the issue of welfare and well-being of the migrants and their families coming to the fore. The issue often raises concerns about the impact of the market reforms on human development and social justice in the country (cf. Solinger, 1999; Wu, 2004; see also chapters by Cook and Dummer, and by Sanders, Chen and Cao in this volume). Although issues related to social policy and the establishment of a safety net to ameliorate the negative impact of market reforms have started attracting academic and policy attentions both within and beyond China in recent years, much of the new interests have focused on *either* urban *or* rural areas. Examples include new research projects on urban or rural poverty, poverty reduction and reemployment schemes, social policy analysis such as education and healthcare reforms in either urban or rural settings (cf. Anson and Sun, 2005; Bloom and Tang, 2004; Cook and Jolly, 2001). Rural migrants, because of the continued structural constraints of the *hukou* system (albeit considerably weakened in respect of its ability to restrict physical mobility), the mode of their livelihoods, which involves frequent movements across spatial and administrative boundaries, and their lack of resources and power, have found themselves falling into a vacuum of social provision and protection with their citizenship rights scarcely recognised. This is also reflected in academic and policy agendas. For example, little research has been done to examine the health issues, needs and rights of rural migrants. When the health risks of the mobile population are brought into the spotlight, for example, in relation to the HIV/AIDS crisis, the dominant narratives tend to "demonise" the group as the vector and spreader of the deadly virus, and hence, a threat to public health (cf. Tan, 2005).

The above analysis demonstrates an urgent need to study a much neglected, but important and relevant dimension of rural-urban migration in China in relation to the theme of marginalisation, that is, the social rights and health needs of the migrants and their families. However, in filling this gap, questions arise regarding the appropriate conceptual tools that we may employ in advancing our knowledge. In the following section I argue that the sustainable livelihood framework is potentially useful in furthering our understanding of the complex changes and relationships involved in China's rural-urban migration. The section reviews the literature on the sustainable livelihood framework as well as other related research, identifies its strengths and weaknesses, and suggests ways in which the approach can be enhanced for better understanding and for addressing the specific issues raised above.

Exploring Links – Migration, Health and Sustainable Livelihoods

Perceptions of Migration

Conventional studies of migration tend to perceive the phenomenon in a rather negative light, especially in terms of its development implications and policy responses (de Haan, 1999). This reflects deep concerns with the situation where large-scale migration sometimes occurs, for example, in devastating circumstances of armed conflicts, civil strife, famine and other disasters of human or environmental causes. Migration under such circumstances is regarded as "forced" or "involuntary", and accordingly referred to as "distress migration". There is also uneasiness about rapid urbanisation, its effects and social cost, manifested, for instance, in the phenomenon of shantytowns surrounding many large cities in Latin America. Related to this is the view that massive rural-urban migration can mean displacement of agricultural labour and a "brain drain" from rural areas, and so forth, which are feared likely to have negative impacts on the rural economy and society. Increased movements of people across national borders in a globalising world, and their potential political and socio-economic impacts both on the sending, but particularly on the receiving societies, lie at the source of concerns and uneasiness about migration as well.

Livelihood analysis with respect to rural development, however, diverges from this line of thinking on migration. It places increasing emphasis on the positive role played by migration, especially rural-urban migration, in poverty alleviation, rural economic diversification and agricultural development. Migration in livelihood studies is viewed as an important rural household strategy for survival, risk reduction, accumulation for investment, or for a combination of all these things (Ellis, 2000; Francis, 2000; Zhang *et al.*, 2006). The economic contributions that migrants have made to both the destination and the origin are highlighted within this line of argument. Rural migrants are responsive to the demands of the urban labour market, contributing to the diversity and dynamics of the urban economy. Instead of competing with urban residents for jobs, as is often assumed, the tasks which rural migrants perform tend to be disdained by urban dwellers, particularly jobs in the informal sector, dirty, difficult or dangerous, but with low pay, low social status and minimum, if any, job security and social protection. At the same time, migrants have remitted a large proportion of their earnings back to the village. The remittances are used for a variety of purposes by their families at origin, functioning to spread and minimise risks, diversify the economy of both the household and local community, invest in agriculture, improve living standards, support children's education, foster social capital through building and consolidating social networks and associations, on which they can draw for support when in need (Davin, 1999; Ellis, 2000; Murphy, 2002; Zhang *et al.*, 2006).

Despite the insights into the positive role of rural-urban migration and the intrinsic link between migration and the household's livelihood strategy, the livelihood approach, while being mainly concerned with agricultural and rural development, has paid insufficient attention to the livelihoods of rural migrants in relation to their urban experiences and how these may reshape livelihood trajectories and outcomes, which can then impact on the poverty or welfare profiles of the migrant individuals and households in rural or urban settings. This omission, however, needs to be understood in a broader context where livelihood analysis has gained currency. The rise of livelihood studies since the early 1990s has been, to some extent, in response to the unsuccessful top-down development approaches adopted by many multilateral development agencies represented in policies such as the Structural Adjustment Programmes of the International Monetary Fund and World Bank. It is recognised that such top-down approaches, instead of promoting growth and reducing poverty, have often had harmful effects on the poorest countries in the world affecting most adversely the poor and the vulnerable therein (Dasgupta, 1998; Zack-Williams *et al.*, 2000). Against this backdrop, livelihood studies, in contrast, have focused attention on the ways in which people in poverty-stricken remote or rural areas have creatively constructed and constantly readjusted their livelihoods, often under unfavourable circumstances, in their struggles for survival and a better life. Through close examination into the ways rural households strive to make a living by creating, managing and maintaining a diverse portfolio of livelihoods, the livelihood approach emphasises the agency of individuals and their families in shaping their own destinies, places the poor at the centre stage in the processes of fighting poverty and bringing about change, and thus reasserts the claims that people make their own history.

The actor-oriented perspective of the livelihood approach seems to fit well in the analysis of rural-urban migration and its related issues in China in the post-Mao era. However, in view of the changed situation, particularly with regard to the more recent shift in the so-called "comparative advantage" possessed by rural migrants in their efforts to seek, secure, improve and sustain livelihoods in an age of increasing globalisation, as discussed earlier, the emphasis on individuals alone becomes insufficient to capture the forces, especially those embedded in institutions and structures of power, that have mapped onto the livelihood pathways, trajectories and outcomes of individuals and families. How can the livelihood framework be enhanced to meet this challenge? Before answering this question, it is necessary to define the notions of livelihood and livelihood analysis.

The Meanings of Livelihood and the Livelihood Framework

A dictionary definition of livelihood is "a means to a living". This suggests that livelihood should be understood in a broader sense than just income and consumption to include the ways in which a living is gained. It is recognised that the more recent rise of livelihood studies is, to some extent, attributable to the influential work of Chambers and Conway in the early 1990s. According to them, "A livelihood comprises people, their capabilities and their means of living, including food, income and assets. Tangible assets are resources and stores, and intangible assets are claims and access" (Chambers and Conway, 1992, p. iii).

The notion of capabilities adopted in this definition derives from the work by Amartya Sen (1984, 1985, 1987, 1992, 2000; Drèze and Sen, 1989), who stressed the human dimension in people-centred development, as against an earlier tendency in international development thinking and policy making of an overwhelming emphasis on economic growth, or income-based development alone as the single gauge for "opulence" and "a good life". "Capabilities" and "functionings" in Sen's theoretical work refer to "to be" and "to do", or human potentials and the realisation of such potentials. Scholars utilising the livelihood approach since then, however, have pointed to a confusion that might arise from this definition on the ground that "capabilities" might overlap assets and activities – the other essential components of livelihoods (Ellis, 2000). Accordingly, an alternative definition is proposed, "A livelihood comprises the assets (natural, physical, human, financial and social capital), the activities, and the access to these (mediated by institutions and social relations) that together determine the living gained by the individual or household" (Ellis, 2000, p. 10).

The livelihood activities in this definition are those familiar to us, including farm, off-farm and non-farm activities performed by rural people. What needs more elaboration here, perhaps, is the other elements of livelihoods, namely assets and access. Indeed, Ellis' definition of livelihood highlights, among other things, the "assets pentagon", that is, the five kinds of "capital" as stated above. There is considerable literature on livelihood, the meanings of its various "capital components", and particularly social capital. Current research generally agrees that *natural capital* refers to the natural resource base for making a living; *physical capital* refers to assets resulting from human productive activities, such as agricultural machinery, land improvement and rural infrastructure; *human capital* comprises labour, education and health of individuals and populations; *financial capital* refers to cash, including credit and loans, which can be accessed for survival, consumption, or accumulation and investment; *social capital* is defined as familial and kinship ties and informal social networks and associations that people have developed, nurtured and are involved with, and to which they can resort for support in their livelihood activities and strategies (Carney, 1998; Ellis, 2000; Scoones, 1998).

The attention paid to access to assets and *economic opportunities* in the definitions of livelihood and its constituents calls for the exploration of a wide range of factors and forces that can either facilitate or constrain people's livelihood, and shape and reshape their livelihood pathways, trajectories and outcomes. Access is perceived as being mediated by institutions and social relations, including the market, the state, formal and informal rules and social and cultural norms which together can affect or determine the differential abilities of individuals, men and women, and households, rich and poor, to own, control, or lay claims to various resources, including land, communal property and other assets. It is arguable, therefore, that the incorporation of access in the livelihood approach allows for the potential of an analytical strength which connects different levels of analysis – the micro, meso and macro across disparate sectors, such as urban and rural, transcending the structure-agency dualism in a dynamic and holistic manner in an attempt to understand and explain shifting and multiple livelihoods and their outcomes in the broader historical, socio-economic and political context. In the meantime, scholars have pointed out that the means whereby such a potential can be translated into research projects and policy interventions in reality remains unclear so long as assets, rather than access, are the actual focus of the livelihood approach (Murray, 1999; de Haan and Zoomers, 2005).[3]

A policy framework has been developed to further an appreciation of the nature of livelihood, the process of its diversification and household livelihood strategies, especially of the poor, as shown in Figure 11.1.

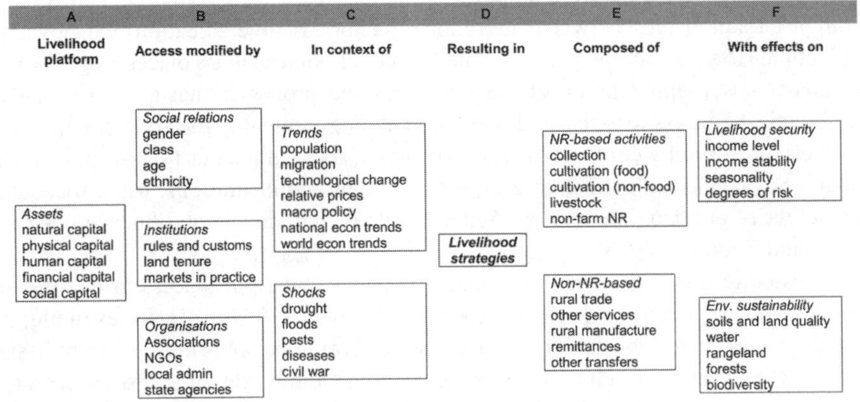

Figure 11.1 A framework for livelihood analysis
Source: Ellis, 2000, p. 30.

The framework is construed as representing the "assets-access-activities" connections (Ellis, 2000, p. 45) and regarded as most suitable for analysing micro-policies concerned with rural poverty alleviation at the local level, although it is suggested that it may also hold the potential of mapping out the impact of macro-level policies and larger forces on the micro-level processes and outcomes. The starting point in this framework is the assets that rural people possess, control or can rely on in supporting their livelihoods. Much research has focused on this dimension with stress being placed on the intangible assets indicated, for instance, in the growing body of literature on social capital (cf. Bebbington, 1997; Bezemer and Lerman, 2004; Mathie and Cunningham, 2005; Wu and Pretty, 2004). While drawing attention to the quantity, quality and mix of the "capital pentagon", and linking this closely to livelihood diversification for poverty reduction, this focus on assets as the basis of livelihood may lead to a downplaying of the other essential elements of livelihood, particularly access, which often raises important issues of equity and social justice, and, as such, poses more challenging questions about existing socio-economic and political arrangements, institutions and power (de Haan and Zoomers, 2005; Murray,

3 See also a critique of the concept of "social capital" by Fine (1999, 2001).

2001).[4] Related to this is the danger of falling into a trap where insufficient analytical space is allowed for the role of the state and public action in facilitating diversification or protecting, securing and sustaining livelihoods and where people, particularly the poor, are left to themselves for sorting out their own livelihood problems.

The Access Problem

The above analysis has shown that rural-urban migration conceptualised as a household livelihood strategy has featured more positively within the livelihood framework. The strength of this approach lies in its potential to deepen our understanding of the nature, components and strategies of livelihoods and of the complex relationships between migration, livelihoods diversification and poverty reduction. However, although it is claimed that livelihood analysis places a significant emphasis on an appreciation of the structures and processes that govern socially differentiated access to assets and livelihood choices, in reality the approach has not yet been able to fully confront the issue of power. As such it tends to downplay such features as connected with structures, organisations and institutions, while focusing on activities and tangible and intangible assets of individuals and households (de Haan and Zoomers, 2005).

Related to this is the need to broaden an understanding of access in livelihood studies. Access, in the work of Chambers and Conway (1992, p. 5), for example, is interpreted as "being able to find and make use of *livelihood opportunities*" (emphasis added), which suggests a bias towards the economic dimension of access (necessary but not sufficient) in livelihood analysis. Many other livelihood researchers stress access to markets, productive assets, natural or environmental resources, credits and loans, transport, and so forth in agricultural/rural settings (cf. Bah *et al.*, 2003; Becker, 2001; Bryceson, 2003; Ponte, 2001). Still others, such as Bebbington (1999) and de Haan and Zoomers (2005), emphasise the importance of *access to resources*, which is interpreted in such a way that resources and assets are frequently mingled together and used in an interchangeable manner. This wider sense of access helps bring to the fore the question of social justice in relation to the role of institutions and other economic, social and political agents, including the market, civil society and the state, in governing and shaping the possibilities, choices, conditions and outcomes of livelihoods. Despite this broadening of the concept, understanding of access within livelihood studies has barely taken account of a health and well-being perspective, which has thus far remained a separate sphere of inquiry for social policy studies. My point here is that like the concept of "livelihood" or "poverty", "access" entails multiple dimensions and, therefore, understanding and analysis of *access* in

4 It should be noted, however, that although much research on "social capital" in livelihood studies has explicitly or implicitly displayed such a tendency, a few scholars do pay particular attention to access and interpret it in a wider sense. For example, Bebbington (1999) argues that the ability to gain access (to resources) is one of the critical assets/resources for sustainable livelihoods in Latin America, and that it involves complex relationships and negotiations around entitlements and claims among different economic, social and political actors.

the livelihood approach need to transcend the single-dimensional "economism", and incorporate political, social and human dimensions. For the purpose of this research, broadening the concept of access should include health and well-being as the basis of livelihoods.

Sustainability and Sustainable Livelihoods

A parallel and very often overlapping development in livelihood studies is the related concept of "sustainable livelihood". Research on sustainable livelihood has gained prominence following the 1992 UN Conference on Environment and Development held in Rio de Janeiro, and particularly through an increasing number of projects on rural livelihood, its sustainability within the immediate environment and their relations to poverty reduction. These projects are supported by multilateral development agencies, donor governments and international NGOs, such as UNDP, Food and Agriculture Organisation of the UN, UK government's Department for International Development (DfID), Oxfam, and CARE (an anti-poverty humanitarian organisation).

Sustainable livelihood within this approach is frequently defined in terms of flexibility, adaptability and resilience of livelihood in conjunction with longer-term environmental soundness as suggested in the following, "A livelihood is sustainable when it can cope with and recover from stress and shocks and maintain or enhance its capabilities and assets both now and in the future, while not undermining the natural resource base" (Carney, 1998, p. 2).

It follows that literature on this approach is largely confined within the environment-development paradigm, focusing on macro- or micro-economic agrarian policy issues, natural resource management or globalisation and its environmental impact (such as climate change) on local livelihood systems (cf. Acevedo, Barry and Rosa, 1995; de Haan, 2000; Kramer, 1988; Low, 1994). Despite the suggestion that sustainability in this framework should be interpreted holistically from a multi-dimensional perspective, embracing, for instance, not only environmental, but also economic, social and institutional aspects (Chambers and Conway, 1992; DfID, 1999; Hussein, 2002), a close look at relevant researches reveals a bias towards environmental issues, particularly those in relation to natural resource management, biodiversity, agricultural diversification, and sometimes indigenous knowledge (cf. Birch-Thomsen, Frederiksen and Sano, 2001; Dubois, Dalai-Clayton and Dent, 2003; Sporton and Thomas, 2002). As Colin Murray (2000) has rightly noted, the notion of sustainability in this framework is vague since it begs many unanswered questions, such as sustainability for whom? by what criteria? or for the short or longer term? On the whole, within sustainable livelihood research, sustainability is defined more as environmental than as human sustainability.

There are some important exceptions, however. For example, the DfID-sponsored "Sustainable Livelihoods in Southern Africa" (SLSA) project coordinated by the Institute of Development Studies (IDS) in Sussex has examined new dimensions of livelihood sustainability, such as governance, institutions and land tenure arrangements and reforms (Scoones and Wolmer, 2003). Elizabeth Francis' work (2000, 2002a, 2002b) on livelihoods in Southern Africa has paid special attention to the complex relationship between livelihood and access to information, social networks and the state, and the ways in which livelihoods are mediated by cultural values and gendered power as important constituents of institutions. More recent research by Ellis and Freeman (2004) has examined the problems with livelihood diversification, security and poverty reduction in four African countries by bringing specific national and local institutional changes into the picture, particularly with regard to decentralisation and local taxation regimes and practices. However, in general, researches on sustainable livelihoods are not much differentiated from livelihood studies except that environmental and natural resource management issues (or "natural capital") are more frequently highlighted. In addition, sustainability in this framework has not yet been linked to health or human capital. Therefore, a much-enriched understanding of the concept is required and the possibility of such a project is explored below.

Missing Linkages: Human Capital, Migration, Health and Sustainable Livelihoods

The above discussion suggests that while new frontiers have been spearheaded and increased sophistication built into livelihood and sustainable livelihood studies, health, conceptualised as human capital and an individual's most valuable asset – and hence an essential livelihood component – has barely featured in this approach. Conceptual links between, and empirical studies on, such key livelihood concepts as migration, diverse or multiple livelihoods, sustainability and sustainable livelihoods from a health and well-being perspective, in either academic debates or policy arenas, are almost absent.

As discussed above, Frank Ellis, one of the most influential analysts in livelihood studies, defines livelihood as comprising five types of "capital", that is, natural, physical, human, financial and social capital (Ellis, 2000, p. 10), amongst which human capital is conceived as labour, education and health. In spite of this apparent recognition, in Ellis' own research as well as that of many other scholars, human capital has not been given serious attention. When the notion of sustainability is applied in livelihood approaches in relation to migration, it again falls into the conventional environment-development discourse with little emphasis on human capital interpreted as essentially linked to health as the very basis of livelihoods and livelihoods diversification process (cf. Ellis, 2000; Goldman, 1995). In addition, studies on migration within this framework tend to focus on an examination and understanding of, for example, the ways in which social capital, in the form of familial and kinship ties, informal social networks, and so forth, is fostered, utilised and enhanced by migrants and their families in their pursuit of intended livelihood outcomes in diverse development contexts (cf. Xiang, 1999).

It should be noted, however, that, in a sense, human capital is not an underdeveloped concept, or a unique notion emerging only or mainly from livelihood studies. In fact, there is a huge and ever increasing body of literature distinct from livelihood research utilising human capital as a core concept. This literature, however, falls into the subject areas of business and management or organisation and administration studies, economics, demography and education, with emphasis being placed on human resources, skills, knowledge, education and sometimes human "qualities" (cf. Bell, Devarajan and Gersbach, 2005; Boxall and Purcell, 2003; Hatch and Dyer, 2004; Lee, 2004; Lutz, Sanderson and Serbov, 2004; Thang and Quang, 2005). Health is not much a concern in human capital research, nor is it given sufficient attention in the livelihood framework, despite the fact that compared with schooling and skills, health may be even more essential for livelihood and its sustainability. A simple example can illustrate this point: a person who lacks schooling can still work as unskilled labour and thus earn a basic living for him- or herself and his or her family, whereas a person with ill health may well lose labour power, then livelihood, and may even impoverish his/her family through incurring high healthcare expenses for the household, in particular in the context of deregulated or privatised healthcare systems.

That said, migration and health is not a blank area of intellectual inquiry. There is, indeed, a considerable but rather separate body of research on migration and health. This literature has several strands. The main focus is very much on the effectiveness of intervention and prevention programmes created in response to the health hazards provoked by infectious diseases like HIV/AIDS, STIs, TB, and so forth, in the context of both increased internal and transborder migration in developing regions of the world (cf. Lyttleton and Amarapibal, 2002; Prothero, 2002). Much of this literature therefore tends to approach migration and health from a policy perspective, with much of the analysis being concerned with how to achieve "better control" of diseases associated with migration in such areas. Another literature strand examines the health problems of transnational migration from developing regions into developed regions of the world. Some of this research, however, tends to stereotype the groups studied, like refugees and asylum seekers, either as vectors or spreaders of infectious diseases or as a drain on the resources of the receiving society (cf. Kesby *et al.*, 2003; Prothero, 2001). A very different approach, however, is taken by researchers who define health and access to healthcare as fundamental rights for migrants, irrespective of their origins: this research tends to be situated in a challenging discourse about needs, rights, citizenship and identity and their policy implications (cf. Boran and Zhang, 2003; Johnston and Murray, 2003). Nonetheless, transnational migration, and its related health problems and challenges analysed and discussed from different perspectives and policy domains tend to dominate the themes of the literature on migration and health. Researches linking migration (both domestic and international), human capital, health, and diverse and sustainable livelihoods are limited in this area of migration studies.

The analysis thus far suggests that a broader understanding of human capital incorporating health and well-being is required in human capital research, and should have taken a much more prominent position in sustainable livelihood studies. This then can help build conceptual links between migration, health, multiple livelihoods and livelihoods sustainability, as well as lead us to a more challenging set of questions, such as issues about access to and accessibility of public good/ social services, particularly healthcare, equality, equity, citizenship, institutions and power. This enhanced framework, then, can be applied to the investigation, understanding and explanation of the ways in which institutions and structures embedded in complicated economic, social and political relations have shaped livelihood trajectories and outcomes, produced and reproduced poverty/wealth, the marginalised/the core, and mapped onto vulnerability/sustainability of livelihoods in the rural-urban spaces and interactions in China and elsewhere.

Conclusion

While experiencing rapid and sustained economic growth for the past 28 years, China has been less successful in narrowing inequalities and promoting equity and social justice. This is particularly the case for the country's massive and ever-increasing numbers of rural migrants, whose equal citizenship and rights to welfare and well-being have scarcely been recognised. Whereas post-Mao reforms have significantly undermined the *hukou* system in terms of controlling and restricting physical mobility of rural people, the barriers that the regime has erected for migrants' access to public good, as well as to various forms of institutions and power have not been fundamentally challenged. This, combined with intensifying globalisation, accompanying changes in the labour market pay structure and the resultant shifting social stratification, has seen diminishing "comparative advantage" for rural migrants in making a living and negotiating their livelihoods in urban settings. It is feared that in the absence of strong political will and effective public action, this large group will continue to suffer from increasing discrimination, marginalisation and social exclusion, and may become a new urban underclass in China. This scenario, together with the many emerging health hazards, particularly TB, SARS, STIs and HIV/AIDS, in a context of *de facto* privatisation of healthcare and worsening health inequalities, has exacerbated the vulnerabilities of rural migrants to ill-health and thus constituted serious threats to livelihoods and well-being of migrants and their families.

Although more recent changes in relation to China's rural-urban migration necessitates the issue of welfare and well-being of the migrants and their families coming to the prominence, limited research, if any, has been done on the social rights and health needs of migrants. I have argued in this chapter that the conceptual framework of livelihood studies holds the potential to fill this gap in our knowledge and understanding, and then inform policy spheres to address the relevant and imminent issues. Drawing on a critical review of literature on livelihood analysis and related researches, the chapter identifies the missing links in livelihood studies between such core concepts as migration, health, multiple livelihoods, sustainability and sustainable livelihoods. The analysis also shows that although rural-urban migration is connected positively to livelihood and poverty reduction in the livelihood approach, limited attention has been paid therein to the close relationship between this and health, particularly the role of health in livelihood sustainability. While studies on migration and health, which is distinct from livelihood analysis, may tackle this omitted dimension, a close look at this literature reveals that it has not been concerned with issues associated with livelihood and poverty alleviation.

While identifying such conceptual missing links, the chapter suggests ways in which the livelihood framework can be further enhanced in advancing our understanding and knowledge of the complex and multi-dimensional relationships between migration, health and sustainable livelihoods in China and beyond. It argues that this can be achieved by broadening our understanding and interpretation of (a) access – to go beyond the emphasis on a single economic dimension to include, in particular, access to public goods, (b) sustainability – not merely environmental but also, and perhaps more importantly, human sustainability, and (c) human capital – to perceive health as a key constituent basis of livelihood, by incorporating a health and well-being perspective, which has so far been absent, and by paying greater attention, beyond individuals and households, to the dynamic relationships and interactions between livelihood and its sustainability on the one hand, and institutions, structures and power on the other.

References

Acevedo, Carlos, Barry, Deborah and Rosa, Herman (1995) 'El Salvador's agricultural sector: Macroeconomic policy, agrarian change and the environment', *World Development* 23(12), pp. 2153-72.

Adams, William Mark (1990, 2001) *Green Development: Environment and Sustainability in the Third World*, 2nd edn (London and New York: Routledge).

Anson, Ofra and Sun, Shifan (2005) *Healthcare in rural China: Lessons from Hebei Province* (Aldershot: Ashgate).

Bah, Mahmoud; Cisse, Salmana; Diyamett, Bitrina; Diallo, Gouro; Lerise, Fred; Okali, David; Okpara, Enoch; Olawoye, Janice and Tacoli, Cecilia (2003) 'Changing rural-urban linkages in Mali, Nigeria and Tanzania', *Environment and Urbanisation* 15(1), pp. 13-23.

Bebbingtonm, Anthony (1997) 'Social capital and rural intensification: Local organisations and islands of sustainability in the rural Andes', *The Geographical Journal*, 163, pp. 189-97.

Bebbingtonm, Anthony (1999) 'Capitals and capabilities: A framework for analysing peasant viability, rural livelihoods and poverty', *World Development*, 27(12), pp. 2021-44.

Becker, Laurence C. (2001) 'Seeing green in Mali's woods: Colonial legacy, forest use, and local control', *Annals of the Association of American Geographers*, 91(3), pp. 504-26.

Bell, Clive, Devarajan, Shantayanan and Gersbach, Hans (2005) *Thinking about the long-run economic costs of AIDS*, paper presented at the Annual World Bank Conference on Development Economics: Securing Development in an Unstable World, Amsterdam, 22-23 May.

Bezemer, Dirk J. and Lerman, Zvi (2004) 'Rural livelihoods in Armenia', *Post-Communist Economies*, 16(3), pp. 333-48.

Bhalla, Ajit S., Yao, Shujie and Zhang, Zongyi (2003) Causes of inequalities in China, 1952 to 1999, *Journal of International Development*, 15(8), pp. 939-55.

Birch-Thomsen, Torben, Frederiksen, Pia and Sano, Hans-Otto (2001) 'A livelihood perspective on natural resource management and environmental change in semiarid Tanzania', *Economic Geography*, 77(1), pp. 41-66.

Bloom, Gerald and Tang, Shenglan, eds. (2004) *Health Care Transition in Urban China* (Aldershot: Ashgate).

Boran, Anne and Zhang, Heather Xiaoquan (2003) *No respecter of borders: The globalisation of disease*, paper presented at the conference Implications of globalisation: present imperfect, future tense? University of Chester, Chester, England, 17 November.

Boxall, Peter and Purcell, John (2003) *Strategy and Human Resource Management* (Basingstoke: Palgrave Macmillan).

Bryceson, D., Maunder, D., Mbara, T., Kibombo, R., Davis, A. and Howe, J. (2003) *Sustainable livelihoods, mobility and access needs*, TRL Report TRL544 (London: Transport Research Laboratory).

Carney, Diana (1998) 'Implementing the sustainable livelihoods approach', in Diana Carney (ed.) *Sustainable livelihoods: What contribution can we make?* Chapter 1 (London: DfID).

Chambers, Robert and Conway, Gordon, R. (1992) *Sustainable rural livelihoods: Practical concepts for the twenty-first century*, IDS discussion paper 296 (Brighton: Institute of Development Studies, University of Sussex).

Chan, Kam Wing (1999) 'Internal migration in China: A dualistic approach', in Frank N. Pieke and Hein Mallee (eds.) *Internal and international migration: Chinese perspectives*, pp. 49-72 (Surrey: Curzon).

Chinese Academy of Social Sciences (CASS) (1998) *Blue book of the Chinese society, 1998* (Beijing: Social Sciences Documentation Publishing House).

Christiansen, Flemming (1990) 'Social division and peasant mobility in mainland China: The implication of the *hu-k'ou* system', *Issues and Studies* 26(4), pp.23-42.

Cook, Sarah and Jolly, Susan (2001) *Unemployment, poverty and gender in urban China: perceptions and experiences of laid-off workers in three Chinese cities*, IDS research report 50 (Brighton: Institute of Development Studies, University of Sussex).

Croll, Elisabeth (1997) China's rural-urban mobility, part I, *China Review* 6, pp. 22-26.

Croll, Elisabeth (1997) China's rural-urban mobility, part II, *China Review* 7, pp. 19-23.

Dasgupta, Biplab (1999) *Structural adjustment, global trade and the new political economy of development* (London: Zed Books).

Davin, Delia (1999) *Internal migration in contemporary China* (Basingstoke: Macmillan).

de Haan, Arjan (1999) 'Livelihoods and poverty: The role of migration – a critical review of the migration literature', *Journal of Development Studies* 36(2), pp.1-47.

de Haan, Leo (2000) Globalisation, localisation and sustainable livelihood, *Sociologia Ruralis* 40(3), pp.339-65.

de Haan, Leo and Zoomers, Annelies (2005) 'Exploring the frontier of livelihoods research', *Development and Change* 36(1), pp.27-47.

Dennis, Carina (2004) 'Asia's tigers get the blues', *Nature* 429(17) June, pp.696-98.

Dobson, Andrew, ed. (1999) *Fairness and futurity: Essays on environmental sustainability and social justice* (Oxford: Oxford University Press).

Dong, Zigang, Hoven, Christina W. and Rosenfield, Allan (2005) 'Lessons from the past: Poverty and market forces combine to keep rural China unhealthy', *Nature* 433, February 10, pp. 573-74.

Drèze, Jean and Sen, Amartya (1989) *Hunger and public action* (Oxford: Clarendon).

Dubois, Olivier, Dalai-Clayton, Barry and Dent, David (2003) *Rural planning in developing countries: Supporting natural resource management and sustainable livelihoods* (London: Earthscan).

Ellis, Frank (2000) *Rural livelihoods and diversity in developing countries* (Oxford: Oxford University Press).

Ellis, Frank and Freeman, H. Ade (2004) 'Rural livelihoods and poverty reduction strategies in four African countries', *The Journal of Development Studies* 40(4), pp. 1-30.

Fine, Ben (1999) 'The developmental state is dead – long live social capital', *Development and Change* 30(1), pp.1-19.

Fine, Ben (2001) *Social capital versus social theory: Political economy and social science at the turn of the millennium* (London and New York: Routledge).

Francis, Elizabeth (2000) *Making a living: Changing livelihoods in rural Africa* (London and New York: Routledge).

Francis, Elizabeth (2002a) 'Gender, migration and multiple livelihoods: Cases from eastern and southern Africa', *The Journal of Development Studies* 38(5), pp.167-90.

Francis, Elizabeth (2002b) 'Rural livelihoods, institutions and vulnerability in North West Province, South Africa', *Journal of Southern African Studies* 28(3), pp 531-50.

Goldman, A. (1995) 'Threats to sustainability in African agriculture: Searching for appropriate paradigms', *Human Ecology* 23(3), pp. 291-334.

Guan, Xinping (2001) 'Globalisation, inequality and social policy: China on the threshold of entry into the World Trade Organisation', *Social Policy and Administration* 35(3), pp.242-57.

Hatch, Nile W. and Dyer, Jeffrey H. (2004) 'Human capital and learning as a source of sustainable competitive advantage', *Strategic Management Journal* 25(12), pp. 1155-178.

Hussein, Karim (2002) *Livelihoods approaches compared: A multi-agency review of current practice* (London: DfID).

Johnston, Vanessa and Murray, Sally (2003) 'Musings and mutterings on migration, citizenship, identity and rights', *Development* 46(3), pp.124-29.

Kesby, Mike, Fenton, K., Boyle, P. and Power, R. (2003) 'An agenda for future research on HIV and sexual behaviour among African migrant communities in the UK', *Social Science and Medicine* 57(9), pp.1573-92.

Kramer, John Michael (1988) 'Sustainable rural livelihoods: enhanced resource productivity', in Czech Conroy and Miles Litvinoff (eds.) *The greening of aid: Sustainable livelihoods in practice*, pp. 47-56 (London: Earthscan).

Lee, Gwanghoon (2004) 'The quality of human capital, educational reform and economic growth', *International Economic Journal*, 18(4), pp. 449- 465.

Li, Peilin (2002) 'The projected impact of the WTO accession on Chinese society', in Ru Xin, Lu Xueyi and Li Peilin (eds.), *Blue book of the Chinese society 2002*, pp. 57-65 (Beijing: shehuikexue wenxian chubanshe).

Li, Qiang (2002) 'New changes in China's social stratification', in Ru Xin, Lu Xueyi and Li Peilin (eds.), *Blue book of the Chinese society 2002*, pp. 133-43 (Beijing: shehuikexue wenxian chubanshe).

Li, Qiang (2004) *Urban migrant workers and social stratification in China* (Beijing: shehuikexue wenxian chubanshe).

Low, A.R.C. (1994) 'Environmental and economic dilemmas for farm-households in Africa – when low-input sustainable agriculture translates to high-cost unsustainable livelihoods', *Environmental Conservation* 21(3), pp. 220-24.

Lutz, Wolfgang, Sanderson, Warren C. and Serbov, Sergei, eds. (2004) *The end of world population growth in the twenty-first century: New challenges for human capital formation and sustainable development* (London: Earthscan).

Lyttleton, Chris and Amarapibal, Amorntip (2002) 'Sister cities and easy passage: HIV, mobility and economies of desire in a Thai/Lao border zone', *Social Science and Medicine* 54(4), pp. 505-18.

Mallee, Hein (1995) 'China's household registration system under reform', *Development and Change* 26(1), pp. 1-29.

Mallee, Hein (2000) 'Migration, *hukou* and resistance in reform China', in Elizabeth J. Perry, and Mark Selden (eds.) *Chinese society: Change, conflict and resistance*, pp. 83-101 (London and New York: Routledge).

Mathie A. and Cunningham, G. (2005) 'Who is driving development? Reflections on the transformative potential of asset-based community development', *Canadian Journal of Development Studies* 26(1), pp. 175-87.

Murphy, Rachel (2002) *How migrant labour is changing rural China* (Cambridge: Cambridge University Press).

Murray, Colin (2000) 'Changing livelihoods: The Free State, 1990s', *African Studies* 59, (1), pp. 115-142.

Murray, Colin (2001) *Livelihoods research: Some conceptual and methodological issues*, paper presented at the Development Studies Association Annual Conference, University of Manchester, Manchester, 10-12 September.

National Statistics Bureau of China (NSBC) (2001) *China statistics yearbook 2001* (Beijing: NSBC).

Ngai, Pun (2005) *A new practice of labour organising: Community-based organisation of migrant women workers in South China*, paper presented at the international conference on Membership Based Organisations of the Poor: Theory, Experience and Poverty, Ahmedabad, India, 17-21 January.

Pieke, Frank N. and Mallee, Hein, eds. (1999) *Internal and international migration: Chinese perspectives* (Surrey: Curzon).

Ponte, Stefano (2001) Trapped in decline? Reassessing agrarian change and economic diversification on the Uluguru Mountains, Tanzania, *Journal of Modern African Studies* 39(1), pp. 81-100.

Prothero, R. Mansell (2002) Population movements and tropical health, *Global Change and Human Health* 3(1), pp. 20-32.

Putman, Robert (2000) *Bowling alone: The collapse and revival of American community* (New York: Simon and Schuster).

Scoones, Ian (1998) *Sustainable rural livelihoods: A framework for analysis*, IDS working paper 72 (Brighton: Institute of Development Studies, University of Sussex).

Scoones, Ian and Wolmer, William (2003) 'Introduction: livelihoods in crisis: Challenges for rural development in southern Africa', *IDS Bulletin Special Issue: Livelihoods in Crisis? New Perspectives on Governance and Rural Development in Southern Africa* 34(3), pp. 1-14.

Sen, Amartya (1984) *Resources, values and development* (Oxford: Basil Blackwell).

Sen, Amartya (1985) 'Well-being, agency and freedom', *The Journal of Philosophy*, 132(4), pp. 169-221.

Sen, Amartya (1987) *The standard of living*, The Tanner Lectures, Clare Hall (Cambridge: Cambridge University Press).

Sen, Amartya (1992) *Inequality reexamined* (Cambridge, Massachusetts: Harvard University Press).

Sen, Amartya (2000) *Development as freedom* (New York: Anchor Books).

Solinger, Dorothy J. (1999) 'Citizenship issues in China's internal migration: Comparisons with Germany and Japan', *Political Science Quarterly*, 114(3), pp. 455-78.

Sporton, Deborah and Thomas, David S. (eds.) (2002) *Sustainable livelihoods in Kalahari environments: A contribution to global debates* (Oxford: Oxford University Press).

State Council (2006) *A research report on China's migrant workers* (Beijing: Yanshi chubanshe) (in Chinese).

Tan, E.L. (2005) China's migrant workers a high AIDS risk, Reuters: http://www.reuters.com/newsArticle.jhtml?type=topNews&storyID=8740702, accessed 23 June.

Thang, Le Chien and Quang, Truong (2005) 'Human resource management practices in a transitional economy: A comparative study of enterprise ownership forms in Vietnam', *Asia Pacific Business Review* 11(1), pp. 25-47.

Wu, Bin and Pretty, Jules (2004) 'Social connectedness in marginal rural China: The case of farmer innovation circles in Zhidan, north Shaanxi', *Agriculture and Human Values* 21, pp. 81–92.

Wu, Fulong (2004) 'Urban poverty and marginalisation under market transition: The case of Chinese cities', *International Journal of Urban and Regional Research* 28(2), pp. 401-23.

Xiang, Biao (1999) 'Zhejiang village in Beijing: Creating a visible non-state space through migration and marketised networks', in Frank N. Pieke and Hein Mallee (eds.) *Internal and international migration: Chinese perspectives*, pp.215-50 (Surrey: Curzon).

Yang, Dongping (2001) *Zhongguo: ershiyi shiji shengcun kongjian* (*China: Spatial existence in the twenty-first century*) (Beijing: Yiyuan chubanshe).

Yang, Yiyong and Xin, Xiaobai (2002) 'Current income distribution and trends in China', in Ru Xin, Lu Xueyi and Li Peilin (eds.), *Blue book of the Chinese society 2002*, pp.144-52 (Beijing: shehuikexue wenxian chubanshe).

Mohan, Giles, Browns, Ed, Milward, Bob and Zack-Williams, Alfred B. (2000) *Structural adjustment: Theory, practice and impacts* (London: Routledge).

Zhang, Heather Xiaoquan (1999a) 'Understanding changes in women's status in the context of the recent rural reform in China', in Jackie West, Minghua Zhao, Xiangqun Chang and Yuan Cheng (eds.) *Women of China: Economic and social transformation*, pp.45-66 (London: Macmillan).

Zhang, Heather Xiaoquan (1999b) 'Female migration and urban labour markets in Tianjin', *Development and Change* 30(1), pp.21-41.

Zhang, Heather Xiaoquan (2004) 'The gathering storm: AIDS policy in China', *Journal of International Development* 16(8), pp.1155-68.

Zhang, Heather Xiaoquan (2004) 'Globalisation and its challenges to rural women in China', paper presented at the international symposium *Women's Experience of Policy and Institutional Change in Rural China*, Institute of Contemporary Chinese Studies, University of Nottingham, UK, 14-15 April.

Zhang, Heather Xiaoquan, Kelly, Mick, Locke, Catherine, Winkels, Alex and Adger, W. Neil (2006) 'Migration in a transitional economy: Beyond the planned and spontaneous dichotomy in Vietnam', *Geoforum* 37(6): 1066-81..

Zhang, Heather Xiaoquan and Lin, Gu (2002) 'Facing up to the AIDS challenge', *China Review* 23, pp.11-13.

Zhou, Kate (1996) *How the farmers changed China: Power of the people* (Boulder: Westview).

Chapter 12

Spatial and Social Marginalisation of Health in China: The Impact of Globalisation

Ian G. Cook and Trevor J.B. Dummer

Introduction

Globalisation has now been with us for at least 25 years or so in its modern form, whilst arguably embryonic globalisation has a history of at least several hundred years. The speed of change unleashed by globalisation is dramatic:

> Globalisation is advancing with a speed scarcely imaginable before now. Economist Edward Luttwak describes the new age as the 'unification of the sloughs, ponds, lakes and seas of villages and provinces, regional and national economies, into a single global economic area, which exposes small areas to giant waves of competition instead of yesterday's little ripples and calm tides (Martin and Schumann, 1997: 21).

Foreign direct investment (FDI) is a key causal factor in globalisation as capital flows unceasingly across borders to new locations in the global quest for profit. Space and time are reshaped in what David Harvey called space-time compression, although *space-time warping* might be more accurate because the process is fundamentally spatially uneven, at all scales (Cook, 1999). Globalisation ratchets up inequalities between places and people as these flows of FDI are place-specific, including some but excluding others. As Wu notes, 'From the perspective of a longer temporality, globalisation is a millennium transformation in each ordinary place' (Wu, 2006: 6). Uneven outcomes are produced, these being particularly obvious in the transition economies:

> The transition from a planned to a market economy has been accompanied by *one of the biggest and fastest increases in income inequality ever recorded.* [our emphasis] Branko Milanovic showed that, on average, inequality in Eastern Europe, the Baltics, Russia and other countries of the former Soviet Union has increased rapidly, as measured by a rise in the Gini coefficient from 25-28 to 35-38 in less than 10 years ... In some countries, such as Bulgaria, Russia and Ukraine, the increase in inequality has been even more dramatic, outpacing by three to four times the yearly rate of increase in the Gini coefficient in the United Kingdom and the United States in the 1980s (Nsouli, 1999: 4-5).

The reasons for these growing inequalities were identified as greater wage inequalities in the new private sector compared to the old public sector, a higher percentage of incomes from self-employment and property, both inegalitarian, and a decline in incomes for the unemployed former state sector workers. Spatially, 'even in the fastest-growing economies, such as China and India, vast areas remain poor and underdeveloped' (Burton, Tseng and Kang, 2006: 12).

It is in the light of such pressures as these that the 'excluded' are vulnerable. As Giddens notes, 'There is a real parallel between exclusion between nations and regions and exclusion on a global scale. Increased prosperity for many leaves others stranded and marginalised' (Giddens, 1998: 152). The excluded are often defined by gender and ethnicity, by age or disability and almost always by poverty. They are peripheral – perhaps in the geographical sense, but also in the social, economic and political senses. It would seem that capital not only actively underdevelops but also actively 'overdevelops' contemporaneously (Cook, 1999, op.cit.). Thus, in China the overdevelopment is in the 'Gold Coast' of the Eastern seaboard, in the honeypots of the major cities especially, while the underdevelopment is in remote rural areas of the interior in particular. The honeypots attract the younger, more mobile and better educated from the rural areas in a process of what years ago the Swedish economist Gunnar Myrdal termed a 'cycle of circular and cumulative causation', nowadays exacerbated by globalisation. Unemployment, for instance has been highest in the Western or Central Provinces of China, compared to the Eastern Provinces (Wu, 2006: 299), and although the Chinese state is working hard to overcome such problems it remains an uphill struggle to reduce unevenness across the vast space of China.

In terms of health in China, marginalisation is on the increase. For instance, in common with other sectors the health care system is being subject to reduction of state subsidy and increased privatisation. This will be examined in more depth below, but here we note that globalisation increases the pressure to marketise, to modernise and to bring in new technologies to monitor and tackle health issues. Health and income become more closely related, and access to health care becomes highly uneven, spatially and socially, with a rich middle-aged male Han urbanite generally having greater access than a poor elderly female rural dweller for example, especially if the latter is from an ethnic minority. In the next section we summarise major health issues that are linked to these issues of marginalisation and globalisation in the People's Republic.

Major contemporary health issues

We begin this section via consideration of mortality rates. In the pre-revolutionary era, mortality rates were at a very high level due to the perennial threats of flood and famine, added to by systemic breakdown (Murray and Cook, 2002; Worth, 1973), and it is to the credit of the Chinese Communist Party (CCP) that significant successes were achieved in tackling health issues and increasing longevity, notwithstanding the high death rates in the several years following the Great Leap Forward of 1958. From 1989 to 1999 the overall death rate in China remained around the 6.5 per 1000 population level, but there was a marked divergence between rates in counties and cities (China Statistical Yearbook 2000), see Table 12.1. The death rate in cities declined by 4.7% between 1989-1999, but by contrast the death rate in counties increased by 1%. During this time period the relative risk (RR) ratio between counties and cities was consistently greater than 1.20. Further, the RR ratio between city and county widened – a pattern also shown by Gao *et al* (2002) using data for urban and rural areas for the period 1990-1998. Mortality rates by urban and rural status are not produced in the China Statistical Yearbook: however, cities and counties roughly approximate to urban and rural and hence provide a reasonable surrogate indicator for urban / rural status.

Table 12.1 City and county death rates, 1989-1999

	Death rate per 1000 population			County-city
Year	**Total**	**Cities**	**Counties**	**RR**
1989	6.54	5.78	6.81	1.18
1990	6.67	5.71	7.01	1.23
1991	6.70	5.50	7.13	1.30
1992	6.64	5.77	6.91	1.20
1993	6.64	5.99	6.89	1.23
1994	6.49	5.53	6.80	1.23
1995	6.57	5.53	6.99	1.26
1996	6.56	5.65	6.94	1.23
1997	6.51	5.58	6.90	1.24
1998	6.50	5.31	7.01	1.32
1999	6.46	5.51	6.88	1.25
% change over time	-1.2	-4.7	+1.0	--

Source: *China Statistical Yearbook, 2000*, Beijing: China Statistics Press.

It also seems to be the case that infant mortality is increasing in poor rural areas (Blumenthal and Hsiao, 2005). The 1% Sample Survey on Population Change in 2003 within the *China Statistical Yearbook 2004* (no such data is recorded in the most recent yearbook, for 2005) shows that 4,228 children in this 1% sample did not survive birth. Although there is not a simple urban-rural split evident in these data, those provinces with highest rates are much more likely to be the least urbanised provinces such as Yunnan, Guizhou, Hunan and others (Table 12.2). The combination of high numbers of live births allied to high rates of infant mortality means that hundreds of infants die in such provinces, compared to relatively few in

Table 12.2 Population and health indicators by province, 2003 and 2004

Province	No of women in sample aged 15 to 49[a]	Birth rate[b]	Number of live births[a]	Live births per woman[a]	Infant mortality rate[c]	Death rate[b]	Population growth rate[b]	Life expectancy[b]
Anhui	17204	11.62	20401	1.19	10.0	5.50	6.12	71.85
Beijing	4128	6.10	2947	0.71	4.8	5.40	0.70	76.10
Chongqing	8311	9.45	8696	1.05	15.3	6.60	2.85	71.73
Fujian	10002	11.58	12719	1.27	9.7	5.62	5.96	72.55
Gansu	7041	12.43	9043	1.28	8.0	6.52	5.91	67.47
Guangdong	21031	13.13	30175	1.43	4.9	5.12	8.01	73.27
Guangxi	12543	13.32	15715	1.25	7.7	6.12	7.20	71.29
Guizhou	9640	15.08	13766	1.43	23.8	6.35	8.73	65.96
Hainan	2135	14.77	2897	1.36	7.9	5.79	8.98	72.92
Hebei	19322	11.98	22117	1.14	5.5	6.19	5.79	72.54
Heilongjiang	11551	7.27	11635	1.01	6.1	5.45	1.82	72.37
Henan	25779	11.67	31671	1.23	5.6	6.47	5.20	71.54
Hubei	16349	8.43	19448	1.19	8.8	6.03	2.40	71.08
Hunan	17960	11.89	21546	1.2	14.3	6.80	5.09	70.66
Inner Mongolia	6891	9.53	8216	1.19	6.1	5.98	3.55	69.87
Jiangsu	20022	9.45	20690	1.03	9.8	7.20	2.25	73.91
Jiangxi	11810	13.61	15634	1.32	12.7	5.99	7.62	68.95
Jilin	8428	7.39	7479	0.89	4.0	5.63	1.76	73.10
Liaoning	12320	6.51	10899	0.88	6.1	5.60	0.91	73.34
Ningxia	1580	15.97	2342	1.48	15.8	4.79	11.18	70.17
Qinghai	1466	16.32	1931	1.32	18.1	6.45	9.87	66.03
Shaanxi	10106	10.59	12201	1.21	8.5	6.33	4.26	70.07
Shandong	25743	12.50	27793	1.08	7.4	6.49	6.01	73.92
Shanghai	4276	6.00	2947	0.69	4.4	6.00	0.00	78.14
Shanxi	9090	12.36	12012	1.32	7.1	6.11	6.25	71.65
Sichuan	23505	9.05	24759	1.05	11.3	6.27	2.78	71.20
Tibet	790	17.40	1017	1.29	27.5	6.20	11.20	64.37
Tianjin	2903	7.31	2519	0.87	7.9	5.97	1.34	74.91
Xinjiang	5408	16.00	6954	1.29	41.4	5.09	10.91	67.41
Yunnan	11469	15.60	16642	1.45	27.8	6.60	9.00	65.49
Zhejiang	12986	10.71	13516	1.04	7.8	5.76	4.95	74.70
National	351789	12.29	410327	1.17	10.3	6.42	5.87	71.40

Sources:
[a] *China Statistical Yearbook 2004*. Beijing: China Statistics Press, Table 4.15. Sample Survey on Population Changes, 2003. The sampling fraction was 0.982‰. (person).
[b] *China Statistical Yearbook, 2005*. Birth rate per 1000 population, death rate per 1000 population, life expectancy calculated for the year 2000.
[c] Infant mortality per 1,000 live births, authors' calculation, source: *China Statistical Yearbook 2004*. Beijing: China Statistics Press, Table 4.15. Sample Survey on Population Changes, 2003.

cities in the 'Gold Coast' such as Beijing, Shanghai and Tianjin. Overall mortality and life expectancy show a similar distribution, with higher death rates and lower life expectancy in the rural, poor and western provinces compared to the more urbanised provinces (*China Statistical Yearbook 2005*). For example, the death rate in Yunnan was 6.6 per 1000 population and life expectancy 65.5 years compared to a death rate of 5.4 and life expectancy of 76.1 in Beijing. See Figure 12.1 for details of the geographical distribution of these data.

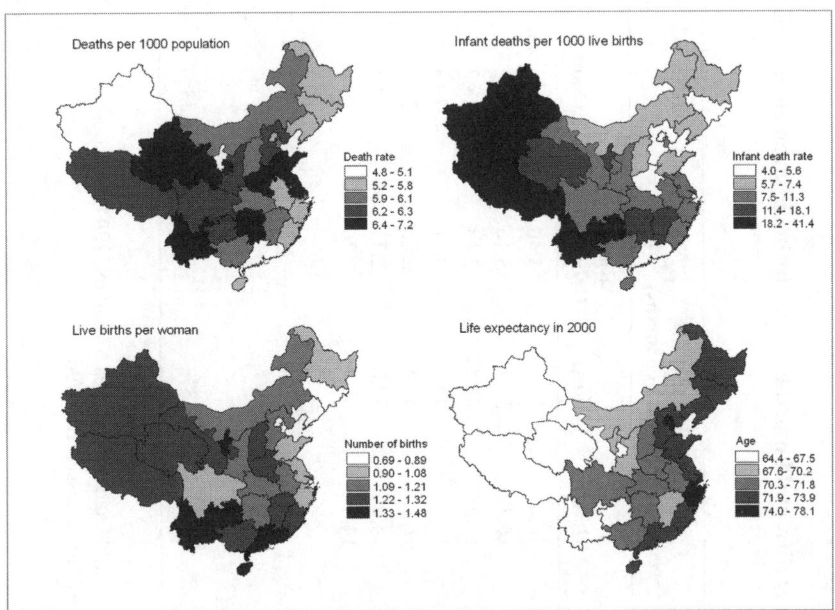

Figure 12.1 Variation in social and health indicators by province
(see Table 12.2 for data sources)

The World Health Organisation (WHO) (2006) and official data from the Ministry of Health (MoH) (2004 and 2005) both identify alarming disparities between urban and rural areas in infant, child and maternal mortality (see Table 12.3). Despite health care improvements, infant and child mortality rates in rural areas remain more than twice as high as the rates in urban areas (rural-urban RR 2.43 for infant deaths and 2.26 for child deaths). In contrast, maternal mortality declined much more slowly in rural areas (18%) compared to urban areas (33%), and the rural-urban relative risk actually widened from 1.94 in 1995 to 2.41 in 2004. Amongst the contributing factors to these disparities in infant and maternal mortality is the relatively low number of births taking place in hospital in rural areas compared to urban areas: for example, in 1992 87% of births in urban areas were in hospital, compared to only 22% of births in rural areas (WHO, 2006). Although by 2002 this had increased to 62% of births in rural areas taking place in hospital (compared to

Table 12.3 Urban and rural variations in infant mortality, child mortality (deaths in children aged under 5 years old) and maternal mortality by year

	Infant mortality (per 1000 live births)			Child mortality (per 1000 live births)			Maternal mortality (per 100,000 live births)		
Year	Urban	Rural	Rural-Urban RR	Urban	Rural	Rural-Urban RR	Urban	Rural	Rural-Urban RR
1991	17.3	58.0	3.35	20.9	71.1	3.40	--	--	--
1995	14.2	41.6	2.93	16.4	51.1	3.16	39.2	76.0	1.94
1997	13.1	37.7	2.88	15.5	48.5	3.13	38.3	80.4	2.01
2000	11.8	37.0	3.14	13.8	45.7	3.31	29.3	69.6	2.38
2001	13.6	33.8	2.49	16.3	40.4	2.48	33.1	61.9	1.87
2002	12.2	33.1	2.71	14.6	39.6	2.71	22.3	58.2	2.61
2003	11.3	28.7	2.54	14.8	33.4	2.26	--	--	--
2004	10.1	24.5	2.43	--	--	--	26.1	63.0	2.41
% decrease over time period	42%	58%	--	29%	53%	--	33%	18%	--

Sources: Chinese Health Statistical Digest, Ministry of Health, 2004 and 2005, pages 67 and 69. 2004 data source: WHO (2006) Maternal and Child Health in China. www.wpro.who.int/china/sites/mnh/overview.htm accessed 22/07/06.

93% in urban areas) this still represents a large proportion of women in rural areas being potentially disadvantaged during childbirth. There are also rural-rural contrasts as well as urban-urban ones to further complicate the pattern, with remote rural areas populated heavily by ethnic minorities exempt from the Single Child Family Programme in the western region being much more likely to suffer from higher rates of mortality than similarly remote Han rural areas in the eastern regions.

The advent of the PRC brought a strong and successful assault on such historic infections as hookworm or schistosomiasis, directly via improved healthcare provision and indirectly via improved socioeconomic conditions in the countryside. Improvements in sanitation, water conservancy and control, inoculations, use of 'barefoot doctors' and other initiatives were successfully used to combat poor environmental and hygiene conditions in rural areas, often by 'mobilising the masses' to combat the threats of five main parasitic diseases (Worth, 1973). Nonetheless, by the early 1990s it was estimated that 60 million rural Chinese were still suffering from such endemic diseases as malaria and schistosomiasis, with the latter reappearing after decades of attempts to wipe out the snail vector (Hillier and Zheng, 1994). Snail infestation is actually on the increase, such that 865,000 people are now infected with schistosomiasis in the provinces where this disease is prevalent (Ross *et al* 2001). China's dealing with this disease is paradoxical; whilst there has been an undeniably successful campaign, funded by the World Bank, this support has now ended and there is a real fear that because the epidemic stations put emphasis on treatment (for income generation) rather than prevention, the problem has not been eradicated. The World Bank programme did not tackle underlying environmental issues (snail habitats) or focus enough on education (Bian *et al* 2004; Chen *et al* 2005).

Similarly, the incidence of TB is steadily increasing in China: in 1999 the rate was 39.03 per 100,000, after not being recorded at all in 1994, rising to 44.06 per 100,000 in 2001 and 71.95 in 2004 (Cook and Dummer, 2004; *China Statistical Yearbook 2005*). There is a strong rural and regional dimension to this increase: TB rates in rural areas are double that of urban areas, and there are particularly high rates in western areas (China Daily, 2003a; Li, 2003). Official estimates indicate that 80% of TB patients live in rural areas (Xinhua News Agency, 2006). Table 12.4 shows the most common causes of death in urban and rural areas, 1995-2004 (*China Statistical Yearbooks 1995, 2000, 2002, 2005*); pulmonary tuberculosis appears as the tenth most common cause of death in rural areas in 2004, although it does not appear in the top ten common causes of death in urban areas – or indeed any areas – in 1995, 1999 or 2001 (the *2004 China Statistical Yearbook*, data not shown in the table, shows that TB was also the tenth most common cause of disease in rural areas in 2003). Meng *et al* (2004a) identify increasing problems with controlling TB, especially in the poor (often rural) counties, problems which relate particularly to issues with TB control programmes and the inability of the local government in poorer counties to finance the appropriate control programmes. There is evidence that more than 60% of hospital patients in rural areas leave hospital too early (before they are fully cured) due to the cost of treatment (*China Daily*, 2003a), even though the government asserts that no-one who has TB will be charged for diagnosis and treatment (Li, 2003). The latter author noted that TB now kills 130,000 per annum, and will plague 20 to 30 million people in the next decade, at huge economic cost. Two million people in China are estimated to be contagious with TB, many in rural areas. We also note that at the time of writing a new strain of TB has been identified at the global level, especially concentrated in South Africa among HIV patients, a strain that is currently resistant to conventional antibiotic treatment. If this spreads widely in China this will pose enormous difficulties for treatment of TB.

Table 12.4 Death rates from major causes, urban and rural areas, selected years 1995-2004 (as percentage of total deaths)

	2004		2001		1999		1995	
Cause of death	**Urban**	**Rural**	**Urban**	**Rural**	**Urban**	**Rural**	**Urban**	**Rural**
Malignant tumour	23.9	23.7	24.9	17.7	23.9	18.4	21.8	16.5
Cerebrovascular disease	19.1	14.8	20.44	19.0	21.6	18.4	22.1	16.35
Heart disease	18.8	12.5	17.6	13.1	16.8	12.4	14.9	10.4
Respiratory disease	13.1	13.3	13.4	22.5	13.9	22.0	16.1	25.3
Trauma and Toxicosis	5.9	6.6	5.9	10.7	6.3	11.0	6.7	12.0
Digestive diseases	3.2	2.8	3.1	4.1	3.0	4.0	3.5	4.8
Urinary disease	1.8	1.61	1.6	1.5	1.5	1.5	1.5	1.3
Mental disease	–	–	1.0	–	1.1	–	–	1.8
Neuropathy	–	–	1.0	–	0.9	–	0.9	–
Internal System, Nutrition, Metabolite and Immunity	2.8	2.5	3.2	1.1	2.9	1.1	2.2	–
Pulmonary Tuberculosis	–	0.64	–	–	–	–	–	–

Source: *China Statistical Yearbook 1995, 2000, 2002, 2005.*

Table 12.4 shows that for all time periods studied (except the most recent) respiratory problems emerge as the main cause of death in rural areas, contrasting with malignant tumours being the main cause of death in urban areas 1995-2004. In 2004 malignant tumours became the biggest cause of death in rural areas, indicating the move in the countryside through the epidemiological transition towards increased prevalence of disease of old age, such as cancers (Cook and Dummer, 2004).

Official data show that the overall death rate from infectious diseases climbed between 2001 to 2004, following decline in the 1990s, up to 235.85 per 100,000 in 2004 compared to 188.62 in 2001, 197.63 in 1999 and 203.68 in 1994 (*China Statistical Yearbooks 1995, 2000, 2002, 2005*). The diseases of the past, once thought to be on the wane if not wholly eradicated, are once again on the march. Thus, we find Malaria, up from 2.0 in 2001 to 2.78 in 2004, viral hepatitis likewise from 65.15 to 85.49, while Kala-Azar had crept in to the table at 0.02 by 2004, as did Dengue Fever also at 0.02. Such diseases affect poor and rural people disproportionately, and are far removed from the glitter and glamour of China's emerging cities.

There is also danger from new diseases such as HIV/AIDS, SARS and Avian Flu. For years the Chinese authorities denied that they had a problem with HIV/AIDS, with just a few cases largely caused by 'foreigners'. The same authorities also at first categorically denied the existence of SARS (it was first reported in February 2003 but atypical cases of pneumonia had been identified in Guangdong Province in November 2002 and were hushed up). In a growing climate of openness, the new leadership of Hu Jintao and Wen Jiabao have encouraged officials and others to face these issues and also apologised for hiding the true facts of the SARS epidemic, unprecedented for leaders of a society so concerned with losing 'face' (Cook and Dummer, 2004). As regards HIV/AIDS there is conflicting evidence over the current scale of the epidemic. Estimates for HIV/AIDS have ranged from one million up to 10 million or even 20 million (Watts, 2004). Most recently, however, UN estimates have suggested that its own upper figures may have been too extreme and that the lower figures are more likely to be the case, while official figures now show 650,000 cases and the WHO regards the target to restrict HIV/AIDS to 1.5 million by 2010 to be a 'good challenge' (Watts, 2006); some believe the true figure to be 1.5 million in China today.

As regards the geographical dimension of this disease, specific provinces – Hunan and Qinghai especially – have been mapped as being particularly at risk of the spread of HIV from needle-sharing by infected drug-users (Donald and Benewick, 2005: 76), while the United Nations Development Programme (UNDP) website notes:

> By the end of November 2005, Henan and Yunnan have each reported over 30,000 cumulative HIV cases. Guangxi, Xinjiang and Guangdong have each reported over 10,000 cumulative HIV cases. In some areas of Xinjiang, Yunnan and Sichuan and other provinces, HIV present among injection drug users exceeds 50% while in Jiangsu, Zhejiang, Inner Mongolia and Liaoning and other provinces HIV prevalence among IDU remains under 5% (UNDP, 2006).

A new feature of tackling this health threat has been at long last an acknowledgement by the authorities that China has a gay community, again after years of denial, and this community is beginning to be involved in educational projects to reduce the threat of transmission of the virus amongst its members (China Daily, 2006b).

A related issue pertains to China's huge migrant population (*liudong renkou*), estimated to be in the region of some 120 million people (Hong *et al*, 2006). This group consists of predominantly rural-urban migrants but also migrants moving between cities of various sizes. These workers, often lacking health insurance and relatively poor, bring with them health problems and health needs linked to a range of economic, social and cultural factors that remain relatively unexplored (Hong *et al*, 2006). As shown above, China has a growing problem with HIV/AIDS and the migrant population has been shown to be at greater risk of sexually transmitted diseases and HIV/AIDS owing to an increase in sexual risk-taking activity (He *et al*, 2006). Lin *et al* (2005) found that levels of alcohol use were higher amongst rural-urban migrants compared to the general population. Moreover, alcohol intoxication was found to be associated with sexual risk-taking activity for this group of migrants (including unsafe sexual practice), and hence this group is at a higher level of risk for sexually transmitted diseases such as HIV/AIDS (Lin *et al*, 2005). In addition to health problems related to alcohol use and sexual risk-taking rural-urban migrants show a higher level of smoking prevalence compared to other groups (Chen *et al*, 2004). In particular, female migrants have been found to have very high rates of smoking (Chen *et al*, 2004), linked inevitably to economic, social and cultural stresses associated with their urban lives. Thus, rural-urban migrants represent a highly marginalised population whose health and social care needs remain unmet. This large and diverse – but mostly disadvantaged and vulnerable – population remain a major public health concern.

Another major health problem globally is now Avian Flu, with the threat of a pandemic should the virus mutate to spread via human-human contact worrying health planners across the planet. At first it was thought that SARS would be the lethal global epidemic that has been feared for some time, but the response worldwide proved to be adequate to reduce and eventually stop the spread of this virus. Now, Avian Flu, with outbreaks mapped for China in Beijing Review in 2004 (Ren Tong, 2004) is feared. By the end of March 2006, 103 people had died in Asia and the Middle East of the Avian Flu H5N1 virus, including 10 in China (China Daily, 2006a). At the time of writing, it seems that the essential policy of openness by China is holding firm, with the reporting of a possible bird-flu death of a migrant worker being reported in late March and another death in Guangdong in early March. However, bird flu was identified in Hong Kong in February 2006 from Guangdong poultry even though at that time it was reported that there was no bird flu there. The tradition of cover up is embedded at all levels and it remains crucial that openness of reporting is the norm rather than the exception, even with the risk of inducing panic among the people. If globalisation obligates greater openness in China then at least there are some saving graces of the process for public health.

The threat of Avian Flu is in part an ecological threat due to rural population and animals living cheek by jowl, often in sub-tropical conditions in which disease vectors thrive. Other ecological threats include the huge scale of coal burning which releases toxins that pose such a severe health hazard across the country that respiratory disease was the main cause of death in rural areas until 2004, whereas it was fourth in the cities (*China Statistical Yearbook 2005*; Cook and Dummer, 2004). Unless there are major changes, the World Bank estimates that by 2020 'China will be paying $390 billion to treat diseases indirectly caused by burning coal…an astounding 13 per cent of its predicted GDP at that time. That suggests that something has to give' (Walker, 2006). Another major issue is water quality, with between 300 and 360 million people in rural areas, depending on estimates, not having access to clean water. But the other main threat to people's lungs and heart among other organs comes more voluntarily via smoking. It is forecast by the World Health Organisation that there could be 2 million deaths per annum from smoking-related diseases by 2025. Perhaps up to one-third of China's men could die eventually of smoking-related conditions, according to one estimate (Cook and Dummer, 2004).

Immunisation rates in China have declined since the 1990s official high of 98% of the target population. The official estimates indicate declining coverage for a range of vaccines – including BCG and Polio – ranging from 87% to 84% coverage in 2005, down from 90% to 99% in 2004 (WHO, 2005). A study by Xie and Dow (2005) found that immunisation uptake was strongly associated with degree of urbanicity, household wealth and maternal education, with lower uptake in rural areas and amongst poorer, less educated households.

Finally in this dismal catalogue of health threats, we note mental health and stress-related problems, including propensity to suicide among young rural females (Cook and Dummer, 2004). Suicide rates are three times higher in rural areas compared to urban for both males and females (Phillips *et al* 2002). The highest rates are in the elderly (aged 60-84 years). Overall there is a 25% higher rate of suicide amongst women compared to men, but this is largely explained by a particularly high rate of suicide for young rural women. Conflicting with trends in other countries towards higher suicide rates among young males, this may be related to pressures upon females as a result of feudal legacies, with traditional Confucian ideas, reinforced by patrilocal residence, demeaning females. Allied to opportunity via access to lethal pesticides and a lack of medical staff trained to deal with pesticide poisoning, this is a worrying sign of the pressures of rural life upon young women and the elderly. 'Gerontocide' is a concern, and although the authorities introduced a law forcing sons and daughters to care for their parents, some elderly have taken their own lives for shame of neglect by their family, in marked contrast to Confucian tradition. With Jason Powell, Cook has explored this and other issues concerning the prospects for the elderly in China (e.g. Cook and Powell 2005, 2007a, 2007b; Powell and Cook 2006, 2007).

Health care provision in China

Following the formation of the PRC, health services in China became owned, financed and run by the government. Working from the ethos of centralised ownership and control, health care provision was structured on a basic "three-tiered" mode (see Feng in this volume). In rural areas almost all villages had a village clinic or health station, served by several part-time staff that provided basic health services and organised public health campaigns, including immunisation programmes (Meng *et al*, 2004b). Township (formerly commune) health centres were larger, with full time doctors providing primary health care and supervising the public health and medical care services provided by the local clinics (Bloom, 2005). The final level in the rural hierarchy was the county hospital, a larger medical centre with referral and speciality services. A similar three-tiered model was also created in urban areas. Here the basic level of health care provision was provided by street health stations, which supplied medical care similar to the rural health stations/clinics. In urban areas district hospitals provided primary health care and administrative organisation. The final tier in the urban hierarchy was the municipal and provincial hospital, which provided specialist and referral care. The aim of the hierarchical health care structure was to ensure equitable access to affordable health care for all members of China's society.

After 1949 the newly formed PRC adopted a prevention-first approach to health; the focus of public health was on health promotion, health education and infectious disease eradication. Public health initiatives – such as campaigns to wipe out the schistosomiasis snail vector – were co-ordinated by the Chinese Academy of Preventive Medicine. This centralised organisation supported the work of many public health institutions operating at different administrative levels. As with the arrangement for health care provision the structure was, and still is, hierarchical. At the provincial and county levels some 3600 anti-epidemic stations monitor epidemics, organise public health campaigns and carry out environmental health inspections. Alongside the anti-epidemic stations some 1800 specialised institutions handle specific diseases, including TB and schistosomiasis (Liu and Mills, 2002). At the local level of the hierarchy public health care becomes integrated with the township health centres and clinics, thus unifying curative and preventative services for rural areas.

Important components of health care policy in China were the strategies for tackling epidemics of infectious diseases (such as TB, hepatitis and schistosomiasis), coupled with an emphasis on preventative medicine, including large-scale immunisation programmes. Although some specific health campaigns were ended during the Cultural Revolution, by the mid 1960s affordable and accessible health care was available to most of the population, both rural and urban (Anson and Sun, 2002).

The PRC's ambition of providing country-wide accessible health care to its entire people was achieved between the 1950s and the early 1980s through the health insurance schemes, which supported a publicly funded and centrally run health service (Gao *et al*, 2001). In urban areas the two most important health insurance schemes were then known as the Labour Insurance Scheme (LIS) and the Government Insurance Scheme (GIS). The LIS covered workers in state-owned and collective owned enterprises whilst the GIS covered civil servants, government workers and college and university students. In rural areas the most important health insurance scheme was the Cooperative Medical System (CMS), a commune-based insurance scheme covering agricultural workers. Through the CMS rural workers had their health care financed via the collective, with the collective retaining money from its sales to fund local health services and meet most hospital costs. Although there were small gaps in coverage (for example, some urban schemes did not cover a worker's dependents), during the 1970s some 90% of the rural population and most urban residents were covered by health insurance (World Bank, 2005a), enabling near universal access to medical care.

A striking feature of health care financing in China is that government money has traditionally supported the full cost of public health institutions in the PRC (Liu and Mills, 2002), including preventative services, environmental health inspections and the provision of treatments. In the past the full cost of all treatment, including drugs for infectious diseases such as leprosy, malaria and schistosomiasis, has also been met by government money.

Health and health policy consequences of economic restructuring

Whilst the health systems established by the PRC were associated strongly with the immense improvements in population and public health throughout the country they proved unsustainable alongside the drive for economic reform. During the 1980s, China's health care policy followed its economic policy – private initiatives and market forces replaced state planning, funding and centralised control. Importantly, public health institutions became recognised as economic bodies, in direct contrast to their traditional role as public welfare resources, and as such their finances were reformed to treat them as income generating entities (Liu and Mills, 2002). Unfortunately, the transition towards a market-based economy had profound impacts on the health of the population and placed a tremendous strain on China's impressive health care system (see Feng's chapter in this volume).

Between 1978 and 1990 the government reduced its share of national health spending by over half, from 32% to 15% (Blumenthal and Hsiao, 2005). Responsibility for health care funding was devolved to provincial and local government (funded via local taxation), which had the side effect of favouring the wealthier coastal and urban provinces at the expense of the western and rural areas (ibid.). Allocation of public funds became heavily skewed towards urban areas, for example, in 1998 rural areas received just 30% of total government health funding despite accounting for 70% of the country's population (Zhao *et al*, 2003). Latest figures from the Ministry of Health show that spending per capita in urban areas is now 3.5 times higher than spending in rural areas (China Health Statistical Digest, 2005). However, despite an apparently simple split between higher levels of health funding for urban areas compared to rural areas, inequalities in health care financing are spatially complex, displaying a high degree of variation within rural areas and within urban areas. Thus, the problem of inequalities in health care funding is not simply an "urban-rural" issue, it is also a "rural-rural" problem and an "urban-urban" problem, whereby the western and poorer regions of rural China, and the poorer parts of urban centres, are heavily disadvantaged with regards to health care.

The rush to a market-based economy inevitably acted as a detriment to health and health care in China, with a greater impact on marginalised people. In particular, three inter-linked processes played out: reduced public funding of health care, financial independence for hospitals/health centres and the privatisation of many health care systems (Hsiao, 1995). Each process resulted, almost inevitably, in a decline in service provision and service coverage. Reduced public funding led service providers to seek alternative modes of finance, and fee paying for services became the norm. However, the emphasis on fee paying for health services (to support service provision) clearly limits the use of such services because usage is often governed by the patient's ability (or willingness) to pay, rather than his/her need. For the poor, especially the large proportion of rural poor, the rural-urban migrants, and the uninsured, fee paying effectively curtails access to health care. Market-orientated financing of China's public health infrastructure – again, with an emphasis on fee paying – has also led to decreases in the demand for many crucial services, in particular a reduction in immunisation take-up because of an inability (or unwillingness) to pay for such services. Thus a reduction in public health campaigns and health awareness initiatives, due to financial constraints, has been an undesirable outcome of the marketisation of services without adequate safeguards and regulation. Problems have been exacerbated further because public health services have seen their share of the government health budget decline from between 15-18% in the 1970s to 12.4% in 1980 and to 10.6% in 1995 (Liu and Mills, 2002). Clearly, any decrease in important public health services increases the risk of infectious disease transmission: the problems outlined earlier of resurgent infectious diseases (such as

TB and schistosomiasis) and newly emerging diseases (including HIV/AIDS) are important indicators of a failure of preventative medical care.

The financial independence of hospitals and township health centres in China's new economic structure has also promoted fee paying for services because fees now provide the backbone of hospital funding. In addition to driving inequalities in access to services (controlled by the ability or willingness to pay) fee paying as a means of hospital income generation has also had the knock-on effect of an over-provision of unnecessary services and over-use of treatments and drugs. This has resulted in greater inefficiency in service provision and delivery (Liu and Mills, 2002), as well as issues associated with unnecessary drug prescribing and unnecessary use of certain medical and surgical procedures.

The privatisation of services, without adequate state control and planning, has resulted in disjointed and fragmented service provision. The quality of care has also suffered as a result of privatisation; although the skills of health care workers has improved in both rural and urban areas the qualifications of workers, and the quality of services, in rural areas now lags behind urban areas (Meng *et al*, 2004b). Thus, the move to a privatised and market-based economy has led to problems of inequity and inefficiency in health care and health service provision. Inevitably, marginalised people (marginalised both socially and geographically) are affected most by such problems.

By 2003, the director of the National Institute of Health Economics under the Ministry of Health, Cai Renhua, was admitting via the state-run Xinhua News Agency that although the national budget for public health had been rising for a decade, nevertheless the proportion spent on this had been steadily declining: 'Statistics from the Ministry of Health show that China spent 5.3% of its gross domestic product (GDP) on sanitation and medical sectors in 2000, slightly higher than the 5% floor set by the World Health Organization (WHO), but much lower than in developed countries' (Xinhua News Agency, 2003). Even this figure includes sanitation, and WHO data estimated China's input in public health in 2000 as only 2.7% of GDP (Beijing Review, 2004). This leaves China well down the global rankings, being 144th in the world in terms of its general level of public health and 188th in the global ranking of fairness in the distribution of public health resources (Beijing Review, 2004). The SARS outbreak focused attention on this low level of state expenditure, with the government forced to supplement normal expenditure via emergency funding in order to deal effectively with this threat. The official China Daily also noted such issues, with the WHO China representative Henk Bekedam linking ill-health to poverty (April, 2003), and the article stating that the 70% of the population in rural areas consumes only 30% of the country's medical resources. This led to the outcome that 'there are many rural families without assets who do not even try to seek treatment when sick' (China Daily, 2003a), a point supported by a survey in three provinces in 2001, that showed that half the respondents had foregone health care in the previous year because of the cost (Blumenthal and Hsiao, 2005). Between 1980 and 2003 per capita spending on health increased six-fold in urban areas (from 158.8 to 932.9 yuan) and seven-fold in rural areas (from 38.8 to 268.6 yuan) (China Health Statistical Digest, 2005). Despite these increases urban areas still receive some 3.5 times more health spending, despite the majority of the population living in rural areas.

Changes in funding has altered health care provision in China, with the urban areas gaining (in terms of numbers of hospital beds, trained personnel and qualified doctors) despite the fact that the majority of China's population is still rural based (China Statistical Yearbook, 2005). Table 12.5 and Figure 12.2 highlight a bias in provision of medical care in more recent years towards urban areas. Until the late 1980s, counties (which still provide the majority of China's population) had higher numbers of hospital beds, trained medical workers and doctors compared to cities. At the beginning of the 1990s cities saw a dramatic increase in their numbers of hospital beds and medical workers, an increase that continued to such an extent that there are now far more hospital beds and medical workers (including doctors) in cities compared to counties (Dummer and Cook, 2007). By contrast, counties are now beginning to see their numbers of hospital beds and medical workers declining in terms of raw numbers. Cleary this pattern reflects partly a process of centralisation of resources and expertise to major centres, similar to processes that have occurred elsewhere in developed nations. However, given the vastness of China's rural countryside the centralisation of health care to major (urban) centres poses serious concerns about accessibility and equity. Further scrutiny of the data on health care provision and utilisation (Table 12.5 and Figure 12.2) highlights the emergence of the rural-rural health care problem, whereby the poorest (often western) provinces fare worst in terms of provision of doctors, nurses and hospital beds as well as utilisation of township health centre beds and length of stay. Often the poorer provinces have less take up of township health centre beds, and also shorter stays once a patient is admitted. Clearly these issues link to problems of cost and payment of fees.

The introduction of the household responsibility system in the late 1970s/ early 1980s – allowing individuals to develop their own agricultural activities and sell their own goods – led to the demise of the collective system. Inevitably this resulted in the collapse of the CMS, which by the mid 1990s saw only 10% of rural residents covered by medical insurance (World Bank, 2005a). By contrast, 55% of urban residents still have their medical care financed by employee insurance schemes (Wang *et al*, 2005) and, despite declining coverage of these schemes, significantly more of the urban population is covered by health insurance compared to the rural population (Gao *et al*, 2002), although some urban residents are now insured through private schemes. However, within urban areas there are wide disparities in both health insurance provision, and the level and depth of funding the insurance provides. The marginalised groups in urban areas (the poor, the unemployed, the migrants) represent a large swathe of this group of urban uninsured. For example, the World Bank estimates that only 12% of the poorest 20% of the urban population is covered by health insurance (World Bank, 2005b). For these people health care needs are frequently unmet because they lack sufficient finances to pay for their health care. Indeed, most of the rural-urban migrants are effectively excluded from health care as they do not have health insurance and they are currently not included in urban health insurance policies (Meng *et al*, 2004b). Of those rural-urban migrants who have health insurance it is usually under the rural scheme, and workers are often required to return to their rural home to gain medical treatment (a situation that is often not

Table 12.5 Health care provision by province, 2004

Province	Doctors per 1000 population	Nurses per 1000 population	Village doctors and assistants per 1000 population	Hospital beds per 1000 population	Utilisation of beds in Township Health Centres (%)	Average length of stay in Township Health Centres (days)
Anhui	1.00	0.70	0.86	0.72	47.9	3.8
Beijing	4.21	3.57	1.20	1.21	38.3	6.7
Chongqing	1.16	0.64	0.88	0.68	41.3	4.5
Fujian	1.29	0.97	1.08	0.72	37.0	2.4
Gansu	1.33	0.86	0.89	0.65	28.8	5.0
Guangdong	1.45	1.18	1.06	1.28	48.5	4.7
Guangxi	1.10	0.89	0.89	0.53	36.7	3.7
Guizhou	0.96	0.56	0.82	0.44	30.9	3.2
Hainan	1.51	1.31	0.37	0.69	23.8	3.9
Hebei	1.48	0.79	1.36	0.73	28.4	3.9
Heilongjiang	1.72	1.21	1.16	0.67	33.7	4.3
Henan	1.11	0.76	1.09	0.66	36.5	5.1
Hubei	1.49	1.10	0.81	0.74	33.8	5.5
Hunan	1.36	0.87	0.73	0.69	33.6	4.5
Inner Mongolia	2.12	1.12	1.20	0.87	40.9	6.7
Jiangsu	1.45	1.06	1.21	1.35	45.5	2.4
Jiangxi	1.15	0.82	0.88	0.59	22.6	3.8
Jilin	2.18	1.48	0.84	0.81	32.2	3.7
Liaoning	2.21	1.75	1.16	0.94	37.9	4.4
Ningxia	1.82	1.21	0.98	0.50	35.7	3.5
Qinghai	1.74	1.25	1.49	0.61	27.4	5.2
Shaanxi	1.62	1.02	1.16	0.64	34.7	4.6
Shandong	1.51	1.05	1.56	0.80	76.9	13.2
Shanghai	3.24	2.82	1.05	3.84	28.9	7.3
Shanxi	2.08	1.24	1.39	0.96	36.0	3.9
Sichuan	1.32	0.71	1.04	0.85	39.1	4.1
Tibet	2.69	2.09	1.02	0.59	46.5	5.9
Tianjin	1.66	0.70	0.65	0.76	34.1	4.2
Xinjiang	2.25	1.61	0.47	1.07	33.4	5.7
Yunnan	1.26	0.87	0.99	0.69	13.0	6.2
Zhejiang	1.82	1.20	0.49	0.64	27.3	3.7
National	1.50	1.03	1.02	0.77	37.1	4.4

Source: *Chinese Health Statistical Digest 2005*, Ministry of Health, Tables s16, s24, s28 http://www.moh.gov.cn/public/open.aspx?n_id=8006 accessed 22/07/06.

viable) or only receive limited payments. Hence, a crucial consideration for reforming the health insurance schemes is the need to make health insurance more portable, this would support the large numbers of rural-urban migrants (World Bank,

2005b). However, the salient urban-rural disparities in all aspects of life, especially in levels of social provisioning including healthcare, has remained a major obstacle to reforming the urban health insurance schemes to the benefit of migrants.

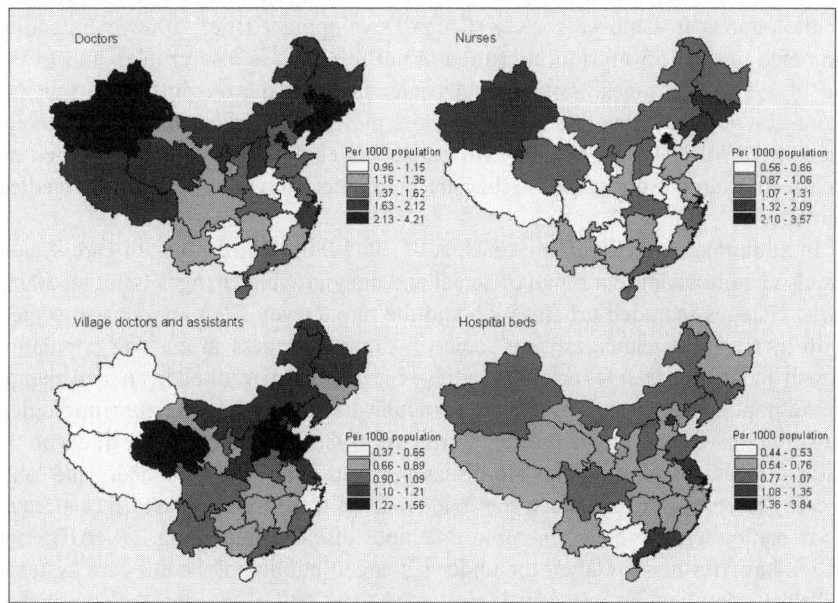

Figure 12.2 Regional variation in health provision indicators
(see Table 12.5 for data sources)

Recognising the serious issues facing the provision and utilisation of health care following the collapse of the CMS and problems surrounding inequalities of provision of health insurance in urban areas various attempts were made in the late 1990s and the early twenty-first century to resurrect health insurance in rural areas and reform the urban schemes. However, despite small improvements, by 2003 some 80% of the rural population (640 million people) and 45% of the urban population lacked medical insurance (World Bank, 2005a, Wang *et al*, 2005). Further, those covered have been required to pay an increasingly larger proportion of their medical costs out of their own finances, rather than directly from their insurance cover (World Bank, 2005a) – an issue that is likely to impact on the take-up of such schemes. The latest attempt to reintroduce a more unified health insurance scheme in rural areas, the new community-based health insurance scheme, is voluntary, with the government providing a subsidy of 10-20 yuan (US$ 1.25-2.50) per year to encourage joining. Contributions from households are at the same level. The scheme is currently being piloted in 300 counties and enrolment is reported to be at 70% (World Bank, 2005a). However, Zhang *et al* (2006) found that the willingness to join the scheme reached only 50% in Fengsan Township, Guizhou Province. A particular issue is that the scheme will only cover around 20% of average spending on medical costs and may not be seen by many as a good buy in terms of insuring against health expenditure (World Bank, 2005a). The PRC government announced in April 2006 that increased funds (4.7 billion RMB) would be put into rural health provision, including the rural health care insurance scheme. It will still cost the farming families some money of their own, however, and it remains to be seen whether this will solve the problems for the poorest in Chinese society (China Development Brief, 2006). Extending insurance to the 155 million uninsured urban residents is also crucial, and to this end in 1998 the Chinese government began merging the old insurance schemes into a new unified urban insurance scheme, the Basic Medical Insurance Scheme (the BMI) (World Bank, 2005b). However, these reforms have not yet halted the decline in insurance coverage in urban areas, or indeed the growth of private medical insurance.

In addition to the economic reforms of the 1980s, China's health care system has also had to adapt to a range of social and demographic changes (Bloom, 2005). These changes included urbanisation and the move away from an agrarian society to an increasingly industrialising society. China's success in curbing population growth and its impressive increases in life expectancy has resulted in an increasingly ageing population that brings with it particular health needs. The epidemiological transition that China moved through during the 1980s has placed new strains on the existing health system, as chronic diseases of old age (such as cancers and heart disease) have begun to replace the epidemics of infectious diseases that affected pre-transition China. New emerging infectious diseases, including HIV/AIDS and SARS, have further stretched the under resourced public and health care systems. A further complication is that it is estimated that 20% of the population still live in areas where the epidemiological transition has not occurred (Hsiao, 1995). In these poor (often rural) areas the burden of illness remains infectious diseases, bringing problems that need to be tackled by the declining public health systems, immunisation campaigns and health education.

Health care facilities and the quality and skills of the health workers employed in rural areas have also been eroded. The services that remain now compete increasingly for patients, relying on fee paying for their survival. Inevitably the poor suffer the most. A paradox of China's rural health care crisis is that a strong network of local, rural-based facilities still exist throughout the country, and despite losing many of the best staff to the urban centres, these facilities still provide reasonable services (Bloom, 2005). The biggest problem is access to these services, access that is governed by the ability and willingness to pay.

Linking globalisation, development and health

The vulnerability of marginalised and disadvantaged people in China's poorer areas reflects the decline in medical insurance coverage and related issues concerning the restructuring and refinancing of the country's health systems, processes that have aggravated access to medical care for many people. After the impressive health successes of previous decades, in the early 1980s 'China virtually dismantled its apparently successful health care and public health system overnight, putting nothing in its place' (Blumenthal and Hsiao, 2005: 1166). Owing to the wider context within China of reform policies that sought to dismantle the communes, introduce a new rural responsibility system (Cook and Murray, 2001) and reduce the role of the state, government expenditure on health care was reduced from 32% in 1978 to only 15% in 1999 (Blumenthal and Hsiao, 2005). Many millions of rural dwellers especially, and the urban poor, lost their insurance against ill health, and the barefoot doctors turned to more lucrative ways of making money, including provision of technical services for which they were untrained, and to selling pharmaceuticals (Blumenthal and Hsiao, 2005). Coinciding with these issues are problems associated with China's ageing population and its epidemiological transition towards chronic diseases of old age that puts increasingly heavy pressures on its already under-funded health care systems.

Globalisation, and more closely China's development trajectory and economic policies, has affected the health of its population through a complex series of interlinked processes: (i) the financing and cost of health care, (ii) the efficiency of service provision, (iii) health policy and health sector regulation, (iv) equity and equality of access to services and (v) quality of service provision (Meng *et al*, 2004b). We deal with each of these five issues in turn.

As a result of a series of changes (fee paying, weak regulation, government funding, use of high technology equipment and expensive drugs) medical care costs have risen dramatically in the past two decades (Meng *et al*, 2004b), rising much quicker than income or inflation. These cost increases have coincided with a decline in medical insurance and low wages and now seriously impinge on equality of health care provision. Meanwhile, the historical legacy of the three-tiered health system has, arguably, played a role in the failure of health care. The three-tiered system worked well when people sought medical care locally, but as transport systems have improved some (wealthier) rural residents now choose to travel further to county or regional hospitals to receive medical care (Hsaio, 1995). Hospitals encourage such flows of patients to help them remain financially viable. However, this movement of patients between higher tiers of the health system impacts on the quality and availability of local services, services that are relied upon by the rural poor. The hierarchical organisation of services also encourages duplication and inefficiencies within the system, as well as confusion and overlapping and unclear responsibilities (Hesketh and Zhu, 1997; World Bank, 2004). The increased use of unnecessary treatments – itself a direct outcome of fee paying for services – further add to inefficiencies within the system.

Health policy in post-reform China has tended to lack coordination between appropriate sectors. Meng *et al* (2004b) highlight poor coordination, low skill levels and inadequate financing within the departments responsible for managing public health (such as the departments of health, security and business administration). Further, curative and preventative services are now organised separately, leading to deficiencies in the coordination of vital services that are complimentary as opposed to distinct. Hospitals could take a more central role in administrating preventative services, for example immunisation programmes, but they are reluctant as they do not generate income. Stronger regulation of practitioners and health service providers is required given the growing evidence of inappropriate and unnecessary prescribing and treatment.

We have shown increasing inequalities in health both geographically and socially, these inequalities manifest as problems between regions and provinces and between the poor and the wealthy. These health problems relate primarily to inequalities in access to appropriate and good quality health care – access that is related to the ability to pay, rather than need or a desire to provide equity to all.

Finally, problems of health care for the poor and marginalised groups have become exacerbated due to a decline in the quality of services offered. Whilst the quality of care in China is generally adequate, and even in the remote rural areas good local services still exist, the quality of service delivery (both in terms of the trained personnel and the number of hospital beds) varies greatly, especially between urban and rural areas. As we have shown, urban areas now have more trained doctors than rural areas, and service provision (including the number of hospital beds and utilisation of township health centre beds) is currently biased towards urban areas and the wealthier provinces.

Conclusions

The outcome of the changes we have explored has been a decline in the health (and health care coverage) of China's marginalised people: a population marginalised both geographically and socially. Whilst there is evidence of a simple urban-rural divide in health status (Dummer and Cook, 2007) the health problems China currently faces are in reality spatially much more complex and relate to intra-urban problems and rural-rural issues linked to the development of China's western and poorer provinces. Thus geographical marginalisation exists within both rural and urban areas. Socially, these marginalised people are China's poor: the rural-urban migrants, the elderly, and the unemployed. Somewhat paradoxically, despite the economic pressures to reduce funding to such vulnerable groups, 'policies to improve the poor's access to quality health care, education, and infrastructure will also assist in enhancing their economic contribution' (Burton, Tsang and Kang, 2006, op.cit.12). Globalisation brings threats and opportunities to China; it is our belief that support for those marginalised people most affected by the negative aspects of globalisation would bring both economic and social benefits, and thus be of crucial importance in terms of alleviating poverty and upholding social justice in the country.

References

Anson, O. and Sun, S. (2002) Gender and Health in Rural China: Evidence from Hebei Province, *Social Science and Medicine*, 55: 1039-1054.

Beijing Review (2004) A Sound Health System Needed, 5th February.

Bian, Y., Sun, Q., Zhao, Z., Blas E. (2004) Market Reform: a Challenge to Public Health – the Case of Schistosomiasis Control in China. *International Journal of Health Planning and Management*, 19: s79-s94.

Bloom, G. (2005) 'China's Rural Health System in Transition: Towards Coherent Institutional Arrangements?', in Huang Y., Saich T., Steinfeld E. (Eds) *Financial Sector Reform in China.* Cambridge, Mass.: Harvard University Asia Centre.

Blumenthal, D. and Hsiao, W. (2005) 'Privatization and its Discontents – the Evolving Chinese Health Care System', *The New England Journal of Medicine*, 353, 11:1165-1170.

Burton, D., Tseng, W., Kang, K. (2006) 'Asia's Winds of Change', *Finance and Development*, 43, 2: 8 15.

Chen, X.G., Li, X.M., Stanton, B., Fang, X.Y., Lin, D.H., Cole, M., Liu, H.J., Yang, H.M. (2004) 'Cigarette smoking among rural-to-urban migrants in Beijing', China, *Preventive Medicine* 39, 4: 666-673.

Chen, X., Wang, L., Cai, J., Zhou, X., Zheng, J., Guo, J., Wu, X., Engels, D. and Chen, M. (2005) 'Schistosomiasis Control in China: the Impact of a 10-year World Bank Loan Project' (1992-2001), *Bulletin of the World Health Organisation*, 83: 43-48.

China Daily (2003a) 'Rural Areas Need Help to Fight TB', 25th March.

China Daily (2003b) 'World Health Day: Safety of Children Emphasized', 8th April.

China Daily (2006a) 'Now, Two Deadly Strains of Virus', 24th March.

China Daily, (2006b) www.chinadaily.com.cn, accessed April 2006.

China Development Brief (2006) http:/www.chinadevelopmentbrief.com, accessed April 2006.

Cook, I.G. (1999), 'Pressures of Globalization: Can These be Managed', *IFSAM World Management Conference Proceedings*, Beijing.

Cook, I.G. and Dummer, T.J.B. (2004), 'Changing Health in China: Re-evaluating the Epidemiological Transition Model', *Health Policy*, 67: 329-343.

Cook I.G. and Murray G. (2001) *China's Third Revolution: Tensions in the Transition to Post-communism*, London: Curzon.

Cook, I.G. and Powell, J.P. (2005) 'China, Aging and Social Policy: The Influences and Limitations of the Bio-Medical Paradigm', *Journal of Societal and Social Policy*, 4, 2: 71-89.

Cook, I.G. and Powell, J.P. (eds) (2007a) *New Perspectives on Aging in China*, New York: Nova Science Publishers, forthcoming.

Cook, I.G. and Powell, J.P. (2007b) 'Ageing Urban Society: Discourse and Policy', Chapter in Wu, F. (ed.), *China's Emerging Cities*, London: Routledge, forthcoming.

Donald, S.H. and Benewick, R. (2005) *The State of China Atlas*, London: University of California Press.

Dummer, T.J.B. and Cook, I.G. (2007) 'Exploring China's Rural Health Crisis: Processes and Policy Implications', *Health Policy*, in press.

Gao J., Qian J., Tang S., Eriksson B., Blas E. (2002), 'Health Equity in Transition from Planned to Market Economy in China', *Health Policy and Planning,* 17: 20-29.

Gao, J., Tang, S., Tolhurst, R., Rao, K. (2001) 'Changing access to health services in urban China: implications for equity', *Health Policy and Planning*, 16, 3: 302-312.

Giddens, A. (1998) *The Third Way: The Renewal of Social Democracy*, Polity Press, Cambridge.

He, N., Detels, R., Chen, Z., Jiang, Q.W., Zhu, J.D., Dai, Y.Q., Wu, M., Zhong, X., Fu, C.W., Gui, D.X. (2006) 'Sexual behavior among employed male rural migrants in Shanghai, China', *Aids Education and Prevention*, 18, 2: 176-186.

Hesketh T. and Zhu X. (1997) 'Health in China: from Mao to Market Reform', *British Medical Journal*, 314: 1543-1549.

Hillier S., Zheng X. (1994) 'Rural Health Care in China: Past, Present and Future', in: Dwyer D.J. (ed.), *China: the Next Decades*, Harlow, England: Longman Scientific & Technical Publishers.

Hong, Y., Stanton, B., Li, X.M., Yang, H.M., Lin, D.H., Fang, X.Y., Wang, J., Mao, R. (2006), 'Rural-to-urban migrants and the HIV epidemic in China', *Aids And Behavior*, 10, 4: 421-430.

Hsiao, W. (1995) The Chinese Health Care System: Lessons for Other Nations, *Social Science and Medicine*, 41, 8: 1047-1055.

Li L. (2003) *No Charge for TB Victims, Ministry of Health Reiterates*. http:/www.China.org.cn. Accessed 26th March 2003.

Lin, D.H., Li, X.M., Yang, H.M., Fang, X.Y., Stanton, B., Chen, X.G., Abbey, A., Liu, H.J. (2005) Alcohol intoxication and sexual risk behaviors among rural-to-urban migrants in China, *Drug And Alcohol Dependence*, 79, 1: 103-112.

Liu, X. and Mills A. (2002) 'Financing reforms of public health services in China: lessons for other nations', *Social Science and Medicine*, 2002, 54: 1691-1698.

Martin, H.P. and Schumann, H. (1997) *The Global Trap: Globalization and the Assault on Prosperity and Democracy*, Zed, London.

Meng, Q., Li, R., Cheng, G., Blas, E. (2004a) 'Provision and Financial Burden of TB Services in a Financially Decentralised System: a Case Study from Shandong, China', *International Journal of Health Planning and Management*, 19: s45-s62.

Meng, Q., Shi, G., Yang, H., Gonzalez-Block, M., Blas, E. (2004b) *Health Policy and Systems Research in China.* UNICEF/UNDP/World Bank/WHO Special programme for research training in tropical diseases (TDR). China Health Economic Institute, WHO, China, 2004.

Ministry of Health, *Chinese Health Statistical Digest 2004, 2005*. http://www.moh.gov.cn/public/open.aspx?n_id=8006 accessed 22/07/06.

Murray, G. and Cook, I.G. (2002) *Green China: Seeking Ecological Alternatives*, London: RoutledgeCurzon.

National Bureau of Statistics, *China Statistical Yearbooks 1995, 1999, 2000, 2004, 2005*, Beijing: China Statistics Press.

Nsouli, S.M. (1999) 'A Decade of Transition: An Overview of the Achievements and Challenges', *Finance and Development*, 36, 2: 2-5.

Phillips, M.R., Li, X., Zhang, Y. (2002) 'Suicide Rates in China, 1995-99'. *The Lancet*; 359: 835-840.

Powell, J.P. and Cook, I.G. (2006) 'Unpacking Performativity and Patriarchy in China', *International Journal of Sociology and Social Policy*, 26, 7/8: 277-283.

Powell, J.P. and Cook, I.G. (2007) 'Theorizing Trust: Governmentality and Aging in China', in Cook, I.G. and Powell, J.P. (eds), *New Perspectives on Aging in China*, New York: Nova Science Publishers, forthcoming.

Ren Tong (2004) 'Minor Setback for Poultry Production', *Beijing Review*, 19th February.

Ross, A.G.P., Sleigh A.C., Li Y.S., Davis G.M., Williams G.M., Jiang Z., et. al. (2001) 'Schistosomiasis in the People's Republic of China: Prospects and Challenges for the 21st Century', *Clinical Microbiology Reviews*, 14, 2: 270-95.

United Nations Development Programme (UNDP) (2006) http://www.youandaids.org/Asia Pacific at a Glance/China/ accessed 8/9/2006.

Walker, M. (2006), 'A Nation Struggling to Catch its Breath', *Newscientist*, 190, 2549: 8-9.

Wang, L., Kong, L., Wu, F., Bai, Y., Burton, R. (2005) 'Preventing chronic diseases in China', *The Lancet*, 366: 1811-1824.

Watts, J. (2004) 'Chinese Walls Come Down', *Guardian*, 11th September.

Watts, J. (2006) 'HIV Epidemic Less Severe than Feared', *Guardian*, 26th January.

WHO (World Health Organisation) (2005) *Immunisation Profile – China*, 2005. http:/www.who.int/immunization_monitoring/en/globalsummary/countryprofileresult.cfm?c='chn' accessed 22/07/06.

WHO (World Health Organisation) (2006) *Maternal and Child Health in China*. http:/www.wpro.who.int/china/sites/mnh/overview.htm accessed 22/07/06.

World Bank (2004) 'Taking Stock of China's Rural Health Challenge', *Rural Health in China: Briefing Note Series*, note 1, October.

World Bank (2005a) 'Rural Health Insurance – Rising to the Challenge', *Rural Health in China: Briefing Note Series*, note 6, May.

World Bank (2005b) *China's Health Sector – Why Reform is Needed: Briefing Note Series*, note 3, April.

Worth, R.M. (1973) Health and Medicine, in Wu Y. (ed.), *China: a Handbook*, Newton Abbot, England: David & Charles: 657-68.

Wu, F. (ed.) (2006) *Globalization and the Chinese City*, London: Routledge Contemporary China Series.

Wu, Z. (2006), 'Urban Unemployment in China: Some Stylized Facts', in Chen, J. and Yao, S. (eds), *Globalization, Competition and Growth in China*, London: Routledge Studies on the Chinese Economy: 298-307.

Xie, J. and Dow, W.H. (2005) 'Longitudinal Study of Child Immunization Determinants in China', *Social Science and Medicine*, 61: 601-611.

Xinhua News Agency (2003) *Experts Urge to Improve Public Health System,* 5th May.

Xinhua News Agency (2006) *TB Tops List of China's Killer Diseases*, 10th May.

Zhang, L., Wang, H., Wang, L., Hsaio, W. (2006) 'Social Capital and Farmer's Willingness to Join a Newly Established Community-based Health Insurance Scheme in Rural China', *Health Policy*, 76: 233-242.

Zhao Y., Wan, Gao, J. (2003) 'Health expenditure in China 2001', *Chinese Journal of Health Economics*, 22: 1-3.

Chapter 13

Civil Society and Marginalisation: Grassroots NGOs in Qinghai Province

Katherine Morton

Introduction

This chapter explores the linkages between civil society, social justice, and marginalisation. In keeping with the central aims of this book, it looks behind the 'China development miracle' to the people and places that have become marginalised rather than emancipated as a consequence of China's modernisation drive. In taking a historically informed perspective, I suggest that marginalisation is best understood as a form of social injustice. This forces us to consider the possible solutions for preventing its expansion. Non-governmental organisations (NGOs) and other civil society organisations are commonly seen as agents of social justice. But what exactly is the relationship between civil society and marginalisation? Can NGOs genuinely represent the interests of disadvantaged groups, or are they more likely to reinforce the power structures that lead to marginalisation in the first place? And how important are global connections in determining outcomes on the ground?

In addressing these questions, special attention is given to the emergence of Chinese NGOs working at the grassroots. I begin the chapter with a theoretical discussion of the meaning of marginalisation and the way in which it has been interpreted in Western intellectual history. At a general level, I then consider the potential for civil society organisations to act as a force for social justice advocacy. This leads into a more focused discussion on the current situation in China followed by the presentation of two case studies detailing the activities of grassroots NGOs working to alleviate hardship amongst poor ethnic communities in Qinghai province. These cases are not intended to be representative. Instead, they provide illustrative examples of successful efforts to promote social justice in some of the poorest and most remote areas of China.

Marginalisation as an Inevitable Consequence of Modernisation

How we define marginalisation is often guided by concerns relating to inequality and social justice. A common theme in the literature is that of relative material and social deprivation. From an historical perspective, marginalisation has been commonly seen as an inevitable consequence of modernisation. Powerful discourses with their origins in nineteenth century political philosophy have promoted a utilitarian logic that discounts the negative social costs of modernisation on the basis that it serves the many rather than the few. Understanding this historic legacy is critical to an appreciation of the challenges involved in seeking solutions to marginalisation. This is particularly the case in the context of developing and transitional states because often the assumption is that injustices can be redressed once the standard of living improves.

In the late-nineteenth century, much of the discussion on marginalisation was located in the broader discourse on modernisation.[1] Proponents of the theory that modernisation would lead to greater prosperity for all tended to view economic inequality and social exclusion as temporal and unavoidable. Underpinned by an evolutionary linear logic, discourses on modernity and progress dominated Western philosophy and social science until the Great Depression in the 1930s.[2] This is not to suggest that concern for the disadvantaged did not exist. W.W. Willoughby wrote the first book on social justice in 1900 (Miller, 1979). Following in its wake, many liberals and progressives such as John Stuart Mill and Henry Sidgwick argued that industrialisation and economic growth needed to go hand in hand with distributive social welfare. However, it was not until the global economy collapsed in the 1930s that Keynesian economics was introduced to provide capitalism with a social safety net (Stiglitz, 2002, p.249). Disillusionment with the costs of economic modernisation did not set in until the second half of the twentieth century culminating in the dependency school of underdevelopment in the 1960s and 1970s (Frank, 1979; Chilcote and Johnson, 1984).

Three decades or so later, the contemporary debate over globalisation reflects and builds upon this earlier discourse on modernisation. Increasing global economic and social interdependence combined with technological change has brought extensive benefits to diverse peoples across the globe. The actual and potential gains have been widely documented, reinforcing a faith in 'the infinite advance towards social and moral betterment' (Habermas, 1985, p.3). The processes of modernisation and globalisation thus need to be viewed as two sides of the same coin, or as overlapping discourses infused with the same irrefutable logic.

It is also important to recognise that the overriding belief in an evolutionary notion of progress has not been confined to the West. In the context of Southeast Asia, Christopher Duncan (2004) asserts that modernisation theory and the myth of the 'primitive' as quintessentially backward pervade most development agendas. In the case of China, the nineteenth century reform movement that created the intellectual force behind the late Qing modernisation drive drew heavily upon the Western understanding of progress. In challenging the dominant Confucian understanding of socio-political order, reformist thinkers such as Yan Fu (1853-1921) promoted a new faith in 'progressive cosmic evolution' (Goldman and Lee, 2002, p.100).

In his essay on contemporary Chinese thought and the question of modernity, Hui Wang argues that the teleology of modernisation has dominated Chinese thinking for

1 For a more complete account of the meanings attached to the concept of marginality from an historical Western perspective see Bailly and Weiss-Altaner (1995).

2 For an excellent overview of the idea of progress throughout European history see Nisbett (1980, Chapter 8).

over a century. In seeking wealth and power towards the establishment of a modern nation state, he maintains that the Chinese discourse on modernity has been located 'within the binary paradigms of "China/West" and "tradition/modernity"' (Wang, 1999, p.144). These binary conceptions remained in place during the Maoist phase of socialist modernisation and are still apparent in the current Chinese discourse on globalisation. Hence in China, as in the West, the dominant idea of human progress, manifest in the desire for greater material wealth, has a strong tendency to overlook the inequities and social injustices that occur as a direct consequence of the transition from the old to the new.[3]

Marginalisation as an Unacceptable Form of Social Injustice

The continuing legacy of nineteenth century modernist thinking in contemporary debates over globalisation is an important consideration, but we should be careful not to overstate its significance. Over time, increasing awareness that globalisation has its downside in the form of growing income disparities, ecological destruction, cultural oppression, and the curtailment of human rights has cautioned against exaggerated claims of human progress, at least in the shorter term. There now exists a growing body of literature that offers a more critical analysis (Pieterse, 2000; Petras and Veltmeyer, 2001; Stiglitz, 2002). More importantly, the contradictory impacts of globalisation are now widely recognised amongst scholars and policymakers alike. Continuing uncertainty over the likely consequences of globalisation has led, in turn, to a heightened interest in the parallel process of marginalisation. This has been further reinforced by a renewed concern for greater social justice at both the domestic and global levels.

Recent studies on marginalisation have looked at the process in a wide variety of contexts including urban spaces in the developed world (Harrington, 1984), rural and peripheral areas in developing countries (Wu, 2003; Tsing, 1993; Duncan, 2004), between countries (Murshed, 2002), and within regions (Hadjimchalis and Sadler, 1995). These studies have contributed significantly to our understanding of the complexities of economic, social, and spatial differences. For a more complete understanding of marginalisation, however, we need to take into account the importance of power differentials that can reinforce social injustices by preventing certain individuals and groups from participating in social life.

In her book on justice and the politics of difference, Iris Young argues that marginalisation is one of the 'five faces of oppression' (1990, p.53).[4] Her interpretation of marginalisation is based upon 'structural issues of justice, in particular concerning the appropriateness of a connection between participation in productive activities of social cooperation, on the one hand, and access to the means of consumption, on the other' (1990, p.55). Young's understanding of the relationship between marginalisation and social justice shares much in common with the capabilities

3 For a good overview of the notion of social justice from a Chinese perspective see Wu (2004).

4 The other four faces include exploitation, powerlessness, cultural imperialism and violence.

approach taken by Amartya Sen (1999) and Martha Nussbaum (2000). In analysing social justice, Sen advances the argument that, 'there is a strong case for judging individual advantage in terms of capabilities that a person has, that is, the substantive freedoms he or she enjoys to lead the kind of life he or she has reason to value' (1999, p.87). Thus poverty 'must be seen as the deprivation of basic capabilities' rather than merely as a lack of adequate income (Sen, 1999, p.97).

In drawing on the above perspective, in this chapter I interpret marginalisation as *a process of social exclusion from the dominant socio-economic, cultural, and political structures which when combined with constraints on self-development prevent individuals, groups, and communities from fully participating in social life.* Marginalisation as a form of social injustice allows us to consider the structural conditions of inequality and the subsequent need for new institutional forms and opportunities that recognise human differences. In other words it forces us to think about the possible solutions for preventing its spread (Bailly and Weiss-Altaner, 1995). In the discussion that follows I argue that an important impetus for resisting marginalisation might well be found amongst the diverse agencies of civil society.

Civil Society as an Answer to Marginalisation?

Many scholars and activists view NGOs and other civil society organisations as important agents of social justice and development: they provide essential social services by filling the void left by the state; they act as an important conduit for exposing injustices and abuses of political and economic power; and they can improve the lives of marginalised groups by involving them in developmental activities. In many cases, civil society organisations arise out of a 'sense of marginalisation, injustice, and exclusion' (Cox, 2001, p.49).

But how effective are civil society organisations in resisting marginalisation in practice? A major problem in addressing this question is that the concept of civil society itself is highly contested, especially in the context of non-Western developing states. In consideration of the fact that civil society has its origins in Western social and intellectual history, we need to be cautious about raising expectations of its potential to bring about increasing freedom and democracy outside of the West. As noted by Sunil Khilnani, 'taken at its boldest, the idea of civil society embodies the epic of Western modernity' (2001, p.14).

In describing the rapid expansion of Third World social movements during the 1990s, Smitu Khotari (1996, p.13) reminds us that initial expectations at the end of World War II that the struggles against colonialism would lead to more democratic and just societies with the development of civil society to hold the state accountable have not been realised. He argues that instead societies across the Third World have become more conflict-ridden and factionalised. Resistance to marginalisation has brought mixed results – often leading to the rise of religious fundamentalism (Khotari, 1996).[5]

5 For an excellent discussion of the relevance of civil society to developing states see Hawthorn (2001).

Civil society clearly has its limits. It may well lack sufficient capacity to act as a bulwark against the excesses of political power and rampant global capitalism on a large scale. But it does contain demonstrated potential to serve the needs of those who have become marginalised though the process of globalisation. A wealth of literature supports the argument that NGOs and civil society organisations are important facilitators of inclusive participation, empowerment, and community development (Eber, 1998; and Epstein, 1995). The very process of marginalisation itself can have a catalytic effect in that the only realistic option open for disadvantaged groups is to self-organise in a collective manner to address grievances.

In the case of Africa, Fantu Cheru (2000, p.123) suggests that marginalisation should be seen in a more positive light – in the sense that it reinforces a connection with social needs. In the words of Claude Ake: 'perhaps marginalisation so often decried, is what Africa needs right now. For one thing it will help the evolution of an endogenous development agenda, an agenda that expresses the aspirations of the people and can therefore elicit their support' (cited in Cheru, 2000, p.123). This perspective, based on the experiences of some of the most marginalised regions in the world, has relevance when thinking about the challenges of marginalisation in the context of China. It serves to remind us that solutions to marginalisation do not only lie in the reform of the development agenda from above, in the redistribution of wealth and resources, but also in social innovation and collective action from the margins.

Resisting Marginalisation in China

One of the most significant transformations over the past decade in China has been the expansion of civil society and the growth of NGOs. In the wake of China's economic reforms, scholars have employed a number of concepts to identify the changing nature of state–society relations. In the 1990s the general consensus, as epitomised in the benchmark study by White *et al.* (1996), was that little empirical evidence existed to support the emergence of an Anglo-American style liberal civil society. Instead, civil society was seen as predominantly state corporatist with social organisations merely acting as an extension of state interests (Chan, 1995; Unger, 1996).

A decade after these initial studies were conducted it is becoming clearer that Chinese civil society (*gongmin shehui*) is both an expression of the continuing consolidation of social power by the state and an expression of the needs, grievances and aspirations of the Chinese people. Above all, civil society reflects the broader socio-economic transformations that are taking place in China with the old mass-based organisations (*qunzhong tuanti*) co-existing comfortably with the new more autonomous organisations (*minjian zuzhi*).[6]

From a government perspective, the latter are tolerated primarily for their service delivery role. As in many other developing countries, NGOs are stepping into the

6 For a good analysis of the ways in which the state and civil society overlap in China see Saich (2000).

void left by the state to provide basic social and environmental services. For political reasons, turning a blind eye to these organisations has something to do with the fact that they are a controllable means of absorbing grievances – or energies that might take on a more dangerous form.

From an NGO perspective, the motivations to self-organise are in part a response to the relaxation of state controls, but also a reflection of growing public concerns over the downside of China's modernisation drive. It is now common knowledge that the economic rise of China over the past 28 years has not been without its costs (see Wang and Hu, 1999; Khan and Riskin, 2001). Rapid economic growth has left in its wake serious environmental problems, social dislocation, rising unemployment, rising crime, a growing divide between rich and poor, and more recently the intensification of the spread of HIV/AIDS. The victims, or those marginalised from the benefits, have little choice but to self-organise.

Nevertheless, they face a number of political, legal, and organisational constraints. National security interests continue to outweigh social concerns.[7] The Chinese authorities are intolerant of any social movement or organisation that is perceived to pose a direct threat to the regime and the stability of the nation. Government regulations on social organisations were first promulgated by the State Council following the student-led pro-democracy campaign in 1989. These were updated in 1998 but remain restrictive: first, before registering with the Ministry of Civil Affairs organisations must be sponsored by a government-owned unit (*zhuguan danwei*); second, only one social organisation is permitted for any single sphere of activity; third, organisations can only operate at the administrative level at which they are registered; and fourth, organisations must have at least 50 individual members with initial assets of US$ 12,000.[8]

The new Foundation Law promulgated in 2004 is in some respects a step forward. It provides an opportunity for Chinese organisations to register as a public or private foundation. In the former case, public fundraising within China is permitted thus resolving a major financial constraint on the capacity of NGOs to sustain their operations on a long-term basis. It is doubtful, however, whether smaller grassroots organisations will be able to raise the necessary initial endowment in order to register.[9]

Many Chinese NGOs also face considerable challenges from within. Very often they lack sufficient resources, managerial expertise, and organisational capacity. As in the case of NGOs in general, the pursuit of a particular cause tends to overshadow professional imperatives relating to accountability and transparency. More cynically, NGO practitioners have been criticised for promoting their own self-interests, and

---

7 For example, in Xinjiang Uighur Autonomous Region and the Tibetan Autonomous Region grassroots organisations are not allowed to register as formal legal entities.

8 Ministry of Civil Affairs (2000).

9 Public foundations require an initial endowment of 8 million RMB (US$ 1 million) to register at the national level and 4 million RMB (US$ 500,000) to register at a lower level of the administration. For private foundations this sum is significantly higher at the national level (20 million RMB or US$2.5 million) but only 2 million RMB (US$ 250,000) at the lower administrative level. The dual registration system still applies. For a comprehensive analysis of the New Foundation Law see China Development Brief (2004).

conflicts between NGO leaders and their staff are believed to be widespread (Lu, 2005).

Despite the constraints and limitations, it is becoming increasingly clear that Chinese NGOs are playing an important role in representing the interests of marginalised groups.[10] Although independent human rights NGOs in China do not, as yet, exist, human rights concerns are often embedded within other issue-based organisations working on the environment, gender equality, health or poverty alleviation. Legal aid organisations are expanding rapidly and many NGOs work directly to support the rights of the vulnerable (*ruoshi qunti*) such as migrant workers, the victims of HIV/AIDS, women and children.[11]

Research on these organisations across diverse regions of China is still limited. Those studies available have tended to focus on China's urban areas. With the exception of a few notable works (Wu, 2003; Wang, 2003; Zhang and Baum, 2004), far less attention has been given to assessing the role of grassroots organisations in rural and poorer areas of China.[12] In the section that follows I will address this gap by focusing on the activities of grassroots NGOs working in rural areas of Qinghai province in western China. The discussion draws upon my fieldwork visits to Qinghai between October 2003 and August 2005. These visits involved close observation of the work of NGOs on a daily basis, semi-structured interviews with village leaders and government officials, as well as focus group discussions with villagers and nomads living in Yushu prefecture and the counties of Minhe and Zaduo.

My reasons for focusing on this region of China are three-fold: first, there exist a growing number of genuine grassroots organisations that are relatively autonomous from the local government. At the time of writing in 2005, a total of ten officially registered NGOs were operating in Qinghai. Four of these were government organised NGOs (GONGOs)[13] and the other six were independently organised.[14] Second, many of the Qinghai NGOs share an interest in improving the conditions of disadvantaged groups based on the common ideals of self-development, equality, and compassion. They are pioneers of social justice and provide exemplary cases of an enduring commitment to their constituents. Third, Qinghai province is located in one of the poorest, most ecologically fragile, and isolated regions of China. It presents a major challenge for advocates of social justice because the dual tensions between tradition and modernity and growth and sustainability are particularly stark. Insights into the ways in which grassroots NGOs are attempting to reconcile these tensions can enhance our understanding of their broader potential to resist the spread of marginalisation.

---

10 See Howell (2004).

11 There exists a growing literature in Chinese on vulnerable and marginal groups. See Jin (2002), Shi (2004) and Yan (2005).

12 For an analysis of environmental NGOs working in rural Qinghai and the transnational dimension of their activities, see Morton (forthcoming 2007).

13 These include the Red Cross, Women's Federation, Qinghai Disabled Organisation and the Social Welfare Organisation.

14 These include three organisations focused on environmental protection, and three working on poverty alleviation.

Pioneers of Social Justice in a 'Backward' Province

The western province of Qinghai is generally considered to be one of the most backward regions in the People's Republic. Recent government efforts towards integrating the province with the rest of China as part of the 'Develop the West' (*xibu da kaifa*) campaign are proving to be only partially successful. This is largely because development planning has been economically driven with insufficient attention given to the province's unique socio-cultural and political diversity (Goodman, 2004). Moreover, environmental concerns remain subordinated to economic goals, and little attempt has been made to draw upon the rich traditions of the ethnic minorities that make up almost half of the 5.3 million population. In the minds of many government officials, tradition is equated with backwardness (Miller, 2000; Namgyal, 2004). Consequently, if current attitudes persist, it is highly likely that the push towards modernisation will lead to new forms of marginalisation and worsening inequities and divisions. The problem is particularly acute in the remote areas of the Qinghai–Tibetan plateau that are populated by nomadic and semi-nomadic pastoralists.

Resettlement programmes for nomads were introduced in the 1960s (Goodman, 2004) and continue to this day. More recent concerns over the degradation of the grasslands have reinforced a sense of urgency.[15] It is estimated that one-third of the grassland in Qinghai is seriously degraded (United States Embassy Beijing, 2003, p.2). Rapid desertification threatens Qinghai's abundant water resources, which, in turn, has important implications for the more densely populated provinces downstream. Climate change is clearly a causal factor. But the complex nature of ecosystemic degradation on the plateau has meant that disproportionate blame has been placed upon the more visible problem of overgrazing. This assumption also feeds off the misperception that traditional lifestyles are backward, irrational and unsustainable. In reality, as aptly expressed by David Miller: 'The very existence of nomads on the Tibetan Plateau – undoubtedly the world's harshest pastoral area – is itself proof of the rationality and efficacy of many aspects of traditional practice' (2000, p.5).

The current policy to return pasture to grasslands (*tui mu huan cao*) is directly linked to expanding the resettlement of the nomads through the privatisation of collectively managed grasslands. The *si pei tao* (four ways) programme aims to fence rangeland, construct houses for nomads, build sheds for livestock, and secure artificial pasture. Anecdotal evidence suggests that the scheme is leading to social conflicts and alienation. Without an education and the new skills necessary to secure alternative employment, nomads can find themselves alienated from their modern surroundings.

The actual and potential consequences of modernisation in Qinghai, however, are not all negative. A reorientation of China's development path paying greater attention to the western provinces has helped to create a space for the establishment of grassroots organisations taking alternative and more sustainable paths towards

15 According to Goodman (2004, p.396) the current goal of the provincial government is to settle all nomadic herdsmen by 2011.

fulfilling the development mandate imposed from above. It is to two of these organisations that we shall now turn.

Sanchuan Development Association

Sanchuan Development Association (*sanchuan fazhan cujin hui*) (SDA) was formally registered with the civil affairs bureau of the local county government in March 2002. It is located in Guanting township, Minhe Hui Tu autonomous county, near the border with Gansu province. The county's mountainous terrain and poor transportation links severely curtail agricultural productivity. Hence the central driving force behind the establishment of the association was the desperate need to alleviate rural poverty (average household income is below US$100 per annum, see Zhang and Baum, 2004). SDA was founded by Zhu Yongzhang, a middle-school teacher from the nearby mountain village of Zhoujiala.[16] He was supported in his efforts by Dr Kevin Stuart who runs an English language-training programme at Qinghai Normal University in Xining, the provincial capital.

SDA has a number of unique characteristics that sets it apart from many other NGOs currently operating across China. First, it has developed organically from the margins. All of the 50 members are from poor villages in Qinghai. As the introductory profile to the organisation makes clear: 'Poverty is … not an academic or "development jargon" abstraction, but rather, something that was personally experienced throughout childhood in all its ugliness and which continues to be a reality for relatives of group members' (SDA, 2002). Most of the members work on a voluntary basis with only four staff (including Zhu Yongzhang) employed full-time. The county education bureau, which acts as SDA's government sponsor, continues to pay the salaries of these full-time staff.

A second unique characteristic is the multi-ethnic nature of the association's membership that includes Mangghuer (Tu), Tibetan, Hui, and Han ethnic groups. The aim is to work on behalf of marginalised peoples regardless of ethnic background. On a visit to Guanting in October 2004, Mr Zhu expressed concerns over Mongolian and Hui communities living in other parts of Qinghai that were currently beyond the reach of NGOs.

A third unique characteristic of the organisation is its 'people first' policy. Decisions over development priorities, activities, and funding are made on the basis of a democratic process of consultation. Villagers participate directly in projects to ensure a sense of ownership. A common criticism made of government-led development activities by locals is that too much money is wasted on unnecessary expenditure. For example, one village leader explained that if he needed 10,000 RMB (US$1250) to invest in the construction of a road, he would have to spend 5,000 RMB (US$625) wooing governmental officials with expensive banquets to secure the funding. Moreover, when the local government provides funding for a school, real needs are often overlooked. Instead of investing in basic educational

16 For local media coverage of SDA see 'Soaring Sanchuan's Modern Folksong', *Qinghai Ribao*, 6 April 2004.

materials, funds are diverted towards purchasing computers, building high walls, and arranging memorial plaques.[17]

In contrast, SDA works with the beneficiaries of its development projects to ensure that real needs are always addressed. A project management committee is set up for each project with membership drawn from the community and local people contribute in kind to bring down project costs. Relative to its limited resources, SDA has been able to demonstrate a high degree of professionalism with a strong emphasis on transparency and accountability.

Relations with the government remain cordial; seemingly because SDA's particular focus on education meshes with the government's plan to provide primary school education for all by 2006. Poverty alleviation bureaux often send their members to observe SDA activities as part of their training. The demonstration effect helps to consolidate support. Moreover, a proven capacity to solicit external funding raises the organisation's profile in the eyes of government officials.[18] However, working with government agencies outside the education sector has proven to be more difficult, especially at the county level. According to Zhu Yongzhang, ethnic divisions between senior county officials often lead to conflicts over development planning. A further problem is that county officials are reluctant to support NGOs unless they can see direct and immediate benefits. Given their proximity to the issues at stake, township officials are more easily convinced. It is also the case that government agencies at both levels can be circumvented when implementing projects in remote villages.[19]

To carry out its work, SDA relies heavily on funding from outside donors. These include the Trace Foundation, the Bridge Fund, the Kadoorie Charitable Foundation, Save the Children Fund Hong Kong, and various embassies in Beijing. Buddhist monks provide an additional source of income as well as a means for closely identifying the needs of the worst off. As of 2003, SDA had implemented over 90 poverty alleviation projects ranging from the construction of schools, to solar cookers, and water supply at a total cost of nearly 7 million RMB (US$875,000). Zhoujiala mountain village primary school provides a good exemplar of SDA's success. In 1996 the school had only 12 children in grades 1-3. After receiving support from SDA to greatly improve the poor conditions of the school, by 2004 the number of children had expanded to over 100 across all grades.

One of the problems that SDA faces is that its identity is inextricably linked to the drive and ambition of its charismatic leader. As in the case of other grassroots NGOs operating in China, staff turnover tends to be high with many graduate students attracted by the opportunity to gain first-hand experience before moving on to work for foreign NGOs or larger Chinese organisations located in the cities. The future plan is to expand SDA's reach beyond the county. In particular, Zhu Yongzhang is keen to work more with the Mongolian community living in the northeast of Qinghai that currently lacks NGO representation. But scaling up activities will require a significant change in the way in which the organisation operates. It will

---

17 Discussion with village leader, 3 October 2004.

18 Interview with county education bureau, October 2004.

19 Interview with Zhu Yongzhang, August 2005.

no longer be possible for the director to take a 'hands on' approach to managing projects. Moreover, working outside the county is likely to expose the organisation to additional political and legal restrictions. At this stage, it is difficult to tell whether such a plan will succeed. Although the future remains uncertain, what is clear is that to date SDA has remained true to its mission in alleviating hardship.

Snowland Service Group

Some of the most remote and poorest villages in China are to be found at an average altitude of 4000 meters at the centre of the Qinghai–Tibet plateau in Yushu Tibetan autonomous prefecture. Yushu has a population of around 270,000, 98 per cent of whom are ethnically Tibetan. Largely inhabited by semi-nomadic herdsmen, this region, known locally as Sanjiangyuan, lies at the source of China's three main rivers – Yangtze, Yellow, and Lancang (Mekong). Over the past two decades, both the region's unique ecosystem and its rich cultural heritage have come under threat.

In 2001, in recognition that sustainable livelihoods and the maintenance of cultural values depended upon the active participation of the people, Rinchen Darwa forfeited his position as deputy-governor of Zaduo county to set up the Snowland Service Group (*jiangyuan fazhan cujin hui*) (SSG).[20] His decision was motivated in part by his exposure to local government corruption. During the heavy snowstorms of 1998 and 1999 when many pastoralists lost up to 80 per cent of their livestock, international funds for rehabilitation were siphoned off by unscrupulous local officials. On the positive side, during this period he was also able to witness the work of Oxfam in practice. Having being introduced to the idea of an NGO, it soon became apparent that the only way to help the people was to work directly with them.[21]

SSG currently has 180 volunteers, most of whom are herdsmen, and a permanent staff of 11. As a consequence of the director's standing in the local community, the organisation benefits from having close government connections. Very often the local government depends upon SSG rather than the other way around. According to Rinchen Darwa, 'in some remote parts of Yushu villagers know SSG but they don't know the government'.[22] My visits to several of the poorest villages revealed that families much preferred to work for themselves rather than depend on government handouts. The efforts of SSG to draw upon the experiences of the poorest members of any given community and include them in development work were widely appreciated.

The central mission of the NGO is to mitigate hardship without destroying tradition. As in the case of SDA, education is deemed to be particularly important. Access to education in Yushu is severely limited, and with average per capita income around US$50 per annum most households require their children to work. Education is also seen as a matter of survival for the Tibetan people. This is clearly expressed

20 The Group was granted official NGO status by the Civil Affairs Bureau of Yushu prefecture.

21 Interview with Rinchen Darwa, 12 October 2004.

22 Ibid.

in the introductory profile to the organisation: 'all too often, modernisation comes at the expense of tradition. With carefully chosen technologies and a reconceived educational platform for non-Mandarin speaking Chinese, the Snowland Service Group will prove that this need not to be true' (SSG, 2003).

Other activities focus on installing solar power, providing loans for yaks, healthcare and cultural restoration. More recently, attention has been given to the importance of legal rights. For example, in 2004 SSG lent its support to a village that was taking the local government to court over its misappropriation of land. It translated the relevant laws pertaining to the case into Tibetan. Then, in 2005, it launched a new project aimed at raising legal awareness as a means of reducing conflicts amongst nomadic communities. A particular emphasis was placed upon clarifying user rights to the land. In collaboration with the county justice bureau, throughout the summer months SSG carried out 'rights promotion' meetings in remote villages that attracted a sizeable audience. Raising legal awareness is considered to be a long-term project. From my observations most of the participants at the meetings felt too inhibited to express their views, especially the women. A village leader in one village was more forthcoming. He told me that in his view the benefit of the law was that 'it made life more equal for the people – Tibetans, Han, rich and poor.'[23] That said, the local government in his area still maintains the right to take back the land.

As a consequence of Rinchen Darwa's former status, SSG experiences fewer problems in its dealings with the county government than SDA. Instead, one of the biggest difficulties that it faces is in identifying the greatest need. On an average day families line up outside the office in Jiegu township, having walked all day to plead their cases to SSG staff. As one member remarked, 'we cannot help everyone, but sometimes being willing to listen can in itself make a difference'.[24] All requests are initially sent to the investigation department, which carries out on-site feasibility studies. Viable requests are then passed on to a management committee whose members are determined by a democratic election at annual meetings. These internal democratic processes are important. They distinguish the NGO from its government counterpart. However, responding to need in the longer term also requires a fundamental shift away from ad hoc development projects and towards sustainable development programmes that encourage a greater sense of ownership on the part of the beneficiaries.

In comparing the two NGOs there is little difference in the way in which they carry out their activities: participation by the people is central; all projects require a contribution from the beneficiaries; and democratic decision-making is deemed essential. Both organisations also depend upon international support. In this regard, SSG works in partnership with the Bridge Fund – an international NGO dedicated to the pursuit of sustainable development in Tibetan areas with its headquarters in the United States. The partnership works because the Bridge Fund has localised its operations. With the exception of the current country director, all personnel working

23 Focus group meeting with nomadic community in Dora village, 90 km from Jiegu township.

24 Discussion with staff from SSG, October 2004.

in Qinghai and Tibet are local Tibetans. Additional funding support is currently being provided from the Trace Foundation and Oxfam.

A major concern for the future, beyond the obvious challenge of ensuring financial viability, is to attract the involvement of the younger generation of Tibetans in development work. It is for this reason that SSG has set up a Development Institute in Jiegu township that can provide a home not only for members of the organisation and its international partners, but also for young Tibetans returning from overseas with new skills and aspirations. The Institute will provide training for NGO practitioners as well as government officials. Training is taken very seriously by SSG members because it is generally assumed that education is the necessary prerequisite for successful advocacy.

Opportunities and Future Challenges

The above cases are significant because they demonstrate how civil society organisations at the grassroots can make a difference to the lives of marginalised peoples. They also reveal how justice is being interpreted and implemented on the ground. In both cases the motivation lies in the desire to alleviate hardship by working with the people concerned. The goals are largely pragmatic but also principled in evoking the ideals of compassion and self-development. Above all, in some of the poorest areas of Qinghai, the pursuit of social and economic justice alongside more democratic forms of participation are seen as important means of dealing with the downside of China's modernisation drive. This is a potentially important finding because it runs counter to conventional wisdom that it is difficult, if not impossible, to construct meaningfully just societies in materially poor societies because people need to focus their physical and intellectual efforts on the struggle for survival.

So what are the local factors behind the success of these grassroots organisations? How significant are the influences of globalisation? And what are the future challenges involved in resisting marginalisation? Clearly the strength of both NGOs lies in their genuine grassroots potential. It is commonly understood within the field of development studies that the risk of imposing inappropriate development solutions recedes according to the degree of direct local knowledge. Indeed, both organisations run on the basis of a self-help philosophy that keeps them rooted within the community. The majority of the members have themselves experienced extreme poverty, which helps to strengthen their resolve and commitment. I was also aware during my visits to project sites of the pre-existing capacity for communal self-help amongst the poorest communities. This is in part driven by religion. Buddhist beliefs in particular nurture a sense of human compassion. But it is also the case that communal participation is a way of ensuring survival. Many families lack food for at least part of the year and it is common practice to borrow from others.

Local expertise and a strong community spirit are critical conditions of success but they are not sufficient. As in the case of many NGOs in general, charismatic leadership is central to the achievements of both SDA and SSG. A particular strength of both leaders is their ability to bridge the gap between remote local communities and the outside world. As mentioned earlier, this has been greatly facilitated by the efforts of Dr Kevin Stuart who runs a development network aimed at implementing small-scale projects in rural communities. As mentioned earlier, Zhu Yongzhang is one of his former students, and other graduates now work for SSG.

It is also clear that these organisations could not function without the support of international funding; they not only depend upon international NGOs and development agencies for financial support but also for the transfer of new ideas, appropriate technologies, and moral support. At a broader level, networking via the Internet and participating in international conferences and workshops provide a global platform for the articulation of local priorities and needs.

Any assessment of the value of these kinds of global connections has to take into account the potential downside of international support. It is widely acknowledged that international dependency can distract attention away from local concerns, skew the agendas of grassroots NGOs, and stifle the potential of civil society agencies to genuinely represent the interests of the people (Howell and Pearce, 2001; Dicklitch, 2002). Particularly in the case of transitional states, one cannot assume that international engagement will automatically lead to improved conditions on the ground. International agencies are just as likely to reinforce injustices, as they are to alleviate them.

In the context of grassroots NGOs operating in Qinghai, it would appear that international engagement presents more of an opportunity than a constraint. This is because local NGOs provide donors with an effective mechanism for delivery which cautions against too much interference from outside. In the case of local–international NGO partnerships, it is also clear that the agenda is being driven from the bottom up. In effect, cooperation works because both partners are bound by the same logic: that modernisation should not come at the expense of social justice. The two NGOs discussed in this chapter do more than simply plead their causes; they are able to actively demonstrate how alternative and more sustainable paths to development can be taken. Advocacy by example is critical.

A note of caution, however, is required. It is by no means clear that NGOs and other civil society groups in China share the same motivation, or indeed capacity, as these grassroots groups in Qinghai. A more representative picture of the relationship between civil society and social justice in China is just as likely to reveal failure, as it is to reveal success. One of the problems the analyst is likely to encounter is that many groups may be involved in promoting social justice but not necessarily describing themselves in this way. Further difficulties will arise from trying to establish the legitimacy of those groups claiming to work for the greater cause but with little evidence to suggest that they are genuine representatives of the marginalised and disadvantaged. Naturally, as guardians of social justice, civil society groups must also be accountable and transparent in their actions. We should also be aware that social justice advocacy is a slow and incremental process. Positive outcomes cannot simply be equated with deliverables on the ground. Within political science the impact of NGO advocacy is often assessed in relation to policy outcomes. The problem with this approach is that it overlooks the importance of bringing about broader attitudinal change.

At a deeper level, the fundamental challenge for social justice advocacy at the grassroots is to convince the Chinese government of the need to re-examine pre-existing notions of modernisation. A serious problem here is that local government officials tend to insist on the need for development based upon GDP growth. They typically view the downside of modernisation as an inevitable sacrifice that must be made for the sake of the nation. Party leaders in particular remain intransigent. Addressing this problem will require reform from above as well as an impetus from below.

To conclude, the challenges that grassroots NGOs face in the struggle against marginalisation in China are inextricably linked to dominant ideas about progress and modernity. I have argued that these ideas need to be critically re-examined if we are to more effectively address marginalisation. In particular, rather than framing poor communities as 'backward' or 'failed', it is important to re-think the boundaries between tradition and modernity, national and ethnic identity, and centre and periphery.[25] For this to happen, marginalisation needs to be widely endorsed as an 'unacceptable' rather than an 'inevitable' consequence of modernisation. Progress in this direction is likely to be slow and incremental. The importance of NGOs lies in their ability to negotiate alternative development solutions that can, in turn, demonstrate just outcomes. This, in itself, is a major step forward to making justice a reality for all.

Acknowledgements

I would like to thank the Department of International Relations in the Research School of Pacific and Asian Studies, Australian National University, for providing the financial assistance for my fieldwork. A special thanks to Miwa Hirono for her valuable research assistance and to Mary-Louise Hickey for her editorial assistance. For my fieldwork investigation, I am particularly indebted to Dr Kevin Stuart, Zhu Yongzhang, Rinchen Darwa, Kunchok Gelek Jackson and Tashi Haiyuan. I do of course take full responsibility for any factual errors in the chapter.

References

Bailly, Antoine and Weiss-Altaner, Eric (1995), 'Thinking about the Edge: The Concept of Marginality', in Costis Hadjimichalis and David Sadler (eds), *Europe at the Margins: New Mosaics of Inequality*, John Wiley and Sons, Chichester.

Chan, Anita (1995), 'Revolution or Corporatism? Private Entrepreneurs as Citizens: From Leninism to Corporatism', *China Information*, vol. 10(3/4), pp. 1-28.

Cheru, Fantu (2000), 'The Local Dimensions of Global Reform', in Jan Nederveen Pieterse (ed.), *Global Futures: Shaping Globalisation*, Zed Books, London and New York.

Chilcote, Ronald H. and Johnson, Dale L. (eds) (1983), *Theories of Development: Mode of Production or Dependency?*, Sage, Beverly Hills.

China Development Brief (2004) 'Blurred law may be better than none' 6 October.

25 Here I am drawing on the work of anthropologists Veena Das and Deborah Poole (2004) who offer a new perspective on the state from the vantage point of the margins.

Cox, David Ray (2001), 'Marginalisation and the Role of Social Development: The Significance of Globalisation, the State and Social Movements', in Debal K. Singha Roy (ed.), *Social Development and the Empowerment of Marginalised Groups: Perspectives and Strategies*, Sage Publications, New Delhi.

Das, Veena and Poole, Deborah (eds) (2004), *Anthropology in the Margins of the State*, School of American Research Press, Santa Fe.

Dicklitch, Susan (2002), 'NGOs and Democratisation in Transitional Societies: Lessons from Uganda', in Daniel N. Nelson and Laura Neak (eds), *Global Society in Transition: An International Politics Reader*, Kluwer Law International, The Hague.

Duncan, Christopher (2004), 'Legislating Modernity among the Marginalised', in Christopher Duncan (ed.), *Civilising the Margins: Policies for the Development of Minorities*, Cornell University Press, Ithaca and London.

Eber, Christine E. (1998), *Seeking Justice, Valuing Community: Two Women's Paths in the Wake of the Zapatista Rebellion*, Michigan State University, East Lansing, Michigan.

Epstein, Barbara (1995), 'Grassroots Environmentalism and Strategies for Social Change', *New Political Science*, vol. 32, pp. 1-24.

Frank, Andre G. (1979), *Dependent Accumulation and Underdevelopment*, Monthly Review Press, New York.

Goldman, Merle and Lee, Leo Ou-fan (eds) (2002), *Intellectual History of Modern China*, Cambridge University Press, Cambridge.

Goodman, David (2004), 'Qinghai and the Emergence of the West: Nationalities, Communal Interaction and National Integration', *China Quarterly*, vol. 178(June), pp. 379-99.

Habermas, Jürgen (1985), 'Modernity – an Incomplete Project', in Hal Foster (ed.), *Postmodern Culture*, Pluto, London.

Hadjimichalis, Costis and Sadler, David (eds) (1995), *Europe at the Margins: New Mosaics of Inequality*, John Wiley and Sons, Chichester.

Hawthorn, Geoffrey (2001), 'The Promise of Civil Society in the South', in Sudipta Kaviraj and Sunil Khilnani (eds), *Civil Society: History and Possibilities*, Cambridge University Press, Cambridge.

Harrington, Michael (1984), *The New American Poverty*, Holt, Rinehart and Winston, New York.

Howell, Jude and Pearce, Jenny (2001), *Civil Society and Development: A Critical Exploration*, Lynne Reinner, Boulder.

Howell, Jude (ed.) (2004) 'New Directions in Civil Society: Organising around Marginalised Interests' *Governance in China,* Lanham, Md, Rowan and Littlefield Publishers.

Jin, Shuangqiu (2002), 'Yi shehui xue de "shehui zhichi" lilungoujian ruoshi qunti de shequ zhiyuan zonghe wangluo' (Comprehensive network of community support for vulnerable groups constructed by sociological 'social support' theory) in Yan Qingchun (ed.), *Shehui fuli yu ruoshi qunti* (Social welfare and vulnerable groups), Zhongguo shehui kexue chubanshe, Beijing.

Khan, Azizur Rahman and Riskin, Carl (2001), *Inequality and Poverty in China in the Age of Globalisation*, Oxford University Press, Oxford.

Khilnani, Sunil (2001), 'The Development of Civil Society', in Sudipta Kaviraj and Sunil Khilnani (eds), *Civil Society: History and Possibilities*, Cambridge University Press, Cambridge.

Khotari, Smitu (1996), 'Rising from the Margins: The Awakening of Civil Society in the Third World', *Development*, no. 3, pp. 11-19.

Lu, Yiyi (2005) 'The Growth of Civil Society in China: Key Challenges for NGOs' Briefing Paper, The Royal Institute of International Affairs, February.

Miller, David (1979), *Social Justice*, Clarendon Press, Oxford.

Miller, David (2000), 'Tibetan Pastoralism: Hard Times on the Plateau', www.cwru.edu/affil/tibet/booksAndPapers/plateauhard.htm, retrieved 14 June 2006.

Ministry of Civil Affairs (2000) *Minjian Zuzhi Guanli Zuixin Fagui Zhengce Huibian* (Collection of the Latest Regulations and Policies on the Management of Popular Organisations) internal documents, Popular Organization Management Bureau of the Ministry of Civil Affairs, People's Republic of China.

Morton, Katherine (2007), 'Transnational Advocacy at the Grassroots: Risks and Opportunities' in Peter Ho and Richard Louis Edmonds (eds.) *Embedded Environmentalism: Opportunities and Constraints of a Social Movement in China*, Routledge, London and New York, forthcoming.

Murshed, Mansoob (ed.) (2002), *Globalisation, Marginalisation and Development*, Routledge, London.

Namgyal (2004), 'China's West Development Strategy and Rural Empowerment: Is There a Link? A Case Study of the Tibetan Plateau Region', in Ding Lu and William A.W. Neilson (eds), *China's West Region Development: Domestic Strategies and Global Implications*, World Scientific Publishing, Singapore.

Nisbett, Robert (1980), *History of the Idea of Progress*, Basic Books, New York.

Nussbaum, Martha (2000), *Women and Development: The Capabilities Approach*, Cambridge University Press, Cambridge.

Petras, James and Veltmeyer, Henry (2001), *Globalisation Unmasked: Imperialism in the 21st Century*, Zed Books, London.

Pieterse, Jan Nederveen (ed.) (2000), *Global Futures: Shaping Globalisation*, Zed Books, London and New York.

SDA (Sanchuan Development Association) (2002), *Sanchuan fazhan cujin hui*, June, Guanting township, Qinghai.

Saich, Tony (2000), 'Negotiating the State: The Development of Social Organisations in China', *China Quarterly*, no. 161(March), pp. 124-42.

Sen, Amartya (1999), *Development as Freedom*, Oxford University Press, Oxford and New York.

Shi, Tong (2004), *Zhongguo shehui zhuanxing shiqi de shehui paiji: yi guoqi xiagang shiye nugong wei shijiao* (Social exclusion during China's transition: from the perspective of the SOE laid-off female workers), Beijing daxue chubanshe, Beijing.

SSG (Snowland Service Group) (2003), *Jiangyuan fazhan cujin hui*, October, Jiegu township, Qinghai.

Stiglitz, Joseph (2002), *Globalisation and its Discontents*, W.W. Norton and Company, New York and London.

Stonequist, Everett V. (1957), *The Marginal Man: A Study in Personality and Culture Conflict*, Russell and Russell, New York, first published 1937.

Tsing, Anna Lowenhaupt (1993), *In the Realm of the Diamond Queen: Marginality in an Out-of-the-Way Place*, Princeton University Press, Princeton.

Unger, Jonathan (1996), '"Bridges": Private Business, the Chinese Government and the Rise of New Associations', *China Quarterly*, no. 147(September), pp. 795-819.

United States Embassy Beijing (2003), 'Defending China's "Water Tower": Environmental Protection in Qinghai Province', www.usembassy-china.org.cn/sandt/ptr/Water-Tower-prt.htm, retrieved. 20 June 2006.

Wang, Hui (1999), '*Dangdai zhongguo de sixiang zhuangkuang yu xiandaixing*' (Contemporary Chinese thought and the question of modernity), *Tianya* (Frontiers), vol. 5 (translated by Rebecca Karl) in Wang Hui (edited by Theodore Huters) (2003), *China's New Order: Society, Politics, and Economy in Transition*, Harvard University Press, Cambridge, Mass. and London.

Wang, Libin (2003), 'Rural Development and NGOs in China', paper presented at Third ISTR Asia and Pacific Regional Conference, Beijing, 23 October.

Wang Shaoguang and Hu Angang (1999), *The Political Economy of Uneven Development: The Case of China*, M.E. Sharpe, Armonk.

White, Gordon, Howell, Jude and Shang Xiaoyuan (eds) (1996) *In Search of Civil Society: Market Reform and Social Change in Contemporary China*, Clarendon Press, Oxford.

Wu, Bin (2003), *Sustainable Development in Rural China: Farmer Innovation and Self-Organisation in Marginal Areas*, RoutledgeCurzon, London and New York.

Wu, Zhongmin (2004), *Shehui gong zheng lun* (Theory of social justice), Shangdong renmin chubanshe, Jinan.

Yan, Wenxiu (2005), *Liudong mingong de bianyuan hua wenti zongshu* (Overview of the issue of marginalisation of migrant workers), *Qiushi*, 2, pp. 85-7.

Young, Iris Marion (1990), *Justice and the Politics of Difference*, Princeton University Press, Princeton.

Young, Iris Marion (2000), *Inclusion and Democracy*, Oxford University Press, Oxford.

Zhang, Xin and Baum, Richard (2004), 'Civil Society and the Anatomy of a Rural NGO', *The China Journal*, no. 52(July), pp. 97-107.

Index

Note: *italic* page numbers denote references to Figures/Tables.